This series is the official book series of IMISCOE, the largest network of excellence on migration and diversity in the world. It comprises publications which present empirical and theoretical research on different aspects of international migration. The authors are all specialists, and the publications a rich source of information for researchers and others involved in international migration studies.

The series is published under the editorial supervision of the IMISCOE Editorial Committee which includes leading scholars from all over Europe. The series, which contains more than eighty titles already, is internationally peer reviewed which ensures that the book published in this series continue to present excellent academic standards and scholarly quality. Most of the books are available open access.

For information on how to submit a book proposal, please visit: http://www.imiscoe.org/publications/how-to-submit-a-book-proposal.

More information about this series at http://www.springer.com/series/13502

IMISCOE Research Series

Anna Amelina • Kenneth Horvath
Bruno Meeus
Editors

An Anthology of Migration and Social Transformation

European Perspectives

Springer

Editors
Anna Amelina
Department of Social Sciences
Goethe-University Frankfurt
Frankfurt, Germany

Kenneth Horvath
University of Education of Karlsruhe
Karlsruhe, Germany

Bruno Meeus
Cosmopolis Centre for Urban Research
Vrije Universiteit Brussel
Brussels, Belgium

ISSN 2364-4087 ISSN 2364-4095 (electronic)
IMISCOE Research Series
ISBN 978-3-319-23665-0 ISBN 978-3-319-23666-7 (eBook)
DOI 10.1007/978-3-319-23666-7

Library of Congress Control Number: 2015957383

Springer Cham Heidelberg New York Dordrecht London

Printed on acid-free paper

Springer International Publishing AG Switzerland is part of Springer Science+Business Media (www.springer.com)

Acknowledgements

The list of people who have supported the publication of this book in one way or the other is very long. First of all, we as the editors would like to thank all the authors who have contributed to this project and have made this project an illuminating and fascinating endeavour. We would like to express our deep appreciation to the whole IMISCOE team whose enthusiasm and encouragement for this project have guided us through the process. In this context, we owe special thanks to Warda Belabas and Michelle Luijben for their reliable, competent, and patient assistance. Bernadette Deelen-Mans and Evelien Bakker from Springer have done a marvellous job in turning our academic manuscript into a market-ready product. We are also very grateful to William White and René Reinholz who were of great help during the editing process.

Special acknowledgements go to the association 'Freunde und Förderer der Goethe-Universität' – the 'Friends and Sponsors of Goethe-University Frankfurt' – who have provided important financial assistance for the publication process.

Last but not least, we are extremely grateful to the anonymous reviewers who have taken their job very seriously and have provided impressively rigorous and constructive feedback!

Frankfurt, Germany Anna Amelina
Karlsruhe, Germany Kenneth Horvath
Brussels, Belgium Bruno Meeus

Contents

Contributors

Anna Amelina Department of Social Sciences, Goethe-University Frankfurt, Frankfurt, Germany

Başak Bilecen Faculty of Sociology, Bielefeld University, Bielefeld, Germany

Alicja Bobek Trinity College, University of Dublin, Dublin, Ireland

Ayşe Çağlar Department of Social and Cultural Anthropology, University of Vienna, Vienna, Austria

Stephen Castles Department of Sociology and Social Policy, University of Sydney, Sydney, NSW, Australia

Sally Daly Trinity College, University of Dublin, Dublin, Ireland

Nicholas De Genova Department of Geography, King's College London, London, UK

Ricarda Drüeke Department of Communication, University of Salzburg, Salzburg, Austria

Martin Geiger Department of Political Science, Carleton University, Ottawa, ON, Canada

Leila Hadj-Abdou Department of Politics, University of Sheffield, Sheffield, UK

Raimund Haindorfer Department of Sociology, University of Vienna, Vienna, Austria

Benno Herzog Department of Sociology and Social Anthropology, University of Valencia, Valencia, Spain

Kenneth Horvath University of Education of Karlsruhe, Karlsruhe, Germany

Ayhan Kaya Department of International Relations and Political Science, Istanbul Bilgi University, Istanbul, Turkey

Helma Lutz Goethe-University Frankfurt am Main, Frankfurt, Germany

Bruno Meeus Cosmopolis Centre for Urban Research, Vrije Universiteit Brussel, Brussels, Belgium

Georg Menz Goldsmiths College, University of London, London, UK

Elaine Moriarty Trinity College, University of Dublin, Dublin, Ireland

Federico Oliveri Sciences for Peace Interdisciplinary Centre, University of Pisa, Pisa, Italy

Christoph Reinprecht Department of Sociology, University of Vienna, Vienna, Austria

Michael Samers Department of Geography, University of Kentucky, Lexington, KY, USA

Elisabeth Scheibelhofer Department of Sociology, University of Vienna, Vienna, Austria

Paul Scheibelhofer Department of Sociology, University of Vienna, Vienna, Austria

Nina Glick Schiller Department of Social Anthropology, University of Manchester, Manchester, UK

Gabriele Tomei Dipartimento di Scienze Politiche, University of Pisa, Pisa, Italy

Nicolas Van Puymbroeck Faculty of Social Sciences - Center on Inequality, Poverty, Social Exclusion and the City, University of Antwerp, Antwerp, Belgium

Roland Verwiebe Department of Sociology, University of Vienna, Vienna, Austria

William Walters Department of Political Science and Department of Sociology & Anthropology, Carleton University, Ottawa, ON, Canada

James Wickham Trinity College, University of Dublin, Dublin, Ireland

Laura Wiesböck Department of Sociology, University of Vienna, Vienna, Austria

Chapter 1
Migration and Social Transformation: Interdisciplinary Insights and European Perspectives

Anna Amelina, Kenneth Horvath and Bruno Meeus

1.1 Introduction

There is little doubt in the field of migration research that patterns of international migration and forms of their political regulation have undergone far-reaching changes over the past decades. The social-transformation perspective used throughout this volume seeks to relate these profound changes in the field of migration to the analysis of more general societal constellations. The theoretical and empirical studies selected for this volume provide insights into how practices of migration and mobility are structured by changes in political-economic orders of power and inequality, by political dynamics, and by ongoing struggles over identity and belonging.

The current European context provides a challenging field of enquiry for researching the interplay of migration and social transformation. Europe, as a political, economic, cultural, and social entity, has seen various significant developments over the past few decades, including the rise of post-Fordist relations of production, the end of the Cold War, European integration, EU enlargement and processes of supranationalization. However, the literature on the interdependencies between international migration and the social transformation of Europe is, in a sense, fragmented. Interdisciplinary European studies (e.g. Rumford 2009) seek to reconstruct the processes of integration and supranationalization linked to the European Union

A. Amelina (✉)
Department of Social Sciences, Goethe-University Frankfurt, Frankfurt, Germany
e-mail: amelina@soz.uni-frankfurt.de

K. Horvath
University of Education of Karlsruhe, Karlsruhe, Germany
e-mail: horvath@ph-karlsruhe.de

B. Meeus
Cosmopolis Centre for Urban Research, Vrije Universiteit Brussel, Brussels, Belgium
e-mail: bruno.meeus@kuleuven.be

A. Amelina et al. (eds.), *An Anthology of Migration and Social Transformation*, IMISCOE Research Series, DOI 10.1007/978-3-319-23666-7_1

and its enlargement; urban-governance literature enquires into rescaling processes that result from general social transformations and institutional macro-shifts (Brenner 2004); and current (critical) politico-economic studies analyse the character and scope of these general transformations, and examine how they affect and are informed by changing relations of political power and economic inequalities (Sum and Jessop 2013). Despite the many ways in which the processes mentioned above are intertwined with the social reproduction of migration, mobilities and borders, none of these bodies of literature explicitly addresses changing patterns of migration and mobility. At the same time, empirical studies and theoretical concepts to describe contemporary migration flows within, to, and from Europe have been proliferating in recent years (see e.g. Fassmann et al. 2009), but few of them have considered the significance of processes of *social transformation*, particularly in what could be called the new European context (Doomernik and Jandl 2008).

This volume has been compiled to bridge this gap in the current body of literature. It has four major objectives:

1. To provide an overview of influential and relevant *social theories* of ongoing social transformation processes as well as of how these theoretical frameworks incorporate migration processes in their analyses;
2. To give special attention to newly emergent forms and scales of the *political regulation of migration* against the background of profound societal change in general, and in the new supranationalized European context in particular;
3. To provide detailed insights into current varieties of migration and mobility in Europe, including temporary, circular, and multidirectional patterns; and
4. To illuminate current conflicts relating to the politics of belonging, including new forms of transnational belonging as well as prevailing forms of racism and xenophobia.

In the following, we discuss the conceptual ideas that inform the selection of studies in this volume in relation to these four general objectives.

1.2 Theorizing Social Transformation: Elements of an Integrative Approach

By putting the concept of social transformation center-stage, we follow a specific way of theorizing and studying the manifold relations between migration and societal change. Stephen Castles has prominently argued for adopting such a perspective in migration research (see Chap. 2). The notion of social *transformation* signifies profound structural modifications of societal relations. It has been proposed as an analytical alternative to other forms of conceptualizing social change. Most importantly, it aims to break with the normative underpinnings and biases of the concept of *development*. The latter expresses a modernist, Eurocentric view on social change that involves a 'Western' rhetoric of progress which uses dichotomous categories such as 'developed' vs 'backward', 'rational' vs. 'non-rational', and so on to classify national societies or macro-regions (Alexander 1994). At the same time, the focus on social transformation signifies more than just undirected and unsystematic social *change*. It directs our attention to the structural embedding of societal shifts, to globalized relations of power and inequality and to the complex interplay between social, cultural, political, and economic dynamics.

In Chap. 2 of this volume, Stephen Castles emphasizes that such a transformation perspective implies the need for a strong theoretical anchoring, for reconnecting empirical studies in migration to social-theory building. There are a number of starting points for such a theoretical embedding. After all, the concept of transformation has seen a long and variegated history of theory building. It was, for example, prominently used by Karl Polanyi (2001[1957]) in his analysis of major historical shifts in the political economy of industrial capitalism and the liberal nation-state. A few decades before Polanyi, Marxist thinkers introduced the basic idea that practices, conflictual relations, and structural tendencies that mark a particular societal order can cause deep crises and may finally lead to the establishment of completely new societal formations. Some decades later, based on such an understanding, the French regulation school prominently diagnosed a shift from the Fordist to the post-Fordist era (Boyer and Saillard 2002), accompanied by the emergence of new neoliberal political projects (Foucault 2008).

The social-transformation perspective that informs the selection of studies in this volume follows Stephen Castles' general heuristic that approaches social transformation, 'as a convenient label to facilitate discussion of the *complexity, interconnectedness, variability, contextuality, and multilevel mediations of global change'* (see Chap. 2). According to this understanding, social transformation processes are not naturally occurring phenomena; rather, they are regarded as processes that are continuously socially produced and generated. Social transformation processes are necessarily located in time(s) and space(s). Therefore, special attention should be given to the configurations of power and inequality in which societal changes unfold. Such a transformation approach will have to be sensitive to both the strategic agency of social actors and the structural frameworks they are confronted with, and it will need to consider the concrete historical settings in which transformation is socially generated. Political discourses play a key role in these processes of social change: they signify hegemonic narratives about society and its social reproduction, they define dominant problem understandings, and they are the basis on which shared political objectives are formulated. For example, the restrictive tendencies in current European migration regulations are embedded in securitization discourses: the political definition of migration (in particular, from the non-EU countries) as an existential threat to social security and public order is a necessary condition of the remarkable change that manifests itself in the manifold deprivation of migrant rights in Europe (Huysmans 2006). In a nutshell, when social transformation is approached in this manner as something that is actively produced by a variety of social actors in a variety of social contexts (state, non-state, collective, and individual actors), it becomes possible to avoid naturalizing understanding of transformation processes.

1.3 Migration, Mobility, and Social Transformation: Aspects of a Complex Interplay

Diagnoses of change play a prominent role in migration research. Obvious examples are the emergence of transnationalism (e.g. Levitt and Glick Schiller 2004) or the identification of ever more flexible mobility patterns (Engbersen et al. 2013). Concerning migration politics, the politicization of migration (Hammar 2004), the rediscovery of guestwork (Menz 2009), or the (often conflicting) assessments of whether the nation-state has lost control over international migration or not are important examples for such diagnoses (Messina 2007). A social-transformation perspective in migration research would attempt to relate the analysis of recent migration and mobility patterns to *fundamental* changes in social, political, and economic orders.[1] The added value of such a perspective for migration research is that it moves beyond mere diagnoses of change towards analyses with a stronger anchoring in social theory. Such an analytical endeavour must pay specific attention to the complexity of the ways in which migration and social transformation interplay. According to Stephen Castles (Chap. 2), it would be misleading to assign causal primacy to either of the two in the analysis of their mutual shaping. Castles criticizes a number of scholars for their 'failure to understand the historical character of migration, false assumptions of one-way causality, and an inability to understand the overall dynamics of migratory processes and their embeddedness in processes of societal change'. Building on such an understanding, we suggest that analyses of the interplay between migration and social transformation require four crucial elements that mirror the main objectives of this volume.

First, any social-transformation perspective requires a conceptual framework to address societal relations. Such a theoretical grounding is all the more necessary, the more we relate our empirical studies to general social transformation(s). There is quite a variety of possible theoretical starting points. For example, the Varieties-of-Capitalism approach (Chap. 3) and the Cultural-Political-Economy approach (Chap. 4) can provide useful analytical tools to examine how politico-economic shifts depend on and facilitate specific forms of geographical movement. Michel Foucault's rich theoretical framework offers another possible conceptual starting point. Over the past few years, Foucauldian approaches have become very important for analyses of past as well as present social transformations. Apart from shifting our attention to the interplay of power relations, discourses, and social practices, Foucault's analysis of neoliberal governmentality has proven to be a fruitful point of reference for analyzing these very recent transformations (Chaps. 10 and 11). A critical Foucauldian framework, for example, may lead us to ask how the recent emergence of harsh deportation and detention policies could be linked to neoliberal political projects and post-Fordist economic orders (De Genova and Peutz 2010; De Giorgi 2010; Horvath 2014a).

[1] Since transformation always implies social change processes, there is of course no reason to avoid the term 'change' entirely: in fact, many important discussions of recent transformation processes revolve around it (see, e.g., Chap. 3, in this volume). The important point is that the analytical focus of this volume is on the interlinked societal, political, and economic dynamics that mark different historical societal constellations.

Second, the analysis of the social generation and reproduction of migration, mobilities, and borders in the context of social transformation processes necessarily has to incorporate the manifold and complex forms of *political regulation of migration*, including concrete policies, administrative procedures, and legal frameworks initiated by state and non-state actors, such as recent migration management programs or new guestworker and cross-border labour migration policies (Chaps. 3, 8, 9, and 11). The political regulation of migration, mobility, and borders is always linked to political discourses and institutions which selectively organize human mobility and immobility, evidence of which can be found in the institutionalized strategies of migration management and changing forms of border control (Chaps. 9 and 10). Because of this complexity, the field of migration politics is ripe with unintended consequences and contradictory constellations (Amelina and Vasilache 2014; Horvath 2014b). For example, temporary mobility in the enlarged Europe is organized by very restrictive border regulations (as in the case of third-country nationals, whose temporariness is enforced) as well as by very liberal regulations of free-movement (as in the case of EU citizens, whose temporary mobility is not restricted).

Third, research on how migration is informed and structured by processes of social transformation must of course also consider individuals' practices of migration, mobility, and immobility, including temporary, circular, and multi-directional patterns (Chaps. 12, 13, 14, 15, and 16). Such analyses of individual practices give consideration to how individuals organize both their mobility and their post-migration settlement. Migration as an overarching societal phenomenon, is, in this sense, also produced by the often (but not necessarily) 'recalcitrant' practices of migrants themselves. Insofar as migrants challenge dominant framings, administrative procedures, and political regulations, their agency involves more than just border-crossing geographic mobility. By directly interacting with migration regulations they also contribute to the production of changed conditions for future orders of borders and mobilities. Thus, practices of mobility challenge and transform not only normative discourses about nationalism (Chap. 13), family coherence, and the gendered division of labour within households (Chap. 16), but also the forms of political regulation of borders and mobilities (Chaps. 7, 8, 9, 10, 11, 12, 13, 14, and 15). However, we should keep in mind that the undeniable increase in flexible and temporary patterns of migration and mobility in the context of the enlarged Europe and its close peripheries goes hand in hand with an actual immobilization of large parts of the world population which is due in part to restrictive immigration policies in the globalized 'North' and 'West'. A transformation perspective would encourage us to analyse how this immobilization is connected to profound societal changes and transformations of politico-economic orders (De Giorgi 2010).

Fourth, the interplay of migration dynamics and processes of social transformation involves not only migration and mobility practices and their political regulation but also *symbolic struggles over belonging* (Yuval-Davis 2011). The notion of symbolic or discursive struggles refers to the provisional quality of dominant problem definitions in respect to migration and related practices. It points to the fact that, although discourses of belonging produce boundaries between (imagined) groups and communities, these dominant narratives can be contested. Recent demands made by migrant protest movements in Western Europe that struggle for access to social, cultural, and political rights (Chap. 17) and the continuing discourse about the role of Islam in Europe in relation to migration (Chap. 18) are examples of current topics that are subject to such contestation. Politics of belonging and membership appear to be relevant in various different spheres and sites: they emerge in media discourses (Chap. 21), in negotiations over ethnic differences in urban contexts (Chap. 20), and particularly in the form of migrants' protest movements (Chap. 17). Most importantly, politics of belonging also emerge in xenophobic discourses of right-wing populists and in state-organized integration courses, which often interlink the categories of ethnicity/race and sexuality (Chaps. 18 and 19).

1.4 Contextualizing the Migration-Transformation-Nexus: towards a Multiplicity of European Perspectives

Europe and the European Union provide an extraordinarily challenging context for enquiring into the interplay of migration and social transformation. The transformation of Europe is intimately linked with changing patterns of migration and mobility and with the re-arrangement of national borders and boundaries of belonging. Again, this is not a unidirectional relation: practices of migration and mobility shape Europe as a political and economic order—as well as the other way around. Furthermore, a social-transformation perspective allows us to dispense with the concept of Europe as a fixed container, and thus to avoid *methodological Europeanism* and *methodological EU-ropeanism* (Garelli and Tazzioli 2013) which involve a static and essentializing view of Europe and confound the social space of Europe with the territorial boundaries of the EU (see Chap. 22 for a detailed critique). Acknowledging that the EU is one among many social actors involved in the social production, reproduction and transformation of Europe, we can consider various institutional and non-institutional sites that are involved in building the current European project. Such a perspective implies the need for nuanced perspectives on the EU as a political project that itself envisions and aims for specific forms of social transformation. A good example for these subtle imaginaries are the enlargement strategies of the European Union that are officially defined as "processes of change" (EU 2012). The documents of the European Commission indicate that the "enlargement strategies" involve a positive *rhetoric of change*, using categories such as "priorities" and "progress", thus contributing to transformation processes they themselves depict in a positive manner.

Rather than approaching Europe as a stable and consistent social space, we propose to analyse (1) the specific social orders and formations, (2) the political regulations, (3) the social practices, and (4) the symbolic struggles by which the social landscape of Europe is produced and transformed—specifically focusing on the myriad forms in which these processes are intertwined with the social generation of migration, mobilities, and borders. The complex constellation of issues that such an endeavour implies may, again, be approached by pointing to the four main dimensions that organize this volume and that may now be made more concrete with regard to the European setting.

First, one of the key questions that arise is how the social transformation of Europe and the emergence of new migration patterns are structured by changing *societal* and *political-economic landscapes*, especially in the aftermath of the fall of the Iron Curtain (Chap. 6). There are different theoretical answers to this question. The Varieties-of-Capitalism approach (Chap. 3) emphasizes the varying logics of national capitalisms, while analyses that follow a Cultural-Political-Economy perspective (Chap. 4) concentrate more on overarching structural dynamics of global capitalism and the emergence of post-national social, economic, and political formations. Both approaches warrant an increasing sensitivity to the interplay of different sociospatial scales and levels of policymaking involved in current migration patterns (see also Chap. 5).

Second, the question of different levels of *policymaking* remains highly relevant when we turn to how international migration is being governed in the context of the post-1989 European political economy. On the one hand, there are clear indicators for the Europeanization of migration policies (Chap. 7), on the other hand nation-state are still relevant actors for the regulation of migration, evidenced by the example of new guest-worker regulations (Chap. 8). Regardless of whether we consider the supranational or the national level more important, there are a number of noteworthy trends in the political regulation of migration in Europe: the increasing use of smart border devices, in particular in the context of migration management programs (Chap. 9), the reconfiguration of borders and their control (Chap. 10), and the increasing differentiation of political and social rights are crucial elements of these developments.

Third, against this societal and political background, we need to understand specific individual *practices of migration and mobility*, such as new cross-border labour mobility (Chap. 12), international retirement migration (Chap. 14), international student mobility (Chap. 15), or transnational care-work relations (Chap. 16). The concrete forms these migration practices take depend, among others, on the regional context: Europe is not a homogeneous social space, but rather a complex and stratified social phenomenon that may produce very different and seemingly contradictory forms of international migration (Chap. 11).

Fourth, current forms of political regulation and social practices of migration and mobility are informed by both EU and national *narratives of belonging*. These narratives, in turn, reinforce the complex stratification of the legal statuses of mobile populations in general and of third-country nationals in particular. Discourses and struggles over belonging structure beliefs about who should be entitled to be a member of the new Europe, and with what processes of subjectification mobile and immobile populations are to be confronted. Two trends can be observed in the transformation of the debates around 'European' belonging and (political) membership. The first is a struggle for hybrid and cosmopolitan forms of belonging (Chap. 20),

1.5.3 Part III. Complexities of Mobilities: From One-Way Migration to Multiple Patterns

Whereas Part I and II focus on societal and political shifts, Part III explores how forms and practices of migration themselves have changed. Various concepts, including 'seasonal workers', 'commuters', 'tourists', 'suitcase traders', and 'temporary workers', have been proposed in the past few decades to account for the discrepancy between the taken-for-granted idea of more or less permanent one-way migration and actually existing mobility patterns (Black et al. 2010; Engbersen et al. 2013). Part III provides an overview of the emergence and development of relatively new migration and mobility patterns and discusses them in relation to social and political transformations. Chapters 12 and 13 introduce different forms and implications of temporary *labour mobility* in Europe, while Chaps. 14, 15, and 16 pay attention to specific categories of mobile subjects.

Chapter 12 by Laura Wiesböck and her colleagues analyse cross-border commuting in the Central European region, building on findings from a recent empirical study. Chapter 13 continues the analysis of the relationship between cross-border labour mobility and the distribution of life chances. Elaine Moriarty and her colleagues use a study of transnational movement from Poland to Ireland to analyse migrants' access and transfer of social-security rights in the context of EU (post-) enlargement. Chapter 14 provides a detailed overview of the emerging phenomenon of retirement migration in Europe. Focusing on the case of Spain, Benno Herzog discusses the social backgrounds of retirement migrants, the wide range of pensioners' transnational lifestyles, social issues, and the ways in which local, regional, and national care schemes respond to the growth of this particular category of mobile individuals. In Chap. 15 Başak Bilecen analyses the case of international student mobility, pointing, among others, to tensions between different forms of cosmopolitan attitudes and corresponding ideas of flexibility. In Chap. 16 Helma Lutz provides insights into the significance of gendered narratives which influence the current transnational migration and mobility of Eastern European migrant women seeking employment in the care sector in 'Western' Europe while still providing care at a distance to their significant others in their country of emigration.

1.5.4 Part IV. Shifting Politics of Belonging

Part IV addresses the question of how practices of migration and mobility as well as their political regulation are linked to struggles over belonging and (political) membership. Highlighting the symbolic and discursive dimensions, this part speaks to all previous parts. The chapters do not only identify the most noticeable current struggles over belonging and identity but also shed light on the relevant actors and significant institutional and non-institutional sites of their social generation. One of the crucial issues in this context is the conflict between essentialist and non-essentialist modes of membership construction. Some researchers have observed a rise of hybrid, diasporic, and cosmopolitan identities encouraged by cross-border migration flows and EU identity politics (e.g. Rumford 2008); others have drawn attention to persistent and even increasing manifestations of racism and Islamophobia (e.g. Korteweg and Yurdakul 2014).

The first chapter of this part, Chap. 17, addresses the agency of migrants in the context of symbolic struggles over belonging. Federico Oliveri discusses the increasing significance of migrants' demands for political and social rights in Europe, and provides a theoretical account of those mobilizations as 'acts of citizenship' by which migrants attempt to legitimize themselves as rights-bearing subjects. The following two contributions, Chaps. 18 and 19, address processes of racialization in contemporary Europe. In Chap. 18 Ayhan Kaya proposes the concept of 'Islamophobism' to explore current processes involved in the governance of migration and settlement by neoliberal states. In Chap. 19 Paul Scheibelhofer focuses on ways in which racialized attributions are interlinked with the sexualization of mobile subjects.

Chapters 20 and 21, finally, provide insights into a variety of institutional and geographical sites that are significant for contemporary discourses on belonging and identity. In Chap. 20 Nina Glick-Schiller and Ayşe Çağlar reiterate their call for studies that avoid an ethnic bias in urban migration research, arguing for their concept of migrants' emplacement that points to the positioning of cities within global networks of power as well as to the strategies that migrants use to find or create a place for themselves in a specific locality. Chapter 21 by Ricarda Drüeke argues that scholars should question binary-coded concepts used in some approaches of current media research which regard 'nation' and 'identity' as linear constructs.

1.5.5 Part V. Outlook for Researching Migration and Social Transformation beyond Eurocentrism

In an endeavour to link accounts of migration and social transformation, we are confronted with the specific challenge that migration scholars are 'part of the world they analyse' (Burawoy 2003: 668), meaning that migration scholars' positionality is inseparably related to their choice of theoretical accounts. This nexus between positionality, theoretical choices, and possible research strategies is the subject of the volume's concluding part, in which Nicholas De Genova (Chap. 22) reflects on the epistemological foundations of any future research on migration and social transformation. In essence, the author addresses the question of how to conceptualize migration studies in the European context without overgeneralizing and essentializing the European project. Building on postcolonial theories, he proposes a strategy of de-ethnicizing and de-naturalizing the European project.

1.6 Conclusion

This volume takes an interdisciplinary approach to the analysis of social transformations in relation to changing migration dynamics within, to, and from Europe that have become evident over the last few decades. By drawing on perspectives from various disciplines, including sociology, political science, social geography, and social anthropology, it provides tools to understand current migration dynamics in a fragmented and constantly changing social space. Taken as a whole, this volume makes a number of important contributions.

First, it proposes that phenomena of migration, social transformation, and Europe be analysed as socially generated and relationally interlinked. This heuristic allows researchers to avoid attributions of causal primacy in the relationship between migration and social transformation. It shifts our attention to the historical, political, and economic embeddedness of the social production of migration, borders, and mobilities. At the same time, it emphasizes the role of political agency as well as of existing structures of power and inequality and, hence, prevents us from conceiving of current developments—including the political projects underlying the European Union—in a naturalizing, essentializing, or teleological fashion.

Second, the volume identifies a number of analytical levels that are relevant for linking the analysis of the social generation of migration to diagnoses of ongoing societal transformations. These analytical levels are mirrored in the volume's structure: (1) influential social theories and accounts of significant social shifts, (2) strategies of political regulation, (3) social practices of migration and mobility on the individual level, and (4) symbolic and discursive dimensions.

Third, the analytical heuristics underlying the volume allows for the identification of a variety of social actors (including migrants themselves) and institutional sites (e.g. governments, state administration, or labour markets) involved in the nexus of migration and social transformation. It sheds light on the most recent theoretical concepts and the most recent results from quantitative and qualitative empirical research.

References

Alexander, J. C. (1994). Modern, anti, post, and neo: How social theories have tried to understand the "New World" of "Our Time". *Zeitschrift für Soziologie, 23*(3), 165–197.

Amelina, A., & Vasilache, A. (2014). Editorial: The shadows of enlargement: Theorising mobility and inequality in a changing Europe. *Migration Letters, 11*(2), 109–124.

Bigo, D. (2011). Freedom and speed in enlarged borderzones. In V. Squire (Ed.), *The contested politics of mobility: Borderzones and irregularity* (pp. 31–50). Abingdon: Routledge.

Black, R., Engbersen, G., & Okólski, M. (Eds.). (2010). *A continent moving west? EU enlargement and labour migration from Central and Eastern Europe*. Amsterdam: Amsterdam University Press.

Boyer, R., & Saillard, Y. (Eds.). (2002). *Regulation theory: The state of the art*. London/New York: Routledge.

Brenner, N. (2004). *New state spaces: Urban governance and the rescaling of statehood.* Oxford: Oxford University Press.

Burawoy, M. (2003). Revisits: An outline of a theory of reflexive ethnography. *American Sociological Review, 68*(5), 645–679. doi:10.2307/1519757.

De Genova, N., & Peutz, N. (2010). *The deportation regime. Sovereignty, space, and the freedom of movement.* Durham/London: Duke University Press.

De Giorgi, A. (2010). Immigration control, post-Fordism, and less eligibility: A materialist critique of the criminalization of immigration across Europe. *Punishment & Society, 12*(2), 147–167. doi:10.1177/1462474509357378.

Doomernik, J., & Jandl, M. (Eds.). (2008). *Modes of migration: Regulation and control in Europe.* Amsterdam: Amsterdam University Press/IMISCOE.

Engbersen, G., Leerkes, A., Grabowska-Lusinska, I., Snel, E., & Burgers, J. (2013). On the differential attachments of migrants from Central and Eastern Europe: A typology of labour migration. *Journal of Ethnic and Migration Studies, 39*(6), 959–981. doi:10.1080/1369183X.2013.765663.

EU. (2012). *Enlargement strategy 2011–2012.* http://eur-lex.europa.eu/legal-content/EN/TXT/?qid=1415382848775&uri=URISERV:el0031

Fassmann, H., Haller, M., & Lane, D. (Eds.). (2009). *Migration and mobility in Europe: Trends, patterns and control.* Cheltenham/Northampton: Edward Elgar.

Foucault, M. (2008). *The birth of biopolitics: Lectures at the Collège de France: 1978–1979.* Basingstoke/New York: Palgrave Macmillan.

Garelli, G., & Tazzioli, M. (2013). Migration discipline hijacked: Distances and interruptions of a research militancy. *Postcolonial Studies, 16*(3), 299–308. doi:10.1080/13688790.2013.850048

Hammar, T. (2004). The politicisation of immigration. In T. Abbas & F. Reeves (Eds.), *Immigration and race relations: Sociological theory and John Rex* (pp. 99–110). London: I.B. Tauris.

Horvath, K. (2014a). Policing the borders of the 'Centaur State': Deportation, detention, and neoliberal transformation processes—The case of Austria. *Social Inclusion, 2*(3), 113–123. Open access: http://www.cogitatiopress.com/ojs/index.php/socialinclusion/article/view/36

Horvath, K. (2014b). Securitisation, economisation and the political constitution of temporary migration: The making of the Austrian seasonal workers scheme. *Migration Letters, 11*(2), 154–170.

Huysmans, J. (2006). *The politics of insecurity: Fear, migration and asylum in the EU.* London/New York: Routledge.

Korteweg, A., & Yurdakul, G. (2014). *The headscarf debates: Conflicts of national belonging.* Stanford: Stanford University Press.

Levitt, P., & Glick Schiller, N. (2004). Conceptualizing simultaneity: A transnational social field perspective on society. *International Migration Review, 38*(3), 1002–1039.

Menz, G. (2009). *The political economy of managed migration.* Oxford: Oxford University Press.

Messina, A. (2007). *The logics and politics of post-WWII migration to Western Europe.* Houndmills: Palgrave Macmillan.

Polanyi, K. (2001[1957]). *The great transformation: The political and economic origins of our times.* Boston: Beacon Press.

Rumford, C. (2008). *Cosmopolitan spaces: Europe, globalization, theory.* New York/Abingdon: Routledge.

Rumford, C. (Ed.). (2009). *The SAGE handbook of European studies.* London/Thousand Oaks/New Delhi/Singapore: SAGE.

Sum, N.-L., & Jessop, B. (2013). *Towards a cultural political economy: Putting culture in its place in political economy.* Cheltenham/Northampton: Edward Elgar.

Yuval-Davis, N. (2011). *The politics of belonging: Intersectional contestations.* London/Thousand Oaks/New Delhi/Singapore: SAGE Publications.

Part I
Theorizing About Migration and Social Transformation in Europe

Kenneth Horvath and Bruno Meeus

Introduction to Part I

For many years, migration research has been largely delinked from general theories of social transformation: Current theories of societal transformation offer little discussion of migration, mobilities, and borders; conversely, migration researchers have become rather hesitant to embed their analyses in 'grand theories'. As Stephen Castles (Chap. 2) notes in the first chapter of this part, these gaps in the literature represent a real lacuna. However, the re-linking of migration research and theories of social transformation does not have to start from scratch. Early migration research was often informed by historical or critical politico-economic theorizing. Three names should be noted in this context. Important parts of early migration research were, first, inspired by Marxist thinking, of which Castles and Kosack's (1973) book on guest workers in Europe is a prominent example; second, Polanyi's (2001) seminal work has informed numerous migration scholars (e.g. Zolberg 1991); and, third, Wallerstein's world system theory continues to influence scholars such as Saskia Sassen (2008).

Part I includes five chapters which discuss aspects that are essential for the re-linking of migration research and theories of social transformation. The selection of texts is based on four objectives. First, the whole idea of conceptually concentrating on transformation itself requires a theoretical justification (Chap. 2). Considering the central role of political economy for any transformation perspective, the second

K. Horvath (✉)
University of Education of Karlsruhe, Karlsruhe, Germany
e-mail: horvath@ph-karlsruhe.de

B. Meeus
Cosmopolis Centre for Urban Research, Vrije Universiteit Brussel, Brussels, Belgium
e-mail: bruno.meeus@vub.ac.be

Chapter 2
Understanding Global Migration: A Social Transformation Perspective

Stephen Castles

2.1 Introduction

More than 15 years ago Douglas S. Massey and his colleagues noted that:

> The theoretical concepts now employed by social scientists to analyse and explain international migration were forged primarily in the industrial era and reflect its particular economic arrangements, social institutions, technology, demography and politics [...]. The classical approach has now entered a state of crisis, challenged by new ideas, concepts, and hypotheses (Massey et al. 1998: 3).

Although, as they pointed out, 'these new ways of thinking have not yet cohered into a single theory', Massey et al. believed that 'the time has come [...] to reassess theories of international migration and bring them into conformity with new empirical conditions'. The 'post-industrial, post–Cold War world' needed a new theory of migration appropriate for 'a brand new century' (Massey et al. 1998: 3). This was the programmatic statement of a very important book which did indeed set out to present a new synthesis as a basis for a 'single' (and implicitly general) theory.

Seventeen years later the exponential growth of social-scientific research into the international mobility of people shows no sign of abating: we have more researchers, university courses, students, research projects, institutes, conferences, journals, and publications than ever before. Yet the quest for a generally accepted theoretical framework for migration studies remains elusive. We still lack a body of cumulative knowledge to explain why some people become mobile, while most do not, and

This chapter originally appeared in *Journal of Ethnic and Migration Studies*, *36*(10), 1565–1586, 2010.

S. Castles (✉)
Department of Sociology and Social Policy, University of Sydney,
Sydney, NSW 2006, Australia
e-mail: Stephen.castles@sydney.edu.au

A. Amelina et al. (eds.), *An Anthology of Migration and Social Transformation*,
IMISCOE Research Series, DOI 10.1007/978-3-319-23666-7_2

what this means for the societies concerned. Although there does seem to be widespread agreement on some matters—the importance of migration networks, for example—we do not have a common conceptual framework that could serve as a starting point for intellectual debates and the formulation of hypotheses and research questions.

This chapter starts by examining the 'sedentary bias' in migration debates, and goes on to discuss why it is so difficult to develop and agree on a conceptual framework for migration studies. A key problem is the tendency to see migration as quite distinct from broader social relationships and change processes. I will argue for the need to embed migration research in a more general understanding of contemporary society. This requires forms of inquiry that start from a situation of rapid and generalized changes. I refer to these processes as '*social transformation*' as a convenient label to facilitate discussion of the *complexity, interconnectedness, variability, contextuality, and multilevel mediations of global change*. The chapter links the analysis of migration to important trends in the theory and methodology of various social-scientific disciplines, and illustrates interdisciplinary social-transformation research by looking at the example of labour force change in Northern economies. My analysis points to rather different conclusions than Alejandro Portes' article (2010), which argues that migration does not generally change fundamental structures and institutions of developed societies. By contrast, I will argue that migration is actually one part of the process of the transformation of these structures and institutions, which arises through major changes in global political, economic, and social relationships.

2.2 Migration, Mobility, and the 'Sedentary Bias'

Some analysts have suggested that we should abandon the term 'migration' because it is thought to imply permanent (or at least long-term) movement from one nation state to another, following the patterns of labour migration and settlement migration seen as typical of the nineteenth and twentieth centuries. The twenty-first century, by contrast, is seen as an era of fluidity and openness in which changes in transportation, technology, and culture are making it normal for people to think beyond borders and to cross them frequently (Urry 2007). Movements for purposes of study, professional advancement, marriage, retirement, or lifestyle are assuming greater significance so that older ideas on migration are thought to be no longer relevant.

But this picture seems overdrawn: indeed, as Bauman (1998) has pointed out, the right to be mobile is more class-specific and selective than ever. National border controls and international cooperation on migration management have become highly restrictive. Most people have neither the economic resources nor the political rights needed for free movement. Only 3 % of the world's population are international migrants (UNDESA 2005). The postmodern utopia of a borderless world of mobility has not yet dawned so that it still seems appropriate to focus on the analysis of migration as a process based on inequality and discrimination and controlled and limited by states.

The migration–mobility debate can be located in a political discourse. For demographic, economic, and social reasons, all highly developed economies found themselves increasingly reliant on immigrant labour in the years leading up to the financial crash of 2008 (Castles 2006; CEC 2005b). International recruitment of highly skilled personnel was considered valuable, while lower-skilled migrant workers were seen as out-of-place in shiny new postindustrial economies. Public opinion was largely hostile towards migrant workers, asylum seekers, and poor people from the South. Movements of the highly skilled were celebrated as professional *mobility*, while those of the lower-skilled were condemned as unwanted *migration*. 'Mobility' equalled 'good' because it was the badge of a modern open society; 'migration' equalled 'bad' because it re-awakened archaic memories of invasion and displacement. It seems to me that a focus on migration, rather than mobility, better reflects real power relations. There is little reason to believe that the structural factors driving labour migration—particularly from low- and middle-income countries to richer countries—have changed fundamentally after the global financial crisis (GFC) of 2007–2009.

There is a further important point here: a dominant political discourse today is that migration is a *problem* that needs to be fixed by appropriate policies. The repressive variant is tight border control, the more liberal one is addressing the 'root causes' of migration—usually defined as poverty and violence in origin countries—so that people do not have to migrate (Castles and Van Hear 2010). Either way, migration is seen as harmful and dysfunctional—something to be stopped. Bakewell (2007) has shown how this discourse—which he calls the '*sedentary bias*'—continues a long tradition which started with colonial policies and is continued by most contemporary development agencies, according to which the poor constitute a threat to prosperity and public order if they move, and should therefore stay at home. The sedentary bias has become dominant in the analysis of contemporary migration. However, because rich countries need migrant workers, its current expression is not a prohibition on South–North movements of the lower-skilled but rather the idea that *circular migration* is a 'win-win-win situation': for labour-importing countries, origin countries, and the migrants themselves (CEC 2005a).

Yet historical perspectives show that migration has been a normal aspect of social life—and especially of social change—throughout history. The reason for the expansion of migration—especially over long distances—since the sixteenth century was the accelerated pace of change connected with the development of the capitalist world market. Nation state formation, colonial expansion, and imperialism involved conflict, violence, development-induced displacement, and the growth of forced migration. Migration in the colonial period took both the form of movement of administrators, traders, and military personnel (in modern terms, professional mobility), and the form of migration based on inequality and coercion: slaves, indentured workers, and so on (Cohen 1995). But migration also often has positive consequences for migrants and their communities of origin. People may move from areas where there are low incomes and few opportunities to places where economic growth and innovation present them with new opportunities. Return flows of remittances, technology, and ideas may, under certain circumstances, lead to positive changes in areas of origin. The UN Development Programme's 2009 *Human Development Report* draws attention to the potential of migration to enhance human capabilities and wellbeing (UNDP 2009).

The great wave of industrialization from the nineteenth to the early twentieth century led to what Hatton and Williamson (1998, 2005) call the first 'age of mass migration', while the accelerated globalization of the post-1945 period led to a second 'age of migration'. As Mark Miller and I argue (Castles and Miller 2009), this current wave has gone much further than the first because it has drawn in virtually all regions of the world, while the first focused mainly on the 'Atlantic economy'. Migration has grown more than ever in the last 30 years because of the accelerated pace of globalization. The 'only 3 % of global population' figure (see above) obscures the significance of migration as an expression of social change and a ferment for further change because it glosses over the highly concentrated nature of migration: cultures of emigration have become established in certain origin areas, while settlement of immigrants is concentrated in developed countries (10–25 % of the population of the OECD states) and cities (20–45 % in many global cities). Moreover, far more people move within their own countries than internationally (Skeldon 2006), although they too may encounter legal, economic, cultural, and social obstacles. The problem is not migration itself but rather the conditions of inequality under which most South–North migration takes place. These lead to marginalization and exploitation for many migrants. Development will not reduce migration (De Haas 2006). If there were less inequality (and therefore less poverty and human insecurity), there would not be less migration, but it would take place under very different circumstances.

These considerations reflect the difficulty of separating the social-scientific from the political in understanding migration. Claims of academic neutrality can mask a sedentary bias—an unquestioning assumption that migration is a bad thing. Yet theories of global migration should not be based on the normative objective of finding ways to help people to stay at home. Rather, theories of global migration should be based on the postulate that migration is a normal part of social relations. They should help us analyse the dynamics of migration not in isolation but as part of complex and varied processes of societal change. If there is a normative goal, it should not be to reduce migration but to find ways in which it could take place under conditions of equality and respect for human rights.

2.3 The Rocky Road Towards a 'Single Theory' of Migration

This section discusses some of the formidable obstacles to theoretical advancement in migration studies. These topics have been dealt with extensively in the literature, so they will only be addressed briefly here. This section will go on to ask if a general theory of migration is actually possible and desirable.

2.3.1 *Interdisciplinarity*

The natural sciences build on an accepted and cumulative body of knowledge arising from past theoretical and empirical work and serving as a basis for formulating hypotheses and research questions and suggesting methodology for new research. This does not imply static and dogmatic theory because 'scientific revolutions' (Kuhn 1996) may lead to a revision of fundamental ideas. Some social sciences (such as economics and demography) try to emulate the natural sciences by putting forward models based on quantitative data, but others (such as anthropology and sociology) cannot, due to the unpredictability and complexity of the groups and relationships with which they deal, and due to the frequent lack of quantifiable data. Indeed, it could be argued that the models used in economics and demography actually reflect oversimplification of complex and diverse patterns of behaviour (Castles 2008), and therefore need to be linked to the insights of other disciplines if they are to help in the understanding of social behaviour, but the point here is that other social sciences cannot even try to avoid the complexity and 'messiness' of the real world.

It is difficult for an interdisciplinary field such as migration studies to develop an agreed body of knowledge, and this problem has been compounded by the rapid growth of the field over the last 20–30 years. As new researchers have been drawn to the study of migration, they have, not surprisingly, applied the conceptual and methodological tools of their disciplines. The incentive structures of the discipline-based academic hierarchy make this difficult to avoid. The result is that migration research is compartmentalized, with little analytical and methodological collaboration across boundaries. The disciplinary bias has often meant reductionist approaches that focus on limited aspects of migratory experiences, blocking understanding of the migratory process as a whole.

Migration embraces all dimensions of social existence, and therefore requires an interdisciplinary approach. Efforts have been made to achieve this through interdisciplinary research teams, as well as through theoretical work designed to 'talk across disciplines' (Brettell and Hollifield 2007). However, all too often attempts at interdisciplinarity have been more additive than integrative—with each discipline contributing aspects susceptible to its mode of analysis but without an overarching synthesis. Indeed, the problem of fragmentation exists not just between but also within disciplines. For instance, the schisms between neoclassical economic theory and the 'new economics of labour migration', or between functionalist and historical-institutional approaches in sociology, seem as profound as those between, say, economic and legal approaches to migration.

2.3.2 Fragmentation on the Basis of Spatial or Functional Criteria

Massey and his collaborators point out that migration studies is split into research on the causes, processes, and patterns of migration itself (they speak of 'determinants of migration') and research on how migrants become incorporated into receiving societies ('immigrant assimilation') (cf. Massey et al. 1998: 3). In fact, there are several other divisions.

Researchers working on internal migration often have little interchange with those working on international migration. Studies of migration in less developed countries often take poverty research as a starting point and may be poorly linked to other areas of migration research. Studies of migration in specific regions are often linked to area studies (African Studies, Middle Eastern Studies, and so on) and may be formulated in spatially specific terms, with little dialogue with social scientists working in other areas. Forced-migration research is often quite separate from other areas of migration studies, and has two distinct prongs: work on asylum and refugees in the North and work on humanitarian issues in the South. The emerging subfield of migration and development has tried to cross disciplinary boundaries but has been too bound up with politics and policies in its relatively short history to contribute significantly to theory formation.

Migration scholars tend to be highly specialized, and each subfield has distinct literatures and bodies of knowledge. There are separate research centres, journals, and conferences for different areas. Results include a failure to understand the historical character of migration, false assumptions of one-way causality, and an inability to understand the overall dynamics of migratory processes and their embeddedness in processes of societal change.

2.3.3 Closeness to Political and Bureaucratic Agendas

The social sciences originated in industrial societies where all types of social relationships were seen as politically and culturally framed by the nation state (Connell 1997; Faist 2000). Contemporary social theory is still trapped in the 'dead end of "methodological nationalism"' (Beck 2007). The problem is particularly severe for migration studies (Wimmer and Glick Schiller 2003) because control of belonging to the national community has always been central to nation state sovereignty. Today migration research still tends to be linked to specific historical experiences of managing migration and diversity (Vasta and Vuddamalay 2006).

The recent politicization of issues of migration and incorporation of migrants into receiving societies has made the dilemma of policy-driven research even more difficult. Governments have commissioned a large volume of research on these topics. This has provided funding for empirical work, opened up new research areas, and encouraged the expansion of migration studies. However, government-commissioned work can also mean that research questions, methods, and even findings may be shaped by policy interests. Policy-driven research often provides simplistic short-term remedies to complex long-term social issues. Much policy-driven research is not only bad social science, it is also a poor guide to successful policy formation and one reason for the poor record of many governments in the area (Bhagwati 2003; Castles 2004; Cornelius et al. 1994).

2.3.4 The Receiving-Country Bias

Most migration research has taken the situation in Northern destination countries as its starting point, neglecting the perspectives of origin and transit countries and of migrants. This is not surprising, given that research funding and capacities are concentrated in the North. When the Social Science Research Council (SSRC) held its first major conference on migration theory in 1996 it commissioned papers exclusively from U.S. scholars. The resulting publications (Hirschman et al. 1999; Portes 1997) focused mainly on issues of incorporation of immigrants into society (assimilation, pluralism, etc.) and on the impact on 'American life and institutions'. A few years later the SSRC and Princeton University sought to extend the debate by including 'immigration scholars from both sides of the Atlantic' (Portes and DeWind 2004a: 828). European efforts to review the 'state of the art' in migration theory have also been mainly North-centric (Penninx et al. 2006).

Recent debates on migration and development have led to a broadening of approaches and to the realization of the need for cooperation of scholars from destination, transit, and receiving countries. International agencies (e.g. IOM, ILO, and UNESCO) have tried to build networks that include researchers from the South. Publications such as the Manila-based *Asian and Pacific Migration Journal* increase the dissemination of Southern research. The SSRC's initiative on migration and development in 2008 included several Southern scholars.[1] The Global Commission on Migration and Development (GCIM 2005) and the Global Forum on Migration and Development (GFMD) have included Southern policymakers, civil society, and academics. The 'perspective from the south' (Castles and Delgado Wise 2008; Manuh 2005) is beginning to be included in international debates.

Yet there is little sign that such trends have had much effect on the dominant approaches in migration studies. In Europe the main policy emphasis is still on the costs and benefits for receiving societies and on questions of migration control (or, more euphemistically, 'migration management', see also Chap. 9, in this volume). One reflection of this is the renewed preoccupation with assimilation. In the 1970s and 1980s many countries had shifted away from assimilationist approaches to migrants and minorities. But in the 1990s, in the face of political and media claims of supposed threats to national identity and security from migrants (especially Muslims), the trend towards multiculturalism or pluralism came to a halt.

[1] See http://essays.ssrc.org/developmentpapers/?page_id=3

New policy trends are reflected in a revamping of social-scientific theories of assimilation. Neoassimilationist approaches (Alba and Nee 1997; Entzinger 2003; Joppke and Morawaska 2003) have recently been joined by discourses on social cohesion and social capital which claim that diversity endangers the solidarity on which democratic nation states are founded (see Vasta 2007). Such social-scientific accounts have in turn helped to justify changes in national policies, such as the introduction of 'integration contracts' and citizenship tests in several countries, including France, Germany, the United Kingdom, the Netherlands, and Australia.

2.3.5 Isolation of Migration Studies from Broader Trends in Contemporary Social Theory

For a long time, migration scholars have found themselves marginalized within the social sciences because migration was not seen as an important area of investigation by many leading social theorists. As mentioned above, the fact that migration studies has to cut across disciplinary boundaries is one reason why it has so far gained little acceptance in mainstream departments. Although this situation might be changing, migration research still often takes place outside core social-science research contexts, usually in dedicated research centres heavily dependent on external funding. This forces migration researchers to take on policy-driven consultancy work, which in turn confirms the prejudice against interdisciplinary study on the part of mainstream social scientists.

To understand this fully would require a detailed study of the institutional and intellectual characteristics of the social sciences in each country. In the United Kingdom, for instance, the initial response to the New Commonwealth immigration of the 1950 and 1960s was the reworking of the pre–World War II Chicago School of sociology's theories of assimilation and acculturation. However, by the 1970s issues of racism, culture identity, class, and gender—influenced considerably by black, feminist, and Marxist scholars—began to play an important role. In the meantime such approaches have become parts of the accepted body of social analysis but have not always moved on to embrace the newer, complex forms of global mobility affecting the UK. In recent years the problem of disciplinary barriers has got worse because the United Kingdom's Research Assessment Exercise has put such a premium on publication in disciplinary journals that young academics fear the consequences of publishing in migration journals.

Globalization theory is now at the centre of international social-science debates, and the mobility of people is a crucial form of globalization. Yet many of the seminal works on globalization, such as those of Castells (1996, 1997, 1998), Albrow (1996), and Beck (1997), pay scant attention to the mobility of people. There are contrasting examples, as will be discussed below, but analysis of migration as a central element of global social change is still the exception.

2.3.6 *Complexity, Diversity, and Context*

A major obstacle to theory formation is the complexity and diversity of migration experiences. This has posed particular problems for economists. The Harris–Todaro model that underpins the neoclassical approach to migration assumes that movement is motivated by the desire for individual income maximization, based on rational comparison of the relative costs and benefits of remaining at home or moving. The mere existence of economic disparities between various areas should be sufficient to generate migrant flows. In the long run such flows should help equalize wages and conditions in underdeveloped and developed regions, leading to economic equilibrium (Massey et al. 1998: Chap. 2). This model was developed to analyse internal movements in developing countries but is seen as applicable to international migration as well, provided that consideration is given to constraints arising from the role of states and their uneven power. This model suggests a long-term transition to 'a one-sector, relatively full-employment neo-classical world' (Ranis 2009: 5).

But the neoclassical model has not proved very useful for analysing and explaining actual migration experiences. Its narrow focus on income maximization and its assumption of rational economic decision-making based on full information have little to do with the reality of most migration flows. This led some economists to criticize the methodological individualism of the Harris–Todaro approach. The proponents of the 'new economics of labour migration' (NELM; see Stark 1991; Taylor 1999) focus on family strategies for income maximization and risk diversification. NELM researchers use ethnographic research methods (such as qualitative interviews and household studies) to understand migration decisions but retain an emphasis on rational economic decision-making. NELM theories still largely fail to take account of the many non-economic factors that shape migration.

Collinson (2009) suggests that there is a need for a political-economy approach to migration that links the analysis of local-level factors that influence people's migration decisions and livelihood strategies, with political, economic, and social factors at various levels that affect the agency of migrants. That would mean, as Collinson (following Gold 2005) suggests, examining

> the inter-linkages between different migration streams; the importance of agency, autonomy, perceptions, cultural and historical factors and institutional constraints; the complex multi-level and transnational nature of migration; and the importance of social groups and relationship—including migration networks—for shaping migration dynamics and migration experiences, straddling migration 'sending', 'receiving' and 'transit' locations, and a range of actors within them (Collinson 2009: 5–6).

This list indicates the great *complexity* of migratory processes. Economic factors are important but hardly ever sufficient to understand any specific experience. But this is not just an issue for one discipline: economic data and models are popular with policymakers, but any monocausal explanation is equally problematic because it cannot do justice to the complexity of migration.

Complexity also implies *diversity*: if there are so many factors at work, the possible combinations become infinite. This in turn points to the crucial role of *context*—the links between migration and the other economic, social, political, and cultural relationships at work in particular places at a particular historical juncture. A historical understanding of societies and the relationships between them is crucial. For instance, no analysis of migration to the United Kingdom could be complete without an understanding of the history of British colonialism and racism; no analysis of Mexican migration to the United States could be valid without consideration of the historical expansion of the country and its past labour recruitment policies.

2.3.7 From Grand Theory to Interdisciplinary Middle-Range Theory

Migration theory needs to provide a framework for understanding the dynamics of international migration and incorporation in a situation of rapid and complex transformation (cf. King 2002). But can general theory do this? General theories are rarely crossdisciplinary; rather, they tend to postulate logical structures that cover all conceivable forms of behaviour from the theoretical perspective of a single discipline. That is why the label of 'grand theory' is often applied in sociology to Talcott Parson's 'social system' (Parsons 1951) or Niklas Luhman's idea of a 'world society' (Luhmann 1990). The 'messiness' (or complexity) of migratory behaviour, which goes across all areas of human existence and therefore concerns all the social sciences, cannot be readily accommodated within such elegant structures.

As discussed in Castles (2007), Alejandro Portes has argued strongly against the idea of an all-embracing general theory for migration studies. Rather, researchers should focus on the complexity, contradictions, and unintended consequences of social action (Portes 1997; Portes and DeWind 2004b). This implies returning to Merton's concept of 'theories of the middle range': 'special theories applicable to limited ranges of data—theories for example of class dynamics, of conflicting group pressures, of the flow of power and the exercise of interpersonal influence' (Merton 1957: 9).

In migration research a middle-range theory would allow analysis of the regularities and variations in specific types of migration that share some important common characteristics such as flows of different types (e.g. labour migration and asylum migration) belonging to a single migratory system (e.g. the system linking France and Algeria, or the United Kingdom and Nigeria). Another example is labour migration flows from poor to rich countries in a specific economic phase (e.g. the period of neoliberal globalization from the 1970s to 2008) across a range of migration systems (such as that linking South Asia and the Gulf, and that linking Southeast and East Asia). Such middle-range theories could bring together the insights provided by all the different social sciences concerned with migration.

What middle-range theories could not—and should not—aspire to do is to provide rules for analysing all types of migration regardless of time or location.

In *Worlds in Motion* Massey and his colleagues state that, 'Our review suggests the outlines of what an integrated theory of international migration should look like' (Massey et al. 1998: 281). It should contain

> four basic elements: a treatment of the structural forces that promote emigration from developing countries; a characterisation of the structural forces that attract immigrants into developed countries; a consideration of the motivations, goals and aspirations of the people who respond to these structural forces by becoming international migrants; and a treatment of the social and economic structures that arise to connect areas of out- and in-migration. Any theoretical explanation that embraces just one of these elements will necessarily be incomplete and misleading (Massey et al. 1998: 281).

These four elements cover the key aspects of an interdisciplinary conceptual framework for migration studies because they embrace not only macrostructures in origin and destination areas but also include the mesostructures developed to link these in migratory processes, and—importantly—the human agency of the migrants themselves. However, a serious problem remains: that of linking this overarching perspective with the specific disciplinary theories reviewed so ably in *Worlds and Motion.* Massey and colleagues note that

> all theories play some role in accounting for international migration in the contemporary world, although different models predominate at different phases of the migration process, and different explanations carry different weights in different regions depending on the local circumstances of history, politics and geography (Massey et al. 1998: 281).

Thus, they argue that world systems theory is best for explaining emigration from developing countries, while bits of world systems theory, segmented labour market theory, and neoclassical macroeconomics can be cobbled together to explain the forces attracting migration to developed destination countries—and so on for the rest of the four 'basic elements' (Massey et al. 1998: 281). It is difficult to see this eclectic approach as the basis for 'integrated theory' or even for a coherent analytical framework. Indeed, there seems to be a risk of making fairly arbitrary choices about which bit of theory to use in which circumstances.

Such considerations help to clarify the requirements for migration theory: it should take the form of a broad conceptual framework which can help to integrate the analyses of specific migratory processes by the various social-science disciplines. However, this framework cannot use various theoretical approaches in an arbitrary way by choosing the bits that fit and leaving out those that do not. A conceptual framework needs to be capable of accommodating all the factors and interactions that shape a given migratory process. However, this does not mean producing a contradiction-free analysis. A lack of consistency in findings across disciplines, paradigms, and methodologies may be an important indicator of knowledge and research gaps but can also show the need to revise the conceptual framework. This is how middle-range theory develops - without ever aspiring to present a universally valid truth.

2.4 A Social-Transformation Framework for Migration Studies

Awareness of complexity, diversity, and the importance of context might lead to the idea that theory formation is pointless because each case appears specific. This could encourage a postmodern fragmentation of knowledge, based on the idea that everything is specific, and that there are no broad social trends or institutional patterns. Yet such a perspective would ignore the reality of global integration processes that lead to higher and more pervasive levels of economic, political, social, and cultural integration than ever before. Contemporary social relations do offer great diversity, but it is diversity within increasingly universal relationships of power and inequality. Thus, the most important way to achieve advancement in migration studies is to link it more closely to wider social theory.

2.4.1 Re-embedding Migration in Social Transformation

Analysis of processes of social transformation could provide the basis for a new understanding of the links between human mobility and global change. Social transformation can be defined as a fundamental shift in the way society is organized that goes beyond the continual processes of incremental social change that are always at work. This implies a 'step change' in which all existing social patterns are questioned and many are reconfigured. Social transformations are closely linked to major shifts in dominant economic, political, and strategic relationships.

Therefore, a useful point of departure for a contemporary theory of social transformation is Polanyi's (2001) work (first published in 1944) on the 'great transformation' of European societies. According to Polyani, the market liberalism of the nineteenth century ignored the *embeddedness* of the economy in society (i.e. its role in achieving social goals laid down by politics, religion, and social custom). The liberal attempt to *disembed* the market was a 'stark utopia' leading to a *double movement*—a protective countermovement to re-subordinate the economy to society. Unfortunately, in the early twentieth century the countermovement inevitably led to fascism and world war (Block 2003; Polanyi 2001).

The closely linked processes of accelerated economic globalization and the reshaping of political and military power relationships since the end of the Cold War represent a contemporary step change—a new 'great transformation'. These fundamental economic and political shifts are closely interwoven with a transformation of social relationships. At the structural level social transformation in developed countries can be seen in the closure of older industries, the restructuring of labour forces, the erosion of welfare states, the fragmentation of communities, and the reshaping of social identities. In less developed countries forms of social transformation include intensification of agriculture, destruction of rural livelihoods, erosion of local social orders, and formation of shanty towns within new megacities.

Polanyi's idea of the 'double movement' can be seen through the modern lens of the concept of agency. Social-transformation processes are mediated by local historical and cultural patterns, through which people develop varying forms of agency and resistance. These can take the form of religious or nationalist movements but also of individual- or family-level livelihood strategies, including rural–urban and international migration. The recent upsurge in South–North migration can best be understood by examining these complementary changes and their complex linkages. Here, too, we can examine agency, for instance in the new social movements which have emerged in many places: in 2006 alone there were strike movements of South Asian workers in Gulf states, demonstrations of migrants in the United States for legalization and rights, and movements of youth of migrant origin against police repression in France.

Research on migration has had little impact on core theories of social order and differentiation. However, in recent times globalization has challenged national models in the social sciences and drawn attention to cross-border flows as key instruments of change. There are signs of a new emphasis on human mobility, and some major works on global change (e.g. Bauman 1998; Beck 2007; Cohen and Kennedy 2000; Held et al. 1999) have stressed the centrality of migration in contemporary social relations. This shift is not surprising: if the principle of the 'container society' in which all social relationships take place within the nation state (Faist 2000) is no longer sustainable (even as a myth), then flows across borders become a crucial area of investigation for the social sciences.

The concept of *embeddedness* can play an important part in understanding globalization and its consequences for human mobility. Just as nineteenth-century liberals portrayed economic affairs as separate from the rest of society, so neoliberals have promoted globalization as a predominantly economic phenomenon. The emergence of a new economy was depicted as the result of increasing foreign direct investment; the deregulation of cross-border flows of capital, technology, and services; and the creation of a global production system (Petras and Veltmayer 2000: 2). According to the neoliberal ideology, the superior efficiency of this new economic world was guaranteed by the rationality of decision-making in multinational corporations (MNCs) and by the 'invisible hand' of global financial and commodity markets. The basic premise of globalization was 'the leadership of civilization by economics' (Saul 2006: xi). This ideology was summed up in the 'Washington Consensus' on the importance of market liberalization, privatization, and deregulation (Stiglitz 2002: 67).

But the neoliberal attempt to disembed economic globalization from its societal context was in fact deeply political because it made global change appear as an inevitable and desirable form of modernization—one that could only be resisted by backward peoples or fundamentalist leaders. Clearly globalization was not just about economics; it was also a *political process*, conceived in ideological terms:

> For the theorists of this process and its many advocates these flows [...], together with the resulting economic integration and social transformation, have created a new world order with its own institutions and configurations of power that have replaced the previous structures associated with the nation-state, and that have created new conditions of peoples' lives all over the world (Petras and Veltmayer 2000: 2).

The globalization paradigm emerged in the context of the political strategies of the Reagan–Thatcher era designed to roll back the welfare states and the relatively high wage levels of the post-war boom period. Economic deregulation, the opening of markets, and the weakening of trade unions led to major social changes in the United States and the United Kingdom. Other developed countries were compelled to review their welfare states and 'social wages' to remain competitive, leading to a decline in labour protection and an increase in labour market segmentation by gender, ethnicity, origins, and legal status (see below).

Even a neoliberal world economy needs control mechanisms, but these were to be provided not by national governments (which, in some cases at least, were democratically elected) but by international institutions, especially the International Monetary Fund, the World Bank and the World Trade Organization. Their task was not to protect weak economies or vulnerable social groups but, rather, to ensure that all economies and societies would be opened up to the cold winds of competition, particularly through the mechanism of 'structural adjustment programmes'. These institutions had—and still have—close links with the U.S. Department of the Treasury, and their policies are strongly influenced by U.S. and European interests (Stiglitz 2002). The neoliberal dream was undermined by the near-meltdown of the global finance sector in 2007–2009. Although economists and politicians now speak of a 'post-Washington consensus' approach to world trade and investment, fundamental changes in economic power and governance have yet to emerge.

A theory of global change in which the economy is seen as disembedded from society, and the political and social consequences are treated as inevitable 'externalities' (as economists put it), also leads to a disembedded understanding of migration. In a narrow economistic view this means seeking the determinants of migration in a range of rational choices based on economic interests. The essential link to massive changes in global economic and political power relationships and the resulting social transformation processes is absent.

An alternative approach is to conceptualize migration not merely as a result of social transformation nor as one of its cause but as an integral and essential part of social-transformation processes. This means that theories of migration should be embedded in broader social theory. It also means that research on any specific migration phenomenon must always include research on the societal context in which it takes place. Finally, because awareness of change usually starts at the local level, it is important to link local-level experiences of migration (whether in origin or receiving areas) with other sociospatial levels—and particularly with global processes.

2.4.2 Social-Transformation Theory and Migration Theory

We can draw on emerging ideas from a range of disciplines to develop a new approach to understanding transformation–migration relationships. In economics Stiglitz has provided a critique of neoliberal economic globalization derived from

Polanyi's concept of transformation (Stiglitz 1998, 2002). To him the 'double movement' is represented by anti-globalization activism (see Stiglitz's foreword to Polanyi 2001). Milanovic (2007) shows that the neoliberal claim of improving economic outcomes for poor countries has masked a vast increase in inequality. In political economy the neoliberal model is criticized as a new utopia of a self-regulating world economy (Freeman and Kagarlitsky 2004; Petras and Veltmayer 2000; Weiss 1998). Such ideas echo Polanyi's critique of attempts to disembed the economy from society, but they are essentially top-down critiques which fail to analyse the local effects of global economic and political forces. In this respect critical theories and neoliberal approaches show a certain similarity in their determinism and exclusion of agency.

This one-sidedness can be countered by applying concepts and methodologies suggested by sociologists, geographers, and anthropologists. The International Sociological Association Research Committee on 'Social Transformation and Sociology of Development' (Schuerkens 2004) use the concept of 'glocalization' to analyse links between global forces and local life-worlds, and has applied this approach to the study of migration and ethnicity (see e.g. Berking 2003; Binder and Tosic 2005; Schuerkens 2005). Other sociologists show how identity movements arise in response to globalization (Castells 1997). Social geographers have developed new ways of understanding the changing meaning of 'territory' and the relationships between spatial levels (e.g. Lussault 2007; Sassen 2006). Social anthropology has moved away from older ideals of authenticity and singularity to study individual and group reactions to globalizing forces (e.g. Levitt and Glick Schiller 2004). This implies analysing 'a simultaneous dialectic of indigenisation [...] and cosmopolitanisation' (Friedman 2004).

Such trends in social theory have already had considerable influence on migration studies. As already mentioned, economists have become increasingly critical of the assumptions of neoclassical theory and are investigating the role of families, communities, and other social actors in migratory processes. The 'new economics of labour migration' (NLEM) seeks to overcome neoclassical methodological individualism by using household surveys to understand how migration can be a collective risk-diversifying rather than an income-maximizing strategy. NELM theorists analyse migration as a strategy to overcome local-market and other development constraints through remitting money, which can serve as investment capital (Stark 1991; Taylor 1999). In political economy a new approach designed to correct the traditional top-down macro-bias is the development of 'micro-' or 'relational' political-economy research on livelihoods and commodity chains in conflict areas (e.g. Collinson 2003, 2009).

One of the most widely accepted innovations in migration theory since the 1980s has been the adoption of network theories which focus on the collective agency of migrants and communities in organizing processes of migration and incorporation (Boyd 1989; Portes and Bach 1985).[2] Informal networks provide vital resources for

[2] In fact, network theories were foreshadowed much earlier by theories of chain migration (see Price 1963).

individuals and groups. In the context of sending countries they are often analysed as mechanisms for the transmission of *cultural capital*, while in the context of migrant incorporation into receiving societies the emphasis is more on *social capital* (Bourdieu and Wacquant 1992: 119), which includes personal relationships, family and household patterns, friendship and community ties, and mutual help in economic and social matters. A newer trend towards analysing migrant agency is to be found in transnational theory (e.g. Guarnizo et al. 2003; Portes et al. 2007; Vertovec 2004).

These brief examples reflect the strength of new thinking about global connectivity in social theory, and show how such ideas are influencing many aspects of migration research. Thus, the project of elaborating a social-transformation framework for the analysis of migration does not require starting from scratch. Rather, the task is to bring together new approaches and insights in a detailed and systematic way so that they can serve as a coherent frame for migration theory and research methodology. This task cannot be attempted here. Instead, one example will be presented to show briefly how the understanding of local experiences of migration can be enhanced through analysis of global social transformations.

2.5 Example: Migration and Labour-Force Dynamics in the New Economy

One of the most dramatic, and perhaps surprising, trends of the last 20–30 years has been the restructuring of labour forces in rich countries through increased use of employment practices such as subcontracting, spurious self-employment, temporary employment, and casual work. Closely linked has been the growth of informal economies. A further trend has been the growth of domestic service and care worker jobs, usually employing women—frequently under highly exploitative conditions. Such forms of work affect natives as well as migrants, but international migration has been crucial to their growth, and migrants are more likely than natives to find themselves in situations of precarious employment (Schierup et al. 2006).

Conventional analyses of such trends often attribute the decline in working conditions and the increasing polarization of labour markets to the ready availability of—frequently irregular—migrant workers. This allows politicians and sections of the media to advocate strategies of tighter immigration control, ostensibly to 'protect local workers'. But some social scientists argue that the causality is the other way round: economic deregulation and employer practices have created informal-sector jobs, forming a pull factor for irregular migrants (Reyneri 2003). This applies most obviously in Southern Europe, but informal work is widespread throughout Northwestern Europe, for instance in agriculture, cleaning, and catering, but also (at least in the United Kingdom) in such occupations as traffic wardens and security guards—both services devolved by public authorities to subcontractors.

Analysis based on a social-transformation framework would start from the position that changes in the work situation and social position of workers in advanced economies are linked to global restructuring of investment, production, and trade.

This has led to simultaneous processes of transformation in the North and in the South. The social transformation in developed countries can be seen in the closure of older industries, the restructuring of labour forces, the erosion of welfare states, and the decline of traditional working-class communities. Combined with demographic change (especially population ageing) and requirements for labour for new types of service industries, this leads to demand for migrant labour. In less developed countries the social transformation of modes of production and social relations already outlined above causes people to emigrate in search of better livelihoods and greater security. The upsurge in South–North migration can best be understood by examining these complementary changes and their complex linkages.

Thus, neoliberal restructuring has led to a new global social geography which favours migration of both the highly skilled and those without formal qualifications. In the 1980s Sassen (1988) showed how foreign investment and displacement of manufacturing jobs abroad had fostered new migratory streams to the United States. Linkages between global cities and distant hinterlands created situations where enormous wealth and highly remunerated professional employment coexisted with growing unskilled service industry employment and Third World–like employment conditions in underground industries. The subsequent development of the new global social geography is perhaps best illustrated by local- or national-level studies.

For instance, Immanuel Ness has examined the economic transformation of New York (Ness 2005: Chap. 2). In the early twentieth century immigrant labour from Southern and Eastern Europe had been crucial to the emergence of the garment, printing, meatpacking, construction, and transportation industries. Industry was concentrated in 'ethnic neighbourhoods', and immigrants came to form the backbone of the city's strong labour movement. In the late twentieth century these traditional industries were restructured, with most production jobs being moved to non-unionized 'sunbelt' states or offshore to the Caribbean, Latin America, and Asia. Many new jobs were created in retailing, personal services, and business services (see also Waldinger 1996). The worst jobs are done by undocumented migrants from the Dominican Republic, Mexico, and French West Africa, who compete for precarious and exploitative posts as supermarket workers, delivery drivers, and kitchen workers (Ness 2005). As in the past, the new economy is heavily stratified on the basis of ethnicity, but this no longer provides a basis for solidarity and unionization because the jobs and the workers are dispersed all over the city.

The construction industry in Berlin provides another example. Following German reunification in 1990 and the move of the government to Berlin the city experienced an unprecedented building boom. Yet by 1996 about 25 % of unemployed persons in Berlin were building workers. Some employers took on workers from Poland, who came through temporary-labour schemes. Another option was to subcontract work to Portuguese firms which could bring their own workers (at lower wages) through EU free-movement provisions. In addition, many workers came as daily commuters from the former East German hinterland of the state of Brandenburg. This competition had adverse effects on unionized building workers, many of whom were long-term foreign residents of Berlin. In the old German model of long-term employment the firm and the trade union had been sites of interethnic communication and integration. Racism against migrants had been less pronounced at work than in other social areas. The decline of this model and its replacement with contract workers thus had negative effects on social integration and intergroup relations. This was no doubt one factor in the increase in racism and racist violence following German reunification (Hunger and Thränhardt 2001).

The garment industry provides many examples of ethnic entrepreneurship and hierarchies based on race and gender around the world (Rath 2002). In the United Kingdom ethnic and gender-based divisions allowed the revival of clothing production after it had seemed doomed to extinction through outsourcing to low-wage economies (see Phizacklea 1990). From the 1970s the management, design, and marketing of clothing became heavily concentrated in a few big and highly capitalized UK retail clothing companies (Mitter 1985). Domestic clothing production declined steeply. During the 1960s and 1970s the immigrant workforce in the garment industry had mainly been first-generation male immigrants: Pakistanis, Indians, Bangladeshis, and others. Many of these workers lost their jobs and then became contractors to the big clothing houses, setting up small, formally independent sweatshops based on cheap ethnic-minority or immigrant-family labour. Migrant women made up the bulk of the workforce in the new sweatshops. Cost reduction was accomplished through this sector's nature as a hidden economy—which also helped the producers to evade taxation. This state of informality suited the economic interests of the big retailers and of the male ethnic middlemen contractors, who managed to keep their female workforce under control through bonds of family and ethnic-community allegiance and dominance (Mitter 1985; Schierup et al. 2006: 235–237).

Each of the above cases has specific characteristics but also reveals recurring patterns that show the connections between specific experiences and global shifts. Taken together, these examples of labour force restructuring add up to a new process of *labour marketsegmentation.* People's chances of getting jobs depend not only on their human capital (i.e. their education and skills) but also on gender, race, ethnicity, origin, and legal status. Each case reflects the complex links between labour force change and processes of social transformation both in the North and in South. Research strategies that concentrate on specific experiences of migrant employment and ignore such connections cannot unravel the broader dynamics of change.

2.6 Conclusion

The central aim of this chapter has been to discuss some of the difficulties of theory formation in the field of migration studies, and to suggest a possible response. The problems include surmounting disciplinary boundaries, preventing fragmentation into isolated subfields, fending off political or bureaucratic cooption, overcoming an overemphasis on receiving country perspectives, and—most important—finding appropriate theories and methodologies to reflect the complexity, diversity, and contextuality of migratory processes. The solution does not lie in seeking to formulate a single (or general) theory of migration, which would almost inevitably degenerate into banality and abstraction. But nor are answers to be found by abandoning the quest for theoretical advancement on the grounds that all migratory processes are different and unique.

The suggested response is that migration researchers should seek to develop middle-range theories that can help integrate the insights of the various social sciences to understand the regularities and variations of a range of migratory processes within a given historical socioeconomic constellation. Such middle-range theories can form the basis for a conceptual framework which takes contemporary social transformation processes as a starting point for understanding shifting patterns of human mobility. Such a conceptual framework would consist of a detailed mapping of the factors that influence migratory processes and of the connections between these factors.

A key aspect of this conceptual framework would be that it should not restrict itself to migration but rather seek to link analysis of migratory processes to broader social theory, and through this to the analysis of societal change in general. The development of migration theory at this historical juncture should therefore be linked to the analysis of social-transformation processes at a range of sociospatial levels: whether a specific piece of research starts with a local phenomenon or a global one, or with something in between, the researchers conducting it must be aware of the connectivity between localities and mediations between levels.

References

Alba, R., & Nee, V. (1997). Rethinking assimilation theory for a new era of immigration. *International Migration Review, 31*(4), 826–874. doi:10.2307/2547416.

Albrow, M. (1996). *The global age: State and society beyond modernity*. Cambridge: Polity Press.

Bakewell, O. (2007). *Keeping them in their place: The ambivalent relationship between development and migration in Africa* (IMI Working Paper 8). Oxford: International Migration Institute. http://afrique-europe-interact.net/files/engl._migration_and_development_-_ob.pdf

Bauman, Z. (1998). *Globalization: The human consequences*. Cambridge: Polity Press.

Beck, U. (1997). *Was ist globalisierung?* Frankfurt am Main: Suhrkamp.

Beck, U. (2007). Beyond class and nation: Reframing social inequalities in a globalizing world. *British Journal of Sociology, 58*(4), 679–705. doi:10.1111/j.1468-4446.2007.00171.x.

Berking, H. (2003). 'Ethnicity Is Everywhere': On globalization and the transformation of cultural identity. *Current Sociology, 51*(3–4), 248–264. doi:10.1177/0011392103051003006.

Bhagwati, J. (2003). Borders beyond control. *Foreign Affairs, 82*(1), 98–104. doi:10.2307/20033431.

Binder, S., & Tosic, J. (2005). Refugees as a particular form of transnational migrations and social transformations: Socioanthropological and gender aspects. *Current Sociology, 53*(4), 607–624. doi:10.1177/0011392105052717.

Block, F. (2003). Karl Polanyi and the writing of *The Great Transformation. Theory and Society, 32*(3), 275–306. doi:10.1023/A:1024420102334.

Bourdieu, P., & Wacquant, L. J. D. (1992). *An invitation to reflexive sociology*. Chicago: University of Chicago Press.

Boyd, M. (1989). Family and personal networks in migration: Recent developments and new agendas. *International Migration Review, 23*(3), 638–670. doi:10.2307/2546433.

Brettell, C. B., & Hollifield, J. F. (Eds.). (2007). *Migration theory: Talking across disciplines* (2nd ed.). New York/Abingdon: Routledge.
Castells, M. (1996). *The rise of the network society: The information age: Economy, society and culture: Vol. I.* Oxford/Malden: Blackwell Publishing.
Castells, M. (1997). *The power of identity: The information age: Economy, society and culture: Vol. II.* Oxford/Malden: Blackwell Publishing.
Castells, M. (1998). *End of millennium: The information age: Economy, society and culture: Vol. III.* Oxford/Malden: Blackwell Publishing.
Castles, S. (2004). Why migration policies fail. *Ethnic and Racial Studies, 27*(2), 205–227. doi:10.1080/0141987042000177306.
Castles, S. (2006). Guestworkers in Europe: A resurrection? *International Migration Review, 40*(4), 741–766. doi:10.1111/j.1747-7379.2006.00042.x.
Castles, S. (2007). Twenty-first century migration as a challenge to sociology. *Journal of Ethnic and Migration Studies, 33*(3), 351–371. doi:10.1080/13691830701234491.
Castles, S. (2008). *Development and migration – Migration and development: What comes first?*http://www.imi.ox.ac.uk/pdfs/SCastlesMigandDevforSSRCApril08.pdf
Castles, S., & Delgado Wise, R. (Eds.) (2008). *Migration and development: Perspectives from the South.* Geneva: International Organization for Migration. http://www.imi.ox.ac.uk/pdfs/migration-and-development-perspectives-from-the-south
Castles, S., & Miller, M. J. (2009). *The age of migration: International population movements in the modern world: Fourth edition: Revised and updated.* Basingstoke/New York: Palgrave Macmillan.
Castles, S., & Van Hear, N. (2010). Root causes. In A. Betts (Ed.), *Global migration governance* (pp. 287–306). Oxford/New York: Oxford University Press.
CEC. (2005a). *Communication from the commission: Policy plan on legal migration: {SEC(2005)1680}.* Brussels: Commission of the European Communities. http://eur-lex.europa.eu/legal-content/EN/TXT/?uri=CELEX:52005DC0669
CEC. (2005b). *Green paper on an EU approach to managing economic migration: COM(2004)811 final.* Brussels: Commission of the European Communities. http://aei.pitt.edu/37783/1/COM_(2004)_811.pdf
Cohen, R. (Ed.). (1995). *The Cambridge survey of world migration.* Cambridge: Cambridge University Press.
Cohen, R., & Kennedy, P. (2000). *Global sociology.* Basingstoke/New York: Palgrave.
Collinson, S. (Ed.) (2003). *Power, livelihoods and conflict: Case studies in political economy analysis for humanitarian action* (HPG report 13). London: Overseas Development Institute. http://www.odi.org/sites/odi.org.uk/files/odi-assets/publications-opinion-files/289.pdf
Collinson, S. (2009). *The political economy of migration processes: An agenda for migration research and analysis* (Working Paper 12). Oxford: International Migration Institute. http://www.imi.ox.ac.uk/pdfs/wp/wp12-collinson/at_download/file
Connell, R. W. (1997). Why is classical theory classical? *American Journal of Sociology, 102*(6), 1511–1557. doi:10.1086/231125.
Cornelius, W. A., Martin, P. L., & Hollifield, J. F. (1994). Introduction: The ambivalent quest for control. In W. A. Cornelius, P. L. Martin, & J. F. Hollifield (Eds.), *Controlling immigration: A global perspective* (pp. 3–41). Stanford: Stanford University Press.
De Haas, H. (2006). *Turning the tide? Why 'development instead of migration' policies are bound to fail* (Working Paper 2). Oxford: International Migration Institute. http://heindehaas.com/Publications/deHaas2006-IMIWP2-DevelopmentInsteadofMigration.pdf
Entzinger, H. (2003). The rise and fall of multiculturalism: The case of the Netherlands. In C. Joppke & E. Morawaska (Eds.), *Towards assimilation and citizenship: Immigration in liberal nation-states* (pp. 59–86). Basingstoke/New York: Palgrave Macmillan.
Faist, T. (2000). *The volume and dynamics of international migration and transnational social spaces.* Oxford/New York: Oxford University Press.

Freeman, A., & Kagarlitsky, B. (Eds.). (2004). *The politics of empire: Globalisation in crisis*. London/Ann Arbor: Pluto Press.

Friedman, J. (2004). Globalization, transnationalization, and migration: Ideologies and realities of global transformation. In J. Friedman & S. Randeria (Eds.), *Worlds on the move: Globalization, migration and cultural security* (pp. 63–88). London/New York: I.B. Tauris.

GCIM. (2005). *Migration in an interconnected world: New directions for action: Report of the Global Commission on International Migration*. Geneva: Global Commission on International Migration. http://www.queensu.ca/samp/migrationresources/reports/gcim-complete-report-2005.pdf

Gold, S. J. (2005). Migrant networks: A summary and critique of relational approaches to international migration. In M. Romero & E. Margolis (Eds.), *The Blackwell companion to social inequalities* (pp. 257–285). Malden/Oxford/Carlton: Blackwell Publishing.

Guarnizo, L. E., Portes, A., & Haller, W. (2003). Assimilation and transnationalism: Determinants of transnational political action among contemporary migrants. *American Journal of Sociology, 108*(6), 1211–1248. doi:10.1086/375195.

Hatton, T. J., & Williamson, J. G. (1998). *The age of mass migration: Causes and economic impact*. Oxford/New York: Oxford University Press.

Hatton, T. J., & Williamson, J. G. (2005). *Global migration and the world economy: Two centuries of policy and performance*. Boston: MIT Press.

Held, D., McGrew, A., Goldblatt, D., & Perraton, J. (1999). *Global transformations: Politics, economics and culture*. Cambridge: Polity Press.

Hirschman, C., Kasinitz, P., & DeWind, J. (Eds.). (1999). *The handbook of international migration: The American experience*. New York: Russell Sage.

Hunger, U., & Thränhardt, D. (2001). Die Berliner Integrationspolitik im Vergleich der Bundesländer. In F. Gesemann (Ed.), *Migration und Integration in Berlin: Wissenschaftliche Analysen und politische Perspektiven* (pp. 109–125). Opladen: Leske + Budrich.

Joppke, C., & Morawaska, E. (Eds.). (2003). *Towards assimilation and citizenship: Immigration in liberal nation-states*. Basingstoke/New York: Palgrave Macmillan.

King, R. (2002). Towards a new map of European migration. *International Journal of Population Geography, 8*(2), 89–106. doi:10.1002/ijpg.246.

Kuhn, T. S. (1996). *The structure of scientific revolutions* (3rd ed.). Chicago/London: University of Chicago Press.

Levitt, P., & Glick Schiller, N. (2004). Conceptualising simultaneity: A transnational social field perspective on society. *International Migration Review, 38*(3), 1002–1039. doi:10.1111/j.1747-7379.2004.tb00227.x.

Luhmann, N. (1990). *Die Wissenschaft der Gesellschaft*. Suhrkamp: Frankfurt am Main.

Lussault, M. (2007). *L'Homme spatial: La construction sociale de l'espace humain*. Paris: Seuil.

Manuh, T. (Ed.). (2005). *At home in the world? International migration and development in contemporary Ghana and West Africa*. Accra: Sub-Saharan Publishers.

Massey, D. S., Arango, J., Hugo, G., Kouaouci, A., Pellegrino, A., & Taylor, J. E. (1998). *Worlds in motion: Understanding international migration at the end of the millennium*. Oxford: Clarendon.

Merton, R. K. (1957). *Social theory and social structure*. New York: The Free Press.

Milanovic, B. (2007). Globalization and inequality. In D. Held & A. Kaya (Eds.), *Global inequality: Patterns and explanations* (pp. 26–49). Cambridge/Malden: Polity Press.

Mitter, S. (1985). Industrial restructuring and manufacturing homework: Immigrant women in the UK clothing industry. *Capital & Class, 9*(3), 37–80. doi:10.1177/030981688502700103.

Ness, I. (2005). *Immigrants, unions and the new U.S. labor market*. Philadelphia: Temple University Press.

Parsons, T. (1951). *The social system*. Glencoe: The Free Press.

Penninx, R., Berger, M., & Kraal, K. (Eds.). (2006). *The dynamics of international migration and settlement in Europe: A state of the art*. Amsterdam: Amsterdam University Press.

Petras, J., & Veltmayer, H. (2000). Globalisation or imperialism? *Cambridge Review of International Affairs, 14*(1), 32–48. doi:10.1080/09557570008400327.
Phizacklea, A. (1990). *Unpacking the fashion industry: Gender, racism, and class in production*. London/New York: Routledge.
Polanyi, K. (2001). *The great transformation: The political and economic origins of our time*. Boston: Beacon.
Portes, A. (1997). Immigration theory for a new century: Some problems and opportunities. *International Migration Review, 31*(4), 799–825. doi:10.2307/2547415.
Portes, A. (2010). Migration and social change: Some conceptual reflections. *Journal of Ethnic and Migration Studies, 36*(10), 1537–1563.
Portes, A., & Bach, R. L. (1985). *Latin journey: Cuban and Mexican immigrants in the United States*. Berkeley/Los Angeles/London: University of California Press.
Portes, A., & DeWind, J. (Eds.) (2004a). Conceptual and methodological developments in the study of international migration. Special issue of *International Migration Review, 38*(3), 828–1302.
Portes, A., & DeWind, J. (2004b). A cross-Atlantic dialogue: The progress of research and theory in the study of international migration. *International Migration Review, 38*(3), 828–851. doi:10.1111/j.1747-7379.2004.tb00221.x.
Portes, A., Escobar, C., & Radford, A. W. (2007). Immigrant transnational organizations and development: A comparative study. *International Migration Review, 41*(1), 242–281. doi:10.1111/j.1747-7379.2007.00063.x.
Price, C. (1963). *Southern Europeans in Australia*. Melbourne: Oxford University Press.
Ranis, G. (2009). *Relationships between migration and development* (SSRC Migration & Development Conference Paper No. 3). New York: Social Science Research Council. http://essays.ssrc.org/developmentpapers/wp-content/uploads/2009/08/3Ranis.pdf
Rath, J. (2002). *Unravelling the rag trade: Immigrant entrepreneurship in seven world cities*. Oxford/New York: Berg.
Reyneri, E. (2003). Immigration and the underground economy in new receiving South European countries: Manifold negative effects, manifold deep-rooted causes. *International Review of Sociology: Revue Internationale de Sociologie, 13*(1), 117–143. doi:10.1080/0390670032000087023.
Sassen, S. (1988). *The mobility of labour and capital: A study in international investment and labor flow*. Cambridge/New York/Melbourne/Madrid: Cambridge University Press.
Sassen, S. (2006). *Territory, authority, rights: From medieval to global assemblages*. Princeton/Woodstock: Princeton University Press.
Saul, J. R. (2006). *The collapse of globalism and the reinvention of the world*. London: Atlantic Books.
Schierup, C.-U., Hansen, P., & Castles, S. (2006). *Migration, citizenship, and the European welfare state: A European dilemma*. Oxford/New York: Oxford University Press.
Schuerkens, U. (Ed.). (2004). *Global forces and local life-worlds: Social transformations*. London/Thousand Oaks/New Delhi: SAGE.
Schuerkens, U. (2005). Transnational migrations and social transformations: A theoretical perspective. *Current Sociology, 53*(4), 535–553. doi:10.1177/0011392105052714.
Skeldon, R. (2006). Interlinkages between internal and international migration and development in the Asian region. *Population, Space and Place, 12*(1), 15–30. doi:10.1002/psp.385.
Stark, O. (1991). *The migration of labour*. Cambridge/Oxford: Blackwell.
Stiglitz, J. E. (1998, October 19). *Towards a new paradigm for development: Strategies, policies, and processes*. Given as the 1998 Prebisch Lecture at UNCTAD, Geneva, 1998. Geneva: The World Bank. http://siteresources.worldbank.org/NEWS/Resources/prebisch98.pdf
Stiglitz, J. E. (2002). *Globalization and its discontents*. London: Penguin.
Taylor, E. (1999). The new economics of labour migration and the role of remittances in the migration process. *International Migration, 37*(1), 63–88. doi:10.1111/1468-2435.00066.

UNDESA. (2005). *Trends in total migrant stock: The 2005 revision*. New York: United Nations Department of Economic and Social Affairs.

UNDP. (2009). *Human development report 2009: Overcoming barriers: Human mobility and development*. New York: United Nations Development Programme. http://hdr.undp.org/sites/default/files/reports/269/hdr_2009_en_complete.pdf

Urry, J. (2007). *Mobilities*. Cambridge/Malden: Polity Press.

Vasta, E. (2007). From ethnic minorities to ethnic majority policy: Multiculturalism and the shift to assimilationism in the Netherlands. *Ethnic and Racial Studies, 30*(5), 713–740. doi:10.1080/01419870701491770.

Vasta, E., & Vuddamalay, V. (Eds.). (2006). *International migration and the social sciences: Confronting national experiences in Australia, France and Germany*. Basingstoke/New York: Palgrave Macmillan.

Vertovec, S. (2004). Migrant transnationalism and modes of transformation. *International Migration Review, 38*(3), 970–1001. doi:10.1111/j.1747-7379.2004.tb00226.x.

Waldinger, R. D. (1996). *Still the promised city? African-Americans and new immigrants in postindustrial New York*. Cambridge: Harvard University Press.

Weiss, L. (1998). *The myth of the powerless state: Governing the economy in a global era*. Cambridge: Polity Press.

Wimmer, A., & Glick Schiller, N. (2003). Methodological nationalism, the social sciences, and the study of migration: An essay in historical epistemology. *International Migration Review, 37*(3), 576–610. doi:10.1111/j.1747-7379.2003.tb00151.x.

Chapter 3
Theorizing About Change: The Promise of Comparative Political Economy for Migration Studies

Georg Menz

3.1 Introduction

In the early 2000s many European governments, having rediscovered the presumed benefits of immigration for economic purposes, began to revise the restrictive-policy approach that had been applied for nearly 25 years. The rhetorical claims used to justify this change in policy stance were related to alleged labour and skill shortages, declining birth rates, and the questionable, conjured-up image of an apparently global competition for skilled migrants.

This chapter seeks to explain what contribution an approach from comparative political economy can make to the study of migration policy formation. This is accomplished by applying a framework that is informed by the varieties of capitalism framework, with a focus on the empirical puzzle of how the drivers of the renaissance of liberal labour migration in Europe can be identified. The chapter contains an empirical study of the rediscovery of labour migration in Sweden and the United Kingdom, the former a coordinated and the latter a liberal market economy. One of the key arguments is that employers are important actors in framing, influencing, and even shaping labour migration policy.

In recent years scholarly efforts have identified a number of factors and actors that are relevant in shaping migration policy design, including 'organised interest groups, courts, ethnic groups, trade unions, law and order bureaucracies, police and security agencies, local actors and street-level bureaucrats and private actors' (Lahav and Guiraudon 2006: 207). This chapter presents a more recent strand of the literature, which emphasizes the role of employers (Caviedes 2006; Cerna 2009a; Menz and Caviedes 2010; Menz 2011).

G. Menz (✉)
Goldsmiths College, University of London, London, UK
e-mail: g.menz@gold.ac.uk

A. Amelina et al. (eds.), *An Anthology of Migration and Social Transformation*, IMISCOE Research Series, DOI 10.1007/978-3-319-23666-7_3

The rest of this chapter is organized as follows: the second section outlines the core contribution that an approach from comparative political economy can make to migration studies. The third section provides an empirical analysis of the politics of migration policy formation in Sweden and the United Kingdom to explore the purchase such an approach affords. The chapter closes with a conclusion.

3.2 What Is Driving Immigration Policy Design?

The politics of migration policy design are by now well-charted territory, yet scholars differ considerably on how much weight should be given to the different driving factors, and there is certainly no consensus on the matter. Some scholars point to the relative policy autonomy of the state in Europe and the fundamentally elitist character of policymaking, which they believe precludes meaningful intervention by non-governmental organizations (Statham and Geddes 2006). This seems somewhat unlikely, and it might be more fruitful to focus on the level of connection to the state apparatus that certain elite non-governmental actors command, which clearly sets them apart from humanitarian and civil-society groups, who are typically kept at arm's length. It is also worth noting that room for manoeuvre in migration policy design, implementation, and administration is limited due to the role of often very liberal court decisions (Joppke 1998; Guiraudon 2001), and that policy implementation in particular is often hamstrung by the fierce resistance from local activists encountered by local governments. In the European context the role of the European Union and of its rapidly growing body of legislation is worth highlighting, which appears to be particularly transformative for countries with underdeveloped migration regulation (Menz 2009; Boswell and Geddes 2010).

Other accounts have been sceptical about the claim that policymaking is elitist and well-insulated. Some scholars have emphasized political salience (e.g. Givens and Luedtke 2005), while others have pointed to the role of public opinion or indeed the role of party politics (e.g. Bale 2008; Hinnfors et al. 2012), and Meyers (2004) has highlighted the significance of national economic performance, specifically that of unemployment. Ultimately, the exact role and degree of agency is highly important because the renaissance of liberal labour migration policies, which had been deemed unlikely earlier (Messina 1990), appears somewhat difficult to account for otherwise. It is still the case that the 'prevailing scholarship […] has been inconclusive with regard to the role and nature of domestic actors [in] national immigration policy-making' (Lahav and Guiraudon 2006: 207). Even if we disregard the sceptical and at times even hostile public opinion, the rise of the Far Right, the serious integration problems among Europe's second-generation immigrants, and the persistently high unemployment rates, the rediscovery of managed labour migration that Europe has witnessed over the past decade seems very surprising. Even more puzzling is the fact that not all European governments have pursued this course despite structural similarities. Somewhat counter-intuitively, the serious economic difficulties experienced since 2008 do not appear to have led to a fundamental revision of the liberal stance.

This chapter explains what contribution an approach from comparative political economy can make to the study of migration. It departs from the assumption that migration policy design is actually elitist and unfolds within an ultimately very limited and confined policy space. Migration regulation being remarkably slow to change and path-dependent, actors interested in pushing for change need to act as strong policy entrepreneurs. The core argument put forward by scholars inspired by approaches from comparative political economy is that the models of capitalism found across Europe have significant ramifications for the parameters and content of immigration policy (see e.g. Caviedes 2006; Cerna 2009a; Menz 2009, 2011). Combining political-economy arguments with the study of migration was common between the early 1970s and the late 1990s, especially in Marxist-inspired analytical contributions (Cole and Dale 1999; earlier: Castles and Kosack 1973; Castells 1975; Piore 1979). Since then, however, scant scholarly attention has been paid to the role of labour market structures, the structural constraints of different systems of political economy, or the agency of economic interest groups. This is particularly true of contributions from the area of migration studies on trade unions and employer associations. This chapter argues that the efforts of organized business and especially their efforts towards the formation of labour migration policy are pivotal.

3.3 Comparative Political Economy and Migration Studies

For the purpose of this chapter, it is worth introducing the basic tenets of the varieties of capitalism approach. In the introductory chapter to their seminal book *Varieties of Capitalism* Peter A. Hall and David Soskice note that their novel approach is 'actor-centered, which is to say we see the political economy as a terrain populated by multiple actors, each of whom seeks to advance his interests', and that it 'is a firm-centered political economy that regards companies as the crucial actors'. With this focus, the authors then proceed to suggest five spheres in which 'coordination problems' need to be resolved: industrial relations (especially wage setting), vocational training and education, corporate governance, inter-firm relations, and intra-firm relations between management and staff. Effectively, there are two basic avenues to address coordination in any of these spheres, depending either on 'competitive market relationships' or on 'non-market relationships', which entail 'more extensive relational or incomplete contracting [...] and more reliance on collaborative [...] relationships' (Hall and Soskice 2001: 6–8). The authors note that the United States and Germany, the former a liberal market economy (LME) and the latter a coordinated market economy (CME), represent these two ideal types most accurately; however, most of the other OECD countries can be similarly classified according to this typology. The case selection is informed by this categorization, Sweden being a CME and the UK being an LME. The respective category is self-reinforcing over time and influences firms' behaviour. This is because there are important *complementarities* between the respective positions that firms may take in these five spheres. It follows that 'institutional practices of various types should not be distributed randomly across nations' (Hall and Soskice 2001: 18); instead, one would expect to find some clustering of certain characteristics according to the overall variety to which an individual country adheres (Hall and Gingerich 2004). Thus, we now have a typology of classification that describes in considerable detail how different political economies are organized. Firms consider it advantageous to adhere to their given model of capitalism in view of the advantages that complementary features of a given variety provide. Because the approach postulates that the distinct varieties also reflect different competitive strengths, firms will also try to maintain or will modestly adjust their distinct variety in the face of pressures for change. This is a neo-Ricardian argument in that it is based on the assumption that the outcome of change can be predicted: firms will prefer *modest, system-affirming renovation* to *radical overhaul*.

Now that the core tenets of the varieties-of-capitalism argument have been clarified, it is necessary to explore to what extent this approach can help the different areas of migration studies to mutually enrich one another. Earlier studies that emphasized the importance of employer associations were concerned with the pluralist policy environment of the United States, in which organized interest groups play a highly important role in lobbying for their preferred outcome. However, it should be noted that—to modify Freeman's (1995, 2002) famous analysis somewhat—in the European context employers will not simply lobby for a more liberal policy but for migrants with certain skill profiles that correspond to the predominant production strategy. Above all, employers seek to achieve *complementarity* with respect to recruitment via labour migration and therefore do not univocally advocate the recruitment of identical profiles of economic migrants. Nor do they simply advocate a more liberal labour migration policy, because certain groups of labour migrants may prove to be ill-suited to labour market requirements. It is worth noting that, unlike in the earlier era of labour recruitment in Europe between the 1950s and 1970s, unskilled and low-skilled manufacturing jobs are no longer plentiful, and simply clamouring for liberalization across the board is difficult politically and of dubious benefit economically. *Instead, employers' interest will be conditioned by the model of capitalism (and thus by the production strategy) in which they are embedded, which will ensure complementarity*. Migrants' skill sets differ along two dimensions: level (low-skilled vs. highly skilled) and specificity (sector-specific vs. generalist). Sector-specific skills are skills that are linked to one specific sector of the economy; they are acquired either through applied tertiary education or through post-secondary vocational training. Generalist skills are not specific to any one particular economic sector, and they are transferable. While Salt (1997: 5) defined 'highly skilled' as 'tertiary level education or its equivalent in experience', I use the term here in a somewhat broader sense to include graduates of post-secondary vocational training programmes. Consequently, unskilled and low-skilled workers are workers who do not possess such formal qualifications. Apart from skills, labour shortages will also influence employer positions, but will be filtered by considerations of results produced by present educational and vocational systems. While it is true that 'countries' policies cannot thus be deduced from a simple division into [... variety-of-capitalism] groups' (Cerna 2009a: 146), the advocacy position of employers is indeed shaped by the production system and the respective model of capitalism. However, it should be noted that employers may also use labour migration to escape the confines imposed by training systems. Employers in LMEs may encounter skill shortages among the domestic labour pool, which result from the traditionally low ability of LME education systems to generate vocational-training schemes. Employers in CMEs face a different challenge: in certain sectors, especially in those rapidly evolving due to technological change, CME education and training systems may perform inadequately because they are geared towards gradual, rather than towards radical product innovation. 'Importing labour' to overcome or 'circumvent institutional constraints' has been recognized as an explicit business strategy in recent studies that have taken the varieties-of-capitalism approach (see Herrmann 2008). Employers will thus seek to recruit employees with skills that are complementary in the first instance, creating obvious *synergy* effects, but they will also turn to labour migration as a source of *supplementarity* to overcome the limitations of domestic training systems.[1]

Employers in CMEs will lobby for skilled migrants who can either complement existing production modes directly or provide valuable synergies if they permit the 'import' of skills that are not or not sufficiently generated domestically, thus permitting radical product innovation. Highly skilled foreigners may have skills equivalent to CME-style vocational training or tertiary education; they may thus either possess generalist or specific skills. In contrast, there is no interest in unskilled migrants. Because there is no low-skill low-wage service sector of notable size, low-skilled and unskilled individuals are rendered difficult to employ. Employers have no institutional incentive to upset the 'high-skill equilibrium' (Culpepper 1999; Culpepper and Finegold 1999) – a crucial component of the CME model – and would face potentially very costly consequences if they did.

The embedded environments of the respective varieties of capitalism thus shape the preferences of actors and create a demand for different sets of labour migrants. Different national production strategies influence employer advocacy coalitions. Recent economic liberalization notwithstanding, the differences in production strategies are more pivotal today than they were during the post-war phase of labour recruitment when labour migration was not driven exclusively by economic factors but often was more influenced by colonial and/or post-colonial ties (Castles and Miller 2003).

However, it has also been argued that the recruitment preferences of employers do not differ so much along national as along sectoral lines (Caviedes 2006), which suggests that employers in similar sectors will share similarities with their international competitors and thus may diverge from the opinions held by other sectoral employer associations or their umbrella association. Employers in the food and beverage sector, for example, may well be interested in relatively unskilled employees,

[1] The terms 'complementarity' and 'supplementarity' are taken from Deeg (2007), who uses them slightly differently. I propose to broaden his term 'supplementarity' to include the 'import of input factors' (Herrmann 2009: 18) that is missing or underprovided due to the institutional particularities of domestic institutions.

not only because skills are defined in less than conventional ways in the hospitality industry but also because long and anti-social working hours, poor working conditions in many cases, and relatively low pay are impediments to the recruitment of local staff. In addition, sectoral employers feel ambiguous about or even hostile to the prospect of fresh immigration into their sector because they are afraid to upset a fine-tuned equilibrium between skills and remuneration (Menz 2005). Immigration can also lead to lower wages and thus allow more aggressive strategies, an outcome the sectoral employers who are inclined to support protectionism might fear. If we are to take these considerations seriously, we need to study the internal politics and the power resources of European employer associations. In countries with relatively highly centralized and very hierarchical employer associations such diverging views carry little weight because dissenting voices are either marginalized or simply ignored (see Menz 2005). This is typically the case in countries with traditions of neocorporatism, such as Austria, the Netherlands, Germany, and the Scandinavian countries. Different dynamics emerge in countries with weaker umbrella associations and lower levels of hierarchy. Finally, it is instructive to 'follow the money' and study the position of the financially and organizationally most potent single sectoral employer associations because they often have a strong influence on the position the umbrella associations are likely to assume regarding economic migration.

The approach to migration studies that is inspired by comparative political economy attaches great significance to the position of employer associations but gives relatively little attention to the role of trade unions. Of course, this is largely a pragmatic reflection of the considerably weaker position of trade unions throughout Europe, which is related to well-known structural challenges such as deindustrialization, privatization, hostile legislators, structural changes to the labour market, and indeed the workforce itself. Nevertheless, it is remarkable how trade unions appear to have changed their original position on the issue of immigration in recent years, abandoning fairly lacklustre and in some cases openly hostile stances that were widespread during the post-war decades. Contrary to what authors such as Watts (2002) and Haus (2002) have assumed, it seems unlikely that this change can be attributed to globalization alone. A much more likely explanation is that the trade unions have adopted a pragmatic stance and have realized that well-managed economic migration is preferable to unmanaged and partially undocumented migration, which can have a negative effect on wages, working conditions, and the unions' bargaining positions (Penninx and Roosblad 2000). Not unlike in the United States (see Milkman 2006), in some European countries unions have embraced migration and have reached out to and organized labour migrants, but the fundamental dilemma identified by Penninx and Roosblad (2000) still persists, namely that between the prerogatives of international solidarity and the often reluctant attitude of rank-and-file members who are wary of the ultimate ramifications of more migrant labour. There is little discernible evidence of a consistent pattern with regard to the stance of the union movement across Europe, and consequently no useful means to categorize them using the varieties-of-capitalism dichotomy; rather, attitudes appear to range from resignation to active embrace and support to reluctance and even hostility.

In the following empirical section we shall explore the role that an approach from comparative political economy can play in illustrating the politics of migration policy design, with the main focus on the agency of employer associations.

3.4 The Liberalization of Labour Migration in Europe

3.4.1 Developments in Sweden: Comprehensive Liberalization

During the first two post-war decades Swedish immigration policy was exceptionally liberal, encouraging permanent immigration, rather than guest worker–style migration patterns. By the late 1960s trade union lobbying, a slight oversupply of labour, and a mismatch between skills required and the skills exhibited by labour migrants, many of whom arrived spontaneously, led to a momentum of change to which employers did not object. The 1968 Immigration Act required that all labour migrants have work permits, which until then had been issued only in exceptional cases. Spontaneous immigration became impossible because both a job offer and proof of appropriate housing had to be presented to receive a work permit. Unsurprisingly, labour migration was reduced to a trickle and was largely limited to recipients of tightly controlled temporary work permits. In many ways this development reflected the Keynesian preoccupation with full employment (Lindvall 2006), but there was also a long-held ideological commitment among members of the dominant Social Democratic Party to enhancing the labour market participation rate among women and the disabled (Johansson 2012), which was deemed more important than immigration.

In the early 2000s the situation changed. The Swedish employer organization Svenskt Näringslivet (SN), finding the highly restrictive state-controlled approach too cumbersome and bureaucratic but above all not liberal enough, developed an appetite for liberalized labour migration. Applications for work permits were handled by the Swedish National Labour Market Board (AMS) in coordination with the unions. SN favoured a demand-driven model that effectively bypassed state control altogether. The organization also sought to minimize union input; a much-debated policy paper drafted by SN board member Bijan Fahimi (Fahimi 2001) articulated precisely this demand. The following year a second policy paper (Ekenger and Wallen 2002) continued the campaign, demanding much more liberal provisions that would permit migrant workers to enter Sweden to seek employment for up to 3 months and to obtain work permits that would no longer be tied to any one sector or even any one single employer. In addition, the paper proposed that migrants be given full permanent-residence status after 3 years of living in the country and demanded that regulation be employer-driven, a move that would completely deprive AMS of its power.

In the meantime the decision had been made to open the labour market to nationals of the A8 countries that were to accede the EU in 2004. However, it was understood that such labour mobility would entail eligibility for standard wages and standard working conditions, which is why the notorious Laval case, which involved Latvian workers who had been seconded to a Swedish construction site and been paid less than their Swedish co-workers, caused such controversy in the country. The insistence on the applicability of Swedish standard wage provisions was meant to placate those who were afraid that Eastern European migration might cause downward pressure on wage levels and to incentivize primarily highly skilled migration, as could be expected from a CME insisting on a strategy to ensure complementarity.

These lobbying efforts eventually bore fruit. Employer claims that changing demographic patterns and rapidly emerging new industries, especially in the field of information technology, required a more liberal approach to immigration regulation began to resonate among the political Right. The employers brought their demands to the political arena and in 2003 Sweden's four centre-right parties and the Greens formed a parliamentary committee to explore immigration legislation with a view to proposing a liberal reform (Cerna 2009b: 14). Given the long-standing ideological hegemony of the Social Democratic Party, the departure from the consensus on favouring domestic workers, including those of immigrant origin, over new immigrants was remarkable. The employers had successfully extolled immigration as crucial in addressing skill and labour market shortages and decried the status quo regulation as cumbersome and excessively bureaucratic. The other parties, deeming the Social Democratic Party's stance anachronistic and out of touch, adopted the employers' argument that a more streamlined and, above all, employer-driven procedure and logic ought to predominate in the administration of work permits.

In 2006 the committee delivered its final report. The timing was fortuitous, for in that year a centre-right government won the national elections. The committee report proposed a slight liberalization of labour migration regulation that would entail a shift of administrative powers over work permits from the national labour board—and thus from the purview of the unions—to the Swedish Migration Board, which was to act at the behest of employers. However, work permit applicants would still require proof of an employment offer and evidence of such an offer being subject to standard wages and working conditions according to the applicable results of collective bargaining. With this explicit nod to the unions, and by dispelling fears of social and wage dumping, the report sought to counter the obvious accusation from the unions or the political Left that this liberalization might jeopardize Swedish standard wage levels. Somewhat remarkably, the Migration Board would not examine any claims regarding labour market shortages independently but simply would take the applicants' and their employers' word at face value and merely monitor compliance with wage laws. In late 2007 Proposition 2007/08:147 was drafted on the basis of the recommendations of the committee report, and it came into effect as of 15 December 2008.

At long last the continuing and skilfully coordinated policy entrepreneur efforts had paid off rather handsomely. Almost overnight Sweden introduced one of the most liberal labour immigration policy regulations in Europe, if not in the world. The employer-driven logic minimized not only union input (and the attendant protectionist stance that could reasonably be expected) but effectively also the administrative discretion of governmental actors. In practice employers proved to be most interested in attracting highly skilled immigrants, and this segment was key to the political debate and to the lobbying efforts. Thus, the overarching strategy is that of a CME focusing on highly skilled immigrants who can easily be accommodated in a complementary fashion with respect to the overall predominant production strategy.

3.4.2 Developments in the United Kingdom: Wholesale Liberalization across the Board in an LME

By the mid-1990s serious concerns about labour shortages in both high-skill and low-skill positions motivated British employers to commence an active lobbying campaign (see CBI 2005). There were no significant signs of internal discord. The advantages identified included flexibility, access to an additional skill base, the superior training and educational standards in many countries, and soft skills such as higher motivation associated with economic migrants. In mid-2005 CBI president Digby Jones stressed the advantage the UK enjoyed owing to its flexible labour markets and pragmatic labour migration schemes.

The new appetite for migrant labour was almost immediately translated into a determined effort to change public policy. In fact, Tony Blair's New Labour government pursued a business-friendly and very liberal stance on migration that almost appeared to pre-empt organized business demands. The 1998 white paper *Our Competitive Future: Building the Knowledge-Driven Economy* published by the Department of Trade and Industry was indicative of the new public-policy approach in that it questioned the restrictive policy towards highly skilled migrants and entrepreneurs. Beginning in 2000, the skill range covered by the work permit scheme was gradually broadened; at the same time formal requirements were lowered to holding a tertiary degree rather than having a degree plus work experience. As a result, the number of work permit holders rose from 62,975 in 1997 to 137,035 in 2005. In 2000 an Innovator Scheme was piloted with the support of the then Minister of State for Immigration, Barbara Roche, herself an outspoken advocate of liberalized labour migration (Somerville 2007: 30–31). In January 2002 a Highly Skilled Migrant Programme (HSMP) was introduced, an explicit points-based assessment system that took into consideration such aspects as formal level of education, work experience, salary level, overall qualification, and qualification of the spouse. Additional points were added for applicants in sectors with shortages, and applications were to be filed by the applicants themselves rather than by their employer.

Coupling liberalized migration with enhanced competitiveness was a goal shared by the employers and the government. The Nationality, Immigration, and Asylum Act 2002 implemented most of the measures contained in the 1998 white paper. In 2001 responsibility for work permits was transferred to the Home Office. The main aim was to restructure and ultimately limit the schemes pertaining to low-skill migration (on the assumption that Central and Eastern Europeans would fill these jobs from 2004 onwards), while streamlining procedures for high-skilled migrants by introducing a points-based system based on qualifications and labour market needs. Between May 2004 and December 2006 alone 579,000 EU-8 citizens registered with the Department of Work and Pensions, 65 % of whom were Polish (Somerville 2007: 34).

In 2008 the HSMP was replaced by a new points-based system with two tiers for highly skilled and skilled migrants respectively, which also took into account available funds, past UK residence, and educational experience. The introduction of the new system marked a change from the original policy proposal, but its 'flexible, employer-led' logic (Home Office 2005: 9) remained similar to that apparent in the proposal's title, *A Points-Based System: Making Migration Work for Britain*. The original plan would have replaced all of these schemes with a single points-based labour migration system consisting of four tiers. The first tier would have been reserved for highly skilled professionals in fields such as IT, finance, medicine, and engineering, as well as individuals regarded as entrepreneurs. The second tier would have been geared towards applicants in sectors that experienced shortages that cannot be filled domestically or within the EU, especially in nursing and teaching. The third tier would have consisted of short-term, strictly limited quota schemes which could have been opened—and presumably closed—on short notice, and which would have replaced the agricultural and sector-based schemes. This tier was never used. The fourth tier concerned visa for adult and child students; it was implemented in 2012; a fifth one focused on temporary workers, including the Working Holidays scheme historically targeted at Old Commonwealth countries. The document reiterated 12 times that employers will be consulted and that the scheme is employer-led. It also stated that an independent advisory body on skills would be consulted. The UK's points-based scheme is a paradigmatic example of a business-driven labour recruitment scheme. Immediately after assuming office in July 2010 the Conservative–Liberal Democrat coalition government announced plans to reduce the number of highly skilled non-EU migrants, but the practical ramifications appeared rather limited, with public policy initiatives aiming at soft targets first, notably at foreign students.

British employers developed an interest in immigrants whom they considered to be of economic utility, both in highly skilled service sector jobs, especially in finance, law, health and the natural sciences, and in low-skill jobs such as food processing, agriculture, food and beverage, and construction, and both regarding generalist and sector-specific job skills. In 2005 a publication by the Confederation of British Industry, a UK business organization, highlighted that immigration 'is no alternative to raising the skills levels of the home-grown workforce—nor should immigration be seen as negating the need for effective active labour market policies to tackle the problem of economic inactivity' (CBI 2005: 2). However, the same position paper also conceded that '20 % of the UK workforce lack appropriate levels of functional numeracy and literacy—raising the skill levels of this group would help to ease recruitment difficulties faced by employers.' In 2005 CBI, the Trade Union Congress (TUC) and the Home Office published a joint position paper which emphasized that 'the skills and enthusiasm' of new migrants was welcomed by all parties (TUC 2005: 1).

Along with the unions and certain NGOs, the CBI was invited to the bi-annual user panel planning sessions of the now defunct Immigration and Nationality Directorate of the Home Office. Its representatives were also members of an employer taskforce group, which was responsible for providing policy suggestions to the Home Office's also now defunct Border and Immigration Agency. Recommendations from this group led to the establishment of the Highly Skilled Migrant Programme in February 2008 and of an Illegal Working Stakeholder Group. Actors represented in this taskforce group include a trade union delegate; major businesses such as Shell, Ernst & Young, Tesco, Citigroup, and Goldman Sachs; sectoral employer associations in the areas of engineering, hospitality, and employment services; and NASSCOM, a trade association of Indian IT and BPO businesses. Formal responses to government initiatives as well as informal avenues to the Home Office have been fairly well received, and the CBI is now in a position where it can influence government policy. It is also a member of the stakeholder panel of the Migration Advisory Committee, an academic expert body convened by the Home Office. An added strength of the CBI is that there is a consensus among its members on the desirability of economic migration and its benefits.

Overall, the reforms to the UK's highly restrictive immigration policy have been conditioned by the purported labour needs of an LME. Immigration reform since 1999 has created new channels for unskilled and skilled migrants to work in a complementary and supplementary fashion for a system of political economy that needs both brain and brawn. Successive UK governments, willing to solicit immigrants who could easily be absorbed into a much more loosely structured labour market with only an embryonic vocational training system and a legacy of company-specific in-house and on-the-job training, recast immigration policy to proactively target skilled migrants, many of whom were seen as supplementary to the outputs of the educational system, as well as low-skilled migrants, who could be channelled into a substantive low-skill service sector. The decision to open the UK labour market to A8-country citizens in 2004 was thus accompanied by a phasing out of recruitment categories for unskilled Commonwealth migrants, the expectation being that these positions would be filled by economic migrants from Central and Eastern Europe.

3.5 Conclusion

This chapter has argued that an approach inspired by comparative political economy provides valuable insights into the political dynamics of migration policymaking. This helps to bring back in considerations related to labour markets, structures of political economy, and organized interest groups, notably employer associations. In empirical terms, this chapter has charted the role these actors have played in recalibrating the political regulation of economic migration.

In Sweden and the United Kingdom economic migration regulations were liberalized considerably during the 2000s. The radical modifications to the Swedish system can be attributed to the vigorous and assertive stance of employers who successfully acted as policy entrepreneurs. UK employers, on the other hand, developed an interest in economic migration in the early 2000s and were aided in their endeavours by very business-friendly liberal governmental actors.

However, while it is obvious that economic-migration provisions were liberalized in both countries, there are also some differences that are worth mentioning. Generally speaking, the details of the reforms are conditioned by considerations of political economy, which are operationalized by adherence to the two different varieties of capitalism. Liberal market economies and coordinated market economies will generate different immigration policies, with skill level being the key point of difference. The new regulations in Sweden may seem fairly liberal at first glance, but ultimately their purpose is to ensure relatively easy and convenient access to highly skilled migrants who can easily complement existing production strategies and thus meet the human-resource needs of the country's coordinated market economy. Similarly, preferences in the UK are also influenced by the particularities and exigencies of the respective liberal variety of capitalism. UK employers, interested in recruiting labour migrants at both ends of the skills distribution scale, secured legislation that now permits them to do precisely that. Although one could argue that the comparatively radical Swedish re-regulation is part and parcel of a broader and somewhat aggressive campaign of Swedish employers to push the country in a more neoliberal direction (see Johansson 2012), it is also worth noting that overt wage and social dumping is prohibited, hence there are no obvious incentives to recruit low-skilled labour migrants from abroad. The overall picture of liberalization, which was primarily targeted at highly skilled migrants while also permitting judicious use of unskilled migrants if needed, thus appears to be broadly in line with what one would expect of a regulatory response from a coordinated market economy. Thus, while employers' agency is an important element in understanding the dynamics of migration policy reform, the strategic thrust of their agency is itself conditioned by the variety of capitalism in which the employers are embedded.

References

Bale, T. (2008). Turning round the telescope. Centre-right parties and immigration and integration policy in Europe. *Journal of European Public Policy, 15*(3), 315–330. doi:10.1080/13501760701847341.

Boswell, C., & Geddes, A. (2010). *Migration and mobility in the European Union*. Basingstoke: Palgrave Macmillan.

Castells, M. (1975). Immigrant workers and class struggles in advanced capitalism: The Western European experience. *Politics & Society, 5*(1), 33–66. doi:10.1177/003232927500500102.

Castles, S., & Kosack, G. (1973). *Immigrant workers and class structure in Western Europe*. London: Oxford University Press.

Castles, S., & Miller, M. J. (2003). *The age of migration: International population movements in the modern world* (3rd ed.). New York: Guilford Press.

Caviedes, A. A. (2006). *Cracks in the fortress Europe? How sectoral needs shape labor migration policy*. Ph.D. dissertation. University of Wisconsin, Madison.

CBI. (2005). *Selective admission: Making migration work for Britain*. London: Confederation of British Industry.

Cerna, L. (2009a). The varieties of high-skilled immigration policies: Coalitions and policy outputs in advanced industrial countries. *Journal of European Public Policy, 16*(1), 144–161. doi:10.1080/13501760802453148.

Cerna, L. (2009b). *Changes in Swedish labour immigration policy: A slight revolution? Working paper 2009:10*. Stockholm: The Stockholm University Linnaeus Centre for Integration Studies.

Cole, M., & Dale, G. (Eds.). (1999). *The European Union and migrant labour*. Oxford/New York: Berg Publishers.

Culpepper, P. D. (1999). The future of the high-skill equilibrium in Germany. *Oxford Review of Economic Policy, 15*(1), 43–59. doi:10.1093/oxrep/15.1.43.

Culpepper, P. D., & Finegold, D. (Eds.). (1999). *The German skills machine: Sustaining comparative advantage in a global economy*. New York: Berghahn Books.

Deeg, R. (2007). Complementarity and institutional change in capitalist systems. *Journal of European Public Policy, 14*(4), 611–630. doi:10.1080/13501760701314433.

Ekenger, K., & Wallen, F. (2002). *Invandring för tillväxt och nya jobb*. Stockholm: Svenskt Näringsliv.

Fahimi, B. (2001). *Globalisering och arbetsmarknad – Öppna den svenska arbetsmarknaden*. Stockholm: Svenskt Näringsliv.

Freeman, G. P. (1995). Modes of immigration politics in liberal democratic states. *International Migration Review, 19*(4), 881–902. doi:10.2307/2547729.

Freeman, G. P. (2002). Winners and losers: Politics and the costs and benefits of migration. In A. M. Messina (Ed.), *West European immigration and immigrant policy in the new century* (pp. 77–96). Westport: Praeger Publishers.

Givens, T., & Luedtke, A. (2005). European immigration politics in comparative perspective: Issue salience, partisanship, and immigrant rights. *Comparative European Politics, 3*(1), 1–22. doi:10.1057/palgrave.cep.6110051.

Guiraudon, V. (2001). European courts and foreigners' rights: A comparative study of norms diffusion. *International Migration Review, 34*(4), 1088–1125. doi:10.2307/2675976.

Hall, P. A., & Gingerich, D. W. (2004). *Varieties of capitalism and institutional complementarities in the macroeconomy: An empirical analysis* (MPIfG Discussion Paper 04/5). Cologne: Max Planck Institute for the Study of Societies.

Hall, P. A., & Soskice, D. (Eds.). (2001). *Varieties of capitalism: The institutional foundations of comparative advantage*. Oxford: Oxford University Press.

Haus, L. (2002). *Unions, immigration, and internationalization: New challenges and changing coalitions in the United States and France*. New York: Palgrave Macmillan.

Herrmann, A. M. (2008). *One political economy, one political strategy? Comparing pharmaceutical firms in Germany, Italy, and the UK*. Oxford/New York: Oxford University Press.

Hinnfors, J., Spehar, A., & Bucken-Knapp, G. (2012). The missing factor: Why social democracy can lead to restrictive immigration policy. *Journal of European Public Policy, 19*(4), 585–603. doi:10.1080/13501763.2011.607348.

Home Office. (2005). *Controlling our borders: Making migration work for Britain: Five year strategy for asylum and immigration*. Norwich: The Stationary Office.

Johansson, J. (2012). Swedish employers and trade unions, varieties of capitalism and labour migration policies. *Nordic Journal of Migration Research, 2*(4), 325–334. doi:10.2478/v10202-012-0003-y.

Joppke, C. (1998). Why liberal states accept unwanted migration. *World Politics, 50*(2), 266–293. doi:10.1017/S004388710000811X.

Lahav, G., & Guiraudon, V. (2006). Actors and venues in immigration control: Closing the gap between political demands and policy outcomes. *West European Politics, 29*(2), 201–223. doi:10.1080/01402380500512551.

Lindvall, J. (2006). The politics of purpose: Swedish economic policy after the golden age. *Comparative Politics, 38*(3), 253–272. doi:10.2307/20433997.

Menz, G. K. (2001). Beyond the Anwerbestopp? The German–Polish bilateral labour treaty. *Journal of European Social Policy, 11*(3), 253–269. doi:10.1177/095892870101100304.

Menz, G. (2005). *Varieties of capitalism and Europeanization: National response strategies to the single European market*. Oxford/New York: Oxford University Press.
Menz, G. (2009). *The political economy of managed migration: Nonstate actors, Europeanization, and the politics of designing migration policies*. Oxford/New York: Oxford University Press.
Menz, G. (2011). Employer preferences for labour migration: Exploring 'Varieties of Capitalism'-based contextual conditionality in Germany and the United Kingdom. *British Journal of Politics and International Relations, 13*(4), 534–550. doi:10.1111/j.1467-856X.2011.00451.x.
Menz, G., & Caviedes, A. (2010). Introduction: Patterns, trends, and (Ir)Regularities in the politics and economics of labour migration in Europe. In G. Menz & A. Caviedes (Eds.), *Labour migration in Europe* (pp. 25–53). Basingstoke: Palgrave Macmillan.
Messina, A. (1990). Political impediments to the resumption of labour migration to Western Europe. *West European Politics, 13*(1), 31–46. doi:10.1080/01402389008424778.
Meyers, E. (2004). *International immigration policy: A theoretical and comparative analysis*. New York: Palgrave Macmillan.
Milkman, R. (2006). *L.A. Story: Immigrant workers and the future of the U.S. Labor Movement*. New York: Russell Sage.
Penninx, R., & Roosblad, J. (Eds.). (2000). *Trade unions, immigration, and immigrants in Europe, 1960–1993: A comparative study of the attitudes and actions of trade unions in seven West European countries*. Oxford/New York: Berghahn Books.
Piore, M. J. (1979). *Birds of passage: Migrant labor and industrial societies*. Cambridge/New York: Cambridge University Press.
Salt, J. (1997). *International movement of the highly skilled* (OECD Occasional Paper 3). London: International Migration Unit.
Somerville, W. (2007). *Immigration under new labour*. Bristol: The Policy Press.
Statham, P., & Geddes, A. (2006). Elites and the 'organised public': Who drives British immigration politics and in which direction? *West European Politics, 29*(2), 248–269. doi:10.1080/01402380500512601.
TUC. (2005). *Managed migration: Working for Britain – A joint statement from the home office, CBI and TUC*. London: The Trades Union Congress. Press Release.
Watts, J. R. (2002). *Immigration policy and the challenge of globalization: Unions and employers in unlikely alliance*. Ithaca: Cornell University Press.

Chapter 4
Turning to Grand Theory: Cultural Political Economy and the Regulation of Immigration

Nicolas Van Puymbroeck

4.1 Introduction

Theorizing the relationship between migration and politics continues to be a haphazard and fragmented affair, both in Europe and beyond. Divergent traditions, including Marxism, Realism, and Liberalism, have each grappled with the complex issue in their own ways, thus subverting the formation of a coherent canon. At best, the literature is structured by pragmatic guiding beacons such as Hammar's (1985: 7–9) distinction between 'immigration regulation' and 'immigrant policy', with the former referring to 'the rules and procedures governing the selection and admission of foreign citizens' and the latter being reserved for 'conditions provided to resident immigrants'.

This chapter voices the concern that the lack of an overarching research perspective and agenda prevents scholars from appropriately addressing how migration is implicated in contemporary social transformations. It therefore attempts to look for substantive and methodological similarities between different schools of thought. Ideally, this attempt will transcend Hammar's distinction, which fails to appreciate that immigrant policy can stimulate population flows and that transnational connections surpass simplified ideas of one-way immigration and integration, to name but two of its shortcomings. However, given the limited space, this chapter focuses only on immigration regulation.

My own reading of the literature on immigration policies reveals three important paradigmatic turns. Firstly, various authors like Joppke (1999) and Hollifield (2000) have discredited early political economic accounts of international migration as overly reductionist. Especially in its Marxist variant, political economy neglected

N. Van Puymbroeck (✉)
Faculty of Social Sciences - Center on Inequality, Poverty, Social Exclusion and the City, University of Antwerp, Antwerp, Belgium
e-mail: nicolas.vanpuymbroeck@uantwerpen.be

A. Amelina et al. (eds.), *An Anthology of Migration and Social Transformation*, IMISCOE Research Series, DOI 10.1007/978-3-319-23666-7_4

the role of the state in controlling the flow of people across borders. In response, scholars have 'brought the state back in' (Skocpol 1985) by exploring institutional and ideological determinants of admission policies. Secondly, questions have been raised about 'methodological nationalism' (Wimmer and Schiller 2003). The aims of immigration policy have long been considered to hold homogeneously across the national territory. Yet research has shown that multiple actors dispersed over different scales have been involved in the regulation of entry and exit. Thirdly, material interests have often been considered as the main drivers of policy designs, but cost–benefit calculations misleadingly represent the policy process as entirely rational and mechanical. Authors like Bigo (2001) and Boswell et al. (2011) have therefore called attention to normative convictions and knowledge claims as an additional dimension of immigration policy.

These 'statist', 'scalar', and 'semiotic' turns allow for an interpretation of the existing literature that is different from those provided in reviews which cluster authors in separate theoretical traditions (see e.g. Meyers 2000 or Sciortino 2000). While it has been proposed to integrate the plurality in middle-range theories (see Chap. 2), I plea for an additional 'grand' theory that would hold the respective turns in place. This is necessary because they often stand in a tense relationship. For example, the statist turn drew primarily on methodological nationalist assumptions. Similarly, the multi-scalar regulation of migration has often been discussed as a way to best serve material interests, neglecting the important semiotic scope of migration narratives.

Therefore, a second goal of this chapter is to initiate a grand theoretical convergence drawing on cultural political economy (CPE) as developed by Bob Jessop and Ngai-Ling Sum (2006). I will show that CPE reveals the economic dimension of immigration to be a thematic blind spot, which also rearticulates immigration regulation by embedding it in a broader material-constructivist perspective on the capitalist state. CPE is one contemporary variant of political economy (for an alternative see Chap. 3 on Varieties-of-Capitalism) which identifies the most important societal transformations, such as the rise of neoliberalism and European Integration, and questions how distinct types of migration, from labour to student migration, are implicated in them.

4.2 Theorizing the Political Regulation of Immigration

I shall begin this chapter with my own non-exhaustive overview of the literature on the regulation of immigration, distinguishing between early political economic accounts and the respective statist, scalar, and semiotic turns. In the second part I will introduce CPE as a grand theory that can hold the respective turns together, but I will also identify thematic blind spots with regard to the economic embedding of immigration policy.

4.2.1 The Political Economy of Immigration

Political economy functions as a 'floating signifier' in that it lacks a clearly defined referent. The term dates from a pre-disciplinary past when scholars combined what today would be called political science, sociology, and economics. In the field of immigration theories political economy has been used to refer both to Marxist accounts of international migration and to rational-choice interpretations of political behaviour. While both bodies of research are clearly different, they share some conclusions about the primacy of organized capital with regard to immigration policy designs.

Marxists were among the very first to devote serious attention to international migration, especially in the wake of the labour recruitment in Europe after the Second World War. However, there is no orthodox Marxist concept of migration because Marx himself never wrote on the subject. Nonetheless, his followers have extended certain of his basic concepts to understand the role migration can play in contemporary capitalism, but it should be stressed that they have never explicitly investigated the political regulation of immigration. More broadly, Michael Samers has argued that 'Marxist analyses never developed a very sophisticated understanding of the state *in the context of immigration*' (Samers 2003: 558), which is why Marxism explicitly underscored the state's role.

Marxists' interest in migration was mediated through a concern with the uneven development of capitalism, the class structure of society, and emancipatory struggle. According to their view, it is the structural process of capitalist expansionism that disrupts self-sufficient societies across the globe, forcing people to sell their labour power in a wage relation. From the point of view of Western developed countries, international wage labourers constitute what Marx called a 'surplus labour force'. For capital, temporary immigrants represent particularly cheap and flexible expendable 'commodities'.

Castles and Kozack (1973: 427) specifically focused on the wider implications of the idea that 'migration provides an industrial reserve army which helps retard wage increases and keep profits high'. Most importantly, they argue that migration undermines the cohesiveness of the labour class, and that it brings about a racialized competition between foreigners and natives. In its turn, this helps displace and obscure the root inequalities of capitalism, thus postponing the possibility of emancipatory struggle. Coming to essentially the same conclusion, Manuel Castells noted that migration does not just fill holes in the labour market, but that '*the utility of immigrant labour to capital derives primarily from the fact that it can act towards it as though the labour movement did not exist*, thereby moving the class struggle back several decades' (Castells 1975: 52).

The role of the state in regulating the flow of immigrants is treated only in the margins of these writings. Castles and Kosack (1973: 425) stuck to a descriptive analysis, highlighting that immigration policies 'have not been part of any long-term economic plan. Rather they have been adjusted according to relatively short-run changes in circumstances. Where the policies have followed economic interests, it has been those of capital which have predominated.' Castells (1975: 53) took the analysis a bit further, arguing that the exploitation of immigrant labour depends on 'the State apparatus of capital and [on] the political status given to them in its institutions.' By depriving immigrant workers of industrial rights, among other things, the state turns them into voiceless and easily exploitable labour power.

Immigration theorists inspired by Marxism see immigration policies as an instrument of capitalism in general. They do not devote much attention to the question of why or how states assume this role (differently), nor to the question of which capitalist factions are served in particular. At best, Marxist world system theory acknowledges that immigration by definition implies the involvement of state policies. For example, while, according to Cohen (1987: 26), 'the state plays a central and directing role in the structuring of a division of labour', Sassen (1988: 34) noted that a 'state's position on migration partly reflects its location in the world economy'.

Looking at the issue from a completely different angle, Freeman (1995) also considered immigration policies as a reflection of powerful economic factions, specifically employers organizations and businesses. Freeman's main question is how these groups come to influence the policy process. His analysis extends the ontology and methodology of neo-classical economics to politics. The starting point of this alternative version of political economy states that immigration 'tends to produce concentrated benefits and diffuse costs, giving those who benefit from immigration greater incentives to organize than persons who bear its costs' (Freeman 1995: 885).

In liberal democratic states this has two consequences for the politics of immigration control. Firstly, because the costs of immigration tend to be both diffuse and lagged in time, there will not be a strongly articulated public opinion on immigration due to what Freeman (1995: 883) called a 'temporal illusion'. In order not to arouse the public, it is expected 'for the major political parties to seek a consensus across the political spectrum that has the effect of taking immigration conflicts off the agenda' (Freeman 1995: 884). Secondly, the limited group of beneficiaries of immigration, such as capitalists, will develop a client politics to influence elected politicians, which will be favourably oriented towards expansive immigration politics.

As Boswell (2007: 77) pointed out, Freeman conceptualized policy-makers 'as brokers who have an interest in producing policies that mollify (influential) organized interests'. In Freeman's view, the state is the political extension of broader societal inequalities, such as the asymmetry between capital and labour. Despite a different theoretical background his conclusions thus resonate well with the Marxist instrumental view on the state. This overly reductionist account of politics has provoked considerable criticism, leading several authors to bring the state (back) in.

4.2.2 The Statist Turn

In retrospect the statist turn came quite late, beginning in the early 1990s and reaching its blossom only around the new millennium. Massey (1999: 303) noted that, although 'scholars have surveyed national immigration policies, conducted case studies of state agencies, and compiled legislative histories of immigration law, through 1990 few had attempted to describe the behavior of bureaucrats and politicians with respect to immigration'. This is especially surprising given the clear policy shift during the 1970s, whereby many Western states put an end to labour recruitment. Embedded in the general economic crisis of the time, scholars did not consider the restriction on the import of foreign workers to be in conflict with the interests of capitalist forces. Therefore, the policy reversal did not shake the political economic foundations.

In the mid-1980s the general paradigmatic reorientation to 'bring the state back in' gradually gained momentum. Skocpol (1985: 4) argued that across the political sciences '"Government" was viewed primarily as an arena within which economic interest groups or normative social movements contended or allied with one another to shape the making of public policy decisions'. A new generation of scholars argued against this minimalist view, emphasizing that the state should also be seen both as an autonomous actor and as an institutional configuration which influences society. This general paradigmatic turn extended to immigration theories as well. Paradoxically, however, the discovery of the state was accompanied by doomsday scenarios of its incipient demise.

Despite the political rhetoric of the 'immigration stop' many Western countries experienced an increase in immigration in the 1990s. This inspired Wayne A. Cornelius and his colleagues to speak of a control gap 'between the *goals* of national immigration policy (laws, regulations, executive actions, etc.) and the actual results of policies in this area (policy *outcomes*)' (Cornelius et al. 1994: 3). Scholars increasingly questioned 'why liberal states accept unwanted immigration' (Joppke 1998). The concern was raised that a control crisis would contradict one of the core dimensions of the sovereign legitimacy of the nation state—that is, the regulation of the admission of foreigners to the national territory and of their deportation from it. Many denied that the policy gap was due to the efficacy of border control. Instead scholars started to focus on the state in search for explanations. 'To use a familiar Weberian metaphor, if the speeding train of international migration is fueled by economic and sociological forces, then it is the state that acts as a switching mechanism, which can change the course of the train, or derail it altogether' explained Hollifield (2000: 148–149).

Many processes were considered to be simultaneously at work in the heart of the 'switching mechanism'. For example, while Perlmutter (1996) pointed out the complex role of party politics, Joppke (1998) highlighted judiciary limits to immigration regulation, especially when it involved refugee or family migration. Inspired by historical and sociological neo-institutionalism, Hansen (2002) also revealed the path-dependent impact of national ideological traditions. While the claims of several societal interest groups were not overlooked entirely, the emphasis of the debate shifted to the question of how bureaucratic institutions and partisan politics modify them. The state thus emerged as an ontologically distinct actor, or sphere, that is not analogous to any other. Boswell (2007) argued that states strive to maintain and fulfil unique functional imperatives, such as providing basic security for their citizens, enabling good foreign relations, and ensuring the rule of law. However, conflicting state imperatives can induce short circuits in the control over immigration, leading to unwanted new inflow.

In many respects the statist turn revealed important mechanisms that influenced the regulation of immigration, but it also suffered from a prevailing implicit methodological nationalism. The goals of immigration policy were thought to be national, holding homogeneously across the territory. Correspondingly, only domestic factors were taken into consideration to explain policy gaps. This inspired new theoretical questions about the scalar nature of the political regulation of immigration.

4.2.3 The Scalar Turn

The attention devoted to geography and scale came from two different directions. Firstly, former Marxists became interested in the global regulation of immigration in advanced capitalism. Sassen (2000: 69) observed a 'de facto, rather than de jure, bi- and multilateralism in the handling of specific aspects of international migrations'. For example, the economic unification of Europe spilled over into the establishment of a zone of free movement beyond the control of nation states. In addition, Sassen joined authors such as Soysal (1994) and Jacobson (1996) in stressing 'the invocation of international covenants, particularly human rights instruments', which, she noted, was 'a move away from statism—the absolute right of states to represent their people in international law and international relations' (Sassen 2000: 72). Combined, these global political developments were said to 'denationalize' the Westphalian assemblage of territory, authority, and rights, legitimating rescaled and highly uneven jurisdictional geographies of control across the globe. Standing out in this respect were the global cities of the world in which the unrestricted free flow of capital clashed with attempts to control immigration on a national level.

However, the 'globalist' argument was met with severe scepticism by the dominant domestic theorists. Joppke (1998: 269), for instance, argued that the internationalization of immigrants' rights is usually 'not so strong as to make states fear and tremble [...], lacks implementation and enforcement powers [...] [and] consists of the soft moral power of discourse'. Nevertheless, even among 'domestics' consensus grew that the issue of scale should be acknowledged more explicitly. This inspired a second body of research, which looked into the 'multi-level politics of immigration'.

Jeannette Money's ground-breaking work introduced the importance of the subnational scale. Her basic belief was that the factors driving immigration politics varied within a country. Therefore, to 'explain why states raise or lower their barriers to immigration', Money (1999: ix) argued 'that the uneven geographic distribution of immigrants creates an uneven geographic distribution of the costs as well as the benefits of immigration, thereby providing a spatial context for immigration politics'. Money also noted that, depending on changes in the local support and opposition to immigration, 'local politicians will shift their policy positions in response to changing community preferences, toward either greater openness or greater closure' (Money 1999: 62).

Guiraudon (2000) introduced the issue of scale in her analysis of European immigration politics. She conceived of different vertical institutional venues—in this case the European scale—as a means for politicians to overcome liberal constraints on the national level (see also Chap. 7). National politicians were supposed to search for policy venues where they would experience least resistance (Guiraudon and Lahav 2000).

The scalar turn of the domestics was clearly a less radical version than Sassen's globalist thesis. While Money and Guiraudon still gave preference to the nationalscale in the regulation of immigration, Sassen essentially looked beyond the nation state (for an extended discussion of methodological nationalism, see also Chap. 5).

Despite opening up the geographic scope, the scalar turn was still caught up in the 'classic' approaches to immigration regulation, which either conceived it as a function of (national or class) interests or path dependent political institutions. As such, a more general approach to sense-making and discourse had been neglected for a long time. Most recently, authors have been beginning to experiment with semiotics, thus introducing a third turn in the literature.

4.2.4 The Semiotic Turn

The semiotic turn is not a coherent research strategy. Drawing on divergent theoretical sources, it refers to attempts which introduce the role of 'ideas' broadly defined in shaping immigration policies. The work of Huysmans (2000) and Bigo (2001) on the concept of 'security' has been particularly influential in this regard. They argue that contemporary migration control has been constructed through a securitarian discursive prism, identifying migration as an 'intrusion' and 'trauma' on state territoriality which calls for 'exceptional' measures.

What is characteristic in Bigo's account is that he saw migration not just as an 'objective' phenomenon. He introduced the metaphor of the Möbius strip to deconstruct the generally accepted 'conception of border as a line that must extend into a circle' (Bigo and Walker 2007). The border as circle distinguishes inside from outside, regardless of the practices of border control. In contrast, if a border is understood as a Möbius strip, then there is only a border during practices of border control, and 'the line of separation is not given, it is only a question of perspective and she or he (= the observer) sees some of the people on the Möbius strip as insiders and others as outsiders' (Bigo and Walker 2007: 737). Thus it is especially important to note how the process of immigration is framed both by politicians and by '(in)security professionals'.

While Ellerman (2006) and Van Der Leun (2006) further elaborated on the discursive dimension of policy implementation, others revealed the role of ideas in policy formation. A constructivist approach to immigration regulation has started to supplant the primacy of material interests. Building on the observation that think thanks and scientists are often involved in setting up policy objectives, Boswell et al. (2011) highlighted the role of narratives and cognitive claims, among other aspects. Ideas about the nature of immigration and possible policy interventions cannot simply be deduced from material interests; they also have their own dynamic. In her study on Dutch family migration policies Saskia Bonjour comes to a similar conclusion, stating that ‘it appears that ideas, ideology and ethical considerations play a much more significant role in the making of migration policies than has hitherto been accounted for’ (2011: 111). This has inspired a growing body of literature to study migration ‘frames’ both in public debates (Balch and Balabanova 2011) and in political institutions (Magnani 2012).

The semiotic turn has added one further layer of complexity to the immigration policy literature. It enables research to extend the actors involved (including ‘experts’ and ‘street-level bureaucrats’) and to assess the ways in which immigration is perceived and studied. However, this process of layering has resulted in an empirical ‘trifle’. This is why it seems promising to make the connections between the statist, scalar, and semiotic turns more explicit.

4.3 Cultural Political Economy as Grand Theory

The turns discussed above each shift the focus of study or extend the objects of analysis. This results in an ad hoc layering that offers a complex yet crumbled account of immigration regulation. A ‘grand’ theory such as CPE should take a step back and reflect on the deeper ontological implications of each of the shifts. For example, what does it mean for our conception of the state that the regulation of entry and exit is a scaled and discursive affair? Following Sum and Jessop (2013: 98), a ‘grand’ theory ‘does not denote here the kind of abstract systematic general theory that seeks to integrate and explain everything about humankind and society in a universal, trans-historical manner’; rather, it develops a sensitizing heuristics on how to combine separate thematic or methodological turns. In this sense a grand theory does not explain empirical phenomena.

4.3.1 Why CPE?

CPE is only one of many possible grand theories. Its roots lie in Marxian political economy. However, to Marx a ‘cultural’ political economy would seem tautological. Sayer (2001: 702), for example, argued that cultural political economy ‘is not new. The classical political economists and philosophers did not separate culture from economy; indeed they were concerned with their interrelationship', but to stress that culture is a way to counterbalance 'economism', which has become influential due to the disciplinary differentiation between economics and other social sciences. This is why CPE is 'pre-disciplinary in its historical inspiration and [...] post-disciplinary in its current intellectual implications' (Jessop and Sum 2001: 89).

CPE stands out from the other grand theories because of its continued insistence on the importance of the material conditions of society. It seeks to keep Marxist accounts of the material dynamics of capitalism alive without overlooking the essential discursive imaginaries that stabilize it. Sum and Jessop (2013: 155) argued that 'in so far as they have different emergent properties, the semiotic (cultural) and social (material) are ontologically as well as analytically distinct'. CPE thus tries to steer clear of the Scylla of pure materialism and the Charybdis of soft postmodern sociology.

At first glance, CPE appears to be an unlikely candidate for integrating the three turns in the field of immigration theory. Since the late 1980s migration scholars have neglected the economy, putting more weight on the state and on semiosis. Nevertheless, there are two reasons to reconsider political economy. The first is that a new type of active labour recruitment has been gaining momentum recently. The regime of 'managed migration' has inspired scholars to update political-economic accounts of migration, such as by comparing the effects of various systems of capitalism on the lobbying power of firms and employers' organizations. The second reason, I argue, is that the relevance of political economy can extend beyond understanding how the state can provide capitalists with a supply of cheap and flexible labour. The 'capitalist' state provides for collective consumption, which has a severe impact on the regulation of immigration. Despite a range of studies on migration policy and the welfare state (Freeman 1986; Boeri et al. 2002; Van Puymbroeck and Dierckx 2011), the 'embedded' nature of capitalism and its implications for immigration regulation could receive more attention.

4.3.2 CPE and the Strategic-Relational Approach

What is characteristic of Jessop's theoretical work is that he attempts to integrate several turns in the social sciences into a general social ontology. CPE responds to various versions of the cultural turn, and constitutes the third and most recent phase of what Jessop calls his encompassing 'strategic-relational approach' (SRA). In its two preceding phases, SRA responded to the return of the state and to the spatialization of social relations. In the following I will first explain the SRA in abstract terms, and then I will discuss its implications for how the state, scales, and culture should be studied.

The basic premise of the SRA is that social agents engage in complexity reduction to 'go on' in the world (Sum and Jessop 2013: 148). It distinguishes structuration and semiosis as two generic modes of complexity reduction. Structuration is the process which gives shape to material patterns of interaction both with humans and with the natural world. While many material articulations are possible, they cannot all exist at the same time. Structuration is the way in which the 'compossible' is managed. Semiosis refers to how worldly phenomena are turned meaningful. While the same material patterns can be variably interpreted, semiosis points to the mechanisms of selection of some over others. Both modes of complexity reduction result in the selective neglect or privileging of certain material interactions and semiotic frames.

The crux of the SRA lies in its account of the dynamic of this selectivity. In a classic version of the agency–structure dichotomy selectivity would be understood as the set of external and invariable constraints put on free-willed actions. The SRA, by contrast, transcends the dichotomy, and articulates the dialectical unity of what is called the 'structurally inscribed strategic selectivity' and the 'strategically calculated structurally oriented action' (Jessop 2008: 41). It involves the dialectical process in which actors reflexively adapt their behaviour to what seems structurally possible, while structurally inscribed material forms and meanings reinforce or discourage certain actors.

Importantly, this reciprocal relationship has a temporal dimension. Strategies unfold in time and target sedimented patterns. In the time lapse, variation in material practices and discourses is possible, leading to new selections, structural retentions, and strategic reinforcements. The temporality of complexity reduction therefore both explains path-dependent recursive reinforcement and path-shaping strategic selection, and avoids deterministic, as well as voluntaristic, accounts of social reality. From this abstract conception of SRA important consequences follow for integrating the respective turns.

4.3.3 Integrating the Turns

As a state theorist, Jessop agreed with many of his contemporaries in the 1980s that Marxism had mainly neglected the role of the state. Nevertheless, he was highly sceptical of the guise in which it returned. He denied that the state is an autonomous institutional structure, and responded that one must not assume that 'there are clear and unambiguous boundaries between state apparatus and society, state managers and social forces [...] This reifies and renders absolute what are really emergent, partial, unstable, and variable distinctions' (Jessop 2008: 64). In addition, Jessop reminded those who sought to 'bring the state back in' as an 'actor' in its own right that, 'rather than speaking about *the*power of the state, one should speak about the various potential structural powers (or state capacities)' (Jessop 2008: 37).

The SRA aims to overcome the return of the state as an institutional structure and as an autonomous actor. Jessop, seeing the state as a social relation, defined it as an 'ensemble of socially embedded, socially regularized and strategically selective institutions, organizations, social forces and activities organized around (or at least actively involved in) making collectively binding decisions for an imagined political community' (Jessop 2002: 6). The unity of the state so defined would constitute the object of competing state projects that also distinguish it from other operational systems (Jessop 1990: 7).

This definition bears serious consequences for the statist turn in immigration theories. On the one hand, neo-institutionalists reify the state and are unable to understand change over time. For example, Joppke's argument that a liberal judiciary setup would impede restrictionist immigration policies unduly treats constitutions and laws as unchangeable structures (Joppke 1998). On the other hand, neo-Realists have wrongfully assumed that the state would operate as a unitary actor (see Boswell 2007). From the perspective of SRA one should examine how competences to regulate immigration are dispersed over many state and non-state actors, and how they are held together.

Almost by definition Jessop's conception of the state also raises the scalar question. The state is not only a social relation; it is also spatial (Jessop et al. 2008). Most immigration theories have identified the issue of scale with the demise of the sovereign nation state (see Joppke 1999). The SRA enables a new perspective. According to Jessop (2002: 211), 'the erosion of one form of national state should not be mistaken for its general retreat'. Instead state spatiality can take many forms, with the national scale still holding a strategically selective path-dependent and path-shaping structure. It is also not necessary that the scale of the state be 'spatially fixed', because it depends on its articulation with other operational systems, such as the economy, and their spatial organization.

Lastly, with the advent of CPE, the SRA also puts the semiotic turn in its place. Semiotic immigration theories tend to oscillate between radical poststructuralism, which tends to reduce border control to a factor that is in the eye of the beholder (Bigo 2001), and schizophrenic policy accounts, which simply add ideas to material interests (Boswell et al. 2011). Sum and Jessop (2013), by contrast, claim to retain the material side but seek to study its co-evolution with semiotic processes. In a real-world context this implies that material interests are never objectively given and need interpretation. Nevertheless, this does not rule out that sometimes the semiotic dimension can outweigh the material dimension, and vice versa. Subjectively defined but materially 'hard', economic givens can rule out other possible 'framings'. Similarly, some material structures leave more room for a multiplicity of discourses than others.

Thus, CPE has the potential to integrate the scalar and semiotic turns, which now remain free-floating, with a poststructuralist account of the state. This should involve an adjusted conception of the state as a strategically selective institutional arena that is the result and the starting point of ongoing material and semiotic confrontations in and through space. As well as making the different methodological and substantive turns ontologically sound, it would also give political economy in immigration theories new momentum. CPE accentuates that the state and its policies should never be studied in isolation from other operational systems, such as the economy, given that their form and content are relationally defined.

4.4 Conclusion: New Momentum for Political Economy

In a narrow sense CPE encourages research to re-evaluate how the state was and is involved in the regulation of migration with explicit economic goals. Regarding labour recruitment policies, for example, CPE would deny that 'objective' capitalist interests exist, and that they are automatically served by the state. Rather, it would examine when and how discursive framings of the benefits and costs of labour migration have entered strategically selective state agencies, how they have acquired hegemony (and lost or regained it), and how material structures such as work permits have co-evolved with, and possibly resisted to, discursive variations.

Horvath (2014) recently experimented with the SRA, coming to the conclusion that employers' organizations had to engage in strategic manoeuvring, framing labour migration both as economically beneficial and as harmless. The securitarian trust of the sedimented connotations of migration strategically select restrictive rather than expansionist policies, although policy shifts are not ruled out. Similarly, Menz (2011) showed how new labour migration is legitimated by drawing on the frame of 'competiveness', the implicit threat being that refusal to attract new human resources might jeopardize the competitive race across the globe. In doing so, it also incorporates a securitarian dimension.

CPE has also been stimulating immigration research to go beyond the narrow connection between the economy and the state, which merely focuses on the supply of labour power. Jessop examined how the economy is embedded in a broader ecology of societal systems: 'While Gramsci defined "the state in its inclusive sense" as "political society + civil society" and saw state power in Western societies as based on "hegemony armoured by coercion", my strategic-relational account defined the "economy in its inclusive sense" as "an accumulation regime + social mode of economic regulation"' (Jessop 2008: 24). Ideal-typically, the class compromise of the Keynesian nationalwelfare state is giving way to the emergence of a Schumpeterian rescaled competition state (Jessop 2002). Continued immigration to the West, as a material given, has contributed to the shift of the social mode of regulation in that it has undermined the willingness to redistribute among strangers. Conversely, political actors have also strategically employed the argument of the affordability of the welfare state to promote restrictionist immigration policies. For example, Van Puymbroeck and Vandevoordt (2013) documented how the concept of 'responsibility' was strategically injected into Belgian family migration policies to overcome liberal legal expansionism, and to put economic barriers to reunification policies.

These suggestions for further research are by no means exhaustive. It should also be noted that by turning to grand theory the insights of decades of immigration theories need not be thrown out altogether. Rather, this chapter suggests that they be critically evaluated in the light of a deeper ontological understanding of society in order to avoid disorganized ontological configurations. It thus both aims to stimulate the cross-fertilization of separate substantive and methodological turns, and to reveal thematic blind spots, particularly with regard to the importance of the embedded nature of capitalism for immigration policy regulation.

References

Balch, A., & Balabanova, E. (2011). A system in chaos? Knowledge and sense-making on immigration policy in public debates. *Media, Culture & Society, 33*(6), 885–904. doi:10.1177/0163443711411007.

Bigo, D. (2001). The Möbius Ribbon of internal and external security(ies). In M. Albert, D. Jacobson, & Y. Lapid (Eds.), *Identities, borders, orders: Rethinking international relations theory* (pp. 91–116). Minneapolis: University of Minnesota Press.

Bigo, D., & Walker, R. B. J. (2007). Political sociology and the problem of the international. *Millenium: Journal of International Studies, 35*(3), 725–739. doi:10.1177/0305829807035003 0401.

Boeri, T., Hanson, G., & McCormick, B. (2002). *Immigration policy and the welfare system. A report for the Fondazione Rodolfo Debenedetti.* Oxford: Oxford University Press.

Bonjour, S. (2011). The power and morals of policy makers: Reassessing the control gap debate. *International Migration Review, 45*(1), 89–122. doi:10.1111/j.1747-7379.2010.00840.x.

Boswell, C. (2007). Theorizing migration policy: Is there a third way? *International Migration Review, 41*(1), 75–100. doi:10.1111/j.1747-7379.2007.00057.x.

Boswell, C., Geddes, A., & Scholten, P. (2011). The role of narratives in migration policy-making: A research framework. *The British Journal of Politics & International Relations, 13*(1), 1–11. doi:10.1111/j.1467-856X.2010.00435.x.

Castells, M. (1975). Immigrant workers and class struggles in advanced capitalism: The Western European experience. *Politics & Society, 5*(1), 33–66. doi:10.1177/003232927500500102.

Castles, S., & Kosack, G. (1973). *Immigrant workers and class structure in Western Europe.* London/New York/Toronto: Oxford University Press.

Cohen, R. (1987). *The new helots: Migrants in the international division of labour.* Brookfield: Gower Publishing.

Cornelius, W. A., Martin, P. L., & Hollifield, J. F. (1994). *Controlling immigration: A global perspective.* Stanford: Stanford University Press.

Ellerman, A. (2006). Street-level democracy: How immigration bureaucrats manage public opposition. *West European Politics, 29*(2), 293–309. doi:10.1080/01402380500512627.

Freeman, G. P. (1986). Migration and the political economy of the welfare state. *Annals of the American Academy of Political and Social Science, 485*, 51–63.

Freeman, G. P. (1995). Modes of immigration politics in liberal democratic states. *International Migration Review, 29*(4), 881–902. doi:10.2307/2547729.

Guiraudon, V. (2000). European integration and migration policy: Vertical policy-making as venue shopping. *JCMS: Journal of Common Market Studies, 38*(2), 251–271. doi:10.1111/1468-5965.00219.

Guiraudon, V., & Lahav, G. (2000). A reappraisal of the state sovereignty debate: The case of migration control. *Comparative Political Studies, 33*(2), 163–195. doi:10.1177/0010414000033002001.

Hammar, T. (1985). *European immigration policy: A comparative study.* Cambridge/New York: Cambridge University Press.

Hansen, R. (2002). Globalization, embedded realism, and path dependence: The other immigrants to Europe. *Comparative Political Studies, 35*(3), 259–283. doi:10.1177/0010414002035003001.

Hollifield, J. (2000). The politics of international migration: How can we 'Bring the State back in'? In C. Brettell & J. F. Hollifield (Eds.), *Migration theory: Talking across disciplines* (pp. 137–186). New York/London: Routledge.

Horvath, K. (2014). Securitisation, economisation and the political constitution of temporary migration: The making of the Austrian seasonal workers scheme. *Migration Letters, 11*(2), 154–170.

Huysmans, J. (2000). The European Union and the securitization of migration. *Journal of Common Market Studies, 38*(5), 751–777. doi:10.1111/1468-5965.00263.

Jacobson, D. (1996). *Rights across borders: Immigration and the decline of citizenship*. Baltimore: Johns Hopkins University Press.
Jessop, B. (1990). *State theory: Putting the capitalist state in its place*. Cambridge: Polity Press.
Jessop, B. (2002). *The future of the capitalist state*. Cambridge: Polity Press.
Jessop, B. (2008). *State power: A strategic-relational approach*. Cambridge/Malden: Polity Press.
Jessop, B., & Sum, N.-L. (2001). Pre-disciplinary and post-disciplinary perspectives. *New Political Economy, 6*(1), 89–101. doi:10.1080/13563460020027777.
Jessop, B., & Sum, N.-L. (2006). *Beyond the regulation approach: Putting capitalist economies in their place*. Cheltenham/Northampton: Edward Elgar.
Jessop, B., Brenner, N., & Jones, M. (2008). Theorizing sociospatial relations. *Environment and Planning D: Society and Space, 26*(3), 389–401. doi:10.1068/d9107.
Joppke, C. (1998). Why liberal states accept unwanted immigration. *World Politics, 50*(2), 266–293. doi:10.1017/S004388710000811X.
Joppke, C. (1999). *Immigration and the nation-state: The United States, Germany and Great Britain*. Oxford: Oxford University Press.
Magnani, N. (2012). Immigration control in Italian political elite debates: Changing policy frames in Italy, 1980s–2000s. *Ethnicities, 12*(5), 643–664. doi:10.1177/1468796811432693.
Massey, D. (1999). International migration at the dawn of the twenty-first century: The role of the state. *Population and Development Review, 25*(2), 303–322.
Massey, D. (2009). The political economy of migration in an era of globalization. In S. Martínez (Ed.), *International migration and human rights: The global repercussions of US policy* (pp. 25–43). Berkeley: University of California Press.
Menz, G. (2011). *Framing competitiveness: The advocacy of articulating migration as a human resources strategy*. Paper presented at the biannual conference of the European Union Studies Association, Boston, MA.
Meyers, E. (2000). Theories of international immigration policy – A comparative analysis. *International Migration Review, 34*(4), 1245–1282. doi:10.2307/2675981.
Money, J. (1999). *Fences and neighbors: The political geography of immigration control*. Ithaca: Cornell University Press.
Perlmutter, T. (1996). Bringing parties back in: Comments on 'Modes of Immigration Politics in Liberal Democratic Societies'. *International Migration Review, 30*(1), 375–388.
Samers, M. (2003). Invisible capitalism: Political economy and the regulation of undocumented immigration in France. *Economy and Society, 32*(4), 555–583. doi:10.1080/0308514032000141701.
Sassen, S. (1988). *The mobility of labor and capital: A study in international investment and labor flow*. Cambridge/New York/Melbourne/Madrid: Cambridge University Press.
Sassen, S. (2000). Regulating immigration in a global age: A new policy landscape. *The Annals of the American Academy of Political and Social Science, 570*(1), 65–77. doi:10.1177/000271620057000105.
Sayer, A. (2001). For a critical cultural political economy. *Antipode, 33*(4), 687–708. doi:10.1111/1467-8330.00206.
Sciortino, G. (2000). Toward a political sociology of entry policies: Conceptual problems and theoretical proposals. *Journal of Ethnic and Migration Studies, 26*(2), 213–228. doi:10.1080/13691830050022776.
Skocpol, T. (1985). Bringing the state back in: Strategies of analysis in current research. In P. B. Evans, D. Rueschemeyer, & T. Skocpol (Eds.), *Bringing the state back in* (pp. 3–43). Cambridge/New York/Melbourne/Madrid: Cambridge University Press.
Soysal, Y. N. (1994). *Limits of citizenship: Migrants and postnational membership in Europe*. Chicago: The University of Chicago Press.
Sum, N.-L., & Jessop, B. (2013). *Towards a cultural political economy: Putting culture in its place in political economy*. Cheltenham/Northampton: Edward Elgar.

Van Der Leun, J. (2006). Excluding illegal migrants in the Netherlands: Between national policies and local implementation. *West European Politics, 29*(2), 310–326. doi:10.1080/01402380500512650.

Van Puymbroeck, N., & Dierckx, D. (2011). De Gordiaanse Knoop van Migratie en de (Multiculturele) Welvaartsstaat. In D. Dierckx, J. Vranken, J. Coene, & A. Van Haarlem (Eds.), *Armoede en Sociale Uitsluiting. Jaarboek 2011* (pp. 285–302). Leuven/Den Haag: Acco.

Van Puymbroeck, N., & Vandevoordt, R. (2013). (On)controleerbare migratie: beleidsnarratieven en de zoektocht naar de grenzen van de welvaartsstaat. In D. Dierckx, J. Coene, A. Van Haarlem, & P. Raeymaeckers (Eds.), *Armoede en Sociale Uitsluiting: Jaarboek 2013* (pp. 235–251). Leuven/Den Haag: Acco.

Wimmer, A., & Schiller, N. (2003). Methodological nationalism, the social sciences, and the study of migration: An essay in historical epistemology. *International Migration Review, 37*(3), 576–610.

Chapter 5
Reflecting on Spatiality in European Migration Research: From Methodological Nationalism to Space-Sensitive Observations of Social Transformations

Elisabeth Scheibelhofer

5.1 Introduction

This contribution starts by outlining the discourse on methodological nationalism in migration research (see Wimmer and Glick Schiller 2002), with a focus on sociology and cultural anthropology. The ongoing struggle with methodological nationalism within migration research has revealed that a reflection on spatiality[1] is needed because spatial relations are a product of social inequality and different power relations. In addition, these spatial relations produce and reproduce social and economic inequalities. In Europe political and administrative EU and national regulations produce spatialities that contribute to social inequalities among (and within the heterogeneous groups of) migrants, movers, and stayers. One example is the way the meaning of borders within the EU has altered during the last few years and the effects this has had on the populations (see Sterbling 2008). This contribution highlights four key driving processes that are indicative of the interrelation of migration and spatiality: European integration, EU strategies for the regulation of non-EU immigration EU enlargement, and migrant space-making.[2]

[1] The concept of spatiality—which will be referred to as 'space', 'social spaces', or 'socio-spaces' in the course of this chapter—highlights the understanding that space is a social construct. It implies that geographically defined spaces are always constructed by human action and through social definition processes. While there is also a material side to space (see Löw 2001), geographical space is a social construct as well (for a detailed discussion of spatiality, see Lefebvre 2002).

[2] I want to thank the anonymous reviewers of IMISCOE for their valuable work and thoughtful suggestions on a previous version of this text.

E. Scheibelhofer (✉)
Department of Sociology, University of Vienna, Vienna, Austria
e-mail: elisabeth.scheibelhofer@univie.ac.at

A. Amelina et al. (eds.), *An Anthology of Migration and Social Transformation*, IMISCOE Research Series, DOI 10.1007/978-3-319-23666-7_5

5.2 The Discourse on Methodological Nationalism

The discussion surrounding methodological nationalism has been prominently brought into the focus of migration research by Andreas Wimmer and Nina Glick Schiller. The authors define methodological nationalism as the implicit assumption that the nation state or the society is the natural social and political form of the modern world. They argue that methodological nationalism characterizes mainstream social science, showing how it has influenced research on migration in particular. Wimmer and Glick Schiller (2002: 302ff.) distinguish between three modes of methodological nationalism. The first is the accepted view in the social sciences that the world is naturally divided into societies; this mode ignores the national framing of modernity. The second mode can be found in the empirical research that takes national narratives and practices as givens rather than regarding them as objects of social scientific research. The third mode involves the 'territorialization' of social scientific thinking (Wimmer and Glick Schiller 2002: 307), which results in research that focuses exclusively on social activities within a given nation state and compares it with the situation in other nation states.

The overall importance of their line of argumentation for social scientific research is still to be assessed in light of the results of empirical research on migration and on the 'integration' of a given nationally and/or ethnically defined group of migrants into a specific nation state. Even the comparative research compares different national and ethnic groups within a nation state. However, the methodological framing of many migration studies conducted in Europe and elsewhere continues to be based on methodological nationalism (Amelina 2012).

The argument triggered considerable interest and stimulated debates among scholars from various different social scientific disciplines who are engaged in research on migration phenomena. In the past years discussions have focused on how to overcome the intricacies of methodological nationalism in migration research (see Amelina 2012; Amelina et al. 2012a, b; Glick Schiller 2009; Levitt and Jaworsky 2007; Pries 2005; Weiß 2010). These exchanges among researchers, as well as their contributions, centre around two broad themes. The first strand of the research focuses on more theoretical questions, such as whether or not we are confronted with methodological nationalism at the level of 'grand theory' in sociological thinking (Chernilo 2006, 2011). The second, and much more productive, theme in the ongoing debate on methodological nationalism is the question of exactly how the methodological limitations may be overcome in empirical migration research. Three major approaches can be distinguished in current international migration research:

1. *Shifting the focus from single territorial case studies to studies of the movements of people, ideas, or goods*: Ethnographic research has made particularly valuable contributions to the ongoing methodological debate on how local phenomena can be studied within the context of global conditionality (see e.g. Albrow 1996; Robertson 1992). Because it is no longer clear how to define a case and its context(s) in this discourse, George Marcus made an important contribution by

developing the well-known 'followings' concept that is now used in multi-sited ethnography (see Marcus 1995). This methodological inquiry has been very fruitful, not only for ethnographic research but also for many scholars in migration research (e.g. Zirh 2012).

2. *Starting out from the shared presence of research subjects within a specific place*: In order to overcome the a priori distinction between migrants and non-migrants and to avoid selecting research subjects based on their assumed nationality and/or ethnicity, researchers have begun to start out with an interest in a specific city or neighbourhood (see Glick Schiller 2007). Specific social practices have been brought into focus as a result, such as the level of transnational involvement to be identified in the inhabitants' everyday social networks within a small Swiss town (see Dahinden 2009). This approach allows researchers to explore the meaning of locality for social embeddedness in diverse networks, be they local or transnational. Also, these analyses can be linked to the socioeconomic position of the individuals, as informed by Dahinden's quantitative approach, which is combined with qualitative data analyses.
3. *Focusing on social networks*: By focusing on social networks, such as ego-centred social networks, empirical migration research may also be able to identify a suitable 'way out' of the impasse of methodological nationalism because researchers do not have to use framings such as 'national' or 'ethnic'[3] but can investigate specific social relations instead. This may allow them to shed light on the question of what meaning a specific place or nation state has for the individuals interviewed (see Scheibelhofer 2006). This relational approach also has much in common with the research carried out in accordance with one of the three premises described above.

The discussion of methodological nationalism is by no means over, but it has become obvious that we need new ways of carrying out migration research in order to fully grasp social transformations.

5.3 Spatialities in the Social Sciences and Migration Research

One might argue that the spatial turn within the social sciences has become historical by now, and that in recent years the social sciences have turned to other 'hot topics'. This has been confirmed by the many conferences, lectures, and publications on space in various different social scientific contexts over the last 20 years. Although one would think that migration is a research field that lends itself particularly well to reflecting on spatiality, most disciplines have been very slow to focus on space (Faist 2013).

[3] Recent empirical and theoretical work has provided evidence of the need to constantly perform ethnicity (see Carlson 2013; Moreman 2009).

The fact that spatiality has not been referred to in most migration research may also be due to naturalizing effects: in our everyday lives, as well as in most migration research, space appears to be objectively given, and human beings appear to be unable to alter them at will. This view is based on an understanding of space as a container—it is an essentialist view on spatiality. Although such a conception of space is quite practical in everyday matters, social scientists have shown that it is by no means a theoretically solid position. Georg Simmel (1992) pointed out that space is a capacity of our mind. Integrating the material component of spatiality into social theory as well has been an issue for scholars from various social scientific traditions, such as Pierre Bourdieu (1985, 1991), Henri Lefebvre (1991), and David Harvey (1994). Over the past decades a sociology of space has been established, major proponents of which include such scholars as John Urry (1996), Doreen Massey (2005), and Martina Löw (2001).

Based on these scholars' work, we can distinguish between an essentialist and a relational understanding of space.[4] The latter is based on the assumption that the spatial is constituted within social relations, and that spatial arrangements also have repercussions *for* social relations. These spatial arrangements include neighbourhoods, landscapes, regions, and—always crucial—nation states. However, classic migration research, as well as many recent migration studies, fail to reflect on this spatial character of the social and thus are unable to address the consequences of spatiality (Samers 2010). This has far-reaching implications for the study of inequality and power within societies. Markus Schroer (2006) emphasizes that spatial arrangements can only be understood as power arrangements because they fulfil specific social functions that result in inclusion and exclusion. Whether or not migration researchers will be able to unravel these power relations also depends on whether or not they make use of theoretical concepts and methodologies that allow them to understand the life worlds of the actors under study and the ways these actors construct meaning.

In view of the distinction between these concepts of spatiality and their implications, it is useful for migration research to start out with the assumption that in everyday life actors (migrants, non-migrants, researchers, laypersons) base their views on both essentialist and relational spatial constructions. For the purpose of research, however, it makes sense to start with a constructivist point of view and to regard spatialities as historically embedded conceptions (Scheibelhofer 2011).

Among the first scholars in migration research to explicitly reflect on spatial conceptions were Ludger Pries (1997), who distinguished between geographical and social spaces, and Thomas Faist (2000, 2004), who introduced the concept of transnational social spaces to the migration debate. In their work on the nexus between migration and cities Nina Glick Schiller and Ayşe Çağlar have shown how migrants are involved in the rescaling of cities, while proponents of the concept of rescaling, such as Brenner (2004) and Jessop et al. (2008) regard current social

---

[4] Some scholars have also introduced a constructivist conception of space for the social sciences, one example being Andreas Pott (2002), who regards space as something that is solely enacted through communication.

transformations as a result of late modern capitalism and its effects on nation state agency and urban and rural restructuring. Glick Schiller and Çağlar were also the first scholars to stress the interrelation between migration and rescaling. This approach enabled them to show how migration and cities can be connected to transnational social relations that are not ethnic (see Çağlar 2006, 2013; Glick Schiller and Çağlar 2008, 2009, 2011; Glick Schiller et al. 2006). These findings stress the importance of combining large-scale economic, political, and migration-specific research with one another in order to gain a better understanding of actual social transformations.

5.4 European Migration Research and Spatiality

This section addresses the complex question of how spatial relations and European migration are interrelated. In the European context it may make sense to roughly distinguish four different types of intervention that have spatial implications—from both above and below—that in turn create, reshape, or destroy previous spatialities: European integration, European enlargement, migrant space-making, and new strategies for the regulation of non-EU immigration.

5.4.1 European Integration

When examining the political project of European integration we must also address the question of spatiality to conceptualize how we can understand the changing relationship between migration and Europe. One result of the process of European integration, and of the power struggles among the major political players within the EU that it involves, is that national legislation is increasingly surrendered to the European level. This transfer of legislative powers is based on the rationale of subsidiarity, which also has far-reaching consequences for European mobility and migration. Regulating migration within the EU is historically closely linked to the establishment of an internally free market including the free movement of persons (Papagianni 2014: 377). This key objective of the EU was first realized in 1990 with the intergovernmental framework of Schengen cooperation.

Since the Treaty of Amsterdam entered into force in 1999, migration politics have been Europeanized with regard to the powers of legislation on asylum and border policies and on matters of irregular migration (Buckel 2012: 80). National legislation in these areas has been implemented with variations in the member states (see also Chap. 7 in this volume). This is even more true of so-called 'third-country nationals'. The opportunities for these individuals to access European nation states as labour migrants are highly regulated and limited in number. However, it should be noted that within the European asylum system the national rates of individuals who are recognized as refugees in accordance with the Geneva Refugee Convention vary from country to country. The politically defined areas that by now have become highly regulated through EU law concern entry provisions for asylum seekers set out in the Dublin Regulation (Craig 2013). Even though migrants continue to die in large numbers at EU borders, no agreement has as yet been reached to distribute asylum seekers more evenly across the countries of the EU, nor have common standards for the treatment of asylum seekers been raised significantly, with the result that the living conditions of refugees vary significantly across EU member states.

A closer look at the immigration of third-country nationals not seeking asylum, whether illegal or otherwise, shows that national regulations, such as laws on labour migration, are still in place, and that legalization campaigns have been carried out in countries such as Italy and Spain.

EU legislation uses the term 'free movers' to denote migrating EU nationals. The idea of free movement has been at the core of European integration efforts since the Treaty of Maastricht (Favell 2008). EU regulations were devised to ensure consistent social, political, and labour rights to the largest extent possible. When it comes to migration within its borders, the EU can be regarded as a vast transnationalization project (Verwiebe 2008: 186), which implies that the meaning of national borders is changing as well (see also Chap. 10). But even for these privileged intra-European migrants free movement is still impeded by a lack of common social security systems. Thus, in most cases individuals engaged in migration, remigration, or further migration lose their rights to social security (Carmel et al. 2011). Along with legislation on social security rights and national borders, regulations on migration therefore still play a decisive role even with regard to intra-European migration and the production and reproduction of social inequalities (see also Chap. 13). The political process of European integration has also had implications for mobility and migration, and has redefined the membership status of former European 'guest workers', as they became citizens of the EU with civil, social, and political rights following the Treaty of Maastricht (Buckel 2011). As the EU member states established a complex system of common EU-wide regulations that continue to coexist with the national regulations, a highly complex situation of new and changing spatial orders has been influencing migration itself, as well as the migration experiences and strategies of migrants in their everyday lives. Thus, these political interventions on the European, the national, and even the regional levels have been reshaping the complex European migration regime, and European integration continues to change the meaning of spaces relevant for migration and migrants' experiences.

5.4.2 EU Strategies for the Regulation of Non-EU Immigration

Access to EU territory is highly restricted for immigrants, and the EU's overall political strategy, the Global Approach to Migration and Mobility (GAMM), is to reduce entries before individuals are able to reach the borders of the EU. Another goal is to control the types of mobility and migration. To this end, the EU has entered into 'mobility partnerships' with a number of non-EU states, such as Moldova, Cape Verde, Georgia, and Armenia. These agreements stipulate that the non-EU countries are to tighten security along their borders to ensure that less undocumented migration reaches the EU borders; they also include provisions on development aid and visa entry facilitation for the nationals of these countries (Maroukis and Triandafyllidou 2013). In return, access to the EU is made easier for citizens of the countries that sign these agreements.

GAMM also provides for programmes of circular migration to be put in place. While in scholarly discourses the term 'circular migration'[5] refers to temporally *undetermined* ongoing movements between two (or more) locations in different nation states, the strategy of regulating migration of the EU understands 'circular migration' to mean that migrants, who are seen as workers, are expected to return to their countries of origin after having spent a certain period of time within the EU. If they wish, they may also move on to another non-EU country, but they have to leave the territory of the EU. Thus, from an analytical point of view, these fairly new strategies follow the, empirically speaking, new historical logic of the 'guest worker' system, which allowed national economies to recruit foreign workers and to send them back when they were no longer needed. However, social scientific research shows that migration cannot be that easily planned and managed through legal provisions (Castles 2004). This is connected to the discourse on securitization within migration: Cassarino (2013) notes that the programmes aimed to regulate the movement of international migrants are linked to new security-driven safeguards within GAMM that have been introduced by the EU. Processes of regulating non-EU immigration have thus had effects not only on European migration within the member states but also on other nation states outside the EU in its current form (Lavenex and Uçarer 2003). The 'mobility partnership agreements' have also led to the creation of buffer zones that, from the immigrants' point of view, add new barriers to their movement into the EU.

Many EU member states are also aware that they have a (nationally framed) demand for labour from outside Europe and have adopted national regulations regarding employment of non-EU citizens in addition to the EU-wide Blue Card work permit.[6] Additionally, member states have also adopted national regulations that allow for home care arrangements that involve low pay, few rights, and prolonged working hours, with the gender aspect of current immigration strategies becoming obvious as well (Lutz 2010 and Chap. 16 in this volume).

In the course of the implementation of national immigration schemes for welcomed, potentially welcomed, or even sought-after immigrants who fall under the premises of national immigration schemes, such as the Red-White-Red Card in Austria, new social spaces have developed that have also led to the production of

[5] The term was first used in an essay on African migration by the economist Walter Elkan (i.e. Elkan 1967).

[6] For a detailed overview and comparison of the EU's Blue Card legislation and the various national regulations, see Cerna (2013).

new social inequalities. If these immigrants are admitted to a nation state different limitations still apply for them as they may find it difficult to change employers and to bring their families or partners with them, or they may have to have their work permits renewed several times to maintain their legal status within the country of residence.

The reshaping of the migratory relations with non-EU states has thus led to the establishment of new relevant social spaces for migrants. The EU's GAMM strategy and the various national initiatives to attract immigrants and incorporate them into the labour market to meet national needs also have spatial implications in that new zones of differentiated mobility rights are introduced. Migration researchers who are aware of the dual character of space—meaning that spatial arrangements influence agency, and vice versa—can focus on the implications of such changing migration-related regulations for migrants, potential migrants, and their significant others. It thus becomes obvious that social transformation is promoted by changing EU and national regulations, and that these changes also have an impact on migration.

5.4.3 Enlarging Europe

The enlargement process has been developing over many years, continually creating new interrelationships of mobility patterns and forms of migrant incorporation. In addition, new border regimes[7] have been established in an attempt to exclude the unwanted (Müller 2013). Various degrees of prosperity and poverty can be observed on the regional level, especially in the new EU member states, with social divisions cutting through zones that were once more homogeneous in terms of social and economic development (Sterbling 2008: 143). These new border regimes have created new lines of social division that in some communities within these regions may affect social cohesion. One example are regions with poor economic development, high unemployment, and a low level of social security, where some families receive financial remittances from family members who have emigrated and others do not. Empirical research in Ukraine, for example, has shown that households that receive remittances are more likely to have better furniture, electrical household appliances, cars, and other modern consumer goods than are households that do not receive any remittances from family members abroad (Malynovska 2004). Migration also has a major effect on the division of labour within transnational families, with mobility arrangements and migration regimes shifting along with the changing borders of an enlarging Europe. This process also transforms the very meaning of the borders still in place, with the implication that new migration and mobility patterns are constantly developing. One example of the rapid and ongoing social change that has been brought about are the well-researched migration movements from Poland to

[7] The term 'border regimes' relates to systems of control that regulate behaviour along borders (Berg and Ehin 2006).

the EU before and after the country's accession (Triandafyllidou 2006; White 2011). Until Poland's accession not all social spaces in the EU were equally accessible to Polish citizens because Germany and Austria had restrictions to free movement, and Croatian citizens will not enjoy free movement within the entire EU at least until June 2015 because 13 member states decided to deny free labour market access for at least 2 years after accession. Other formerly new member states confronted with limited labour market access include Romania, Bulgaria, and most of the countries that acceded in 2004. Such restrictions continue to contribute to differentiated migratory spaces within the EU. Thus, summing up this section, the ongoing European enlargement process has had an effect on spatiality aspects of the European migration regime with regard to the outer borders of the EU and also with regard to limitations on the free movement of new EU citizens. By regarding space as socially constructed in this situation, we are able to explore new and changing social inequalities in more detail to contribute to our understanding of social transformation.

5.4.4 Migrant Space-Making

In contrast to the other three driving forces described in this section, which are the result of large-scale political processes, migrant agency is a force 'from below' that also must be taken into account as a distinct and specific way of transforming social spaces. Migrant activities lead to the creation of new social spaces, as has been well documented, especially in the research on transnational migration, with its perspective on migrants' networks, which has highlighted how new social spaces come into being and how they change individuals' social spaces (Dahinden 2009; Haug and Pointner 2007). There is a growing body of literature on the meaning of social relations and social practices in migration research (Plüss 2013). Important factors include new technologies and new modes of low-cost travel such as air travel, as well as the historical dimensions of former migratory movements that still influence mobility today. Even generations later former migrants' social networks continue to influence European migration in different ways, as was the case during the war in Yugoslavia in the 1990s, when many refugees decided to join their family members or friends who were living in other European countries (Kofman et al. 2000). In addition, future generations may decide to emigrate to their parents' country of origin, as has been observed among Germans with a Turkish family background who are moving to various different areas in Turkey (Aydın 2010; Pusch and Aydın 2012).

However, it is not only individuals, families, and households that have come to act as driving forces; intermediary institutions such as hometown associations can play a crucial role in the establishment or reconfiguration of transnational spaces as well (Çağlar 2006). Collective identity formations in such complex social situations have been shown to move towards 'multi-level and multi-local relational references of belonging' (Pries 2013) with regard to spatial configuration. Based on his empirical studies, Pries (2013) has argued that in the future different types of collective identities will exist simultaneously, including various spatial reaches.

In going about their everyday lives and making plans for the future many migrants also decide to send remittances to their countries of origin, be it to help family members, to build houses, to invest in their communities, or to pursue their own economic goals. These remittances are an instrument used to build and secure transnational social relationships and thus to help to establish and maintain relational social spaces (Tolstokorova 2012). The establishment of such relational spaces is also governed by legal provisions, such as the provisions regarding access to dual citizenship and to the rights associated with it (Bauböck 2010). Migrants as individual actors, and even more so migrants within social groups such as kinship, associations, and interest groups, change spatialities within Europe, with relational space becoming increasingly important as a result. These changes have been shown to have impacts on migratory movements and pathways of migrant incorporation (Glick Schiller 2008).

5.5 Current Conceptions of Space-Sensitive Approaches in Migration Research

On the whole, the 'spatial turn' within the social sciences has not yet been fully acknowledged in migration research, despite the fact that giving serious consideration to spatialities enables us to capture the specific character of migration phenomena (Scheibelhofer 2010, 2011). These migration phenomena are complex and diverse in character, which is especially true of the ongoing social transformations in Europe. Taking up a perspective of social transformations means to zoom in on questions of social change. As Castles argues in Chap. 2 of this volume, we need a re-embedding of migration research in a more general understanding of societies. European societies are clearly changing as a result of the various different forms of migration that are part of them. A space-sensitive approach to the study of European migration can help us raise new research questions because 'space' is no longer conceptualized as static but as something that is changing and is relational. As indicated earlier, this approach leads to a spatial turn in migration research, which can build upon the existing discourses on spatiality.

By taking spatiality into consideration, we are able to examine the circumstances and consequences of the complex ongoing social transformations related to European migration, as well as the power relations involved. As this chapter has shown, spatialities within Europe have been changed by four major processes. First, European integration has led to the implementation of common EU-wide legislation and new national regulations that have changed the spaces of potential migration. New opportunities for migration have emerged (e.g. the principle of free movement for EU citizens and a small group of highly qualified individuals), while access to the EU has been restricted for other individuals (as a result of the EU's new border management strategy). If we regard 'space' as socially constructed, we can understand the ongoing social transformations more easily. The second process, the EU strategies for the regulation of non-EU immigration, has changed the EU's migration-specific relations with non-EU-member states and the strategies it uses to attract certain groups of immigrants have led to changes to European migration regimes. Here relational spaces are reinforced if, for example, circular migration is reinforced in EU programmes that are yet to be put in place. The third major process, EU enlargement, has changed the borders of the EU several times, affecting the right of free movement for millions of Europeans and differentiating mobility rights according to the political constraints put in place by some of the EU member states. These changes have resulted in a shift in the meaning of space in that EU citizens have access to rights in other nation states they had no access to before. The fourth major process, migrant space-making, involves the change of spatialities as a result of the activities of the migrants themselves, such as when migrants, through their transnational social relations, create social spaces that are relational and not primarily limited in character by nation states. Transnational migration and the specific pathways of migrant incorporation within EU borders have led to the creation of new spaces that permit migration.

References

Albrow, M. (1996). *The global age: State and society beyond modernity.* Stanford: Stanford University Press.

Amelina, A. (2012). Socio-spatial scales as social boundaries? Or: How do migration studies profit from including 'space' in the sociology of social boundaries. *Migration Letters, 9*(3), 273–288.

Amelina, A., Faist, T., Glick Schiller, N., & Nergiz, D. D. (2012a). Methodological predicaments of cross-border studies. In A. Amelina, D. D. Nergiz, T. Faist, & N. Glick Schiller (Eds.), *Beyond methodological nationalism: Research methodologies for cross-border studies* (pp. 1–19). New York/Oxon: Routledge.

Amelina, A., Nergiz, D., Faist, T., & Glick Schiller, N. (Eds.). (2012b). *Beyond methodological nationalism: Research methodologies for cross-border studies.* New York/Oxon: Routledge.

Aydın, Y. (2010). Der Diskurs um die Abwanderung Hochqualifizierter türkischer Herkunft in die Türkei: Paper 3–9 des HWWI-Kompetenzbereiches Migration Research Group. Hamburg: Hamburgisches WeltWirtschaftsInstitut. https://mediendienst-integration.de/fileadmin/Dateien/Diskurs_um_Abwanderung_von_Tuerken.pdf

Bauböck, R. (2010). Changing the boundaries of citizenship: The inclusion of immigrants in democratic polities. In M. Martiniello & J. Rath (Eds.), *Selected studies in international migration and immigrant incorporation* (pp. 275–314). Amsterdam: Amsterdam University Press.

Berg, E., & Ehin, P. (2006). What kind of border regime is in the making? Towards a differentiated and uneven border strategy. *Cooperation and Conflict, 41*(1), 53–71. doi:10.1177/0010836706060935.

Bourdieu, P. (1985). *Sozialer Raum und "Klassen". Leçon sur la leçon. Zwei Vorlesungen.* Frankfurt am Main: Suhrkamp.

Bourdieu, P. (1991). Physischer, sozialer und angeeigneter physischer Raum. In M. Wentz (Ed.), *Stadt-Räume. Die Zukunft des Städtischen. Frankfurter Beiträge* (pp. 26–34). Frankfurt am Main/New York: Campus.

Brenner, N. (2004). *New state spaces: Urban governance and the rescaling of statehood.* Oxford/New York: Oxford University Press.

Buckel, S. (2011). Staatsprojekt Europa. *Politische Vierteljahresschrift: Zeitschrift der Deutschen Vereinigung für Politische Wissenschaft, 52*(4), 636–662.
Buckel, S. (2012). "Managing Migration" – Eine intersektionale Kapitalismusanalyse am Beispiel der Europäischen Migrationspolitik. *Berliner Journal für Soziologie, 22*(1), 79–100. doi:10.1007/s11609-012-0179-y.
Çağlar, A. (2006). Hometown associations, the rescaling of state spatiality and migrant grassroots transnationalism. *Global Networks, 6*(1), 1–22. doi:10.1111/j.1471-0374.2006.00130.x.
Çağlar, A. (2013). Turkey and Europe: Locating homeland ties and re-scaling migration scholarship. *European Review, 21*(3), 400–411. doi:10.1017/S1062798713000367.
Carlson, M. A. (2013). *Performance: A critical introduction* (2nd ed.). Oxon/New York: Routledge.
Carmel, E., Cerami, A., & Papadopoulos, T. (2011). *Migration and welfare in the new Europe: Social protection and the challenges of integration*. Bristol: Policy Press.
Cassarino, J.-P. (2013). The drive for securitized temporariness. In A. Triandafyllidou (Ed.), *Circular migration between Europe and its neighbourhood: Choice or necessity?* (pp. 22–41). Oxford: Oxford University Press.
Castles, S. (2004). Why migration policies fail. *Ethnic and Racial Studies, 27*(2), 205–227. doi:10.1080/0141987042000177306.
Cerna, L. (2013). Understanding the diversity of EU migration policy in practice: The implementation of the Blue Card initiative. *Policy Studies, 34*(2), 180–200. doi:10.1080/01442872.2013.767587.
Chernilo, D. (2006). Methodological nationalism and its critique. In G. Delanty & K. Kumar (Eds.), *The SAGE handbook of nations and nationalism* (pp. 129–140). London/Thousand Oaks/New Delhi: SAGE Publications.
Chernilo, D. (2011). The critique of methodological nationalism: Theory and history. *Thesis Eleven, 106*(1), 98–117. doi:10.1177/0725513611415789.
Craig, S. (2013). Struggling with EU safe country practices in asylum. In U. Korkut, G. Bucken-Knapp, A. McGarry, J. Hinnfors, & H. Drake (Eds.), *The discourses and politics of migration in Europe* (pp. 53–72). New York: Palgrave Macmillan.
Dahinden, J. (2009). Are we all transnationals now? Network transnationalism and transnational subjectivity: The differing impacts of globalization on the inhabitants of a small Swiss city. *Ethnic and Racial Studies, 32*(8), 1365–1386. doi:10.1080/01419870802506534.
Elkan, W. (1967). Circular migration and the growth of towns in East Africa. *International Labour Review, 96*, 581–589.
Faist, T. (2000). *The volume and dynamics of international migration and transnational social spaces*. Oxford: Oxford University Press.
Faist, T. (2004). The border-crossing expansion of social space: Concepts, questions and topics. In T. Faist & E. Özveren (Eds.), *Transnational social spaces: Agents, networks and institutions* (pp. 1–34). Aldershot/Burlington: Ashgate.
Faist, T. (2013). Elemente einer transnationalen Methodologie jenseits von methodologischem Nationalismus und Essentialismus. In B. Pusch (Ed.), *Transnationale Migration am Beispiel Deutschland und Türkei* (pp. 103–128). Wiesbaden: Springer VS.
Favell, A. (2008). *Eurostars and Eurocities: Free movement and mobility in an integrating Europe*. Malden/Oxford/Carlton: Blackwell Publishing.
Glick Schiller, N. (2007). *Beyond the nation-state and its units of analysis: Towards a new research agenda for migration studies. Essentials of migration theory* (COMCAD Arbeitspapiere – Working Papers No. 33). Bielefeld: Center on Migration, Citizenship and Development.
Glick Schiller, N. (2008). *Beyond methodological ethnicity: Local and transnational pathways of immigrant incorporation* (Willy Brandt Series of Working Papers in International Migration and Ethnic Relations 2/08). Malmö: Malmö Institute for Studies of Migration, Diversity and Welfare (MIM) and Department of International Migration and Ethnic Relations (IMER), Malmö University.
Glick Schiller, N. (2009). *A global perspective on transnational migration: Theorizing migration without methodological nationalism* (Working Paper No. 67). Oxford: Centre on Migration, Policy and Society, University of Oxford.

Glick Schiller, N., & Çağlar, A. (2008). *Migrant incorporation and city scale: Towards a theory of locality in migration studies* (Willy Brandt Series of Working Papers in International Migration and Ethnic Relations 2/07). Malmö: Malmö Institute for Studies of Migration, Diversity and Welfare (MIM) and Department of International Migration and Ethnic Relations (IMER), Malmö University.

Glick Schiller, N., & Çağlar, A. (2009). Towards a comparative theory of locality in migration studies: Migrant incorporation and city scale. *Journal of Ethnic and Migration Studies, 35*(2), 177–202. doi:10.1080/13691830802586179.

Glick Schiller, N., & Çağlar, A. (2011). *Locating migration: Rescaling cities and migrants*. Ithaca: Cornell University Press.

Glick Schiller, N., Çağlar, A., & Guldbransen, T. C. (2006). Jenseits der "ethnischen Gruppe" als Objekt des Wissens: Lokalität, Globalität und Inkorporationsmuster von Migranten. In H. Berking (Ed.), *Die Macht des Lokalen in einer Welt ohne Grenzen* (pp. 105–144). Frankfurt am Main/New York: Campus.

Harvey, D. (1994). Die Postmoderne und die Verdichtung von Raum und Zeit. In A. Kuhlmann (Ed.), *Philosophische Ansichten der Kultur der Moderne* (pp. 48–79). Frankfurt am Main: Fischer.

Haug, S., & Pointner, S. (2007). Soziale Netzwerke, Migration und Integration. In A. Franzen & M. Freitag (Eds.), *Sozialkapital: Grundlagen und Anwendungen. Kölner Zeitschrift für Soziologie und Sozialpsychologie: Sonderheft 47/2007* (pp. 367–396). Wiesbaden: VS Verlag für Sozialwissenschaften.

Jessop, B., Brenner, N., & Jones, M. (2008). Theorizing sociospatial relations. *Environment and Planning D: Society and Space, 26*(3), 389–401. doi:10.1068/d9107.

Kofman, E., Phizacklea, A., Raghuram, P., & Sales, R. (2000). *Gender and international migration in Europe: Employment, welfare and politics*. London: Routledge.

Lavenex, S., & Uçarer, E. M. (2003). *Migration and the externalities of European integration*. Lanham: Lexington Books.

Lefebvre, H. (1991). *The production of space*. Oxford: Basil Blackwell Ltd.

Lefebvre, H. (2002). The production of space. In M. J. Dear & S. Flusty (Eds.), *Spaces of postmodernity. Readings in human geography* (pp. 131–142). Oxford: Blackwell.

Levitt, P., & Jaworsky, B. N. (2007). Transnational migration studies: Past developments and future trends. *Annual Review of Sociology, 33*, 129–156. doi:10.1146/annurev.soc.33.040406.131816.

Löw, M. (2001). *Raumsoziologie*. Frankfurt am Main: Suhrkamp.

Lutz, H. (2010). Gender in the migratory process. *Journal of Ethnic and Migration Studies, 36*(10), 1647–1663. doi:10.1080/1369183X.2010.489373.

Malynovska, O. (2004). *International migration in contemporary Ukraine: Trends and policy* (Global migration perspectives no. 14). Geneva: Global Commission on International Migration.

Marcus, G. E. (1995). Ethnography in/of the world system: The emergence of multi-sited ethnography. *Annual Review of Anthropology, 24*, 95–117. doi:10.1146/annurev.an.24.100195.000523.

Maroukis, T., & Triandafyllidou, A. (2013). *Mobility partnerships: A convincing toll for the EU's global approach to migration? Policy paper 76*. Paris: Jacques Delors Institute.

Massey, D. (2005). *For space*. London/Thousand Oaks/New Delhi: SAGE.

Moreman, S. T. (2009). Memoir as performance: Strategies of hybrid ethnic identity. *Text and Performance Quarterly, 29*(4), 346–366. doi:10.1080/10462930903242855.

Müller, A. (2013). Territorial borders as institutions: Functional change and the spatial division of authority. *European Societies, 15*(3), 353–372. doi:10.1080/14616696.2012.717633.

Papagianni, G. (2014). EU migration policy. In A. Triandafyllidou & R. Gropas (Eds.), *European immigration: A sourcebook* (2nd ed., pp. 15–46). Aldershot: Ashgate.

Plüss, C. (2013). Migrants' social positioning and inequalities: The intersections of capital, locations, and aspirations. *International Sociology, 28*(1), 4–11. doi:10.1177/0268580912468920.

Pott, A. (2002). *Ethnizität und Raum im Aufstiegsprozeß: Eine Untersuchung zum Bildungsaufstieg in der zweiten türkischen Migrantengeneration*. Opladen: Leske + Budrich.
Pries, L. (1997). Neue migration im transnationalen raum. In L. Pries (Ed.), *Transnationale migration* (pp. 15–46). Baden-Baden: Nomos.
Pries, L. (2005). Configurations of geographic and societal spaces: A sociological proposal between "methodological nationalism" and the "spaces of flows". *Global Networks, 5*(2), 167–190. doi:10.1111/j.1471-0374.2005.00113.x.
Pries, L. (2013). Ambiguities of global and transnational collective identities. *Global Networks, 13*(1), 22–40. doi:10.1111/j.1471-0374.2012.00368.x.
Pusch, B., & Aydın, Y. (2012). Migration of highly qualified German citizens with Turkish background from Germany to turkey: Socio-political factors and individual motives. *International Journal of Business and Globalisation, 8*(4), 471–490.
Robertson, R. (1992). *Globalization and social theory*. London: Sage.
Samers, M. (2010). *Migration*. Oxon/New York: Routledge.
Scheibelhofer, E. (2006). Migration, Mobilität und Beziehung im Raum: Egozentrierte Netzwerkzeichnungen als Erhebungsmethode. In B. Hollstein & F. Straus (Eds.), *Qualitative Netzwerkanalyse: Konzepte, Methoden, Anwendungen* (pp. 311–332). Wiesbaden: VS Verlag für Sozialwissenschaften.
Scheibelhofer, E. (2010). *Space-sensible sociology of migration: How migration research can profit of socio-spatial theories* (COMCAD Arbeitspapiere – Working Papers No. 77). Bielefeld: Center on Migration, Citizenship and Development.
Scheibelhofer, E. (2011). *Raumsensible Migrationsforschung: Methodologische Überlegungen und ihre empirische Relevanz für die Migrationssoziologie*. Wiesbaden: VS Verlag für Sozialwissenschaften/Springer Fachmedien.
Schroer, M. (2006). *Räume, Orte, Grenzen: Auf dem Weg zu einer Soziologie des Raumes*. Frankfurt am Main: Suhrkamp.
Simmel, G. (1992). *Der Raum und die räumliche Ordnung*. Frankfurt am Main: Suhrkamp.
Sterbling, A. (2008). Konturen eines europäischen Migrations- und Sozialraums in Südosteuropa. In P. A. Berger & A. Weiß (Eds.), *Transnationalisierung sozialer Ungleichheit* (pp. 137–160). Wiesbaden: VS Verlag für Sozialwissenschaften.
Tolstokorova, A. V. (2012). The woman and sixpence: Gendered impact of remittances on social sustainability of Ukrainian transnational households. *Analytical, 5*(1), 74–97.
Triandafyllidou, A. (Ed.). (2006). *Contemporary polish migration in Europe: Complex patterns of movement and settlement*. Lewiston: Edwin Mellen Press.
Urry, J. (1996). Sociology of time and space. In B. S. Turner (Ed.), *The Blackwell companion to social theory* (pp. 369–394). Malden/Oxford: Blackwell Publishers.
Verwiebe, R. (2008). Statusveränderungen und innereuropäische Wanderungen: Ergebnisse einer Verknüpfung qualitativer und quantitativer Befunde. In P. A. Berger & A. Weiß (Eds.), *Transnationalisierung sozialer Ungleichheit* (pp. 185–210). Wiesbaden: Verlag für Sozialwissenschaften.
Weiß, A. (2010). Vergleiche jenseits des Nationalstaats: Methodologischer Kosmopolitismus in der soziologischen Forschung über hochqualifizierte Migration. *Soziale Welt, 61*(3/4), 295–311.
White, A. (2011). *Polish families and migration since EU accession*. Bristol: Policy Press.
Wimmer, A., & Glick Schiller, N. (2002). Methodological nationalism and beyond: Nation- state building, migration and the social sciences. *Global Networks, 2*(4), 301–334. doi:10.1111/1471-0374.00043.
Zirh, B. C. (2012). Following the dead beyond the 'nation': A map for transnational Alevi funerary routes from Europe to Turkey. *Ethnic and Racial Studies, 35*(10), 1758–1774. doi:10.1080/01419870.2012.659274.

Chapter 6
Migration and Postsocialism: A Relational-Geography Approach

Bruno Meeus

6.1 Introduction

In the two decades that followed the end of the Cold War the mobility of people, objects, and ideas connecting the European 'East' with 'the West' reached an unprecedented intensity and depth. As a result, 'the East' is in 'the West', and 'the West' is in 'the East' (Stenning 2005). However, the analysis of the fall of socialism and the deep changes afterwards tends to stick to the territorial boundaries of the former socialist states. Scholars only rarely emphasize how mobilities between 'the East' and 'the West' have transformed, are transforming, and are transformed by postsocialism. This chapter introduces a relational-geography perspective to analyse how the mobility of people, ideas, and objects between 'East' and 'West' is produced by but also produces particular forms of postsocialist transformation. The relational-geography approach is the result of a recent and broad paradigmatic change in human geography that has roughly two aims: to offer alternative spatial registers to conceptualise the social world beyond imaginaries that tend to contain it in territories like the nation-state. And to critically analyse politics of care and responsibility that go beyond the spatial container of the nation-state.

The chapter begins with a brief overview of the current state of the discussion of the relevance of the concept of 'postsocialism'. It will then introduce the relational-geography approach. In the sections that follow, three examples of relational-geography approaches to post-socialism and migration are discussed in more detail. The first of these examples will illustrate how a 'politics of connectivity' point of view can be used to highlight the historical and contemporary responsibility of the West in shaping particular postsocialisms and migration; the second will illustrate how 'a politics of openness vs. closure' perspective can be used to criticize the

B. Meeus (✉)
Cosmopolis Centre for Urban Research, Vrije Universiteit Brussel, Brussels, Belgium
e-mail: bruno.meeus@vub.ac.be

A. Amelina et al. (eds.), *An Anthology of Migration and Social Transformation*,
IMISCOE Research Series, DOI 10.1007/978-3-319-23666-7_6

terms under which mobility between the East and the West takes place; and the third will illustrate how a 'politics of propinquity' view can be used to emphasize the responsibility of mobile people, ideas, and objects in Europe in the Gramscian struggle for hegemony over postsocialist morality.

6.2 From Transition to Postsocialist Transformation to 'Actually Existing Postsocialism'

Because the Cold-War 'West–East' division was deeply ingrained in the social sciences themselves, Western and Eastern social theorists were in limbo the moment the Iron Curtain fell (Outhwaite and Ray 2005: 22–23). Critical scholars of Western capitalism at the time did not have the appropriate tools to analyse what was happening while theories inspired by 'neoliberalism'—'transitology', as this approach was later conceived—self-confidently informed the marketization, privatization, and deregulation of 'the East'. During the 1990s, critiques of the increasing hegemony of 'transitology' approaches in social theory started to gain influence (see e.g. Burawoy 1992; Lagerspetz 1999; Pickles and Smith 1998; Verdery 1996). The problem with transitology was that it imagined the former communist countries as on their way 'back to normal' on a preconceived path in the direction of a uniform European market economy. It was employed by many powerful actors, such as the World Bank and the IMF. Scholars such as Pickles and Smith (1998) therefore proposed to talk about 'transformation' instead of 'transition' to emphasize a more open-ended point of view. 'Postsocialist transformation' was supposed to bring alternative postsocialist trajectories and outcomes into view to replace transitology's view on change, which was inspired by teleology (only one future is possible) and market fetishism (a future in which competitive markets and individuals were the only relevant social phenomena). The 'transformational' school brought into being a range of ethnographical and sociological studies of life during and after socialism.

Twenty-five years after the collapse of state-socialism, the usefulness of the concepts of 'postsocialism' or 'postcommunism' can be questioned. Some have argued that postsocialism is only a variant of neoliberalism and that therefore capitalism and its current neoliberal variant need to be analysed. Others have stated that by continuously referring to a socialist past the language of postsocialism marginalizes these states and their inhabitants because it implies an ongoing undemocratic, corrupt, and abnormal situation despite the fact that many former state-socialist countries are now part of the European Union and/or NATO, and there is no longer a need to refer to what is now a distant past. It has also been argued that the paths taken by these countries since 1989 are so divergent that putting them all under the umbrella of 'postsocialism' was an unnecessary conceptual reduction (for an overview of these arguments see King 2000; Pickles 2010; Flynn and Oldfield 2006).

However, Stenning and Hörschelmann (2008: 312) argue that there are at least two reasons why the concept of 'postsocialism' is still relevant. First, notwithstanding the diversity of the vast region, there is *a common experience* of dealing with some sort of state-socialism that is shared in the region, which explains for instance similar nostalgic memories of consumption practices and identities, or, similar political standpoints in the region (Ekman and Linde 2005). And indeed, there is a diversity of postsocialist trajectories, but experiences of having been 'transitologized', and possibly other experiences, are shared as well. Second, postsocialist thinking is, just like postcolonial thinking, a particular *vantage point* that brings into view particular aspects of social reality that would otherwise remain out of sight or be only limited understood. For example: 'false hopes of the market, inherited from memories of pre-socialism, nurtured in its absence under socialism and cultivated still further in the particular moment of the late 1980s and early 1990s, combined to structure the very real disappointments of post-socialism' (Stenning and Hörschelmann 2008: 326).

The aim of this 'strategic essentialism' of postsocialism is not to hide the real existing diversity of postsocialist trajectories (Smith and Stenning 2006). Nor is the aim to explain everything by referring to a socialist past. Instead, it envisions the diversity of 'actually existing postsocialism' that results from the articulation of multiple socialist legacies with various other processes and features to explain certain empirical facts.

6.3 The Relational-Geography Approach

In order to get to grips with the way in which 'actually existing post-socialism' extends into the West, space should be understood relationally. The relational-geography approach, developed by, among others, Massey (2004, 2005), Amin (2004), and Harvey (2006), challenges the dominance in social theory of the spatial register in which 'society' is conceived of as contained in a 'territory'. Territorial approaches start from an understanding that people care first and feel most responsible for those that are spatially nearest; this results in a hierarchy of feelings of care and responsibility from the family to the neighbourhood, the region, the country and so on (Massey 2004). Following this territorial approach, care and responsibility for others are to be organised on the basis of hierarchically organized territorial containers to which the politics of care and responsibility are limited. This notion of space as 'containing society' and 'containing politics' appears to be at odds with, for instance, the argument of transnationalism scholars that relations of care and responsibility in practice extend across the borders of nation states (see e.g. Levitt and Glick Schiller 2004; Wimmer and Glick Schiller 2003, for details see also Chap. 5, in this volume).

To reimagine a politics of care and responsibility beyond territorial spatial registers, Massey (2005) proposed an approach to space that radically breaks with the territorial understandings. To Massey, particular places are not containers but are always the product of the throwntogetherness of different trajectories of people, things and ideas. Hence, space is *the sphere of the possibility of the existence of multiplicity* and places such as cities, regions and countries are *always under construction*. Space is being developed and has neither a predetermined future nor a singular past. Particular places are events, 'in the simple sense of the coming together of the previously unrelated, a [temporary] constellation of processes rather than a thing' (Massey 2005: 141). If different trajectories and histories converge in and constitute particular places, then places are implicated in spatial and social relations beyond the bounds of place (Darling 2009: 1938–1939).

Indeed, relational geography emphasizes how other and distant places are implicated in the here-and-now. It points out that a politics of care and responsibility does not stop at the borders of a predefined territory (Amin 2004). Moreover, relational geography offers three 'spatial registers' instead of one through which to understand the politics of care and responsibility*: (i) a politics of connectivity, (ii) a politics of openness vs closure* and *(iii) a politics of propinquity*. Importantly, none of these spatial registers is essentially more progressive or more regressive than the others: 'there are no rules of space and place' Massey (2005: 163).

6.4 Migration and the Responsibility of 'the West': A Politics of Connectivity

A '*politics of connectivity*' builds on the 'outwardlookingness' of places. In a context in which the growing number of Eastern European migrants in Western European cities and regions tends to produce moral panics (Pijpers 2006), unions fearing a 'race to the bottom' (Donaghey and Teague 2006; Krings 2009), and pleas for closing the national borders are heard increasingly often (Amin 2013), a politics of connectivity emphasizes how the 'West' has been and is still implied in the transformation of the 'East'. More particularly, this spatial register politicizes the way in which 'the West' has been coproducing a particular form of postsocialist transformation in 'the East' and, as a result, has been coproducing migration. It emphasizes the responsibility of 'the West' vis-à-vis 'the East' not only in recent history but also in the here-and-now.

The opening of borders after the fall of the Iron Curtain immediately generated new forms of international mobility and led to the intensification of already existing forms of cross-border mobility (Humphrey 2002). However, these forms of mobility intensified and became forms of (temporary and/or undocumented) work migration only as a result of the social damage of 'transitology' in the 1990s. 'Transitology' theories supported policies that mainly served the stakes of Western companies. At the end of the 1980s Western Europe was still struggling with the crisis of the Fordist economic growth model (Harvey 2003). Facing strong union opposition, continental Europe realized the potential of a large reservoir of cheap non-unionized labour from the Eastern neighbourhood (Bieler 2000).

Bohle (2006) and Ivanova (2007) demonstrated the influence actors such as the European Roundtable of Industrialists (ERT)—a club of CEOs of some of Europe's largest non-financial corporations[1]—and the European Commission had on the redevelopment of Eastern Europe. The ERT viewed the developments from the perspective of CEOs; that is, with the aim of maintaining and increasing the profit rates of their companies. According to Ivanova (2007), the successive ERT reports written during the 1990s read like a roadmap to the European Union enlargement project. The central message of the ERT was that Europe had become a 'high-cost, low-growth economy' that was not adapting fast enough and was losing its competitive advantage to other parts of the world. The key to revitalize Europe's competitiveness was cutting the cost of labour. 'Needless to say, Eastern Europe, which offers a large pool of cheap labour in the immediate vicinity, fits nicely into the cost cutting strategy. Not only are the wages there quite low, but Old Europe's labour market "rigidities" are something that the New Europe will probably never know' (Ivanova 2007: 353).

To prepare the East for this role, the postsocialist states had to be restructured in two ways: first, they had to retreat from their redistributive functions and their role as major investors (shock therapy) to produce 'a disempowered, impoverished and spineless working class that would succumb to all forms of flexibilization and could be easily engaged in the "East–West win–win business experience"' (Ivanova 2007: 361); and, second, the state had to be reconstructed to turn it into a legislator and a guardian of the free market that would create and safeguard favourable conditions for business operations. The social damage caused by this shock therapy was part of the transitology policy agenda: 'the immense social cost of this policy could have been and probably had been anticipated. Damage was necessary and pain was necessary because it was part of the design' (Ivanova 2007: 360). But, while the Eastern and Central European 'strong states' came close to meeting the convergence criteria of the EU at the end of the 1990s, the farther East one looked, the more severe was the damage to the state. Bulgaria and Romania, for instance, have been so severely crushed that they have failed to fully develop the capability to defend the interests of the foreign as well as the domestic capitalist class.

All kinds of migratory practices in the direction of the West were part of what Stenning et al. (2010) call the 'domestication' of neoliberalism. Many Eastern Europeans chose the 'flight forward' to organize their welfare by themselves. The practices that had informed everyday life during socialism reconfigured into crucial resources for this endeavour to succeed (Morawska 2001). The informal networks of reciprocal gift giving and market exchange that had secured access to goods and means of production at a time when state socialism had bred chronic shortages (Kornai 1992) turned into transnational networks of care. The ability to 'play against the structures' proved to be a skill necessary to deal with the constraints on sojourn duration in Western countries and to meet the requirement to work mostly in the unofficial or grey segments of the Western labour markets(Morawska 2001). The availability of extensive transnational assistance networks, the know-how of other

[1] Siemens, ThyssenKrupp, Bayer, and Solvay, among others.

migrants, and the realization that the informal life as a migrant is not much different from the informal practices at home, offer subsequent migrants 'a predictable future' as migrants and significantly reduce the uncertainty of the actions.

A politics of connectivity thus opens up a spatial register with which to imagine the claims for resources, care, and concern beyond the imagined nationalcommunity in a territorial and enclosed spatial imaginary. It emphasizes that Western European cities are in the here-and-now related to places in Eastern Europe (May et al. 2007), and that particular places in Eastern Europe relate to labour market conditions in the West (Meeus 2013).

6.5 Mobility on Whose Terms? A Politics of Openness vs. Closure

According to Noel Castree, there is not necessarily anything progressive about translocal connections, just as there is not necessarily anything regressive about all forms of localism that are defined against a putative exterior, such as when indigenous communities organize against land grabs. Projects to erect 'stringent boundaries' around places—both in the imagination and in practice—should not necessarily be deemed as 'regressive' (Castree 2004: 150; see also Wills 2008). The question is: 'Against what are the boundaries erected? What are the power-geometries here; and do they demand a political response?' (Massey 2005: 179). These questions are the realm of a politics of openness vs. closure.

A *'politics of openness vs. closure'* is a central theme in migration research. Various scholars have emphasized that the post-war guest worker regimes, with their restrictions on family reunion, outsourced many of their welfareresponsibilities to the guest workers' places of origin (see e.g. Burawoy 1976; Piore 1979;Castles and Kosack 1973; Freeman 1986; Samers 1999). These migration scholars have argued that post-war Western capitalism created 'closed' welfare systems for their citizens (see also Freeman 1986), but, because capitalist production in the West still needed workers prepared to fill the vacant jobs in mining and construction, such workers were imported, thereby creating a de facto dual labour market (see also Kloosterman et al. 1999). The advantage this guest worker system had for the receiving states was that they did not have to bear the full responsibility for the welfare of the workers, because the workers' families and children were supposed to stay behind. Production in the receiving states thus capitalized on the persistent loyalty of guest workers to their home-states, who were encouraged or forced to leave at moments of economic crisis or when insurgency developed (Samers 1999). The ready availability of new Eastern European 'income-seeking travellers' reproduced this system (Castles 2006).

However, from the perspective of the postsocialist sending states a similar outsourcing of responsibility occurs. If Eastern European workers make use of transnational networks of social support, their home governments do not have to bear full responsibility for the reproduction of their citizens either (Piore 1979). Postsocialist sending states thus also capitalize on migrants' loyalty: their citizens work abroad to secure the welfare of their families 'at home'. Their migrant work acts as a 'safety valve': migrants' welfare is ensured, they do not mobilize against the policies of welfare restructuring, and the postsocialist governments do not have to invest in collectivizing the social risks of all their citizens (Meeus 2013). Indeed, mass emigration was an attractive option to address the problems of mass unemployment that came with transition (May et al. 2008: 67).

But the perspective of the politics of openness vs. closure also sheds light on other postsocialist transformations that result from mass migration. As a result of rural exodus, postsocialist countries such as Hungary, Ukraine, and Romania have become more vulnerable to land speculation and land grabbing (Franco and Borras 2013). Bouniol (2013) showed that, when faced with rural exodus, rural populations and regional governments in Romania are usually enthusiastic to lease or sell their land to transnational or domestic corporations. Supported by massive European Union subsidies for large-scale export-oriented agriculture (a *politics of engendering openness*), the investments of these corporations bring little benefit to local inhabitants and instead cause environmental degradation, undermine food sovereignty, increase the price of land, and drive down the local prices of agricultural commodities. The few collective mobilizations against these land grabs are examples of a *politics of engendering closure*; for example, in Romania social movements have started to emerge which organize resistance to the Roşia Montană Gold Corporation's land grabbing efforts (Alexandrescu 2012).

6.6 Negotiating Postsocialist Morality: Mobility and the Politics of Propinquity

If Zygmunt Bauman's warning of 'liquid modernity'—the radical instability that characterizes postmodernism—does describe an actually existing situation, then the reality of the postsocialist experience probably comes near (Bauman 2000). The increasing speed of change since the 1990s had made it difficult for Eastern Europeans to make sense of the world around them (Humphrey 2002). The struggle over 'sense-making' is therefore part of postsocialist transformation (see also Chap. 16, in this volume). What is particularly interesting is the struggle for Gramscian hegemony over common sense, the struggle to dominate what is taken for granted. Neoliberalism not only aims to design markets, it also aims to enact a moral transformation in which meritocracy and individual success become taken for granted (Rose et al. 2006), and as Peck (2010) convincingly argues, the strength of neoliberalism lies precisely in how it adapts this morality to versatile contexts, namely by capturing local discontents, criticisms, and popular moral ideas and practices (Young 2013, cited in Petrovici 2013). In postsocialist societies neoliberal morality mainly parasitizes on the existing critique of the experience in communist times:

totalitarianism, bureaucratic rule, shortages, and inefficiency (Kornai 1992). In contrast, capitalism—'the only alternative'—is referred to as democratic, just, efficient, and competitive compared with the old system. Thus, for the 'bright future' to come, the old communist habits and practices have to disappear (Petrovici 2013: 24–25). During socialism state ideology dominated over common sense. Capitalist practices such as private trading to make a profit were deemed immoral, a judgment widely shared by ordinary people, though not by everyone (Humphrey and Mandel 2002: 1; Wanner 2005). However, 25 years of transnational mobility of mobile individuals such as professional technocrats, traders, and migrant workers have had an important influence on local discourses on meritocracy and moral justice. If we see places as the juxtaposition of heterogeneous trajectories, then there always has to be negotiation between the different micro-worlds which find themselves thrown together on the same turf. This is what Amin (2004) calls a '*politics of propinquity*'. The perspective of a politics of propinquity is particularly interesting for investigating the negotiation of different moral orders in particular places characterized by the juxtaposition of these orders (Amin 2013). As I will show, the continuous negotiation of their practices and discourses in a diversity of places potentially either enables the neoliberal trajectory to gain traction in the postsocialist context or prevents it from doing so.

Theories, policies, and techniques 'travel' between different contexts, and change during that journey (Peck and Theodore 2010; Collier 2011). For instance, in Poland neoliberal restructuring emerged from 'a complex blend of ideas and practices bought over from Washington and Brussels but [was] reworked by the Polish state and carried through by a newly emergent, indigenous (though fully transnational) capitalistclass' (May et al. 2008: 56). Soon after a small group of foreign economic-policy experts had settled in Ukraine in 1992, international mobility grants facilitated the rise of a small army of academic and professional economists and the emergence of an infrastructure of think tanks, schools, seminars, and publications which produced neoliberal transition scripts for the Ukrainian economy (Swain 2006).

Indeed, in Eastern Europe it has often been through the international mobility of *travellingtechnocrats* that a critical mass of local 'shock therapy' economists has come into being. The infrastructure described by Swain (2006), such as visiting fellowships at Western universities, Master's degrees, and participation in research and teaching projects with Western scholars, created enough transnational dialogue for neoliberal ideas to be embraced by a critical mass of Romanian economists (Ban 2011: 504). A research agenda that would scrutinize to what extent the transnational mobility, the cosmopolitan attitudes, and the individual career aspirations of Eastern European graduate, doctoral, and postdoctoral students (see also, Chap. 15, in this volume) and NGO delegates promote an ethics of meritocracy in the East and in the West has yet to be developed.

However, it is not only in the schools and research institutions that the politics of propinquity influences the struggle for hegemony over common sense. The transforming postsocialist morality is also the result of the work and consumption practices of another mobile group: the mobile 'meritocrats'. Carving out a local ethnic niche when working abroad, Polish construction workers in the UK strategically distinguish themselves from British workers by depicting them as lazy and welfare-dependent, and by emphasizing their own Polish ethics of hard work (Datta and Brickell 2009). By mobilizing this ethnic construction these workers promote the very role neoliberaldiscourses attribute to them: to be accepted as citizens, they are expected to be the new guest workers. Moreover, they also promote the increasing demonization of the British working class (Jones 2011). Similarly, Lopez Rodriguez (2010) shows how Polish mothers in the UK try to achieve what they think is a state of 'normalcy' by teaching their children meritocratic individualism and emphasizing the success of their children in British schools. It is essentially this new work ethic that is often depicted as the 'human capital' form of remittances supported by the World Bank development discourses (Mullings 2012). States and development partners regard these returning migrants as risk-taking individuals that embody the spirit of entrepreneurialism and responsibility, and imagine them as ideal development partners with whom to extend the rationality of the market to everyday social relations and institutions (Mullings 2012: 407). To give an example, in 2004 the then Romanian prime minister, Adrian Năstase, stated that all those working abroad would learn a more rigorous work ethic (Badescu 2004).

The discourses and practices of these *mobile meritocrats* intertwine and come into conflict with other moralities. For instance, the disorderly practices of cross-border traders—one of the first forms of international mobility in the aftermath of the fall of socialism—caused widespread resentment in postsocialist societies (Humphrey 2002). Traders were a heterogeneous group of travellers, many of whom had been outcasts during socialism (Konstantinov et al. 1998). This group, which brought in desired goods but also carried away local valuables and sometimes sold off the state-owned machinery, essentially made a profit by crossing borders. Their practices of buying, transporting, and selling all kinds of goods—or making money 'just for themselves, not for society', as an elderly peasant family cited in Humphrey (2002: 72) put it—were often depicted as immoral by local non-trading citizens. Currently, migrant workers such as Roma are being disapproved of for building conspicuous houses and driving expensive cars. While the consumption of 'Western goods' during socialism often served to demonstrate resistance (Scott 1985), the consumption of the right Western goods is now becoming a form of cultural capital through which moral citizens are distinguished from immoral ones.

It appears, then, that the outcome of the local negotiation between moral and immoral mobile practices resonates with, and even promotes, ethnic prejudice. Instead of fighting against the neoliberal policies that cause social uncertainty, the newly developing postsocialist middle classes—who regard themselves as the 'right' consumers—distinguish themselves from the poor, 'flawed consumers' (Bauman 2005). As a result, certain groups of migrant workers who consume the wrong way, do illegal work, and have a rural or a high-rise urban background are demonized. Hence, in a postsocialist context in which migrating Roma and less educated individuals are particularly vulnerable due to the macroeconomic transformation, the middle classes' critique of 'immoral' behaviour is not so much an expression of resentment at the neoliberal values of individual enrichment as an aspect of the racialization and classification of the work and consumption practices of this particular social group of migrant workers that depoliticises the reality of increasing socioeconomic inequality.

6.7 Conclusion

In this chapter I have shown how academic thinking about the social, cultural, economic, and political transformation of the former socialist states has evolved since the fall of the Iron Curtain. Against the backdrop of a narrow and teleological focus on 'transition' at the beginning of the 1990s postsocialist transformation was introduced to highlight the diversity of transformation processes in the former socialist states of Europe. More recently, the idea of a plurality of 'actually existing post-socialism' has been proposed by Stenning and Hörschelmann (2008). I have supported this idea in this chapter because of its potential to politicize the relationships between postsocialist transformation and migration and mobility in Europe, a relationship that is still largely neglected in social theories which hold that postsocialist transformation is something that happens in 'the East'. Drawing on concepts of relational geography, this chapter has emphasized three forms of politics, or 'spatial registers', that are based on an alternative geographical imagination and that give serious consideration to the role migration and mobility play in shaping transformation, as well as to the role transformation plays in shaping migration and mobility. Each of these politicizing spatial registers can be seen as a potential vantage point for progressive research and action.

A politics of connectivity highlights the translocal aspect of 'actually existing post-socialism'. I have illustrated this by emphasizing the responsibility of 'the West' in the redevelopment of 'the East'. The policies of transitology extended 'the West' into 'the East', and migration practices in turn extend the postsocialist relations of care into 'the West'. Politicizing this connectivity can take different forms. It points Western policy-makers to the historical role they have played in shaping the East but also opens up new avenues for thinking about integration policies in the West that take the transnational relations of care seriously. A politics of openness vs. closure in its turn highlights the power relations through which this connectivity unfolds, considering that not all trajectories are equally powerful. The connectivity between East and West has been leading to unequal development across Europe. In the West employers capitalize on the temporariness of migrant work, while the absence of migrant workers in the East serves as a safety valve for further state restructuring, and facilitates the opening up of the East for speculative investments. This politics of openness vs. closure counters liberal freedom of mobilitydiscourses that neglect the power geometries in which mobility occurs. It helps progressive movements to imagine legitimate politics of closure. A politics of propinquity, finally, examines how difference is negotiated in particular places. In this chapter this abstract notion has been illustrated by pointing out how neoliberal ideas travel back and forth between West and East and are continuously negotiated in particular places. Top-down, travelling technocrats schooled in Western MBA schools negotiated neoliberal ideas with other moral orders when informing and constituting postsocialist restructuring policies. But meritocratic moral orders also grow bottom-up. In the encounter with the dual labour markets in the West migrant workers produce identities of individualist mobile meritocrats. Meritocratic identities are, thus, negotiated with class- and ethnicity-based identities in the East. Hence, as this chapter has argued, postsocialism is not something that happens only in the East. Instead, the history of state-socialism, its moral order, its embeddedness in everyday practice, its frustrations and the way in which diverse postsocialisms have taken and are still taking shape, are part of and continuously transform the European East and West.

References

Alexandrescu, F. M. (2012). *Human agency in the interstices of structure: Choice and contingency in the conflict over Roşia Montană, Romania*. Unpublished PhD dissertation, University of Toronto.

Amin, A. (2004). Regions unbound: Towards a new politics of place. *Geografiska Annaler: Series B: Human Geography, 86*(1), 33–44. doi:10.1111/j.0435-3684.2004.00152.x.

Amin, A. (2013). Land of strangers. *Identities, 20*(1), 1–8. doi:10.1080/1070289X.2012.732544.

Badescu, G. (2004). Romanian labor migration and citizenship. In D. Pop (Ed.), *New patterns of labor migration in Central and Eastern Europe* (pp. 7–18). Budapest: AMM Press.

Ban, C. (2011). *Neoliberalism in translation: Economic ideas and reforms in Spain and Romania*. PhD dissertation submitted to the Faculty of the Graduate School of the University of Maryland, College Park, MD.

Bauman, Z. (2000). *Liquid modernity*. Cambridge: Polity Press.

Bauman, Z. (2005). *Work, consumerism and the poor* (2nd ed.). Maidenhead: Open University Press.

Bieler, A. (2000). *Globalisation and enlargement of the European union: Austrian and Swedish social forces in the struggle over membership*. London/New York: Routledge.

Bohle, D. (2006). Neoliberal hegemony, transnational capital and the terms of the EU's eastward expansion. *Capital & Class, 30*(1), 57–86. doi:10.1177/030981680608800104.

Bouniol, J. (2013). Scramble for land in Romania: Iron fist in a velvet glove. In J. Franco & J. Borras (Eds.), *Land concentration, land grabbing and people's struggles in Europe* (pp. 146–167). Amsterdam: The Transnational Institute (TNI) for European Coordination Via Campesina and Hands off the Land Network.

Burawoy, M. (1976). The functions and reproduction of migrant labor: Comparative material from Southern Africa and the United States. *American Journal of Sociology, 81*(5), 1050–1087. doi:10.1086/226185.

Burawoy, M. (1992). The end of Sovietology and the renaissance of modernization theory. *Contemporary Sociology, 21*(6), 774–785.

Castles, S. (2006). Guestworkers in Europe: A resurrection? *International Migration Review, 40*(4), 741–766. doi:10.1111/j.1747-7379.2006.00042.x.

Castles, S., & Kosack, G. (1973). *Immigrant workers and class structure in Western Europe*. London/New York: Oxford University Press.

Castree, N. (2004). Differential geographies: Place, indigenous rights and 'local' resources. *Political Geography, 23*(2), 133–167. doi:10.1016/j.polgeo.2003.09.010.

Collier, S. (2011). *Post-Soviet social neoliberalism, social modernity, biopolitics*. Princeton/Oxford: Princeton University Press.
Darling, J. (2009). Thinking beyond place: The responsibilities of a relational spatial politics. *Geography Compass, 3*(5), 1938–1954. doi:10.1111/j.1749-8198.2009.00262.x.
Datta, A., & Brickell, K. (2009). "We have a little bit more finesse, as a nation": Constructing the Polish worker in London's building sites. *Antipode, 41*(3), 439–464. doi:10.1111/j.1467-8330.2009.00682.x.
Donaghey, J., & Teague, P. (2006). The free movement of workers and social Europe: Maintaining the European ideal. *Industrial Relations Journal, 37*(6), 652–666. doi:10.1111/j.1468-2338.2006.00426.x.
Ekman, J., & Linde, J. (2005). Communist nostalgia and the consolidation of democracy in Central and Eastern Europe. *Journal of Communist Studies and Transition Politics, 21*(3), 354–374. doi:10.1080/13523270500183512.
Flynn, M., & Oldfield, J. (2006). Trans-national approaches to locally situated concerns: Exploring the meanings of post-socialist space. *Journal of Communist Studies and Transition Politics, 22*(1), 3–23. doi:10.1080/13523270500508320.
Franco, J., & Borras, S. M. J., Jr. (Eds.). (2013). *Land concentration, land grabbing and people's struggles in Europe*. Amsterdam: The Transnational Institute (TNI) for European Coordination Via Campesina and Hands off the Land Network.
Freeman, G. P. (1986). From foreign workers to settlers? Transnational migration and the emergence of new minorities. *Annals of the American Academy of Political and Social Science, 485*, 51–63.
Harvey, D. (2003). *The new imperialism*. Oxford/New York: Oxford University Press.
Harvey, D. (2006). Space as a keyword. In N. Castree & D. Gregory (Eds.), *David Harvey: A critical reader* (pp. 270–294). Malden/Oxford/Carlton: Blackwell Publishing.
Humphrey, C. (2002). *The unmaking of soviet life: Everyday economies after socialism*. Ithaca: Cornell University Press.
Humphrey, C., & Mandel, R. (2002). The market in everyday life: Ethnographies of postsocialism. In R. Mandel & C. Humphrey (Eds.), *Markets & moralities: Ethnographies of postsocialism* (pp. 1–16). Oxford/New York: Berg.
Ivanova, M. (2007). Why there was no 'Marshall Plan' for Eastern Europe and why this still matters. *Journal of Contemporary European Studies, 15*(3), 345–376. doi:10.1080/14782800701683748.
Jones, O. (2011). *Chavs: The demonization of the working class*. London/Brooklyn: Verso.
King, C. (2000). Post-postcommunism: Transition, comparison and the end of "Eastern Europe". *World Politics, 53*(1), 143–172. doi:10.1017/S0043887100009400.
Kloosterman, R., Van Der Leun, J., & Rath, J. (1999). Mixed embeddedness: (In)formal economic activities and immigrant business in the Netherlands. *International Journal of Urban and Regional Research, 23*(2), 252–266. doi:10.1111/1468-2427.00194.
Konstantinov, Y., Kressel, G. M., & Thuen, T. (1998). Outclassed by former outcasts: Petty trading in Varna. *American Ethnologist, 25*(4), 729–745. doi:10.1525/ae.1998.25.4.729.
Kornai, J. (1992). *The socialist system: The political economy of communism*. Princeton: Princeton University Press.
Krings, T. (2009). A race to the bottom? Trade unions, EU enlargement and the free movement of labour. *European Journal of Industrial Relations, 15*(1), 49–69. doi:10.1177/0959680108100165.
Lagerspetz, M. (1999). Postsocialism as a return: Notes on a discursive strategy. *East European Politics and Societies, 13*(2), 377–390. doi:10.1177/0888325499013002019.
Levitt, P., & Glick Schiller, N. (2004). Conceptualizing simultaneity: A transnational social field perspective on society. *International Migration Review, 38*(3), 1002–1039. doi:10.1111/j.1747-7379.2004.tb00227.x.
Lopez Rodriguez, M. (2010). Migration and a quest for 'normalcy'. Polish migrant mothers and the capitalization of meritocratic opportunities in the UK. *Social Identities, 16*(3), 339–358. doi:10.1080/13504630.2010.482422.

Massey, D. (2004). Geographies of responsibility. *Geografiska Annaler: Series B: Human Geography, 86*(1), 5–18. doi:10.1111/j.0435-3684.2004.00150.x.
Massey, D. (2005). *For space*. London/Thousand Oaks/New Delhi: SAGE Publications.
May, J., Wills, J., Datta, K., Evans, Y., Herbert, J., & McIlwaine, C. (2007). Keeping London working: Global cities, the British state and London's new migrant division of labour. *Transactions of the Institute of British Geographers, 32*(2), 151–167. doi:10.1111/j.1475-5661.2007.00241.x.
May, J., Datta, K., Evans, Y., Herbert, J., McIlwaine, C., & Wills, J. (2008). Travelling neoliberalism: Polish and Ghanaian migrant workers in London. In A. Smith, A. Stenning, & K. Willis (Eds.), *Social justice and neoliberalism: Global perspectives* (pp. 61–89). London/New York: Zed Books.
Meeus, B. (2013). Welfare through migrant work: What if the Romanian 'safety valve' closes? *Southeast European and Black Sea Studies, 13*(2), 175–194. doi:10.1080/14683857.2013.802177.
Morawska, E. (2001). Structuring migration: The case of Polish income-seeking travellers to the West. *Theory and Society, 30*(1), 47–80. doi:10.1023/A:1011081228016.
Mullings, B. (2012). Governmentality, diaspora assemblages and the ongoing challenge of "development". *Antipode, 44*(2), 406–427. doi:10.1111/j.1467-8330.2010.00857.x.
Outhwaite, W., & Ray, L. (2005). *Social theory and postcommunism*. Malden/Oxford/Carlton: Blackwell Publishing.
Peck, J. (2010). *Constructions of neoliberal reason*. Oxford: Oxford University Press.
Peck, J., & Theodore, N. (2010). Mobilizing policy: Models, methods, and mutations. *Geoforum, 41*(2), 169–174. doi:10.1016/j.geoforum.2010.01.002.
Petrovici, N. (2013). Neoliberal proletarization along the urban–rural divide in postsocialist Romania. *Studia Universitatis Babes Bolyai – Sociologia, 58*(2), 23–54.
Pickles, J. (2010). The spirit of post-socialism: Common spaces and the production of diversity. *European Urban and Regional Studies, 17*(2), 127–140. doi:10.1177/0969776409356492.
Pickles, J., & Smith, A. (Eds.). (1998). *Theorising transition: The political economy of post-communist transformation*. London/New York: Routledge.
Pijpers, R. (2006). 'Help! The Poles are coming': Narrating a contemporary moral panic. *Geografiska Annaler: Series B: Human Geography, 88*(1), 91–103. doi:10.1111/j.0435-3684.2006.00207.x.
Piore, M. J. (1979). *Birds of passage: Migrant labor and industrial societies*. Cambridge: Cambridge University Press.
Rose, N., O'Malley, P., & Valverde, M. (2006). Governmentality. *Annual Review of Law and Social Science, 2*, 83–104. doi:10.1146/annurev.lawsocsci.2.081805.105900.
Samers, M. (1999). Globalization', the geopolitical economy of migration and the 'spatial vent'. *Review of International Political Economy, 6*(2), 166–199. doi:10.1080/096922999347272.
Scott, J. C. (1985). *Weapons of the weak: Everyday forms of peasant resistance*. New Haven: Yale University Press.
Smith, A., & Stenning, A. (2006). Beyond household economies: Articulations and spaces of economic practice in postsocialism. *Progress in Human Geography, 30*(2), 190–213. doi:10.1191/0309132506ph601oa.
Stenning, A. (2005). Out there and in here: Studying Eastern Europe in the West. *Area, 37*(4), 378–383. doi:10.1111/j.1475-4762.2005.00647.x.
Stenning, A., & Hörschelmann, K. (2008). History, geography and difference in the post-socialist world: Or, do we still need post-socialism? *Antipode, 40*(2), 312–335. doi:10.1111/j.1467-8330.2008.00593.x.
Stenning, A., Smith, A., Rochovska, A., & Swiatek, D. (2010). *Domesticating neo-liberalism: Spaces of economic practice and social reproduction in post-socialist cities*. Malden/Oxford: Wiley-Blackwell.
Swain, A. (2006). Soft capitalism and a hard industry: Virtualism, the 'transition industry' and the restructuring of the Ukrainian coal industry. *Transactions of the Institute of British Geographers, 31*(2), 208–223. doi:10.1111/j.1475-5661.2006.00212.x.

Verdery, K. (1996). *What was socialism, and what comes next?* Princeton: Princeton University Press.

Wanner, C. (2005). Money, morality and new forms of exchange in postsocialist Ukraine. *Ethnos: Journal of Anthropology, 70*(4), 515–537. doi:10.1080/00141840500419782.

Wills, J. (2008). Making class politics possible: Organizing contract cleaners in London. *International Journal of Urban and Regional Research, 32*(2), 305–323. doi:10.1111/j.1468-2427.2008.00783.x.

Wimmer, A., & Glick Schiller, N. (2003). Methodological nationalism, the social sciences, and the study of migration: An essay in historical epistemology. *International Migration Review, 37*(3), 576–610. doi:10.1111/j.1747-7379.2003.tb00151.x.

Young, A. (2013). Inequality, the urban–Rural gap, and migration. *Quarterly Journal of Economics, 128*(4), 1727–1785. doi:10.1093/qje/qjt025.

Part II
Transformations in the Political Regulation of Migration

Kenneth Horvath and Bruno Meeus

Introduction to Part II

The main aspect that the five chapters of Part I have in common is that they all point to political agency as a crucial element of social transformation processes. The field of migration politics thus obviously requires special attention for understanding current constellations and their development. That is all the more true because migration has over the past decades become one of the most salient political issues, especially in Europe (Hammar 2004). This politicization of migration is itself a symptom of the contradictions and complexities of current global capitalism, as prominently expressed in Hollifield's (2007) notion of the liberal paradox: while economic and societal relations tend towards openness, the political form of the nation state leans towards closure.

Hollifield's diagnosis is a viable starting point for the following part. It points to an essential structural feature of the liberal nation state, relates the political to the economic, and leaves room for analyses of how exactly the struggle over the political regulation of borders and mobilities is realized in concrete historical settings. However, Hollifield does not offer a diagnosis of concrete historical constellations. The chapters in this part can be read as an attempt to achieve exactly that: to specify different aspects of the liberal paradox.

Part II is opened by Chap. 7 authored by Leila Hadj-Abdou, who provides an overview of recent tendencies towards the Europeanization of migration politics. Whether Europeanization is a profound political-economic and cultural transformation in and of itself—a standpoint the author endorses—or whether it is an element

K. Horvath (✉)
University of Education of Karlsruhe, Karlsruhe, Germany
e-mail: horvath@ph-karlsruhe.de

B. Meeus
Cosmopolis Centre for Urban Research, Vrije Universiteit Brussel, Brussels, Belgium
e-mail: bruno.meeus@vub.ac.be

and symptom of a more general societal transformation, is open to debate. The chapter outlines the major phases of this process to reveal the contradictory interests and strategies effective in the field of migration politics. According to Hadj-Abdou, national governments have chosen Europeanization as a means to expand their control over migration, but by doing so have been putting constraints on their effective capabilities to restrict and control migration.

As becomes obvious from the analysis presented in Chap. 7, there are counterforces to the tendency towards the political closure of liberal nation states. In Chap. 8 Michael Samers discusses recent developments in the political regulation of labour migration that point in a similar direction. The focus of this chapter is on the recent rise of temporary migrant worker programmes (TMWPs). The author scrutinizes these programmes as they have been introduced in various European countries, arguing that these programmes are not a recent phenomenon. In fact, the late 1980s and early 1990s appear to be more of a turning point than the mid-2000s. Further, it is not at all clear whether the introduction of TMWPs marks a shift in the political regulation of migration—or whether their widespread introduction even qualifies as a regime, at least if we hold to a traditional understanding of the concept of regimes.

An important difference between current labour migration programmes and those of earlier decades is that the very form of how they are governed has profoundly changed. Migration politics do not only shift between the dimension of restriction vs. soliciting (which is discussed by Michael Samers), the scale of policy making (Leila Hadj-Abdou's focus), or the concrete constellation of actors and interests (as outlined by Georg Menz in Chap. 3). There are more profound changes at stake that involve, to use Foucauldian terminology, the political technologies and rationalities of migration politics. In this context the notion of migration management marks a crucial development of the past few decades. In Chap. 9 Martin Geiger draws a detailed picture of how this new form of governing migration is enacted in practice. He uses the example of how Albania and Bosnia-Herzegovina are integrated into the EU's political regulation of migration and mobility. Geiger argues that the key development is a combination of exterritorialization and externalization of border control. A certain increase in freedom of mobility is one side of these new programmes, growing control and surveillance of whole populations mark the other. Martin Geiger also shows how the national is moulded through the supranational, how nation states become realigned with global political-economic orders through, among others, the agency of supranational organizations such as IOM and ICMPD.

In Chap. 10 William Walters continues along the lines of Foucauldian reasoning. Inspired by Deleuze's notion of the 'control society', he inquires into the changing form and function of borders, conceived of as political technologies. This technology perspective results in a shift in the form of problematization: the question is no longer one of openness vs. restriction; rather, the question is how borders are implicated in the production, steering, enabling, and controlling of mobilities.

The last chapter of Part II, Chap. 11, takes a similar analytical approach. Gabriele Tomei shifts our attention back to the economy and global capitalism, examining how the current economic crisis has transformed migration patterns in the European context. Building on Foucault's notion of biopolitics and Emirbayer and Mische's conceptualization of the structure-agency interplay, he demonstrates how post-Fordist economics and migration practices are linked by processes of subjectification, that is, the moulding of desires and self-understandings. This conceptual move allows us to make sense of a suspicious double movement that causes young Southern Europeans to emigrate while migrants from more peripheral parts of the world economy remain in their countries of destination.

Turning back to Hollifield's diagnosis of a liberal paradox, we might summarise that there is a notable counter-tendency to the political closure of nation-states: immigration regulations have been loosened for many (e.g. new guest worker directives or mobility programmes for the 'highly skilled'). On a global scale, however, we are confronted with a very different dynamic. For the vast majority of the world population the alleged age of globalisation and migration is primarily marked by forced immobilization, by deportation and detention rather than mobility regimes. To understand how this differentiation of mobility rights is embedded in changing political-economic relations and how it structures social relations on different scales, can be seen as one of the most challenging objectives of migration research for the coming years.

The notions of smart borders and migration management point to the important role social sciences play for current forms of governing borders and mobilities. This leads to a question migration research will, presumably, be more and more faced with in times of global crisis: how to define its role and responsibility vis-à-vis migration politics? The spectrum ranges from a consultancy-like function to theory-building that is largely delinked from political processes to more radical and critical stances. In any case, as soon as we turn to migration politics, it becomes obvious that migration research itself plays a role in ongoing transformation processes.

References

Hammar, T. (2004). The politicisation of immigration. In T. Abbas & F. Reeves (Eds.), *Immigration and race relations: Sociological theory and John Rex* (pp. 99–110). London/New York: I.B. Tauris.

Hollifield, J. F. (2007). The emerging migration state. In A. Portes & J. DeWind (Eds.), *Rethinking migration: New theoretical and empirical perspectives* (pp. 62–89). New York: Berghahn Books.

Chapter 7
The Europeanization of Immigration Policies

Leila Hadj Abdou

7.1 Introduction: Immigration Policies, the Core of National Sovereignty

> Before 1914 the earth had belonged to all. [...] There were no permits, no visas, and it always gives me pleasure to astonish the young by telling them that before 1914 I travelled from Europe to India and to America without passport and without ever having seen one (Zweig 1943).

The author Stefan Zweig remembers here the changes in the wake of the First World War. Although Zweig's memory is based on the specific experience of the bourgeoisie, and does not accurately capture the surveillance of, and the restrictions on, the movement of other societal groups (Mau et al. 2012: 19), his words are a reminder that with the emergence of modern nation states movement across international borders became a major focus of control. A paradigmatic example is the French revolutionary regime, which issued passports in 1791, in order to establish a sense of national community.[1] Other European states followed its example (Mau et al. 2012: 16). However, as industrialization spread, the control of movement was challenged by the increasing demand for labour, and between 1843 and 1889 passports were abolished in many countries in Europe (Mau et al. 2012: 18). The outbreak of the First World War changed border policies once again. The (re)-imposition of passport controls by many Western European states and the United States enabled

[1] Passports have previously existed, but pervasive and systematic control of movement is closely linked to the emergence of modern nation states, as Torpey (2000) demonstrates. The French revolutionary regime, moreover, initially also used passports to control those considered ideologically unreliable or socially marginal (Mau et al. 2012, 17). For the disciplinary function of border control see Chap. 10, in this volume.

L. Hadj Abdou (✉)
Department of Politics, University of Sheffield, Sheffield, UK
e-mail: l.hadj-abdou@sheffield.ac.uk

A. Amelina et al. (eds.), *An Anthology of Migration and Social Transformation*, IMISCOE Research Series, DOI 10.1007/978-3-319-23666-7_7

governmentss to identify their citizens, to distinguish them from non-citizens, and to fully construct themselves as nation states (Mau et al. 2012: 21). Borders are therefore constitutive of modern statehood, and the regulation of admission and control of people is usually seen as the deepest expression of national sovereignty. From the perspective of sovereignty, it thus seems unlikely that nation states would choose to cooperate in the policy area of immigration (see Messina 2007: 139). Indeed, European Union member states have long been hesitant to Europeanize matters of immigration. Yet in spite of this, in recent years immigration has been increasingly subjected to European integration. This development suggests a major social transformation in itself, a shift away from a national to a post-national framework of immigration politics and immigration policy making. The field of migration and the emergence of a European framework demonstrates that states are changing, but they are not disappearing; or as Sassen (2007: 436) has aptly put it in reference to the European Union, we are witnessing an 'endogenizing of the non-national (the universal) inside national, without eliminating the national state'.

The aim of this chapter is to explore the extent to which EU member states have actually opted to cooperate on the highly sensitive issue of immigration. Focusing[2] on the member states and the EU institutions, the chapter also addresses the question of what effect Europeanization has had on the rights of immigrants. Do we see restrictions on, or an expansion of, their rights? The Europeanization of immigration matters has often been associated in the media with the image of the 'Fortress Europe'—that is, the idea that controls have become ever more restrictive, and the rights of immigrants have been curtailed. Similarly, albeit in a more differentiated way, much migration research has been emphasizing the restrictive effects of the European integration processes in relation to immigration: the so far dominant approach in migration research interprets the devolution of decision-making power to the EU level as a strategy of national governments to pursue restrictive immigration agendas by circumventing liberal forces at the domestic level, such as national courts and pro-immigrant advocacy groups. This chapter emphasizes that, while EU member states have indeed pursued this aim, this does not imply that they have actually achieved it.

To address these issues, the chapter begins with an overview of the development of Europeanization and its dynamics in the domain of immigration, and then discusses the impact of these developments on the rights of immigrants.

[2] The restricted focus on these two sets of actors does not imply that non-state actors do not play an important role in the process of Europeanization of immigration policies. However, national governments, as well as the EU institutions, hold a key position in decision-making and in the implementation of European policies. Moreover, the impact of non-state actors differs considerably. Wunderlich (2011), for instance, showed that international organizations such as IOM and UNHCR are important brokers of Europeanization when it comes to the implementation of immigration policies (see also Chap. 9, in this volume). While acknowledging the importance of think tanks and lobby groups, Boswell and Geddes (2011: 211) noted the irrelevance of grass-roots movements, concluding that mobilization on behalf of migrants (not by them) proves to be successful. Finally, Menz (2011) noted that employers' organizations have little influence on Europeanization in the domain of migration and asylum.

7.2 The Process of Europeanization

7.2.1 Europeanization and Its Complexity

The old dilemma of nation stateshow high to build the walls, and how small to make the doors to protect the nation state from immigration, has remained the same over the years, but the setting of policy-making has ultimately changed, as Geddes (2011b: 87) observed. Previously an exclusive responsibility of the nation state, immigration control and immigrant integration are nowadays of a multi-level nature, and the European Union has become a major player in that realm. As will be demonstrated in the following, immigration matters have become a major issue since the 1980s, and there has been a common EU migration policy since the Treaty of Amsterdam (1997), which was further consolidated by the ratification of the Lisbon Treaty in 2009.

This chapter focuses on this emergence of legal EU competences and on the subsequent sharing of power between national governments and the European Union in migration policy-making. Thus, it is interested in the process by which key decisions about public policies are gradually transferred to the European level (Richardson 2012:1). While this chapter is devoted to a specific aspect of Europeanization, it has to be emphasized that Europeanization involves more than the formal transfer of power. Radaelli (2000:4) defines Europeanization as "the construction, diffusion and institutionalization of formal and informal rules, procedures, policy paradigms, styles, 'ways of doing things' and shared beliefs and norms which are first defined and consolidated in the EU process and then incorporated in the logic of domestic (national and sub-national) discourse, political structures and public policies".

In order to understand the evolution and the nature of Europeanization of immigration policies, it has to be emphasized that the European Union is no monolithic entity. Thus, salient policies such as those of migration are often the object of a range of competing interests (see Boswell and Geddes 2011: 47). When setting and developing policies, different actors and institutions pursue different interests, and face different constraints. While state authorities often tend to frame immigration as a threat, 'Eurocrats' tend to portray immigration in a more positive light, and appear more sympathetic to the rights and freedoms of immigrants (Luedtke 2009: 2). This reflects the potential disjuncture between economic and political interests, which Hollifield (1992) has framed as the 'liberal paradox' of open markets and closed political communities. While the European Commission is predominantly guided by economic considerations and the goal of market-making (see Joppke 2011), as well as by the aim of achieving equality in rights, national governments are first and foremost vote maximization seekers. To put it differently, national governments face pressures from their electorates, who can often hold unfavourable attitudes towards immigrants. Members of the European Commission, by contrast, do not face such direct electoral pressure (Luedtke 2009: 2). The fact that the constituents of national politicians tend to prefer having control over liberalization (Lahav and Luedtke 2013: 113), has spurred cooperation at the EU level in the domain of unwanted (irregular) migration, rather than cooperation in the domain of legal migration (Geddes 2011a: 198). It should be noted that, while the European Parliament has often exhibited a pro-integration and migrant-friendly approach (Boswell and Geddes 2011: 66), until recently its power was very limited (for a discussion of a possible shift of the EP's attitude since its increase of powers, see Acosta 2009).

Different actors also allow for different voices to be taken into account. The European Commission derives much of its credibility from its technical expertise (Boswell and Geddes 2011: 62), and thus allows for a large scope of expert influence on policy-making, meaning that think tanks and lobby groups have more of a say in this area than in policy-making processes at other levels.

Moreover, interests shift over time, either because the actors themselves have changed, such as through elections in member states or other changing circumstances. In the 1990s, for instance, Germany, Austria, and Italy were supporters of EU control over immigration policy but in the new millennium changed their position. France and Sweden, by contrast, shifted in the other direction, from opposition to support. Belgium is one of the few nation states that have constantly favoured the supranationalization of immigration policy (Lahav and Luedtke 2013: 113).

Member states also differ in their capacity to shape EU policy-making. Consequently, some member states have been quite proactive in shaping European policies on immigration, while others have been more passive 'takers' (Börzel 2003) of European demands for domestic change. This is particularly true of newer member states that have joined the EU since 2004. During the accession period the migration policies of some accession states such as Poland became more Europeanized than those of the member states at the time, despite very low levels of immigration (see e.g. Kicinger et al. 2007).

In sum, actors and institutions exhibit different capacities and face different constraints, but they also follow multiple and different, partly even contradictory, policy goals, and this renders policies incoherent and leads to 'deliberate mal-integration'; that is, more or less intentional incoherence in the output of the EU's migration and immigrant integration agenda, as well as in individual policies (Boswell and Geddes 2011: 47). Most notably, there is a manifest tension between economically oriented perspectives focusing on legal labour migration and the security-oriented perspective, which is focused on irregular migration (see Hansen 2010: 91).

7.3 Evolution: From the Treaty of Rome to the Treaty of Lisbon

7.3.1 Immigration: From a Neglected Issue to a Common Concern

As Robert Schuman, one of the founding fathers of the EU, once put it, one of the aims of the European project was to take away the 'rigidity' and 'intransigent hostility' of borders (Schuman 1963 cit. in Geddes and Hadj-Abdou forthcoming). The 1957 Treaty of Rome provided for the establishment of a common market, which would be based on the free movement not only of services, goods, and capital but also of persons. Notwithstanding this fact, immigration matters were of no major relevance in the first decades of the European integration project. The interest of national governments in cooperating on immigration was eventually triggered by the adoption of the Single European Act (SEA) in 1986. With the SEA, the member states decided to establish a single European market, implying the removal of all internal frontiers. The stipulated abolition of internal border control made the issue of immigrants from outside the EC more pressing. In 1985 the European Commission issued a communication to the Council of Ministers on Guidelines for a Community Policy on Migration, with the intention of launching a debate on how to proceed in that area (Talani 2012: 63). However, because of tensions between the different institutions the only viable way of coordinating immigration policies was outside the community system, through intergovernmental arrangements. Consequently, 1 year before the entry into force of the SEA in 1987 the national ministers responsible for immigration established an ad hoc immigration group of senior officials (AHIG). The AHIG emerged from the TREVI group, an intergovernmental body whose objective was to combat terrorism across the European Community (Messina 2007: 141). Thus, from the start the logic embedded in intergovernmental cooperation on immigration was security-driven. The major aim of the AHIG was to emphasize external border control in each member state, to maintain the border security of the Community as a whole, and to facilitate the coordination of national policies (Messina 2007: 141). For the first time ever, in the framework of the AHIG a supranational body, namely the Commission, was invited to take part as an observer in the meeting of a working group on migration matters (Talani 2012: 64). The working group served as a cooperation forum until 1993, when it was substituted by a coordinating committee on immigration matters in the Treaty on the European Union signed in Maastricht in 1992 (Messina 2007: 141). Two of the most important intergovernmental policy agreements in the domain of immigration in that period were the Schengen Agreement of 1985 (implemented in 1995), which abolished border controls among participating members by establishing a common external border and reinforcing control measures, and the Dublin Convention of 1990 (implemented in 1997), which determined which member states would have jurisdiction in matters of asylum.

Taking into account the reluctance of the nation states to communitarize immigration, these agreements represented a feasible solution—albeit one that excluded the European Parliament, the Commission, and the Court of Justice (Talani 2012: 51). The Maastricht Treaty (formally, the Treaty on the European Union), which came into effect in 1993, formalized, but did not supranationalize, cooperation on immigration; It drew cooperation that had been outside the Treaty into an intergovernmental pillar of the newly created European Union (Geddes 2008: 88). The Justice and Home Affairs pillar, referred to as the 'third pillar' by the Treaty, institutionalized prior patterns of ad hoc cooperation on migration, as well as asylum, policing, and judicial cooperation (Geddes 2008: 96). The Treaty's section on the third pillar provided for unanimous voting in the Council of Ministers as the basis for decision-making, a very limited role for the European Parliament, and only a shared power of initiative for the Commission (Peers et al. 2012: 9); in addition, the Court of Justice was stripped of its power of jurisdiction, unless this was specifically allocated under the terms of an international convention (Geddes 2008: 100).

7.3.2 Maintenance of Intergovernmentalism despite Formal Communitarization

The Amsterdam Treaty of 1997 introduced a new era. For the first time, legal competences were given to the EU in the field of migration. By introducing a new title (Title IV), immigration, along with asylum, visa, external border control, and civil law matters, were transferred from the intergovernmental Justice and Home Affairs pillar to the first, the European Community pillar. More precisely, as of May 1, 1999, the Treaty provided power for the Community to adopt measures on immigration policy in the following areas: conditions of entry and residence and standards on procedures regarding long-term visas and residence permits, including those for the purpose of family reunion; and irregular immigration and irregular residence, including the repatriation of irregular residents. The Community was also entitled to set measures defining the rights and conditions under which nationals of third countries who are legally resident in a member state may reside in other member states (Peers et al. 2012: 10). The Schengen Convention and the measures implementing it (Schengen acquis) were incorporated into the legal order of the EU in 1999, when the Treaty of Amsterdam entered into force (Peers et al. 2012: 24). The Amsterdam Treaty also established jurisdiction of the European Court of Justice (CJEU) regarding migration policies, where previously it had not had any competences in the areas of justice and home affairs, and thus had not been entitled to review measures adopted by the Council in that realm (EU 2014).

Since the Amsterdam Treaty the framework for EU migration and asylum policy has been organized into three consecutive 5-year work plans: the Tampere, Hague, and Stockholm action plans (Boswell and Geddes 2011: 52). The first crucial measures in the area were adopted in 2003: Directive 2003/86 on the right to family reunification and Directive 2003/109 concerning the status of third-country nationals who are long-term residents.

However, these developments did not imply that the resistance of member states to communitarizing immigration matters had ended. It is more accurate to say that formal communitarization had de jure started, but de facto intergovernmental modes of regulating immigration matters continued. Three relevant limitations were enshrined in the Treaty of Amsterdam.

First, it introduced a transitional period until the full application of the new competences for the supranational level (Wolff and Trauner 2011: 64). Most importantly, the application of the Community Method, which would have granted the Commission the exclusive right to initiate legislation, and would have included the European Parliament in the legislative process, was suspended (Reslow 2010: 2). During a period of 5 years the Commission would share the right of initiative with the member states, the Council would act unanimously, and the European Parliament was entirely excluded. After 5 years the Commission would be granted the sole right to initiate legislation. However, all immigration issues would remain subject to unanimous decisions of the Council and to consultation of the European Parliament, unless the Council decided unanimously to alter these voting rules and to apply the co-decision procedure,[3] including qualified majority voting in the Council (Reslow 2010: 2). In 2005 the Council decided to apply the co-decision procedure to the adoption of measures regarding irregular migration but prevented its expansion to measures relating to legal migration. The unanimous decision-making procedure was kept for legal economic migration until the adoption of the Lisbon Treaty (Wolff and Trauner 2011: 67).

Second, triggered by the fears of nationalgovernments about the application of the perceived 'overly integrationist outlook' of the CJEU (Guiraudon 2000, cited in De Somer 2012: 11), the Treaty imposed a number of important limitations to the Court's competencies in this area: it could only act if called upon by a national court, the Council, the Commission, or a member state to rule on a question regarding the interpretation of the new title or of measures adopted on its basis (Talani 2012: 69). These provisions prevented direct access to the CJEU by citizens. Comparable limitations did not exist in any other policy field (De Somer 2012: 11).

Third, three EU member states negotiated ways not to take part in measures under Title IV. The UK and the Irish governments opted out of Title IV and maintained the Common Travel Area between the two countries (Geddes 2008: 125), meaning they upheld national controls. Denmark also abstained from taking part in measures under Title IV, with the exception of measures determining the third countries whose nationals must be in possession of a visa when crossing the external borders of the member states and measures relating to a uniform format for visas (Vedsted-Hansen 2004: 65–66).

[3] The co-decision procedure, introduced by the Treaty of Maastricht in 1992, is referred today to as ordinary legislation procedure. In a co-decision procedure the European Parliament and the Council jointly adopt legislation.

7.3.3 The Victory for Supranationalization over National Power

As already indicated, a major feature of the process of communitarization of immigration matters is that member states were much more inclined to cooperate on irregular migration and border control than on measures of legal migration and refugee protection (see Wolff and Trauner 2011: 67). The Tampere Summit in 1999 recognized demographic and sectoral labour market needs, but member states were very cautious about committing to common policies in that realm.

The Commission, in turn, made repeated attempts to put labour migration on the agenda. For instance, in 2001 it had already proposed a directive to establish common conditions for a joint residence and work permit for third-country nationals, with the aim of strengthening the competitiveness of the Community in attracting labour forces. Faced with protests by some member states—most notably Germany, Austria, and France, which protested that there was no legal basis for the adoption of such a measure—the Commission had to withdraw its proposal (Cerna 2014: 78).

The Hague Programme (2004–2009) emphasized anew the need to have an open debate on economic immigration, and thus aspired to a truly common European immigration policy beyond external border controls (Cerna 2014: 69). Alarmed by the incessant demographic changes, the Commission issued COM (2004) 811, a Green Paper on an EU approach to managing economic migration in 2005, and subsequently adopted COM (2005) 669, a policy plan on legal migration. In 2007 the Commission eventually released a draft proposal 'on the conditions of entry and residence of third-country nationals for the purpose of highly qualified employment' (the so-called Blue Card Directive) in order to promote the international competitiveness of the Union. However, the final version, adopted in 2009, provides only a minimum framework for the admission of high-skilled labour, which leaves important decisions to the discretion of member states (Cerna 2014: 77). Christian Joppke poignantly noted that the Blue Card was nonetheless a first and significant crack in Europe's still nationalized control of economic migration, and that 'legal labour migration is by now the last bastion of state sovereignty in Europe, though an end to this is nearing also' (Joppke 2011: 223, 225).

In the same year as the Blue Card was adopted the Treaty on the Functioning of the European Union, more commonly called the Lisbon Treaty, entered into force. The Lisbon Treaty represents a victory for supranationalization over national power in that it extended the co-decision procedure to measures on legal migration (Article 79). Today member states vote on migration issues in the Council according to a qualified majority, and the Commission has the sole right to propose laws. The European Parliament is involved by co-decision; it has the power to propose amendments and the power to veto. Moreover, the European Court of Justice now has an important role to play in immigration matters because the restrictions in this field have been lifted (see Bonjour and Vink 2013: 401). Consequently, for the first time the Commission has brought infringement actions to the Court of Justice, which challenged the substance of national implementation of EU legislation (Peers et al. 2012: 25).

However, member states retained the right to determine the number of migrants entering their territory. Thus, the Lisbon Treaty has significantly widened the cracks of economic migration control, to borrow Joppke's metaphor again, but it has not entirely torn down the national walls. Moreover, the sensitive nature of migration-related issues is still mirrored in the prevalence of soft methods of cooperation in the domain of immigrant integration. Although no binding measures exist, the EU's immigrant integration agenda has effectively stimulated vertical processes of policy diffusion, and triggered processes of policy-learning, particularly in regard to polities which do not have a long history of immigration, such as the newer EU member states.

7.3.4 Why Europeanization? Revisiting the Venue Shopping Approach

The previous sections showed that immigration was at first an issue politicians did not rank highly in the creation of the common market. Later the issue increased in importance at the Community level, but national governments were reluctant to cede any authority in that domain to the supranational level. Instead they opted for intergovernmental cooperation. This cooperation, however, paved the way for the later actual communitarization of migration politics. Today immigration is a competence shared between the member states and the institutions of the European Union. How can we understand this striking evolution from an issue off the table to a deeply Europeanized one?

One strand of the literature has suggested that, in order to explain this development, we have to consider changes brought about by globalization: in a globalizing world the power of individual states to control immigration has diminished; the transaction costs of international migration have declined and, as a result, national borders have become more porous (see Messina 2007: 147 ff.). Such a perspective captures some relevant dynamics of social change and its relation to the political regulation of migration. It is in particular consistent with the initial development of intergovernmental cooperation in regard to border control of European states. However, it is not adequate to entirely grasp the more far-reaching communitarization of immigration policies.

Another strand of the literature, the one based on neo-functionalist theory, has explained the Europeanization of immigration policies as a result of what have become known as 'spillover' effects, according to which cooperation in one policy area often leads to cooperation in others. As the reconstruction of the Europeanization of immigration policies showed, spill-over effects were indeed a crucial driver. The single-market programme was a major trigger for the advancement of a common immigration agenda. The free movement of citizens of EU member states and the abolition of internal border controls contains a strong logic for cooperation on immigration issues. However, 'contrary to neo-functional assumptions, the progress of a European immigration policy regime has been painfully slow and uneven' Messina (2007: 157).

One of the most powerful explanatory approaches, and the most dominant one so far, is the intergovernmentalist approach, which is based on the 'venue shopping' concept (Guiraudon 2000). According to this concept, national governments support European integration because it empowers them in relation to other domestic actors. To put it more specifically, venue shopping at the EU level is considered as a strategy, which enables national governments, in particular restrictive interior ministers, to circumvent domestic constraints imposed by the jurisprudence of higher courts, nongovernmental organizations, interest groups in favour of immigration and migrants, and other pro-immigrant political actors.

Indeed, the EU level initially allowed national policy-makers to prevent constraints (Kaunert et al. 2013: 179): The CJEU had very few competences on migration matters, if any, as was pointed out earlier in this chapter. The fact that immigration policies were mostly dealt with within the separate Justice and Home Affairs pillar, which was governed by intergovernmental mechanisms, also kept the European Parliament and the European Commission—institutions which tend to be in favour of immigration and immigrants' rights—out of the way. This made venue shopping to the EU level a viable strategy for national governments and interior ministers to implement their restrictive agendas (Kaunert et al. 2013: 182). As Geddes (2008: 55) so aptly summarized it, these opportunities have led to a 'politics of Europeanization' rather than a 'Europeanization of policy'.

However, since the Treaty of Lisbon entered into force, these arrangements have ultimately changed. Hence, while intergovernmentalism was able to capture crucial dynamics of European migration politics in the past decades, it is not adapted for capturing recent processes (Bonjour and Vink 2013: 192); the dominant idea that Europeanization has led to securitization and restriction is to a great extent built on such intergovenmentalist perspectives (Bonjour and Vink 2013: 390). Thus, the question is to what extent these conceptions are still appropriate, if they ever actually were, to capture current realities. The following section will shed some light on this question, clarifying whether Europeanization has actually extended or restricted the rights of immigrants.

7.4 Extension or Restriction of Rights?

As was pointed out in the previous section, national governments have chosen the European Union as the level of policy-making in order to maximize control and security. Many studies have argued that the regulations set at the European level were accordingly restrictive, allowing national governments to lower their standards. Lahav and Luedtke (2013: 116), for instance, found that only three of the policies adopted by the EU Council extended immigrants' rights and freedoms significantly, namely the directives on the admission of students, researchers, and highly skilled workers. But in these cases the extension of rights was linked to the fact that directives mentioned regulate only rather low-salience issues and because they address some sort of 'elite' migration, these policies were little contested; indeed, 'overall, EU policy has aided national politicians in enacting stringent measures targeting illegal immigrants' (Lahav and Luedtke 2013: 116–117). However, judgements such as this are often based on an analysis of policy output, ignoring the policy outcomes, that is, the effects of these policies.[4]

The Family Reunification Directive, proposed in 1999 and adopted in 2003, illustrates this point well. The process of policy-making with regard to this Directive is a clear example of an uploading of political preferences by restrictive-minded member states. A particularly crucial element, pushed through in the legislative process by the Netherlands, Germany, and Austria, was the possibility to introduce integration tests for family members aged 13 years and older. Failing the test could be used as grounds for refusing admission to the country. France was among the strongest supporters of the Family Reunification Directive because the adoption of the Directive would provide it with the opportunity to significantly weaken its own domestic legislation (Luedtke 2009: 13)—that is, to restrict immigration. Indeed, immediately after the Directive had been released the French government passed a national immigration law that lowered the state's generous family reunification standards (Joppke 2011: 228). The Spanish government used the Directive in a similar vein, adopting integration tests for minors to reduce family migration (Luedtke 2009: 13).

However, particularly in the newer EU member states the Directive actually led to the raising of standards (Joppke 2011: 228). Thus, while some member states have indeed used the EU as a venue to restrict their domestic policies, in other member states Europeanization has actually led to an extension of rights.

The effects of EU legislation on the rights of immigrants are even more extensive. The communitarization of migration policies is increasingly constraining governments in ways they did not anticipate (Bonjour and Vink 2013: 390), as a further analysis of the Family Reunification Directive reveals: as early as 2008 the European Commission criticized the Netherlands for failing to fulfil their legal obligation to implement family reunification policy (Bonjour and Vink 2013: 394). While the Dutch government rejected this criticism, its conduct was condemned by the ECJ in 2010 (Judgment of the Court C-578/08, Rhimou Chakroun v Minister van Buitenlandse Zaken). The Court held that the Dutch government must not use the margin for manoeuvre given to member states in a manner which would undermine the objective of the Directive: namely to promote family reunification. In 2011 the CJEU dealt with yet another claim against the Netherlands related to the Family

[4] Approaches that equate Europeanization with restriction on migrants' rights also ignore that Europeanization has actually led to a complex stratification of migrants' rights. For a comprehensive discussion of the multidimensionality of migrants' rights produced by EU law, see Carmel and Paul (2013).

Reunification Directive (C-155/11, Bibi Mohammad Imran v Minister van Buitenlandse Zaken). The question was whether the Dutch policy requiring immigrants to pass an integration exam before arrival was compatible with the Directive or not; the Dutch government eventually granted a permit to the wife whose husband had initiated the case in order to prevent a ruling by the Court. The case was dropped, but not before the Commission had delivered its opinion to the Court; the Commission argued that the Directive does not allow for a family member to be denied entry merely on the grounds of having failed the integration exam abroad (Bonjour and Vink 2013: 400). Although the case was subsequently withdrawn, it clearly demonstrated the constraining impact of the CJEU on EU member states' capacity to restrict immigration (Acosta Arcarazo and Geddes 2013: 190). The French government had already attenuated its proposal for integration requirements for family migrants in 2007 to prevent condemnation by the Court (Bonjour and Vink 2013: 405), and a similar dynamic can be observed regarding the rights of migrants who are usually seen by nation states as the least wanted group of migrants, namely irregular migrants (see Acosta Arcarazo and Geddes 2013).

The CJEU has been called upon several times to interpret the Return Directive (2008/115/EC), which establishes common standards and procedures in EU member states for returning irregular third-country nationals, and to establish its scope of application. Most notably in the El Dridi case (C-61/11), concerning the imprisonment of an Algerian national who stayed in Italy without a residence permit, the Court of Justice ruled that national legislation 'providing for a prison sentence for illegally staying third-country nationals in the event of refusal to obey an order to leave the territory' is not in line with EU law. In a later ruling, the Achughbabian case (C-329/11), the CJEU noted that member states may place irregular migrants in detention, but it made clear that – contrary to what had been the practice of quite a few member states – the potential scope of such measures is actually extremely limited.

These recent developments show that 'Europeanization has become a double-edged sword' (Bonjour and Vink 2013: 404). While member states initially chose to communitarize immigration matters to control and restrict immigration, they have, paradoxically, severely constrained this control. Even immigration lawyers underestimated the effects EU law would have on national immigration law (Groenendijk 2006, cited in Joppke 2011: 228): once 'sucked into the ambit of supranational actors within the EU, immigration becomes infused with the liberal rights logic of free movement' (Joppke 2011: 225). Legal principles such as proportionality, effectiveness, and effective legal remedies now apply (Joppke 2011: 228). This ultimately leads to a strengthening of the rights of immigrants, even in the case of EU laws that have been criticized for their restrictive character, such as the family reunification and the return directives.

7.5 Conclusion

The construction of the supranational architecture in the EU has been described as 'the most radical political-economic and cultural transformation of space in Western Europe since the French revolution' (Swyngedouw 2014: 173). This chapter has retraced the evolution of this transformation and the impact it has had on a policy area, which is particularly sensitive because it lies at the very heart of national sovereignty: immigration. It has been shown that the shifting of competencies in that domain to the supranational level was a slow and uneven process, and that nation states eventually ceded power to the EU level to enforce restrictive agendas that would curtail immigration. However, national governments underestimated the long-term dynamics of supranationalization. Far from asserting that nation states have become powerless spectators, this chapter has emphasized that the agency of the European Commission, and especially the increasing competences of the European Court of Justice on immigration matters, have put significant constraints on national governments attempts to pursue their restrictive aims.

The walls built by the European states in the aftermath of the French revolution to insulate them from immigration are still there. Their doors are not open, but national governments are no longer the only ones possessing a key.

References

Acosta Arcarazo, D. (2009). The good, the bad and the ugly in EU migration law: Is the European parliament becoming bad and ugly? *European Journal of Migration and Law, 11*(1), 19–39. doi :10.1163/157181609X410575.

Acosta Arcarazo, D., & Geddes, A. (2013). The development, application and implications of an EU rule of law in the area of migration policy. *JCMS: Journal of Common Market Studies, 51*(2), 179–193. doi:10.1111/j.1468-5965.2012.02296.x.

Bonjour, S., & Vink, M. P. (2013). When Europeanization backfires: The normalization of European migration politics. *Acta Politica, 48*(4), 389–407. doi:10.1057/ap.2013.11.

Börzel, T. (2003). *Shaping and taking EU policies: Member state responses to Europeanization* (Queen's Papers on Europeanisation 01/2003). Belfast: School of Politics, International Studies and Philosophy, Queen's University of Belfast. https://www.qub.ac.uk/schools/SchoolofPoliticsInternationalStudiesandPhilosophy/FileStore/EuropeanisationFiles/Filetoupload,38412,en.pdf

Boswell, C., & Geddes, A. (2011). *Migration and mobility in the European Union.* Basingstoke/New York: Palgrave Macmillan.

Carmel, E., & Paul, R. (2013). Complex stratification: Understanding European Union governance of migrant rights. *Regions & Cohesion, 3*(3), 56–85. doi:10.3167/reco.2013.030304.

Cerna, L. (2014). The EU Blue Card: Preferences, policies, and negotiations between Member States. *Migration Studies, 2*(1), 73–96. doi:10.1093/migration/mnt010.

De Somer, M. (2012). *Enhanced competences for the European Court of Justice: "Re-shuffling" the dynamics of EU migration policy-making?* (LSE Migration Studies Unit Working Paper No. 2012/01). http://www.lse.ac.uk/government/research/resgroups/MSU/documents/workingPapers/WP_2012_01.pdf

EU. (2014). *Treaty of Amsterdam amending the treaty on European Union, the treaties establishing the European communities and certain related acts*. http://www.europarl.europa.eu/topics/treaty/pdf/amst-en.pdf

Geddes, A. (2008). *Immigration and European integration: Towards fortress Europe*. Manchester/New York: Manchester University Press.

Geddes, A. (2011a). Borders and migration in the European Union. In N. Phillips (Ed.), *Migration in the global political economy: IPE yearbook* (Vol. 17, pp. 193–208). Boulder: Lynne Rienner Publishers.

Geddes, A. (2011b). The European Union's extraterritorial immigration controls and international migration relations. In R. Hansen, J. Koehler, & J. Money (Eds.), *Migration, nation states, and international cooperation* (pp. 87–99). New York/London: Routledge.

Geddes, A., & Hadj-Abdou, L. (forthcoming). An unstable equilibrium: Freedom of movement and the welfare state in the European Union. In G. Freeman, & N. Mirilovic (Eds.), *Handbook on international immigration*. Northampton: Edward Elgar Publishing.

Groenendijk, K. (2006). Family reunification as a right under community law. *European Journal of Migration and Law, 8*(2), 215–230. doi:10.1163/157181606777975003.

Guiraudon, V. (2000). European integration and migration policy: Vertical policy-making as venue shopping. *JCMS: Journal of Common Market Studies, 38*(2), 251–271. doi:10.1111/1468-5965.00219.

Hansen, P. (2010). More barbwire or more immigration, or both? EU migration policy in the nexus of border security management and neoliberal economic growth. *The Whitehead Journal of Diplomacy and International Relations, 11*(1, Winter/Spring), 89–101.

Hollifield, J. F. (1992). *Immigrants, markets, and states: The political economy of postwar Europe*. Cambridge: Harvard University Press.

Joppke, C. (2011). European immigration policies: Between stemming and soliciting still. In E. Jones, P. M. Heywood, M. Rhodes, & U. Sedelmeier (Eds.), *Developments in European politics 2* (pp. 220–240). Basingstoke/New York: Palgrave Macmillan.

Kaunert, C., Léonard, S., & Hoffmann, U. (2013). Venue-shopping and the role of non-governmental organisations in the development of the European Union asylum policy. *Comparative Migration Studies, 1*(1), 179–200. doi:10.5117/CMS2013.1.KAUN.

Kicinger, A., Weinar, A., & Górny, A. (2007). Advanced yet uneven: The Europeanization of Polish immigration policy. In T. Faist & A. Ette (Eds.), *The Europeanization of national policies and politics of immigration: Between autonomy and the European Union* (pp. 181–200). Basingstoke/New York: Palgrave Macmillan.

Lahav, G., & Luedtke, A. (2013). Immigration policy. In C. Bretherton & M. L. Mannin (Eds.), *The Europeanization of European politics* (pp. 109–122). New York: Palgrave Macmillan.

Luedtke, A. (2009). Uncovering European Union immigration legislation: Policy dynamics and outcomes. *International Migration, 49*(2), 1–27. doi:10.1111/j.1468-2435.2009.00588.x.

Mau, S., Brabandt, H., Laube, L., & Roos, C. (2012). *Liberal states and the freedom of movement: Selective borders, unequal mobility*. Basingstoke/New York: Palgrave Macmillan.

Menz, G. (2011). Stopping, shaping and moulding Europe: Two-level games, non-state actors and the Europeanization of migration policies. *JCMS: Journal of Common Market Studies, 49*(2), 437–462. doi:10.1111/j.1468-5965.2010.02123.x.

Messina, A. M. (2007). *The logics and politics of post-WWII migration to Western Europe*. New York: Cambridge University Press.

Peers, S., Guild, E., Acosta Arcarazo, D., & Groenendijk, K. (2012). *EU immigration and asylum law* (Vol. 1). Leiden: Brill.

Radaelli, C. M. (2000). Whither Europeanization? Concept stretching and substantive change. *European Integration online Papers (EIoP), 4*(8), 1–25.

Reslow, N. (2010, June 23–26). *Explaining the development of EU migration policy: The case of the mobility partnerships*. Paper prepared for the fifth Pan-European conference on EU politics, Porto, Portugal. http://www.jhubc.it/ecpr-porto/virtualpaperroom/008.pdf

Richardson, J. (Ed.). (2012). *Constructing a policy-making state? Policy dynamics in the EU*. Oxford: Oxford University Press.

Sassen, S. (2007). Response. *European Journal of Political Theory, 6*(4), 433–446.

Schuman, R. (1963). *Pour l'Europe*. Paris: Éditions Nagel.

Swyngedouw, E. (2014). Excluding the other: The production of scale and scaled politics. In R. Lee & J. Wills (Eds.), *Geographies of economics* (pp. 167–176). Oxon/New York: Routledge.

Talani, L. S. (Ed.). (2012). *Globalization, migration, and the future of Europe*. Oxon/New York: Routledge.

Torpey, J. (2000). *The invention of the passport. Surveillance, citizenship and the state*. Cambridge/New York: Cambridge University Press.

Vedsted-Hansen, J. (2004). Denmark. In I. Higgins & K. Hailbronner (Eds.), *Migration and asylum law and policy in the European Union: FIDE 2004 national reports* (pp. 65–87). Cambridge/New York: Cambridge University Press.

Wolff, S., & Trauner, F. (2011). A European migration policy fit for future challenges. In S. Wolff, F. Goudappel, & J. de Zwaan (Eds.), *Freedom, security and justice after Lisbon and Stockholm* (pp. 63–78). The Hague: T.M.C. Asser Press.

Wunderlich, D. (2011). Europeanization through the grapevine: Communication gaps and the role of international organizations in implementation networks of EU external migration policy. *Journal of European Integration, 34*(5), 485–503. doi:10.1080/07036337.2011.611385.

Zweig, S. (1943). *The world of yesterday* (p. 409). New York: Viking.

Chapter 8
New Guest Worker Regimes?

Michael Samers

8.1 Introduction

About 30 years ago, Castles (1986) wrote an 'obituary' for 'guest worker programmes'[1] that reflected upon their precipitous decline since the early 1970s across European countries. Some 20 years later Castles questioned if guest worker programmes were being 'resurrected', fully acknowledging how policy thinking had evolved, especially, but not exclusively, at the level of the European Union (EU). He concluded that despite moves by EU policy-makers and individual states, the argument that guest worker programmes were being resurrected was both 'simplistic and misleading', but he also conceded that 'there is no question of a general return to guest worker policies' (Castles 2006: 760, 742). Indeed, more recently, others have claimed a growing interest in temporary migration in the 'migrant-receiving countries' (e.g. Dauvergne and Marsden 2014; Leach 2013). For example, Dauvergne and Marsden note that in the same year as the publication of Castles' (2006) paper there were three times as many 'temporary migrants' in the OECD countries (about 2.5 million) as there were 'permanent migrants', and that 'temporary migration' increased steadily from 2000 to 2008. Definitional problems aside for a moment, this chapter considers Castles' (2006) discussion in light of discourses and practices of what some observers are casually calling 'new guest worker *regimes*' over the last decade or so.

[1] I have placed 'guest worker' between quotation marks to indicate a critical stance towards the very term 'guest worker' and the 'programmes' or 'policies' themselves. In order to avoid monotony, however, I will no longer use quotation marks when using this term, including any derivative terms such as 'guest worker regimes', 'guest worker' policies, and so on. Subsequently, I discuss the very use of the term 'regime'.

M. Samers (✉)
Department of Geography, University of Kentucky Lexington, KY 40506, USA
e-mail: michael.samers@uky.edu

A. Amelina et al. (eds.), *An Anthology of Migration and Social Transformation*,
IMISCOE Research Series, DOI 10.1007/978-3-319-23666-7_8

Yet in tackling this challenge, one arrives at several problems. The first—as alluded to above—is what exactly constitutes 'a temporary migrant' if we take such a term as the equivalent of the erstwhile 'guest worker'. For the purposes of this chapter, we will define 'temporary migrants' as individuals who are required to have a visa, work permit, or similar document which allows them to take employment through a dedicated set of work-related policies or programmes for a specified period of time in a country other than their own, and who are *not* entitled to permanent settlement. Cumbersome as a definition no doubt, and not without controversy, given that the line between 'temporary' and 'permanent' is frequently blurred and categories such as 'students' or 'intra-company transferees' may also be included in such a definition. In any case, a second and related problem is what precisely constitutes a temporary migrant worker programme (TMWP), which, depending on the conditions of duration and renewal, finish by being rather 'permanent-oriented' in practice. The third problem of analysis concerns whether there are in fact *regimes* in the twenty-first century, and to what extent they can be considered 'new'. Indeed, one could speak of such policies (if not regimes) in Germany in the 1990s (see e.g. Rudolph 1996) well after the official end of the *Gastarbeiter* system in West Germany in 1973, or indeed those programmes in the Benelux countries and Switzerland in the two decades after WWII.

Do such 'new guest worker regimes' exist in the context of more service-based economies, stripped-down social-welfare systems, and judicial practices that often seem to tolerate family reunification (Joppke 1998; Ellermann 2013)? If such 'regimes' persist, what is their form, and how and to what extent are they different from the 'classic' example of the *gastarbeiter* system? Before I turn to answering these questions, it might be worth exploring the idea of 'regime'. As Alexander Betts reminds us, 'regime theory represents a branch of international relations that attempted to understand the role that regimes—as norms, rules, principles, and decision-making procedures—play in influencing the behaviour of states in particular issue-areas' (Betts 2012: 5). In Krasner's (1983) original formulation, the definition of regimes is not necessarily restricted to states alone, and such an expansive definition leaves room for the relevance of non-state and private entities in the formulation and practice of TMWPs. Relatedly, one of the trenchant limitations of regime theory is its 'rationalist' underpinnings, which is argued to weaken its 'explanatory power' (Betts 2012: 5). Thus, the question remains whether the term 'regime' is appropriate when referring to guest worker policies, particularly in the context of national states. Curiously, given the critique of rationality, the term 'global governance' seems to have replaced 'regimes' in international relations, yet at the same time the term 'regime' appears to have crept back into usage over the last few years (for example, Koslowski 2011 speaks of 'global mobility regimes', and Glick Schiller and Salazar 2013 of 'regimes of mobility across the globe'). It may be true that such migration or mobility-related regimes exist in the form of EU institutions, and that European states are constrained or at least shaped by the actions of these institutions, but the argument that national guest worker *policies* or *programmes* should be understood as 'regimes' deserves more scrutiny. In this chapter, then, I will employ the term 'policies' or 'programmes' while acknowledging and documenting how EU developments constrain and shape, but do not *determine*, the practices of national governments and related institutions in the area of TMWPs.

This chapter begins with a seemingly *de rigueur* discussion of the *gastarbeiter* system in post-WWII West Germany, noting how guest worker policies came to be defined, practiced, and understood. I then provide an overview of what might be called 'actually existing guest worker policies' in the twenty-first century at the level of the EU, France, Germany, and the United Kingdom (UK). The problems of 'methodological nationalism' aside, I conclude with an overall assessment of Castles' discussion in light of guest worker policies in the second decade of the twenty-first century.

8.2 A Brief History of the *Gastarbeiter* System

For most observers of immigrant labour recruitment, Germany's *gastarbeiter* (guest worker) system is the iconic example of a guest worker regime. In the late 1940s the German government established a system of migrant recruitment with heavy state involvement through the Federal Labor Office (the *Bundesanstalt für Arbeit*, or BfA), which set up offices in a number of Mediterranean countries. Employers who wanted to hire workers from overseas had to apply to the BfA and pay a fee. The BfA would select workers based on their occupational capacities, administer a medical test, and screen for their political proclivities and any criminal histories. Once accepted, migrants often arrived in groups and were housed near their worksites, frequently in 'substandard' housing. The German government envisaged a 'rotation' system, whereby migrants' rights were to be restricted; they would be discouraged from bringing in their families, would be expected to return at the end of their contract period, and could be deported when no longer needed by their employers (Castles 1984). In fact, in terms of the migration of family members, the reality proved to be somewhat divergent from official rhetoric; that is, some 30 % of foreigners had arrived as 'dependent spouses' by the end of the 1960s. The bulk of guest workers actually held annually renewable permits (rather than short-term seasonal permits) and, oddly, guest workers were entitled to unemployment insurance, although few availed themselves of this benefit given 'full' employment during this period (Ellermann 2013, 2015). The guest worker system began as a means of recruitment for 'low-skilled'[2] work in agriculture, construction, and manufacturing, but recruitment later spread to a range of other industries. From the early 1960s until the end of that decade, the West German government had signed bilateral contracts with Greece, Spain, Portugal, Morocco, Tunisia, Turkey, and Yugoslavia. The number of recruited migrant workers declined precipitously after 1973 with the halt to labour migration in West Germany, and while many migrants returned home, many

[2] Skill (as in 'low-skilled', 'medium-skilled', or 'highly skilled') is socially constructed both spatially and temporarily, and is defined in this case by employers and governments.

chose to stay. By 1975 the number of non-employed 'foreigners' had exceeded the number employed while recruitment continued at a time of widespread unemployment for West German citizens (Castles 1984; Ellermann 2015). In fact, the system began to break down as early as the mid-1960s, and as Castles (2006) notes, by 1966 only 40 % of migrant workers were being recruited through official channels. The recession that became pervasive across the richer countries, and Germany in particular, signified the *de jure* end of the *gastarbeiter* system. Over time the system proved contradictory as employers preferred more permanent employees in light of persistent labour shortages, and male workers began to bring in their wives, often as workers themselves. This led to more permanent settlement, while pervasive governmental discourse insisted that Germany was 'not a country of immigration'. Castles (1984) argues that the guest worker system might be understood as a euphemism for a rotation system which maximizes the benefits for employers and the German state by lowering the costs of production and 'social reproduction'. He contends further that as migrants chose to stay in Germany, this reduced their 'flexibility' and enabled migrant workers (who had acquired substantial rights over time) to further protest their political and social conditions, not only in West Germany but across the EU.

However one theorizes the rapid decline of the *gastarbeiter* system after 1973, variations of such a system through TMWPs have continued in the EU ever since, and it therefore might be worthwhile to understand why they have apparently resurfaced in public discourse and practice.

8.3 Guest Worker Policies and Programmes in the Twenty-First Century

8.3.1 Why the Apparent Turn to Temporary Migrant Worker Policies and Programmes?

What led national policy-makers in the EU to establish new guest worker policies in the twenty-first century? According to Castles (2006), there were two 'major factors'. These 'factors' might be better understood as interlocking but also contradictory processes that motivated various branches of government in the wealthier countries to return to guest worker policies. In any case, Castles' first such 'factor' is 'economic', in which jobs in certain sectors such as construction and personal services could not be 'exported' to low-wage countries (see also Kloosterman 1996), and consequently, employment in such sectors would require a continual pool of migrant workers with varying skills. Castles' second factor is demography, especially the greying of Europe and its consequences for labour shortages, pension shortfalls, and domestic consumer demand.

In addition to these 'two major factors', he cites other more minor reasons. First, the control of apparently growing 'informall abour markets' meant that policy-makers believed guest worker policies would curb employers' propensity to hire undeclared (and often undocumented) workers. Second, and related to the demographic explanations above, fewer children will mean improved educational chances, which will then constrain the number of those who are willing to work in 'low-skilled' jobs. Third, 'globalization' and inequality are driving forces behind migration from poorer countries to richer countries, and richer countries are pressed to have some system of 'legal migration' that may benefit poorer countries. Fourth, the fear of 'brain drain' from the South to the North has led richer countries to allow more cooperative forms of migration. Fifth, there has been a growing recognition that border control by itself will not stop migration; in fact, it is argued that border control will drive migration further underground. Sixth, the events of September 11, 2001, have associated migration with a security threat (but see Boswell 2007), and it would be better to control migration through legal channels rather than for it to occur in a disorganized and clandestine fashion. Lastly, governments promulgated 'migration management' as a response to seemingly endless asylum, economic, and 'mixed-motivation' migration. With this social transformation perspective in mind (see Chaps. 1, 2, and 3, this volume), let us examine the development of guest worker policies in the EU since Castles' assessment in the mid-2000s.

8.3.2 The EU and the Development of a Nascent 'Actually Existing Guest Worker Regime'

In 2005 the EU Green Paper on Migration set out to consider TMWPs (see CEC 2005), and 2 years later the then European Commissioner for Justice, Freedom and Security, Franco Frattini, argued that the EU must develop a common migration policy to attract more highly skilled immigrants. This would be achieved through the creation of an EU Blue Card, which would address EU institutions' concern for 'competitiveness' without allegedly contributing to 'brain drain', and regulate, harmonize, and facilitate the conditions of entry and residence of third-country nationals (TCNs) for the purposes of 'highly qualified employment'. In May 2009 a Council Directive brought this into law (EU 2009), though it did not apply to Denmark, Ireland, or the UK (*Migration News*, January 2012).

Specifically, the Blue Card allows EU member states to admit professionals from outside the EU with a university degree and/or at least 5 years of work experience. Individuals must earn at least 1.5 times the EU member country's average gross salary (or 1.2 times in occupations facing labour shortages), although how this is to be measured in any way remains uncertain. Nevertheless, member states decide whether the employer or the individual applies for the Blue Card. The card involves an individual who wishes to work for more than 3 months, and is valid for 1–4 years for specific sectors to which a cardholder would be confined. Family members of Blue Card holders can come to an EU member state after 6 months, and it is possible for spouses to receive work permits (EU 2009).

After 5 years Blue Card holders can become permanent EU residents, and after 18 months of legal residence, they may move to another EU country, provided the second country agrees to this, based on its quota for highly skilled immigrants. Also inscribed into the EU directive is equal treatment with nationals as regards educational and vocational training, recognition of diplomas, pensions, social security, and working conditions. After 2 years of legal employment they may receive equal treatment with citizens in terms of access to any 'highly qualified' employment. Significantly, the EU Blue Card may be withdrawn if the holders do not have sufficient resources to maintain themselves and their family members without social assistance or if they been unemployed for more than three consecutive months or more than once during the period of validity of the card (EU 2009).

In November 2011, the EU Commissioner announced an EU 'Global Approach to Migration and Mobility' with Egypt, Morocco, and Tunisia. Under EU 'mobility partnerships', guest workers and students would in theory find it easier to enter the EU in exchange for cooperation from North African governments to 'prevent illegal migration' and accept the return of unauthorized migrants (EC 2011; *Migration News*, January 2012). This is partly illustrative of the way in which guest workers are being enrolled in EU processes of 'externalization' (see e.g. Casas et al. 2010).

However, moves by EU institutions have not been restricted to highly skilled migration. In fact, in February 2014 the Council of the EU adopted the Directive 'on the conditions of entry and stay of third-country nationals for the purpose of employment as seasonal workers' (EU 2014) for a stay not exceeding 3 months.[3] The seasonal-workers directive is novel insofar as it is the first EU directive aimed at 'low-skilled' (seasonal) workers. The Directive set out to establish 'fair and transparent rules of entry and stay for seasonal workers who are EU citizens'. It is designed to effectively manage 'migration flows' of temporary seasonal migrants while 'ensuring decent working and living conditions' and 'providing for incentives and safeguards to prevent overstaying or temporary stay from becoming permanent' (EU 2014).

This Directive concerns seasonal workers only (principally in agriculture or tourism), but other sectors may be involved with consent from the relevant 'social partners'. Individuals coming from outside the EU (third-country nationals, or TCNs) must have a work contract that specifies the pay and working hours, and provide evidence of 'appropriate' accommodation that will not be deducted from the wage and that will meet basic health and safety standards. As with the Blue Card Directive, member states are permitted to determine the number of seasonal workers and reject an applicant if an EU citizen is available for the position.

According to the Directive, seasonal workers who are already in an EU member state may extend their work contract or change their employer at least once. Given EU institutions' interest in encouraging circular migration, the annual re-entry of TCNs for seasonal work is also possible. Seasonal workers are entitled to equal treatment with nationals of the 'host' member state, at least with regard to their

[3] However, legislation also states that member states must determine a maximum period of stay for seasonal workers between 5 and 9 months in any 12-month period (see CEC 2014; EU 2014).

employment terms, including minimum working age, pay, hours, dismissal, leave/holidays, and health and safety requirements. They also have the right to join a trade union; to occupational advice, to pensions, to social security, and to training. Member states must provide measures to avoid any abuses of these regulations, punitive measures in case they are flouted, and a means by which seasonal workers can file a complaint against their employer. However, member states will not be required to offer equal treatment on unemployment and family benefits, and equal treatment on tax benefits and on education and vocational training, as well as public housing, can be limited by member states.

The EU Blue Card and the 2009 Directive on seasonal employment appear to be the closest set of policies to what one might call guest worker *regimes*, if we take into account Krasner's (1983) understanding. Yet, it is dependent upon individual member state quotas, and thus it resembles more of a limited supranationalism in practice (a sort of 'actually existing supranationalism') than a supranational regime *per se* (see also Chap. 7, in this volume). Perhaps more importantly, the discussion above about the various rules and regulations says nothing about actual practices, especially at the sub-state level, that might call into question any facile recourse to the term 'regime'.

8.3.3 France and Guest Worker Policies

In part because the French state and employers relied on 'post-colonial' migrants to one degree or another, France could not be said to have a *gastarbeiter* system, at least not along the lines of West Germany's (Ellermann 2013). In fact, most migrant workers in France during the 1950s and 1960s were undocumented but were later regularized, or they were recruited in France through the *Officenationald'immigration* with few restrictions on settlement (Tripier 1990). It was not until Sarkozy became Minister of the Interior that guest worker policies were officially entertained. Sarkozy's 'second law' of 2006 signalled a shift from what he called *immigration subie* (immigration policy under duress) to *immigration choisie* (chosen immigration or immigration by choice). While the restrictive policies for families and 'unskilled' workers continued, he sought to recruit highly skilled migrants. This had antecedents in policy thinking in the 1990s but also coincided with the introduction of the European Blue Card. The push for recruiting highly skilled migrants drew the support of numerous governmental organizations, including the Ministry of Finance, business-friendly think tanks such as the *Institut Montaigne*, and employer associations such as MEDEF. Sarkozy's law sought to streamline the process of recruiting skilled workers, first, by the *Conseil d'État* assessing which regions and professions were faced with labour shortages; and, second, by creating a *Carte compétences et talents* ('skills and talents visa'), which would be spared from the citizenship tests and 'Welcome and integration contracts' (*Contrat d'accueil et d'intégration*) required by other migrants. At the same time employers would be subjected to the requirement that no available French citizens or 'local residents' were available for the position. In response to protests by some sections of the French public about 'brain drain', the French government required recruited migrants to sign a 'co-development agreement' that would impel them to return after 6 years in France. This could be argued to be a rather clever way of appeasing voices of protest while ensuring a 'rotation system' for skilled migrants, albeit one with a rather lengthy duration. In 2009 the French government revised the second Sarkozy law by including a 10-year work and residence permit for those who could demonstrate an 'exceptional economic contribution'. By this the government meant that an individual would have to own a 30 % share in a firm, that they could retain or create 50 jobs, or that they could invest at least €10 million in France. In December 2012 the French government reduced the number of professions requiring recruitment from 30 to 14. In this respect it is crucial to recognize that in contrast to Germany and the UK, France's unemployment rates has remained quite elevated since the emergence of the global financial crisis in 2008, and one might surmise that particularly high unemployment is behind the reduction in quotas (Menz 2010; Murphy 2006; OECD 2008, 2009, 2013).

The example of the French government's policies has similarities with the policies of other EU countries, and we therefore now turn to development in Germany since 2006 to assess the evolution of guest worker programmes, and to discuss what they might say about Castles' (2006) broad admonishment.

8.3.4 Germany and Guest Worker Policies

While Castles (2006) addresses the policy discourses and practices of migration during the mid-2000s, it is worth exploring what has happened since his assessment. To answer this, we might actually begin in the late 1980s and early 1990s, when, as noted briefly above, German employers—especially in the construction sector—relied heavily on cross-border and other migration from Eastern Europe (especially Poland). In 1990 the German government passed a rather obscure government decree to allow labour recruitment despite the official ban on recruitment since the 1970s (Ellermann 2015; Laubenthal 2012). Over the course of the next few years bilateral agreements for 'contract workers' were signed with a number of Eastern European countries. Contract work essentially entailed 'short-term'/project-based employment, usually in the construction industry. Work permits could not exceed 2 years and were based on annual quotas. This was decidedly a 'rotation' system, which sought to severely curtail settlement in light of supposed past 'mistakes' of the *gastarbeiter* system. Furthermore, contract workers were not to be integrated into the system of social insurance, and would not be entitled to housing assistance or language training (Rudolph 1996; Ellermann 2015). Between 1991 and 2000 roughly 50,000 annual project-based work permits and 250,000 seasonal work permits were accorded by the German government (Ellermann 2015). This suggests that despite the official doctrine of the 'end of migration', low-skilled labour recruitment continued, even if no doubt many temporary workers were in fact undocumented and outside official state channels of recruitment (Rudolph 1996). Over the course of the 1990s the system drew criticism from employer associations and trade unions primarily because of the competitive threat that foreign firms posed through 'wage dumping', and because they did not have to pay a 'social wage' as did German employers. Eventually the government reduced the quotas on contract workers, meted out more severe sanctions, and reduced recruitment in regions with higher unemployment. Nevertheless, the contract rotation system—which should not be confused with a guest worker system because it involved foreign-owned firms—continued into the 2000s. By 2005 numbers had declined, and between 2005 and 2012 the annual average number of contract workers had declined from over 42,000 between 1999 and 2004 to approximately 17,700 (Ellermann 2015; Laubenthal 2012). I will return to low-skilled labour migration after 2006, but let us first turn to highly skilled migration.

In the late 1990s employers began to lobby the German government in order to implement recruitment in a variety of industries, especially in the IT sector. In part this led to the Nationality Act (*Staatsangehörigkeitsgesetz*), which permitted the immigration of 10,000 workers and later 20,000 into the IT sector. For employers and other observers of German economic growth, this number appeared to be inadequate. In any case, unlike the EU Blue Card, the German government's Green Card was limited to 5 years' duration, and family reunification was highly restricted, while the application for work permits proved challenging to navigate for potential applicants. In 2001, the then Minister of the Interior, Otto Schily, announced plans for a policy to recruit highly skilled immigrants annually, but on the basis of permanent settlement. This would rest on a quota and be modelled along the lines of the Canadian points system. These plans were buttressed by demands from employers in other sectors, such as engineering. Several years later the Commission's work led to the 2005 Immigration Act, which liberalized highly skilled migration and abolished the previous points-based system. With the interests of employers and interested state elites, the government further liberalized highly skilled migration with the 2009 Labour Migration Control Act (or the 'Law for the Management of Labour Migration'), which in particular, lowered the salary threshold for potential applicants. By 2012 the federal government had replaced the 2009 act with respect to highly skilled migration with the EU Blue Card (Cerna 2014; Laubenthal 2012; Mushaben 2011).

Returning to the question of low-skilled employment, seasonal migration (e.g. in agriculture and tourism) persisted into the latter half of the 2000s with the BfA having signed agreements with the EU-A8 (Czech Republic, Estonia, Hungary, Latvia, Lithuania, Poland, Slovakia, and Slovenia). However, as of 2012, only migrant workers from Croatia remained within a bilateral framework for seasonal employment. Nevertheless, the number of temporary seasonal workers remained relatively stable, even increasingly slightly from 286,940 in 2001 to 293,711 in 2010. In addition to agreements on seasonal employment, the BfA has signed agreements with 'third countries', or A8 countries, which provide that domestic care workers can be employed for up to 3 years. The number of such workers (roughly 75 % of whom were from Poland) doubled from approximately 1,660 to 3,000 between 2005 and 2008 (Laubenthal 2012).

8.3.5 The UK and Guest Worker Policies

In the 1990s the UK began to move towards recruiting migrants for work with a range of skills. At the low end of the skill spectrum recruitment concentrated on agriculture, food processing, and social care. From the 1950s to 2013, agricultural firms in the UK relied on migrant labour to harvest a range of crops through the Seasonal Agricultural Workers Scheme (SAWS). It was designed to meet seasonal fluctuations (e.g. in planting and gathering crops, on-farm processing/packing of crops, and handling livestock). The Home Office managed the scheme and oversaw the selection of operators, and in principle, SAWS workers had to be provided with accommodation and paid the agricultural minimum wage. Operators had a fixed quota of work cards they could issue to eligible applicants each year, and each had a maximum duration of 6 months (UK Gov 2012).

By the 1990s the UK government began to move towards recruiting migrants with a range of skills. At the low end of the skill spectrum, recruitment continued to concentrate on agriculture, but also food processing, and social care. Agricultural firms began to draw heavily on Eastern European workers, particularly, but not exclusively, from Poland. In line with a policy of 'managed migration' set forth in 2002, the government recognized the 'need' for migrant workers but at the same time sought to control immigration very carefully. With migration from Eastern Europe increasing, and the A8 countries joining the EU in 2004, the UK government implemented travel restrictions and the requirement that all A8 migrants register with the Worker Registration Scheme (WRS) as well as restricting their social welfare benefits. Between 2004 and 2007 over a million migrants (largely Polish) were estimated to have entered the UK through the WRS. Despite the UK government's efforts to manage the skill base of immigrants, in 2008 more than half of all new A8 arrivals were employed in unskilled occupations compared with one third of other migrants. In 2008 the UK suspended all unskilled immigration from outside the European Economic Area (EEA) (UK Gov 2013). With the accession of Romania and Bulgaria in 2007, the UK government closed SAWS to non-EEA migrants, and in 2008 restricted SAWS to Romanians and Bulgarians. Employers were officially required to meet certain pay and working conditions (e.g. related to health and safety law), and had to rely on only 'authorized providers/gangmasters' operating in agriculture, food and drink processing/packaging, forestry, horticulture, and shellfish harvesting. Providers who were not licensed by the Gangmasters Licensing Authority risked being fined. Wages were set by the Agricultural Wages Board until October 2013, when the National Minimum Wage became the standard. Nonetheless, the UK government closed the SAWS on January 1, 2014, as it envisioned that agricultural employers could meet their needs for workers from within the UK and the EEA. At the same time the government developed an Agricultural Technologies Strategy to reduce the demand for unskilled labour (UK Gov 2012, 2013).

In the area of food processing the Sector-Based Scheme (SBS) was first introduced in May 2003 and initially covered the hospitality sector as well as the food processing sector, with quotas of 10,000 places for each. These sectors were identified as having labour needs that could not be met by the UK or the EEA workforce. Eventually, only firms within fish, meat, and mushroom processing could use the scheme to employ migrants from any non-EU country (Migration Advisory Committee 2013). In July 2005 "the SBS coverage of the hospitality sector was terminated. This was the result of indications that the labour requirements of the sector could be met without the scheme, in addition to evidence that it was being used as a means to facilitate illegal [sic]entry" (Home Office 2005, 21).

In terms of highly skilled migration, by the 1990s, UK employers were relying increasingly on migration from India to fill highly skilled positions, and the government gradually moved to a points-based scheme beginning in 2008. What is noteworthy about the UK scheme, and which is mirrored in other countries, is its hybrid character, that is, it combines both tiers *and* a points system, with the latter being restricted to those considered to be 'highly skilled immigrants'. As of April 2014 the UK decided to reform its procedures into five tiers, but only Tiers 1, 2, and 5 will concern us here: the first tier consists of five categories, including for entrepreneurs and investors, but again, I will only address two of these. For the first category (the 'Exceptional Talent visa'), individuals who apply should be an 'internationally recognized leader or emerging leader' in STEM-related fields, or the arts and humanities. They are required to be endorsed by a relevant professional body, such as the Royal Academy of Engineering or Tech City UK. The visa duration is initially for 3 years and can be extended for another 2 years, with the annual cap set at 1,000 individuals. The Tier 1 'General' visa mainly involves those who applied under a now terminated highly skilled migrant programme and who are already in the UK. In the 'Graduate Entrepreneur' category are individuals who are recognized by either a UK university or UK Trade and Investment (a government body) as having highly tuned entrepreneurial skills (e.g. by completing a recognized training programme). The initial duration of this visa is 1 year and can be extended for another year. Successful applicants are allowed to bring in family members (including children under 18) so long as they have a visa themselves, and they also meet minimum income requirements (UK Gov 2014a).

Tier 2 has four categories, but we will concern ourselves only with the 'General' category because the others are highly specialized (such as 'Minister of Religion'). A vast number of work permits are granted under this category (the UK government had a 14-page list in April 2014), which includes anything from engineers to internationally recognized ballet dancers to chemistry and physics teachers to specialized neonatal nurses (UK Gov 2014b). Anyone hoping to obtain a visa under the 'General' category is required to have a 'skilled' job offer from a UK employer (generally, but not exclusively, from the 14-page list). Successful applicants in this category may be required to pass an English proficiency test and to have an 'appropriate' salary. As with many other categories, visa holders are allowed to bring in family members under certain financial conditions. In most cases the duration of the visa will be 5 years, and the visa can be renewed, but only for an additional year.

8.4 Conclusions

'New' guest worker policies have their antecedents in post-WWII *gastarbeiter*/labour recruitment policies, yet they have been adapted to reflect concerns by EU member governments that there are skill deficits which range from the 'less skilled' to the 'highly skilled'. One might ask four questions then: first, what sort of economic knowledge has circulated to drive this perception of skill shortages and their relationship to economic development; second, how do institutions, individuals, groups, and power relations (in some sort of tradition of political economy) matter in the formulation and unfolding of TMWPs on the ground; third, to what extent does 'equal treatment', supposedly guaranteed and upheld by EU and member state institutions with respect to TMWPs, actually work in practice; and finally, are the wages, working conditions, and other labour rights that are stipulated under the various guestworker programmes adhered to in practice (e.g. Ruhs and Anderson 2010). While a comprehensive response to these questions lies far beyond the scope of this chapter, I have endeavoured to suggest some changing political-economic forces that point to a social transformation perspective on TMWPs.

More specifically, this chapter has—in an empirical and deductive manner—aimed to assess Castles' (2006) initial pronouncements and caveats concerning some distinctions between TMWPs in the twenty-first century and the post-WWII *gastarbeiter* system. This is not an easy challenge given that definitional ambiguities abound with respect to who precisely constitutes a migrant, what 'temporary' means, how 'skill' is defined over time and space, and, indeed, what exactly a TMWP is. Nonetheless, employing a working definition of a temporary migrant worker, I have examined developments at the level of EU institutions, as well as in France, Germany, and the UK. While Castles is right to be wary of any simple return to guest worker policies, there is certainly evidence of an approximation of neo-gastarbeiter policies in what is arguably a significantly transformed global (and specifically European) political economy since the 'Fordist' years. The wide gamut of skills required then (including the recruitment of 'medium-skilled' migrants such as nurses into European health systems), is one way in which TMWPs in the twenty-first century can be set apart from the *gastarbeiter* system in post-war West Germany. Second, and relatedly, these stratifications, which are refracted through complex forms of administration that we might associate with 'migration management', are a far cry from the laissez faire and poorly administered guest worker policies of the post-war period. A third way in which they may be distinguished is through the effects of EU institutional programme design. That is, the Blue Card and now the seasonal migrant worker directive—the first in the EU's history—suggest that TWMPs are slowly shaping member state TWMPs both at the 'low end' and the 'high end' of the skill spectrum. In this respect, the Blue Card and the seasonal worker directive might even represent an incipient guest worker *regime* not foreseen at the time of Castles' analysis. At the same time we could hardly refer to *national* TMWPs or guest worker policies as *regimes*, but rather must regard them as a set of oscillating policies and programmes, some of them nearly as temporary as migrant workers themselves.

References

Betts, A. (2012). Introduction: Global migration governance. In A. Betts (Ed.), *Global migration governance* (pp. 1–33). Oxford: Oxford University Press.

Boswell, C. (2007). Migration control in Europe after 9/11: Explaining the absence of securitization. *JCMS: Journal of Common Market Studies, 45*(3), 589–610. doi:10.1111/j.1468-5965.2007.00722.x.

Casas, M., Cobarrubias, S., & Pickles, J. (2010). Stretching borders beyond sovereign territories? Mapping EU and Spain's border externalization policies. *Geopolítica(s), 2*(1), 71–90. doi:10.5209/rev_GEOP.2011.v2.n1.37898.

Castles, S. (1984). *Here for good: Western Europe's new ethnic minorities*. London: Pluto Press.

Castles, S. (1986). The guest-worker in Western Europe – An obituary. *International Migration Review, 20*(4), 761–778. doi:10.2307/2545735.

Castles, S. (2006). Guestworkers in Europe: A resurrection? *International Migration Review, 40*(4), 741–766. doi:10.1111/j.1747-7379.2006.00042.x.

CEC. (2005). *Green paper on an EU approach to managing economic migration /* COM/2004/0811 final */*. Brussels: Commission of the European Communities. http://eur-lex.europa.eu/legal-content/EN/TXT/HTML/?uri=CELEX:52004DC0811&from=EN

CEC. (2014). *Council adopts directive on third-country seasonal workers*. Brussels: Commission of the European Communities. http://www.consilium.europa.eu/uedocs/cms_data/docs/pressdata/en/jha/141044.pdf

Cerna, L. (2014). Attracting high-skilled immigrants: Policies in comparative perspective. *International Migration, 52*(3), 69–84. doi:10.1111/imig.12158.

Dauvergne, C. C., & Marsden, S. (2014). The ideology of temporary labour migration in the post-global era. *Citizenship Studies, 18*(2), 224–242. doi:10.1080/13621025.2014.886441.

EC. (2011). *European Commission: Home affairs: What we do: Policies: Africa*. http://ec.europa.eu/dgs/home-affairs/what-we-do/policies/international-affairs/africa/index_en.htm

Ellermann, A. (2013). When can liberal states avoid unwanted immigration? Self-limited sovereignty and guest worker recruitment in Switzerland and Germany. *World Politics, 65*(3), 491–538. doi:10.1017/S0043887113000130.

Ellermann, A. (2015). Do policy legacies matter? Past and present guest worker recruitment in Germany. *Journal of Ethnic and Migration Studies, 41*(8), 1235–1253.

EU. (2009). *Council Directive 2009/50/EC of 25 May 2009 on the conditions of entry and residence of third-country nationals for the purposes of highly qualified employment*. http://eur-lex.europa.eu/legal-content/EN/TXT/PDF/?uri=CELEX:32009L0050&from=EN

EU. (2014). *Directive 2014/36/EU of the European Parliament and of the Council of 26 February 2014 on the conditions of entry and stay of third-country nationals for the purpose of employment as seasonal workers*. http://eur-lex.europa.eu/legal-content/EN/TXT/PDF/?uri=CELEX:32014L0036&from=EN

Glick Schiller, N., & Salazar, N. B. (2013). Regimes of mobility across the globe. *Journal of Ethnic and Migration Studies, 39*(2), 183–200. doi:10.1080/1369183X.2013.723253.

Home Office. (2005, February). *Controlling our borders: Making migration work for Britain – Five year strategy for asylum and immigration*. London: Home Office. Available at: http://www.archive2.officialdocuments.co.uk/document/cm64/6472/6472.pdf

Joppke, C. (1998). Why liberal states accept unwanted immigration. *World Politics, 50*(2), 266–293. doi:10.1017/S004388710000811X.

Kloosterman, R. (1996). Mixed experiences: Post industrial transition and ethnic minorities on the Amsterdam labour market. *New Community, 22*(4), 637–653. doi:10.1080/1369183X.1996.9976565.

Koslowski, R. (Ed.). (2011). *Global mobility regimes*. New York: Palgrave Macmillan.

Krasner, S. D. (1983). Structural causes and regime consequences: Regimes as intervening variables. In S. D. Krasner (Ed.), *International regimes* (pp. 1–22). Ithaca: Cornell University Press.

Laubenthal, B. (2012). *Labour migration governance in contemporary Europe. The case of Germany.* http://www.labmiggov.eu/wp-content/uploads/2012/05/laubenthal_case-study_-Germany_17.05.pdf

Leach, B. (2013). Canada's migrants without history: Neoliberal immigration regimes and Trinidadian transnationalism. *International Migration, 51*(2), 32–45. doi:10.1111/imig.12019.

Menz, G. (2010). Employers, trade unions, varieties of capitalism, and labour migration policies. In G. Menz & A. Caviedes (Eds.), *Labour migration in Europe* (pp. 25–53). Basingstoke/New York: Palgrave Macmillan.

Migration Advisory Committee. (2013). *Migrant Seasonal Workers: The impact on the horticulture and food processing sectors of closing the Seasonal Agricultural Workers Scheme and the Sector Based Scheme.* https://www.gov.uk/government/uploads/system/uploads/attachment_data/file/257242/migrant-seasonal-workers.pdf

Murphy, K. (2006). *France's new law: Control immigration flows, court the highly-skilled.* http://

Mushaben, J. M. (2011). Citizenship and migration policies under Merkel's grand coalition. *German Politics, 20*(3), 376–391. doi:10.1080/09644008.2011.606568.

OECD. (2008). *International migration outlook 2008.* Paris: SOPEMI.

OECD. (2009). *International migration outlook 2009.* Paris: SOPEMI.

OECD. (2013). *International migration outlook 2013.* Paris: SOPEMI.

Rudolph, H. (1996). The new *gastarbeiter* system in Germany. *Journal of Ethnic and Migration Studies, 22*(2), 287–300. doi:10.1080/1369183X.1996.9976539.

Ruhs, M., & Anderson, B. (2010). Semi-compliance and illegality in migrant labour markets: An analysis of migrants, employers and the state in the UK. *Population, Space, and Place, 16*(3), 195–211.

Tripier, M. (1990). *Immigration dans la classe ouvrière en France.* Paris: Ciemi; L'Harmattan.

UK Gov. (2012). *Guidance: Farm workers: Agricultural workers' pay and working conditions, labour and health and safety laws, and recruiting temporary workers from overseas.* https://www.gov.uk/employing-farm-workers

UK Gov. (2013). *Written statement to Parliament: Seasonal Agricultural Workers Scheme and the Food Processing Sectors Based Scheme. Written ministerial statement on the Seasonal Agricultural Workers Scheme and the Food Processing Sectors Based Scheme.* https://www.seasonal-agricultural-workers-scheme-and-the-food-processing-sectors-based-scheme

UK Gov. (2014a). *Tier 1 (Exceptional Talent) visa.* https://www.gov.uk/tier-1-exceptional-talent

UK Gov. (2014b). *Guidance: Tier 2 shortage occupation list from 6 April 2014.* https://www.gov.uk/government/publications/tier-2-shortage-occupation-list-from-6-april-2013

Chapter 9
Identity Check: Smart Borders and Migration Management as Touchstones for EU-Readiness and - Belonging

Martin Geiger

9.1 Introduction

Since December 15, 2010, citizens of Albania and Bosnia-Herzegovina have been able to travel to Schengen states without a visa for a maximum of 90 days, provided they have biometric passports; holders of conventional passports still need a visa. This is a vivid example of how technology helps in creating and separating categories of travellers and citizens, with differentiated freedoms of mobility, degrees of access, and inclusion or exclusion (see Chap. 2, in this volume).

Albania and Bosnia-Herzegovina were able to conclude their visa liberalization following a process of bringing border and migration policies in line with European Union demands that lasted more than a decade. The main prerequisite for lifting the visa requirements and for signing the vital Stabilisation and Association Agreement (SAA) was the ratification of a readmission agreement with the EU. The SAA itself was the EU's main prerequisite for any closer association. At the Santa Maria de Feira European Council in 2000, Albania, Bosnia-Herzegovina, and other countries of the Western Balkans were offered the prospect of becoming members of the EU as part of what is called the Stabilisation and Association Process (see COM 2000; Delegation 2014a, b; EC 2000). While Albania, having been an 'EU candidate country' since June 2014, has a good chance of joining the EU, possibly in a few years, Bosnia-Herzegovina's progress towards membership is currently completely stalled. It is therefore quite interesting to scrutinize the developments in the two countries; both have benefited from visa liberalization more or less at the same time, while their chances of achieving EU membership are quite different.

Since the early 1990s Albania and the former Yugoslavia have featured prominently in EU discussions concerning migration, asylum, refugees, and the return of

M. Geiger (✉)
Department of Political Science, Carleton University, Ottawa, Canada
e-mail: martin.geiger@carlton.ca

A. Amelina et al. (eds.), *An Anthology of Migration and Social Transformation*, IMISCOE Research Series, DOI 10.1007/978-3-319-23666-7_9

migrants and refugees (see e.g. COM 2001: Summary; COM 2003: 4.4.1). As a consequence, the EU has taken a strong and immediate interest in the control and prevention of unwanted ('irregular') migration from Albania and Bosnia-Herzegovina, the latter being one of several successor states of the former Yugoslavia. The EU has been using a set of measures to exert influence on the two countries, their state-building efforts, institutional reforms, and, in particular, their border and migration control strategies.

This chapter argues that, while forced and voluntary migration have profoundly transformed Albania, Bosnia-Herzegovina, and other states in the region (see e.g. Baldwin-Edwards 2006; Pastore 1998; King and Vullnetari 2003), the reform of border and migration control, under pressure from the EU and other states, have had major transformative impacts on the political and social transformation of the two countries and their societies. This chapter highlights the close link that has emerged between the EU's attempts to simultaneously, (a) re-establish peaceful neighbourliness by influencing not only on the political but also the social and economic fabric of countries in the region while, (b) at the same time nevertheless making sure that emigration and transit migration from and through the region towards EU member states are addressed restrictively and become regulated in a supposedly more orderly, humane and balanced way. The latter attempt has, in turn, inevitably profound effects on the socio-political fabric of nation-states in the region and their populations, to the extent that their externally (EU-)induced socio-political transformation and stricter regulation of migration, on the one hand, purportedly brings them closer to the EU (and EU membership), while at the same time the highly exclusionary and restrictive overall approach of EU migration policies is in reality working towards guaranteeing that these countries' citizens (though they are regarded as potential future EU citizens), at least for the time being, remain de facto outsiders and are subjected to improved schemes of bio-political control, surveillance, 'smart bordering', and governance (or 'management') tactics and techniques. Hence, this chapter and the discussion of two EU neighbouring countries on the path to future EU membership vividly demonstrate the close link between migration, political attempts to govern/manage migration and borders, and, at the same time, the extent to which migration policies are embedded in, and, as well, form vital components of more overarching attempts of recreating order, peace, and structure in EU accession trajectories—a clear example and argument why discussions on migration and migration policies necessarily need to be linked to and re-embedded in more general understandings and discussions of contemporary society, e.g., in the case of the EU, accession processes and the processes of building a common European space (see Chaps. 1 and 2 as well as the introduction to Part I of this volume).

From as early as the mid-1980s onwards one of the key features of the EU's common migration and asylum policy, in addition to the emergence of intergovernmental collaboration and a supranationalization between EU member states (see Chap. 7, in this volume), has been the territorial export, or shifting, of border control and other measures to curb illegal migration to non-EU states ('exterritorialization'). This process was accompanied by the outsourcing ('externalization') of these measures to agencies beyond the EU's institutional framework, most notably to international organizations (IOs), which in turn became part of, and started to operate within, the context of a new global and more privatized approach to migration and border control, a new political economy under the umbrella of 'migration management' (see the Chapters in Part II of this volume). The aim of this chapter is to highlight not only the role of the EU but also the contributions of IOs to the process of 'EU-ropeanization', a process that in the case of Albania and Bosnia-Herzegovina extends far beyond EU-style border and migration policies and measures. In fact, border control and the regulation of migration (i.e. the prevention of irregular migration) are still important touchstones not only for the two countries and their societies but also for how the EU itself perceives, and may wish to continue, its relations with the two countries and their citizens. Consequently, the EU's process of 'EU-ropeanizing' border and migration control policies by externalizing (i.e. by outsourcing measures to IOs and other non-EU actors, including e.g. non-governmental organizations) and, based on this, exterritorializing and territorially shifting control and countermeasures to non-EU states deserves to be discussed as an important and powerful element of the general political and social transformation of these two case countries (see also Part III of this volume).

9.2 Migration-Related Interventionism: The EU and International Organizations

Since the 1990s the European Commission has been providing substantial funding to implement countermeasures in both countries through various funding programmes such as Community Assistance for Reconstruction, Development, and Stabilisation (CARDS) and Instrument for Pre-Accession Assistance (IPA) (for an overview, see e.g. Geiger 2011: 215–220). These countermeasures were developed because the Commission has regarded Albania and Bosnia-Herzegovina as important countries of origin of and gateways for irregular migration and human trafficking (see e.g. COM 2001: Summary; COM 2003: 4.4.1). Additional financial and logistical support has been provided by EU member states such as Germany, Greece, and Italy; the United States; and other countries.

The EU Commission began to structure its bilateral relations with Albania and Bosnia-Herzegovina in the field of border and migration control based on demands and recommendations, which were then used to track performance in the form of annual progress reports (see e.g. COM 2005, 2006a). The EU considered a new legal basis concerning border management, migration, trafficking, refugees, and asylum a top priority and urged both countries to adopt laws and regulations in accordance with the Schengen and the EU Acquis. The Commission also demanded new bilateral readmission agreements on the return of irregular migrants (including third-country nationals) and of rejected asylum seekers. Moreover, it called on both countries to effectively strengthen border control; to actively combat irregular migration and trafficking; to increase capacities for receiving asylum seekers and integrating refugees; to improve and guarantee the security of IDs and passports by introducing biometric documents and other measures; to fully disclose and exchange all migration-related data and information with the Schengen states; and, more generally, to assume full 'ownership' in the field of borders and migration (see e.g. COM 2005: 3.3.1, 2006a: 4.3.1, b: Annex 2). By demanding reforms, funding the necessary infrastructure, and facilitating policy development and implementation, the EU worked towards the complete 'Europeanization' of the border and migration policies of Albania and Bosnia-Herzegovina, a process that actually would be more appropriately called 'EU-ropeanization' because the EU was the main driver behind it.

However, in complete contradiction to the statement that the EU's chief interest lay in strengthening sovereignty and facilitating full national ownership, a considerable part of the funding was provided not to the respective government agencies but to IOs. The countries' Europeanization thus went hand in hand with a newly evolving, more multi-actor and multi-approach type of migration governance called 'migration management' (see Chap 2. in this volume). IOs were asked and funded by the EU to partner with local stakeholders including governmental and non-governmental entities (see e.g. Geiger 2010, 2011: 215–229). Unfortunately, it is nearly impossible to obtain precise and complete information on the funding provided, especially on how and for what purposes it was received and how it was spent. Under the regional CARDS programme for all Western Balkan states the Commission alone provided more than €105 million between 2000 and 2005 for measures to improve border security (for an overview, see Geiger 2011: 217). Under another funding programme the International Organization of Migration (IOM), one of the main recipients of EU funding, was provided several annual grants of €600,000 to €700,000 each between 2001 and 2003 for projects to prevent irregular migration, promote regular migration, and facilitate reintegration for returning migrants and refugees; IOM still receives funding from the EU.

UNHCR (the UN refugee agency) has been another major recipient of EU funding. Among other types of EU funding, UNHCR has received several grants, most of them in the range of €500,000 to €700,000 annually, for the reform of national asylum systems, the reception and integration of asylum seekers and refugees, and other activities. Other organizations have also been benefiting from regular EU grants since early 2000, including the International Centre for Migration Policy Development (ICMPD) and the United Nations Development Programme. All of these IOs also received additional funding from individual EU member states, other countries (e.g. the United States), and donors. IOM, UNHCR, and other organizations also collaborated independently with other actors (in some cases with EU funding and in others with additional funding from other institutions), such as the Organization for Security and Co-operation in Europe and the U.S. Agency for International Development. Moreover, in some cases with EU funding and in others with the support of other donors, organizations such as IOM also acted as local 'sponsors' for local NGOs (if only as intermediaries). In this capacity they played an active and important role in shaping a new border and migration system that at first glance seemed 'national', but on closer inspection was fully 'EU-ropeanized'.

9.2.1 Migration Management in the Context of 'EU-Ropeanization'

'Migration management' is a new form of a tool-based multi-stakeholder approach to migration. The main pillars of this new concept were Bimal Ghosh's 1993 recommendations to the Commission on Global Governance, which proposed to take a more 'balanced' political approach to migration, emphasized the need for 'regulated openness', and stated the objective to achieve a 'triple win', namely regulation to the end that migration would be beneficial for migrants, sending countries, and receiving countries (see Ghosh 1993, 2000; for a critical discussion, see e.g. Geiger and Pécoud 2010; Kalm 2010). In the context of the New International Regime for Orderly Movements of People—Ghosh's UN-funded project—in the mid-1990s IOM started to become the global leader in promoting and implementing innovative approaches to 'managing' migration across the world (see e.g. Georgi 2010).

In fact, for migration management to work, functioning state agencies are not necessarily required; it is typically 'put into practice' in what are considered weak states—such as Albania and Bosnia-Herzegovina. It also has little to do with conventional approaches to migration, which would be based on laws and would involve state agencies carrying out democratically legitimated programmes to regulate cross-border flows of people (see Geiger 2013; Kalm 2010; Geiger and Pécoud 2010). The main characteristics of this approach are a high degree of 'privatized' regulation beyond and without the state and the dominance of regulatory activities which, when combined, form a 'system of systems' but can operate independently of one another. It is essentially a market-driven approach: programmes, strategies, and tools are developed and then advertised to potential donors: economically strong countries, migrant-receiving countries, and countries interested in restrictive migration control. Migration management inevitably depends on how creatively the 'vendors' respond to certain issues, develop solutions, and then make use of funding opportunities; in other words, it depends on how successful the 'vendors' are in lobbying and finding 'buyers'. In most cases providers such as IOM also assume the responsibility of implementing the activities 'bought' by states or other donors (e.g. the EU). Activities, programmes, and tools that state and non-state donors can 'buy into' include health checks on migrants; visa processing; the implementation of anti-trafficking campaigns; the provision of training for NGOs and state officials; the upgrading of border checking and surveillance measures; facilitating 'voluntary' return for victims of trafficking, irregular migrants, or rejected asylum seekers; the provision of migration-related data; and the design of migration strategies for countries considered to be struggling with the development or implementation of effective border and migration control.

In 2004 Albania's government agreed on a National Strategy on Migration and only a few months later adopted a lengthy and detailed National Action Plan (Government of Albania/IOM 2004, 2005a; see also Geiger 2010). The main objectives were to extend the possibilities for Albanians to migrate legally; to make better use of migration for developing Albania (e.g. through remittances and diasporas); to improve consular support abroad; and to use the new National Strategy and the Action Plan as a means to bring Albania closer to EU membership (Government of Albania/IOM 2005b). At first glance, the two documents give the impression of strong national leadership and of pronounced political sensibility among national policymakers. However, the main problem is that neither the National Strategy nor the Action Plan were originally proposed or developed by the Albanian government. On the contrary, it was the IOM mission in Tirana that pushed for these projects, and it did so as early as 2001; it creatively used its contacts to the EU Commission to get funding approved for designing ('on behalf of Albania') a 'National' Strategy and an Action Plan, the latter consisting of more than 130 policy measures, with the great majority of these measures more or less directly earmarked for IOM and requiring additional EU funding. Although IOM had already completed its project of developing a 'National' Strategy and an Action Plan, and although Albania could have negotiated with the EU and implemented the suggested activities independently, only a year after the government members' 'approval' (by a vote of hands during a final, end-of-the year meeting) IOM requested yet another grant of €800,000 to implement the National Strategy and the Action Plan (for more details, see Geiger 2010). Since then IOM has been continuously involved in the design and implementation of migration management activities in Albania.

Similar strategies were developed by IOM in other countries neighbouring the EU that will eventually accede to the EU, including Bosnia-Herzegovina. The strategy developed in Albania is a case of 'best practice', a policy model that in the view of EU and IOM officials has been tested successfully and can be used in other 'project countries'. Primarily because of the more difficult political and administrative situation in Bosnia-Herzegovina it was only in 2008 that IOM was also able to finalize a strategy and action plan for this country.

In the cases of Albania and Bosnia-Herzegovina local EU officials and the European Commission viewed the 'national' strategies and action plans positively and congratulated the national governments on their partnership with the EU. The fact that citizens of Albania and Bosnian-Herzegovina have been allowed to travel to the Schengen Area without visas since the end of 2010 clearly shows that the European Commission ultimately regarded the two countries as far 'less concerning' in terms of irregular migration, trafficking, and porous borders than it had done in the 1990s. At least it considered the policy process that had been achieved in the context of massive EU funding and implementation led by IOs such as IOM to be satisfactory—which of course was of great importance for the two countries, not only politically (i.e. with regard to closer association and future membership) but also in broader societal terms in that it permitted free travel for citizens, providing them with a stronger sense of societal belonging to the EU and reducing exclusion.

9.2.2 *Visa-Free Travel in Exchange for Integrated and Smart Border Management*

While visa-free travel opportunities can be regarded as an important milestone towards a better inclusion of the two countries (as political entities) and their citizens in the enlarging 'EU-ropean' community, it is important to note that these opportunities were provided in exchange for a stricter stance on regular and irregular migration and an increased scrutiny and surveillance not only of third-country nationals visiting and transiting the two countries but also of their own citizens. Both countries were forced to act more decisively in dealing with those of their own citizens trying to emigrate or travel without proper authorization. This involved intensified 'filtering' at the borders and stepping up checks, surveillance, countermeasures, and decisive remedial action, such as using physical force, arresting apprehended irregular migrants, and forcibly returning and deporting individuals from EU member states.

The establishment of what has become known as 'integrated border management', which started in early 2002, was a key demand of the EU (see e.g. COM 2002). The term describes the management of borders to provide effective control of and protection against illicit cross-border mobility, while at the same facilitating to the largest extent possible the licit cross-border movement of individuals and goods. In addition, the term 'integrated border management' stresses the importance of close inter-service, inter-agency, and international cooperation, as well as the need for a reliable, fast, and constant exchange of threat-related data and information, facilitated by state-of-the-art information technology. 'Integrated border management' predates the term 'smart borders', at least in the European context; both terms essentially mean the same, although the discussion about smart borders has been more prominent, such as with regard to checks at airports, and is mostly used exclusively to relate to human-mobility flows. In contrast, integrated border management, a concept that was actually developed by the EU, is still based on a broader understanding of border control, which includes land and sea borders, flows of goods and people, and so on.

Important supporters of integrated border management include ICMPD and IOM; EU agencies such as the Police Assistance Mission of the European Commission to Albania (PAMECA) and the European Union Police Mission in Bosnia-Herzegovina (EUPM); and, recently, Frontex, the EU border agency created in 2005, all of which have worked closely with donors such as the EU, individual EU member states, and international sponsors. On several occasions ICMPD and IOM have received EU funding for conducting performance checks, making recommendations for improving control at sites such as the 'blue' (i.e. the Adriatic) border of Albania and the airports of Tirana and Sarajevo, and for facilitating the development and implementation of modern border technology (see e.g. ICMPD 2005).

The provision of expertise and technology was especially important in the case of Bosnia-Herzegovina because the country did not have its own border guard force until 2001. During the time of communism Albania used severe measures to prevent any form of unauthorized emigration, and the death penalty was imposed on many 'traitors' caught trying to leave what was then a 'People's Republic'. In the context of the country's difficult transition the Albanian border guards had to be transformed into a civilian force, a force that is still struggling with corruption, malpractice, and inexperience to this day.

By 2013 the majority of citizens (1.8 million in Bosnia-Herzegovina and 2.6 million in Albania) had acquired 'e-passports'; they can now travel to Schengen states visa-free (COM 2013c: 3.1, 3.2). Along with readers to scan e-passports and identify forged documents, other technologies have been introduced in both countries over the last 10 years, including data systems such as Albania's Total Information Management System, which exchange information on border crossings with each other and with other national and international databases (including Interpol); risk analysis systems with direct connections to Frontex; mobile border units equipped with radar technology and night vision gear; and IT-based equipment that can be used in joint operations centres such as the Albanian–Macedonian one, and that allows for the swift exchange of time-sensitive information. Most of these tools are produced by European corporations such as Sagem Sécurité, which has been developing biometric passports, and are funded in whole or in part by the EU and other institutions and states, while the procurement of technology is based primarily on recommendations and intermediary support provided by Frontex, IOM, and other organizations.

9.3 EU-Ropeanization of Border and Migration Policies as a Process of Social Transformation

9.3.1 *Albania and Bosnia-Herzegovina as Laboratories for EU and Global Migration Management*

As the previous section showed, Albania and Bosnia-Herzegovina can be regarded as specific 'locales', or 'laboratories', where broader—that is, European and global—developments play out in specific ways under the umbrellas of exterritorialized and externalized EU control policies, IO-driven migration management, and modern, technology-based, or 'smart', border enforcement. For a long time EU institutions had the fundamental problem that they tried to have a strong influence on non-member states that were regarded as the 'causers' or 'enablers' of irregular/unwanted migration, such as Albania and Bosnia-Herzegovina. However, their capacity and legitimization to do so was limited. For some time the solution to this problem was to provide funding for non-EU actors (primarily IOs) and of NGOs and other non-EU stakeholders in the context of the emerging EU framework on how to govern the 'neighbourhood', the future 'accession area' (e.g. through the Stabilisation and Association Process), and migratory movements, and to implement generous funding schemes created by the EU. Other, non-EU stakeholders acted on behalf of the EU, 'in the name of EU Europe'. They actively supported, and in the case of Albania's migration strategy even proactively initiated, policy solutions, facilitated their adoption, and monitored their implementation.

In light of the above, and in line with discussions on the 'socialization' or 'teaching' of states by IOs and other organizations (see e.g. Checkel 2005; Finnemore 1993) and Radaelli's (2003) concept of 'Europeanization', one might say that there has been a process of 'socializing' and 'teaching' non-EU states, which has been occurring mostly through the help of IOs (in their capacity as non-EU policy actors), and which had as its primary aim the effective 'EU-ropeanization' of non-EU member states such as Albania and Bosnia-Herzegovina; that is, the alignment of these states with the EU and its policies and demands. Since the establishment of Frontex in 2005, 15 years after the Stabilisation and Association Process was initiated in 1999, the picture has been changing slowly. While direct collaboration between Frontex and state authorities of Albania and Bosnia-Herzegovina has been increasing, IOM and other international stakeholders still play a vital role in continuing the EU's governance of migration 'from within' in Albania and Bosnia-Herzegovina, which may seem 'remote' at first glance but on closer inspection is actually deeply 'embedded' and 'quasi-local'.

9.3.2 *Border and Migration Management, Its Broader Purposes, and Its Costs*

(Forced) migration has undoubtedly transformed Albania and Bosnia-Herzegovina, but this was precisely not the focus of this chapter. Rather, the argument that has been put forward is that the promotion of migration and integrated/smart border management has itself had transformative impacts on the two case countries, their societies, and their citizens.

It appears necessary to broaden the perspective and highlight an often-neglected dimension of migration and border politics, namely that these policies and processes rarely focus exclusively on the political regulation of cross-border mobility and migration, or on the 'policing' of migrants and travellers. In reality most of them are also designed to reach beyond these immediate policy objectives and to achieve other objectives as well, such as providing support to promote the broader social transformation or 'stabilization' of certain countries after the decay of state structures, social unrest, or even war. These broader societal objectives could even be regarded as the 'real' policy objectives.

It is important to remember that the alignment of Albania and Bosnia-Herzegovina with the Schengen and the EU Acquis took place within the EU's broader Stabilisation and Association Process for Albania, Bosnia-Herzegovina, and other successor states of the former Yugoslavia (see e.g. COM 2000). The Stabilisation and Association Process was itself designed as a framework process with the aim of creating more stable state structures, promoting pacification, stimulating new development and, the ultimate goal set from the very beginning, achieving close association with, and even membership in, the EU. Migration, refugee return, asylum, and border security featured most prominently in the Justice and Home Affairs section of this process and its annual progress reports (see e.g. COM 2000, 2005, 2006a). While the ratification of a readmission agreement was made a main condition for achieving closer pivotal association with the EU (and the signing of the Stabilisation and Association agreements mentioned earlier), the progress and performance of border and migration management was the main condition for achieving visa liberalization. Both the Stabilisation and Association agreements and visa liberalization are thus without any doubt ‘public goods’ of extremely high value. At the same time, border security and migration politics were clearly construed as stepping stones, or tests, for the EU readiness of both countries. Functioning border security and migration management were regarded as major drivers of EU stabilization and of integration and enlargement efforts. These policy fields were thus of far greater importance and served broader purposes, and therefore must be regarded as even greater public goods.

Paradoxically, while the substantial investment in border security measures and in capacities to regulate migration effectively contributed to ensuring and strengthening traditional aspects of Westphalian statehood, state building, institution building and capacity building efforts, this came at the price of non-local policy actors (most notably IOs) and their ‘policy implants’ effectively hindering and undermining state sovereignty and blocking progress towards national ownership. Moreover, EU and international efforts simultaneously operated both in the interest of Albanian and Bosnian-Herzegovinian citizens and against them. They undoubtedly provided citizens with more security (e.g. by promoting the rule of law and fighting organized crime in the form of human traffickers and smugglers) in addition to visa-free travel opportunities, thereby creating a sense of belonging to the EU. At the same time, however, these efforts worked to increase state capacities to control citizens and put them under permanent surveillance in the name of regulating migration and preventing irregular migration. They also contributed to the development of capacities to deter citizens from leaving the country without the necessary authorization and of efforts to keep track of their movements more effectively, to store their personal information in databases, and so on. These Albanian and Bosnian-Herzegovinian databases are not yet connected to the relevant European databases on movements, but they have been used to exchange information with databases whose first and foremost aim is to fight crime, such as those of Interpol.

The problem is that in most cases this strengthening of state capacities is done without proper democratic legitimatization, one example being the ‘ratification’ of migration strategies. While it is likely that the EU has actively and successfully promoted its interests and has created institutions and mechanisms that are working for the EU, this does not necessarily mean that they also work in favour of the citizens, the two countries, and long-lasting solutions to their ‘national’ policy challenges. National ownership continues to be a major issue, and for quite some time Albania and Bosnia-Herzegovina will have to face the challenge of creating and supporting stable state institutions and mechanisms to establish and guarantee sustainable solutions. For Bosnia-Herzegovina this will probably be the most pressing challenge.

9.3.3 Border and Migration Management Remain Touchstones for EU-Readiness and Belonging

The final question is whether the introduction of border and migration management has actually been effective in achieving the main goal of these policy projects and in re-establishing order, the rule of law, justice, and home affairs in the interest of citizens. It is very difficult to say whether EU-compliant border and migration management has resulted in a reduction of irregular movements and human trafficking, and in more orderly regular migration to the EU. This regular migration would also refer to authorized labour migration to the EU. However, the lifting of visa requirements did not include direct free access to EU labour markets, so there was actually no real change in most of the EU member states' generally restrictive labour migration policies for citizens of Albania, Bosnia-Herzegovina, and other 'third countries', or at least not for low-skilled labour migrants. In addition, family reunification and other channels involving citizens from Albania and Bosnia-Herzegovina were handled more restrictively by EU members states in recent years. At this point it appears that citizens from these two countries benefit primarily or even exclusively from short-term, non-employment-related visit and travel opportunities.

According to Frontex and the European Commission, estimates or exact data on the extent of irregular migration from Albania and Bosnia-Herzegovina to the EU have become more difficult to obtain in recent years—ironically, precisely because of the progress the two countries have made towards visa liberalization—while irregular migration across the Western Balkans has increased (see e.g. COM 2013c: 17; Frontex 2012: 5, 16). While in 2010, for example, 53,078 Albanian citizens were apprehended at EU borders as irregular migrants, in the 2 years following visa liberalization this number was much lower (6,671 in 2011, and 6,602 in 2012) (COM 2013c: 36). This is believed to be because citizens of Albania and Bosnia-Herzegovina no longer need a visa, and those who previously would have been apprehended as irregular migrants (i.e. those migrating without a visa) can no longer be easily identified as such. Some of them, however, do become 'visible' when they are discovered by EU member state authorities, such as individuals already living within the EU, over-stayers, or irregular migrant workers. If the effect of the EU-ropeanization of non-EU countries is that it makes irregular movements less detectable—as it appears to be doing—the introduction of an EU entry–exit system, which has been promoted as part of the EU Commission's 'smart border package' (see e.g. COM 2013b) could be regarded as an almost logical consequence of, and instrument to 'repair', the effects of a visa liberalization that ultimately was introduced too quickly.

This visa liberalization has become a topic of fierce debate between EU member states and institutions not only because there is less information available about the real extent of irregular migration now than there was before but also, and especially, because of the simultaneous sudden rise of asylum applications in certain EU member states, such as Germany. In 2012 member states of the Schengen Area recorded an increase in asylum applications filed by Albanian citizens of 143 % compared with the previous year (7,705 applications), while the number of citizens of Bosnia-Herzegovina applying for asylum in the same year increased by a staggering 117 % compared with the previous year (6,335 applications). Of the citizens from countries of the Western Balkans, only Serbs and Macedonians filed more asylum applications in that period (20,935 and 10,740 respectively), according to COM (2013c: 13). The sharp increase in the number of asylum applications, the increase in irregular migration transiting both countries, and the suspected simultaneous increase in irregular migration from Albania and Bosnia-Herzegovina to the EU drew sharp criticism from member states, Euro-sceptic, conservative and anti-immigration parties, resulting in a forced response by the European Commission. Since the end of 2013 member states of the Schengen Area have been allowed to temporarily reintroduce visa requirements under specific conditions if they experience a sudden and dramatic increase in irregular migration or asylum abuse (see e.g. COM 2013a).

Albania and Bosnia-Herzegovina are still under close EU observation—despite all of the progress the countries have made, according to the EU, which earlier had undoubtedly encouraged Schengen states to lift their visa requirements for citizens of the two countries. Their border and migration management remains a touchstone for further closer association with the EU and for eventual membership.

However, the EU itself has been under scrutiny as well: there is growing uneasiness about a further massive enlargement of the EU in the near future, which has been used as justification to keep certain countries waiting longer than planned to be allowed to accede. Albania, Bosnia-Herzegovina, and other countries are really putting the EU to the test. The touchstone for the EU lies in the question of whether the EU is able and willing to collaborate more effectively with non-EU states that have applied for membership to address the challenges in these countries in a sustainable manner. The surge of asylum applications and the fear of a further increase in irregular migration from and through Albania and Bosnia-Herzegovina are a clear sign that the ratification of agreements, the alignment of policies and laws with EU standards, and the heavy presence of additional international organizations do not bring about a change of the social and economic situation of the two countries and of the real lives of citizens affected by poverty, widespread unemployment, precarious livelihoods, and stagnating living standards. So far the investment in border and migration management has simply not resulted in any improvement of the general social and economic situation. It is unlikely that border enforcement and migration politics are appropriate means to bring this change about. While Albania and Bosnia-Herzegovina may have obtained 'admission tickets' to the EU by accepting the Schengen and the EU Acquis and international norms and standards, the EU continues to fail the test because it still does not truly welcome citizens of either country—citizens who are supposed to become citizens of the EU someday. All of this may have more to do with misappropriated 'colonial' approaches towards 'Western Balkan' states (see Chap. 22, in this volume), failing EU policies, poor leadership, mismanagement, and wrong investments on the part of the EU—more than with Albania and Bosnia-Herzegovina and with the citizens living in these countries, dreaming of a better life in a united Europe that makes them feel that they belong to it.

References

Baldwin-Edwards, M. (2006). *Patterns of migration in the Balkans* (MMO Working Paper No. 9). Athens: Mediterranean Migration Observatory. http://aei.pitt.edu/7045/1/mmo_wp9.pdf

Checkel, J. T. (2005). International institutions and socialization in Europe: Introduction and framework. *International Organization, 59*(4), 801–826. doi:10.1017/S0020818305050289.

COM. (2000). *EU stabilisation and association process for countries of South-Eastern Europe: Bosnia and Herzegovina, Croatia, Federal Republic of Yugoslavia, former Yugoslav Republic of Macedonia and Albania. COM (2000) 49 final/2.* Brussels: European Commission. http://eur-lex.europa.eu/legal-content/EN/TXT/PDF/?uri=CELEX:52000DC0049&from=EN

COM. (2001). *On the work of the EU/Albania High Level Steering Group, in preparation for the negotiation of a Stabilisation and Association Agreement with Albania. COM (2001) 300 final.* Brussels: European Commission. http://eur-lex.europa.eu/legal-content/EN/TXT/PDF/?uri=CELEX:52001DC0300&from=EN

COM. (2002). *Towards integrated management of the external borders of the member states of the European Union. COM (2002) 233 final.* Brussels: European Commission. http://eur-lex.europa.eu/legal-content/EN/TXT/PDF/?uri=CELEX:52002DC0233&from=en

COM. (2003). *Bosnia and Herzegovina: Stabilisation and association report 2003. COM (2003) 139 final.* Brussels: European Commission. http://ec.europa.eu/enlargement/pdf/bosnia_and_herzegovina/com03_340_en.pdf

COM. (2005). *Albania: 2005 progress report. COM (2005) 561 final.* Brussels: European Commission. http://ec.europa.eu/enlargement/archives/pdf/key_documents/2005/package/sec_1421_final_progress_report_al_en.pdf

COM. (2006a). *Bosnia and Herzegovina 2006 progress report. COM (2006) 649 final.* Brussels: European Commission. http://ec.europa.eu/enlargement/pdf/key_documents/2006/nov/bih_sec_1384_en.pdf

COM. (2006b). *Enlargement strategy and main challenges 2006–2007: Including annexed special report on the EU's capacity to integrate new members. COM (2006) 649 final.* Brussels: European Commission. http://ec.europa.eu/enlargement/pdf/key_documents/2006/Nov/com_649_strategy_paper_en.pdf

COM. (2013a). *Cecilia Malmström on the adoption of a visa waiver suspension mechanism.* Brussels: European Commission.

COM. (2013b). *Regulation establishing an Entry/Exit System (EES) to register entry and exit data of third country nationals crossing the external borders of the Member States of the European Union. COM (2013) 95 final.* Brussels: European Commission. http://ec.europa.eu/dgs/home-affairs/doc_centre/borders/docs/1_en_act_part1_v12.pdf

COM. (2013c). *Fourth report on the post-visa liberalisation monitoring for the western Balkan countries. COM (2013) 836 final.* Brussels: European Commission. http://register.consilium.europa.eu/doc/srv?l=EN&f=ST%2017144%202013%20INIT

Delegation. (2014a). *Key dates in Albania's path towards the EU.* Delegation of the EU to Albania. http://eeas.europa.eu/delegations/albania/eu_albania/political_relations/index_en.htm

Delegation. (2014b). *Key dates*. Delegation of the EU to Bosnia-Herzegovina. http://europa.ba/Default.aspx?id=12&lang=EN

EC. (2000). *Presidency conclusions: Santa Maria da Feira European council: 19 and 20 June 2000*. Brussels: European Council.

Finnemore, M. (1993). International organizations as teachers of norms: The United Nations educational, scientific, and cultural organization and science policy. *International Organization, 47*(4), 565–597. doi:10.1017/S0020818300028101.

Frontex. (2012). *Western Balkans: Annual risk analysis 2012*. Warsaw: Frontex. http://frontex.europa.eu/assets/Publications/Risk_Analysis/WB_ARA_2012.pdf

Geiger, M. (2010). Mobility, development, protection, EU-integration! The IOM's national migration strategy for Albania. In M. Geiger & A. Pécoud (Eds.), *The politics of international migration management* (pp. 141–159). Basingstoke/New York: Palgrave Macmillan.

Geiger, M. (2011). *Europäische Migrationspolitik und Raumproduktion: Internationale Regierungsorganisationen im Management von Migration in Albanien, Bosnien-Herzegowina und der Ukraine*. Baden-Baden: Nomos.

Geiger, M. (2013). The transformation of migration politics: From migration control to disciplining mobility. In M. Geiger & A. Pécoud (Eds.), *Disciplining the transnational mobility of people* (pp. 15–40). Basingstoke/New York: Palgrave Macmillan.

Geiger, M., & Pécoud, A. (2010). The politics of international migration management. In M. Geiger & A. Pécoud (Eds.), *The politics of international migration management* (pp. 1–20). Basingstoke/New York: Palgrave Macmillan.

Georgi, F. (2010). For the benefit of some: The international organization for migration and its global migration management. In M. Geiger & A. Pécoud (Eds.), *The politics of international migration management* (pp. 45–72). Basingstoke/New York: Palgrave Macmillan.

Ghosh, B. (1993). *Movements of people: The search for a new international regime*. Geneva/New York: Commission on Global Governance.

Ghosh, B. (2000). Introduction. In B. Ghosh (Ed.), *Managing migration: Time for a new international regime?* (pp. 1–5). Oxford/New York: Oxford University Press.

Government of Albania/IOM. (2004). *National strategy on migration*. Tirana: Government of Albania/IOM.

Government of Albania/IOM. (2005a). *National action plan on migration*. Tirana: Government of Albania/IOM.

Government of Albania/IOM. (2005b). *The national strategy on migration management*. Tirana: Government of Albania/IOM.

ICMPD. (2005). *Definition of a blue border management system in Albania*. Vienna: International Centre for Migration Policy Development. http://www.anti-trafficking.net/fileadmin/ICMPD-Website/Border_Management/Albania_Blue_Borders/Albania_Blue_Borders_Final_report.pdf

Kalm, S. (2010). Liberalizing movements? The political rationality of global migration management. In M. Geiger & A. Pécoud (Eds.), *The politics of international migration management* (pp. 21–44). Basingstoke/New York: Palgrave Macmillan.

King, R., & Vullnetari, J. (2003). *Migration and development in Albania* (Working Paper C5). Brighton: Development Research Centre on Migration, Globalisation and Poverty. http://www.migrationdrc.org/publications/working_papers/WP-C5.pdf

Pastore, F. (1998). *Conflicts and migrations: A case study on Albania. Written briefing addressed to the conflict prevention network of the European commission* (Revised version – January 1998). Rome: Centro Studi di Politica Internazionale. http://www.cespi.it/PASTORE/Albania1998.PDF

Radaelli, C. M. (2003). The Europeanization of public policy. In K. Featherstone & C. M. Radaelli (Eds.), *The politics of Europeanization* (pp. 27–56). Oxford/New York: Oxford University Press.

Martin Geiger works at Carleton University (Ottawa, Canada) where he is Assistant Professor of "Politics of Human Migration and Mobility". He holds a PhD in Geography from the University of Bonn (Germany) and is a former Banting Post-Doctoral Fellow of the Government of Canada. He has (co-)authored and co-edited numerous publications on different aspects of mobility/migration politics, including *The Politics of International Migration Management (Palgrave Macmillan, hardback 2010, 2012 paperback), Europäische Migrationspolitik und Raumproduktion. Internationale Regierungsorganisationen in Management von Migration in Albanien, Bosnien-Herzegowina und der Ukraine (Nomos, 2011), Disciplining the Transnational Mobility of People (Palgrave Macmillan, 2013)* and *International Organisations and the Politics of Migration (Routledge, 2015)*. He has also founded thew *Mobility & Politics* series with Palgrave Macmillan (co-editors Parvati Raghuram and William Walters).

Chapter 10
Border/Control

William Walters

10.1 Introduction

How might we historicize the idea of border control? If state borders can be understood as institutional sites of governance, what forms and logics of governance do they enact? This chapter asks what insights Foucauldian political sociology might bring to these questions. To do this, it looks not directly to Foucault but to Deleuze, who, building upon Foucault's cartography of power (Deleuze 1988: 23–44), develops an analytic of *control* (Deleuze 1995). Understanding control as a particular technology of power, the chapter pays special attention to the changing topography of border control, as well as the changing subjectivities presupposed by this form of power.

Researching borders using a Foucauldian lens has several benefits. For one thing, this move helps us better understand changing logics and practices of bordering. But it has a second benefit, one that is close to the aims of this book. Foucault's analytics of power are diagrams. They are valuable precisely because they have not been developed within an order of knowledge modelled along the lines of the social-science disciplines or area studies. Instead they operate tranversally to these fields, cutting across disciplinary and specialist areas. We get a better understanding of a practice when we can observe it operating in diverse contexts. By revealing what certain practices of border control might have in common with, say, the governance of a shopping mall or a database, Foucauldian analyses challenge some of the epistemological blinders that otherwise constrain thought unnecessarily when it is based in narrow specialized fields. Put differently, a strong case can be made that Foucauldian political sociology has much to offer any programme of research that

W. Walters (✉)
Department of Political Science and Department of Sociology & Anthropology
Carleton University, Ottawa, ON, Canada
e-mail: william.walters@carleton.ca

A. Amelina et al. (eds.), *An Anthology of Migration and Social Transformation*,
IMISCOE Research Series, DOI 10.1007/978-3-319-23666-7_10

is concerned to situate the study of migration in a wider understanding of societal transformation.

10.2 Rebordering

In reflecting on genealogy as a method, Foucault argued for a form of critical social analysis focused on 'events', moments when an existing regime of practices is reinvested, coopted, and redeployed by new social forces and governmental rationalities. To study events is to rediscover 'the connections, encounters, supports, blockages, plays of forces, strategies and so on which at a given moment establish what subsequently counts as being self-evident, universal and necessary' (Foucault 1991: 76). For instance, one cannot understand the birth of modern punishment without recognizing how an existing, and in many ways ancient, practice such as internment—which could serve multiple functions, including the sequestration of the insane and the suppression of political dissent—was put to new purposes once it was invested by practices of legal punishment.

Something comparable can be said about rebordering today, a useful concept Peter Andreas and his colleagues have developed (Andreas 2003; Andreas and Biersteker 2003; Andreas and Snyder 2000). As Andreas (2003) has noted, borders have long been associated with the military defence of the national territory from opposing, and often neighbouring, armies. They also have a history as privileged sites of commercial regulation, such as customs and excise. But today, it seems, borders are becoming more and more important as machines for the policing of a variety of actors, objects, and processes whose common denominator is their mobility (Adey 2004) or, more specifically, the forms of social and political insecurity that have come to be discursively attached to these mobilities (Bigo 2002; Huysmans 1995).

This chapter will offer some preliminary observations regarding Foucauldian political sociology, and what it might bring to recent studies of the transformation of state borders. Foucauldian political sociology has developed as an important site of theorization about contemporary as well as historical trends in power and governance (Barry et al. 1996a; Burchell et al. 1991; Dean 1999; Rose 1999). Forging productive connections between political and social theory, political economy, criminology, and sociology, it has fashioned a distinctive approach to political power. Among its hallmarks are a concern with the place of expertise within strategies of governance; the pivotal place of self-governance and subjectivity within modes of power; and an eschewal of grand theories of modernity in favour of a more empirical and, in a sense, more situated understanding of governance, understood at the level of various strategies, technologies, programmes, and techniques (Barry et al. 1996b: 4).

Given the keen interest in the political management of population these studies have shown, it is somewhat strange that they have paid little attention to the regulatory functions of borders. One objective of this chapter will be to explore some ways this particular oversight might be addressed.

But there is more at stake than simply extending the empirical scope of Foucauldian political sociology. My bigger claim is that this perspective offers a way to express the 'rarity' (Veyne 1997: 159), and hence raise the intelligibility, of current practices of border control. To pose the question of their rarity is to emphasize that however much we may have come to take political talk of 'border security' for granted, this term actually denotes a very particular and unique set of power relations. Foucault's studies of madness, crime, and sexuality have taught us how to think about power in terms of its 'dispositions, manoeuvres, tactics, techniques, functionings' (Foucault, cited in Deleuze 1988: 25). But what kinds of dispositions and functionings characterize the border today?

Foucauldian political sociology has stressed the polyvalence and multiplicity of power relations. This point bears emphasizing because of the way in which references to Foucault sometimes draw a rather narrow equation with discipline, surveillance, and, more often than not, the stark architectural figure of the panopticon. Yet a quick glance over Foucault's oeuvre, not to mention the countless studies that take up his hypotheses, reveals a strikingly rich and heterogeneous field. Studies of disciplinary power and surveillance are prominent, of course, but far from exhaustive. For we also find such themes as the ancient and modern ethics of the self, agonistic games of citizenship (Isin 2002), the governance of the social (Donzelot 1988), biopolitics (Foucault 1990), sovereignty (Butler 2004), authoritarianism and domination (Dean 2002; Hindess 2001), strategies of governing through risk (O'Malley 1996), crime (Simon 1997), and much else.

While recognizing that Foucauldian political sociology presents us with a complex landscape, in the space of this short chapter I cannot begin to think its possible implications through. Instead I shall confine my discussion to one particular analytic, or diagram, of power: that which Deleuze calls the 'society of control'. The following section offers a brief discussion of control. In the remaining sections I explore some of the ways in which control, understood as an analytic rather than a new type of society, can advance the project of a genealogy of borders and, more broadly, modern systems of power.

10.3 Control

If we can speak of a Foucauldian political sociology that is committed, as I have already suggested, to understanding power in terms of its multiple tactics and functionings, then Deleuze's idea of the control society surely deserves to be seen as an important contribution to such a project. In 'Postscript on Control Societies' Deleuze argues that a new kind of power is coming to define the social and political life of states and citizens in the course of the latter part of the twentieth century. This is a power, a diagram he calls 'control' (Deleuze 1995). The word itself is perhaps unfortunate, invoking as it does images of an Orwellian totally administered society.

While Deleuze certainly does not see the rise of control as a benign phenomenon, neither is it a situation of perfected domination. What, then, is control?

Deleuze theorizes control by comparing its logic, its topology, its assumptions, and its mechanisms to those of the 'disciplinary society' that it challenges and threatens to displace. Foucault associated disciplinary societies with the 18th and 19th centuries. He emphasized that discipline was reducible neither to a particular institution nor to a specific apparatus but rather was 'a type of power, a modality for its exercise comprising a whole set of instruments, techniques, procedures, levels of application, targets; it is a "physics" or an "anatomy" of power, a technology' (Foucault 1977: 215). While discipline would have different objectives and targets depending on its particular site of deployment, it does have more general properties and characteristics. It is oriented by concerns of demographics and economy. Discipline confronts the 'floating population' of eighteenth-century Europe. It is an 'anti-nomadic technique'; this is why it 'fixes, arrests or regulates movements; it clears up confusion; it dissipates compact groupings of individuals wandering about the country in unpredictable ways; it establishes calculated distributions' (Foucault 1977: 218–219).

Deleuze argues that today we are witnessing a generalized breakdown of disciplinary mechanisms. Disciplinary societies are gradually turning into control societies. Discipline involves a power that is concentrated in, if not contained by, sites of confinement. It deploys forms of authority that are exterior to the subject but seek to effect relationships of interiorization and disciplined self-governance within its targets. But in control societies power has become more fluid, less centred. We have gone from moulding to modulation. Now it operates in fluctuating networks of production and consumption. Power has become immanent to social orders that understand themselves as 'consumer societies', 'information societies', or 'risk societies'. According to one influential interpretation, 'mechanisms of command become ever more "democratic", ever more immanent to the social field, distributed throughout the brains and the bodies of the citizens' (Hardt and Negri 2000: 23). We are moving from an analog world in which the citizen circulates between such discrete sites as family, school, and work to a digital order in which the lines between inside and out become blurred, a social order where power is inseparable from mechanisms and circuits of desire which are actualized by systems of advertising, marketing, and self-actualization.

According to Deleuze, the control society can be characterized in terms of certain key transformations. I shall mention three of these since they will enable us to raise new questions about the nature of rebordering. First, there is the shift in the *spatiality of power*: from forms of governance which privilege particular institutional sites of enclosure to open networks of power which operate through variable combinations and productions of desire, lifestyle, anxiety, and fear, and which have the market as their paradigm. I have already discussed this point above and will return to it when exploring the displacement and delocalization of borders.

Second, there is a transformation in the dominant mechanisms and images of social order. If discipline nurtured the impossible dream of governing the state in the image of the well-ordered city (Foucault 1984), control privileges the figure of communication, finding in information technology and computers its 'machine' (Deleuze 1995: 180). Control societies implicate their constituent institutions and subjects in regimes of modulation and feedback. All fixed standards and norms are made to float. 'Money [...] best expresses the difference between the two types of society, since discipline was always related to currencies containing gold as a numerical standard, whereas control is based on floating exchange rates, modulations depending on a code setting sample percentages for various currencies' (Deleuze 1995: 180). Here we might add that modulation finds its expression at the level of politics and the state in the relatively new style and ethos of government which political scientists call 'governance', or what Jessop (1998: 42–43) qualifies as 'meta-governance': a form of political authority that takes as its strategic objective the 'organization of self-organization'.

Third, there is a shift in assumptions about the *subject of power*, concerning what we might call the subject effects of strategies of governance. One of the most distinctive features of Foucauldian political sociology is its ambition to combine an analytics of power and rule with a dynamic and historicized account of the subject. This is certainly evident in Deleuze, who argues that, whereas discipline set up a productive tension between masses and individuals, with control we witness a world of 'dividuals' whose context is not the mass or society but proliferating databases, samples, profiles, and markets.

Deleuze's notion of the dividual is not entirely clear. I want to give it two distinct but related meanings. First, the dividual signifies an apparent thinning-down, or even hollowing-out, of strategies of governance. Disciplinary power was all-embracing, extending itself across the entire social field. Its ambition was to govern *omnes et singulatim*. This meant the marginal elements of society could not be ignored but had to be reformed, moralized, and integrated. If the *individual* signifies a complete, whole person, the *dividual* is partial, fragmented, and incomplete. Control de-emphasizes, or even abandons, the quest to train, moralize, reform, and remake the individual. It relinquishes the dream of an all-encompassing, normalized society. It is less bothered with reforming young offenders than with securing the home or the shopping mall against their presence.

This does not mean that the society of control has abandoned projects of surveillance. On the contrary, surveillance is now '"designed in" to the flows of everyday existence' (Rose 1999: 234). That the tactics of surveillance have multiplied is captured nicely by Deleuze's reference to the technology of the password. Nothing captures the ethos of the control society better than the password, which can materialize in such forms as the credit card, the passport, the reward card, the identity card, and the electronic ankle tag. Even the body itself can operate as a password once imprinted by the indelible sign of the biometric (van der Ploeg 1999). Control resolves its subject matter into 'coded flows' (Diken and Lautsen 2002). If control societies resemble constellations of privatized consumption and information, circuits of desire, and lifestyle, these are networks whose every node is a potential gate or filter. Linked in a dynamic relationship to the database and the risk profile, the password distributes access and status. It constitutes privileged populations who enjoy the rewards of credit, mobility, and information. But at the same time it filters out, and constitutes a risky, excluded remainder.

This leads us to the second meaning of 'dividual', one that Nikolas Rose has clarified. Here the meaning of 'dividual' draws attention to control as a particular strategy of social division. The underside of the control society is the cumulative production of abject populations, those either abandoned or forcibly placed outside the circuits of consumption and lifestyle, deemed to inhabit 'forms of existence [that] are cast into a zone of shame, disgrace or debasement, rendered beyond the limits of the liveable, denied the warrant of tolerability, accorded purely a negative value' (Rose 1999: 253). These populations are excluded from but simultaneously included in the control society. They are included, for instance, every time that political passion cathects itself in the scandal of the 'welfare cheat' or business capitalizes on the labour of the undocumented and the non-citizen. Similarly, they are included whenever the image of these 'outsiders' forms the basis for the calculated mobilization of fear and loathing and, concomitantly, the marketing of ever more ingenious schemes of security, risk management, and societal insulation.

It is better to think of control as a 'diagram' (Deleuze 1988: 34–36) than as a form of society. Diagrams are necessarily abstract and serve to express 'something at work in many different institutions and situations, spread out in several countries, working in a manner not given in the map of social policies and prescriptions, planned as such by no one' (Rajchman 1999: 47). Just as there are multiple ways to diagram a city, so we leave open the possibility of other, equally valid ways of diagramming the present. These include diagrams that point to the revival of older, seemingly archaic forms of power and domination—such as the contemporary phenomenon of indefinite detention (Butler 2004)—which do not accord readily with the idea of control and its image of open, fluid, decentred power relations.

10.4 New Spaces of Border Control

How might this thematization of control illuminate the event of rebordering? Let us first consider the changing topography of the border. In his recent study of the political imagination of the modern state Mark Neocleous notes how the word 'frontier' (*frontière*) originally referred to the façade of a building or the front line of the army. Sometime in the sixteenth century it 'came to mean the boundaries or borders of a particular space and has been associated with state borders ever since' (Neocleous 2003: 99). This is the modern idea of the border: a continuous line demarcating the territory and sovereign authority of the state, enclosing its domain. It corresponds most closely with the historical spatiality of political power which Agnew calls 'field of forces', a geopolitical world of 'rigidly defined territorial units in which each state can gain power only at the expense of the others and each has total control over its own territory' (Agnew 1999: 504). If discipline imagined the state as a city state writ large, then the frontier was its wall.

However, a series of investigations suggest that today we are witnessing a 'delocalization' of the border. If policing and control functions were previously concentrated in this special place, it is argued, currently there is a disaggregation of border functions away from the border (Bigo 2002: 77; Salter 2004: 76). Delocalization has become evident in the case of the United States as part of its government's ongoing campaign against global terrorism. For instance, under the Enhanced Border Security and Visa Entry Reform Act of 2002 greater effort is made to schedule policing and identification functions well before the traveller arrives at the border but also, in certain cases, after they arrive on American soil (Salter 2004: 76). With regard to the EU, Lahav and Guiraudon (2000) point to a cluster of not dissimilar tendencies they call 'remote control'. Remote control, they aver, involves a double displacement in that it moves the locus of control activities away from the geographical borders of the territory and, in cases where functions are delegated to private companies, beyond the formal apparatus of the state.

It is probably fair to say that remote control has become an intrinsic feature of the way in which states and other international agencies imagine and pursue border control. It is written into the conceptual architecture of Europe's Schengen Agreement and, in different ways, the American idea of homeland security. One of the more prominent and in some cases controversial instruments of remote control today is carrier sanctions (Guiraudon 2003: 201–206; IRU 2001). This policy is worth considering briefly since it illustrates quite vividly certain trajectories that are remaking the topography of border control.

Few governments can have used carrier sanctions more vigorously than that of the UK. Under the UK's carrier liability laws private transporters—principally airlines, railway, and shipping companies, and road hauliers—can be fined up to £2,000 for each improperly documented passenger they transport into the national territory. To mitigate their exposure to such financial penalties, and with technical assistance from public and private security experts, the carriers now implement systematic measures to police migrants. In this way carrier sanctions have played a part in turning the check-in desks of airlines and even travel agencies into semi-formal spaces of migration control, a development that threatens to erode the integrity of refugee rights (Gilboy 1997; ECRE 1999).

The case of road haulage is particularly interesting in this regard. If it is the case that cross-border trucking had recently emerged as a key pathway for clandestine migrants and refugees seeking to enter the UK from continental Europe, then carrier sanctions have sought to turn the truck and its entire routeway into a dispersed, mobile border. With trucking, the locus of control is not with the verification of identity, as it is with air travel, but with the prevention of clandestine movements and the detection of hidden bodies. To this end, the UK Home Office now provides companies and their staff with detailed instructions on what we might call the 'securitization' of the truck and its milieu (UK Home Office 2004). The very surface of the truck is to be made impermeable to unauthorized entry; the outer fabric on the vehicle is to be suitably resistant to cutting open; all external storage compartments are to be secured with seals and padlocks; drivers and their supervisors are to be trained in the responsibilities and procedures of regularly inspecting their own vehicles, especially when stopping en route at petrol stations and restaurants. Similarly, scanners and carbon dioxide detectors are to be used to mechanically see and smell every recess within the vehicle.

We can say that with road haulage we have moved beyond even the situation where the UK relocates its borders to the desks of its overseas embassies and consulates where visas are issued, or to the check-in areas of airports in distant countries. Once applied to road haulage, the entire road transportation system becomes a kind of networked border. The border transforms into a mobile, non-contiguous zone materializing at the very surface of the truck and in every place it stops. If the 1980s saw Europe's routeways identified and re-imagined as one of its foremost Trans-European Networks—an instrument to positively integrate Europe along new spatial and social axes (Barry 1996)—then carrier sanctions, and the many little practices this policy insinuates into the everyday conduct of transportation and commerce, aspire to project a regime of surveillance into the very capillaries of these same networks. The project becomes one of the Trans-European Networks of control.

It would be misleading to consider remote control as a recent invention. Aristide Zolberg dates the emergence of remote control to 1924, when, in response to the perception of uncontrolled immigration from Europe and human chaos at its great ports, the U.S. federal government put in place a system requiring 'all foreign nationals coming from overseas to produce an entry visa prior to boarding a U.S.-bound vessel' (Zolberg 1999: 75–76). Similarly, it would be a mistake to see remote control as though it were the expression of some kind of social or technological logic, as though the border were simply one more setting where the inexorable tendency of the control society works itself out. Lahav and Guiraudon (2000) point to an interplay of quite specific political logics that underpin the spread of remote control today. These include a desire on the part of Western governments to intercept refugees before they have an opportunity to activate human-rights claims within the territory. But they also include a concern to decongest border crossings in the interests of further liberalizing and accelerating circuits of transnational tourism, trade, and production.

In short, we should not interpret the control society as the *cause* of the various practices and processes associated with remote control, so much as an account of the terrain on which border control is being effected. It takes us beyond the recognition of the 'securitization' of borders and other spaces, and towards a more precise account of the particular forms and practices that enact security. Like discipline, control is a technology that is capable of materializing at different sites and levels. When governments try to find ways to insulate their territories from unwanted population flows, or ways to reconcile the quest for security with openness to cross-border economic activity, the solution has to come from somewhere. In a sense it comes from *else*where. What is useful about the idea of control is that it theorizes the form, the matter, the diagram of the response. This should become clearer when we consider border control as dividualization.

10.5 The Subjects of Border Control

If in certain (but by no means all) respects border controls are becoming more dispersed, what kinds of subjects do they presuppose? Consider the following two cases, drawn from the lively interdisciplinary field of border studies. Matthew Sparke (2004) has written an illuminating little history of the problematization of border crossing in the heavily urbanized region between Vancouver and Seattle, on the Pacific coast of North America. He recounts how local business elites successfully lobbied the U.S. and Canadian governments to implement an expedited border crossing lane for vehicles in the early 1990s—PACE on the U.S. side and a reciprocal CANPASS for Canadians. Under PACE, for a small fee pre-screened applicants received a decal for their cars authorizing them for expedited border crossing in the so-called PACE (fast) lane. PACE was justified by various arguments to the effect that it would promote cross-border trade, tourism, and even a pan-regional, Cascadian identity. From the perspective of the border guards it was consistent with the objective of distinguishing primary (safe) and secondary travellers.

However, PACE was to experience various political and logistical difficulties. In July 2002 the old PACE lane was replaced by a new scheme, NEXUS. Presented as a response to the 'new security environment', the unveiling of NEXUS was mediated by a new rhetoric. This rhetoric emphasizes the need to reconcile freedom and trade with heightened 'security' or, as the slogan appended to the US-VISIT scheme puts it: 'Keeping America's doors open and our nation secure.' Like PACE, NEXUS seeks to sort pre-screened and self-identified travellers into high-risk and low-risk groups, combining this function with a commitment to expediting the mobility of the latter. But reflecting the new security consciousness, NEXUS incorporates new technologies of control to meet this end. These include a photo-ID and biometric 'proximity card' which relays passenger data from the approaching car to the border authority's computer screen.

In a study of what she calls the 'technological frontiers' of the EU Ginette Verstraete (2001) focuses on the Belgian harbour of Zeebrugge and its joint venture with DielectroKinetic Laboratories (DKL), a U.S. company which markets itself as an authority in 'the Science of Saving Lives'. For most of 1999 the harbour used DKL's most important product, LifeGuard, to assist in the detection of clandestine migrants hiding in trailers. LifeGuard is a remote-sensing device which detects the ultra-low frequency signals of a beating heart's electromagnetic field. This technology was first developed by U.S. military engineers, and came to be used by law enforcement agencies in searching buildings for criminals and in emergency rescue operations. But in Zeebrugge it was used by a private security agency contracted by the port to detect and assist in the removal of refugees and unauthorized migrants hiding in trucks and containers destined for Britain—'"the science of saving lives" became the science of removing them' (Verstraete 2001: 26).

The circumstances under which Zeebrugge formed this commercial and logistical alliance with DKL are quite telling. Zeebrugge was endeavouring to market itself as the preeminent node of transit in the automobile industry, a status it would eventually lose to the Dutch port of Vlissingen. Large numbers of migrants hiding in trucks and containers were posing a significant cost for companies such as Ford and Vauxhall, so that Zeebrugge was under considerable commercial pressure to provide improved security for its clients. At the same time DKL sought to capitalize the possibility of an emerging market in detecting and removing 'illegals' once it became clear there was commercial demand to use its technology in this way.

These are but two short border histories among the many thousands that could no doubt be written for different places, each with their peculiar and unique circumstances. Yet they serve to illustrate certain points I wish to make concerning the way in which particular kinds of subjects are positioned at the border. To begin with, they suggest that today borders operate like filters or gateways. Not borders as Iron Curtains or Maginot Lines but more like firewalls differentiating the good and the bad, the useful and the dangerous, the licit and the illicit; constituting a safe, 'high-trust' interior secured from the wild zones outside; immobilizing and removing the risky elements so as to speed up the circulation of the rest. It might be objected that borders have always served this function. True, but borders did other things besides. Perhaps this sorting function is becoming far more central to the practice of the border than it ever has been. I shall return to this point shortly.

What I find especially interesting is the particular sociotechnical arrangement through which this function of sorting humans and things is sought. Discipline was an assemblage combining certain architectures, expertise, norms, and practices such as training and panoptic surveillance. If control is an assemblage, it is one that combines concepts (e.g. risk), materials which it comprehends as flow, scanners, codes, passwords, security professionals, gateways, and databases. Like discipline, it is a highly mobile, flexible technology capable of materializing in different sites. The port/harbour, the airport, the shopping mall, the city centre, the office building are all quite different functional locales. But inasmuch as each faces certain commercial and public pressures to bring 'security' to its premises and users, to differentiate and manage dense movements of population, each thinks its solutions within the coordinates of these methods and technologies. Within this milieu security becomes something to be marketed—a 'solution'. The technology of discipline placed the school, the prison, the workhouse in a certain series which Foucault called the 'carceral archipelago' (Foucault 1977). It is important to recognize how the border belongs to its own series. Of course, the border remains a special place, its difference marked out in law, history, and geography, and sanctified by rituals of sovereignty. Yet there is a sense in which for many people today the experience of crossing the border is not unlike entering a large corporate building, government ministry, university library, gated residence, or computer network. In each case the subject is scanned, identified, and profiled. A database is accessed, a record created. An entry occurs, or perhaps access is denied. Such is the changing *texture* of borders.

Second, there is a point about the changing ends, and not just the means of surveillance. Some might see developments like NEXUS or DKL simply as further steps towards a panoptical society. But it is important to consider the ways in which these interventions diverge from the formula of discipline. My point is that discipline and the panopticon are specific technologies pertaining to particular historical and social contexts. Consider that NEXUS and DKL are not in the business of individualization, at least not in the sense that they encourage subjects to govern themselves as 'individuals'. In many ways they are less deep, governing persons rather like baggage, mail, or, in the case of LifeGuard, living matter. This is not to suggest that dividualization bears no relationship to practices and processes of identity. As NEXUS suggests, its version of dividualization is continuous with the culture of the reward card, of gold- and platinum-coded club memberships, and their associated 'lifestyle' of mobility and access. By contrast, LifeGuard is legitimated by the idea of 'asylum seekers' and 'illegals' as the new kind of wandering, dangerous classes. But in both cases, as a technology, control expresses little interest in shaping the identity, moulding the subjectivity of its targets—it has got no time for that.

I have argued that today the border governs us as dividuals, with all that that implies in terms of techniques, identities, practices, and power relations. This will no doubt draw the objection: 'So what's new; hasn't this always been a function of borders?' True, the border has served other ends, such as demarcating the sovereign's domain and the limits of the territory. But have the borders not always been in the business of distinguishing the wanted from the unwanted, the safe from the dangerous, the national from the foreigner—at least since the early twentieth century, when passports became the norm and borders became systematic instruments of population management (Salter 2003; Sassen 1999)?

Here we have to emphasize that the border is a multiplicity. It is certainly true that in some minimal sense borders have long been dedicated to the sorting, dividing, and separating of mobilities. But they have had other functions and purposes overlaid; they have formed other machinic connections. Consider, for example, the case of the great countries of immigration and colonial settlement, such as Canada, Australia, the United States, Argentina. By the start of the twentieth century it was clear that, at least in these cases, the border was not just, or even primarily, a gateway into the national territory but into a (regional or national) *society*. Perhaps this is why Ellis Island and Nova Scotia's Pier 21 have taken their place alongside Checkpoint Charlie in what is evidently a thriving border control museum complex, and why The Rocks in Sydney is now a place of tourism and national heritage. If Ellis Island and Pier 21 have become museums, it is because they speak to a time that has passed. If these and other zones of arrival have acquired iconic status, it is not just because of the genius of the marketing industries. It is because they functioned not just as gateways into the territory but also as points of arrival, reception, and integration. Flows of migrants did not simply pass through. There were spaces where public authorities checked the health and social condition of immigrants (Bernard 1998). But at the same time these border sites were linked to public and private networks for arranging travel into the interior, as well as employment, housing, and distribution. There was a real sense in which the edges of the American and Canadian societies and territories coincided in these unique places.

No doubt many of these social-processing functions are still undertaken in international airports today, but far less conspicuously. Nevertheless, the function of receiving the migrant does not define the identity of the airport in the way it once marked the seaport, for the technology and social context of the border has changed. The more that ports resemble nodes moving people in a global network (Heyman 2004); the more that the status of 'immigrant' is officially conferred not upon entering the territory but sometimes only years after arriving in a new land[1]; the more that international travel becomes an everyday experience and not a life-defining event—the more all these things obtain, the less the border appears as a threshold or gateway into a nation/society, and the more it appears as just one among many sorting and switching points. It becomes a node within a wider, albeit thinner, social space. The territorial and the social no longer coincide as neatly as we imagine they once did. Perhaps this is the condition to which Balibar alludes when he notes the 'ubiquity of borders', a condition in which, far from disappearing, borders proliferate, becoming 'a grid ranging over the new social space' rather than a line separating it from the outside (Balibar 2002: 84–85).

10.6 Conclusion

Deleuze argues that it is not difficult to detect a certain 'correspondence between any society and some kind of machine'—as long as we do not see those machines as in any way determining everything about those societies. Control societies 'function with a third generation of machines, with information technology and computers, where the passive danger is noise and the active, piracy and viral contamination' (Deleuze 1995: 180).

In this vein, let us conclude with the observation that border control today is a bit like antivirus software. This is not just because of a desire to filter flows and secure an interior. Nor is it just because the antiviral is not a static device but a dynamic game: no sooner is one border crossing updated, one smuggling route closed down, than another is opening up. It is also because border control today is, as much as anything, a commodity. While this chapter did not thematize relationships between border control and transformations in capitalism, that is surely a zone of relations that has been insufficiently studied. Borders and capitalism, then, is a new research frontier destined to unfold very quickly.

Acknowledgement This chapter originally appeared in the *European Journal of Social Theory*, 9(2), 187–203, 2006. I am grateful to the publishers for permission to reproduce it here. This is a somewhat shortened version. Apart from that, and some minor editing, I have changed only the Introduction and the Conclusion. In the 10 years since I first wrote 'Border/Control' an entire field of critical border studies has matured, greatly advancing our knowledge of a number of the themes addressed here. However, I have resisted the temptation to update my sources. Instead I hope this

[1] For instance, 'in FY 2000, 52 % of immigrants were already in the [U.S.] when their visas became available. This means that being admitted as an immigrant does not equate with traveling to the United States to begin a new life, as was true in the nineteenth century' (Martin 2004: 53, 55). On the decoupling of 'immigration control' and 'border control', see Crowley (2003: 33–34) and Bigo (2000).

chapter can have as one of its functions to show where a certain version of Foucauldian political sociology was at when critical border studies was in its infancy.

References

Adey, P. (2004). Secured and sorted mobilities: Examples from the airport. *Surveillance & Society, 1*(4), 500–519.

Agnew, J. (1999). Mapping political power beyond state boundaries: Territory, identity, and movement in world politics. *Millennium: Journal of International Studies, 28*(3), 499–521. doi:10.1177/03058298990280030701.

Andreas, P. (2003). Redrawing the line: Borders and security in the twenty-first century. *International Security, 28*(2), 78–111. doi:10.1162/016228803322761973.

Andreas, P., & Biersteker, T. J. (Eds.). (2003). *The rebordering of North America*. New York/London: Routledge.

Andreas, P., & Snyder, T. (Eds.). (2000). *The wall around the west: State borders and immigration controls in North America and Europe*. Lanham: Rowman & Littlefield.

Balibar, É. (2002). *Politics and the other scene*. London/New York: Verso.

Barry, A. (1996). The European network. *New Formations, 29*, 26–37.

Barry, A., Osborne, T., & Rose, N. (Eds.). (1996a). *Foucault and political reason: Liberalism, neo-liberalism and rationalities of government*. Chicago: University of Chicago Press.

Barry, A., Osborne, T., & Rose, N. S. (1996b). Introduction. In A. Barry, T. Osborne, & N. S. Rose (Eds.), *Foucault and political reason: Liberalism, neo-liberalism and rationalities of government* (pp. 1–18). Chicago: University of Chicago Press.

Bernard, W. S. (1998). Immigration: History of U.S. policy. In D. Jacobson (Ed.), *The immigration reader: America in a multidisciplinary perspective* (pp. 48–71). Malden/Oxford: Blackwell Publishers.

Bigo, D. (2000). When two become one: Internal and external securitisations in Europe. In M. Kelstrup & M. C. Williams (Eds.), *International relations theory and the politics of European integration* (pp. 171–204). London/New York: Routledge.

Bigo, D. (2002). Security and immigration: Toward a critique of the governmentality of unease. *Alternatives: Global, Local, Political, 27*(1), 63–92. doi:10.1177/03043754020270S105.

Burchell, G., Gordon, C., & Miller, P. (Eds.). (1991). *The Foucault effect: Studies in governmentality*. Chicago: University of Chicago Press.

Butler, J. (2004). *Precarious life: The powers of mourning and violence*. London/New York: Verso.

Crowley, J. (2003). Locating Europe. In K. Groenendijk, E. Guild, & P. Minderhoud (Eds.), *Search of Europe's borders* (pp. 27–44). The Hague: Kluwer Law International.

Dean, M. (1999). *Governmentality: Power and rule in modern society*. London/Thousand Oaks/New Delhi: SAGE.

Dean, M. (2002). Liberal government and authoritarianism. *Economy and Society, 31*(1), 37–61. doi:10.1080/03085140120109240.

Deleuze, G. (1988). *Foucault*. Minneapolis: University of Minnesota Press.

Deleuze, G. (1995). Postscript on control societies. In G. Deleuze (Ed.), *Negotiations 1972–1990* (pp. 177–182). New York: Columbia University Press.

Diken, B., & Lautsen, C. B. (2002). Zones of indistinction: Security, terror, and bare life. *Space and Culture, 5*(3), 290–307. doi:10.1177/1206331202005003009.

Donzelot, J. (1988). The promotion of the social. *Economy and Society, 17*(3), 395–427. doi:10.1080/03085148800000016.

ECRE. (1999). *Carriers' liability: Country up-date on the application of carriers' liability in European states*. Brussels: European Council on Refugees and Exiles. http://www.refworld.org/docid/3c02740b4.html

Foucault, M. (1977). *Discipline and Punish: The birth of the prison* (A. Sheridan, Trans.). London: A. Lane.
Foucault, M. (1984). Space, knowledge, and power. In P. Rabinow (Ed.), *The Foucault reader* (pp. 239–256). New York: Pantheon.
Foucault, M. (1990). *The history of sexuality: Volume one*. New York: Vintage.
Foucault, M. (1991). Questions of method. In G. Burchell, C. Gordon, & P. Miller (Eds.), *The Foucault effect: Studies in governmentality* (pp. 73–86). Chicago: University of Chicago Press.
Gilboy, J. A. (1997). Implications of "third-party" involvement in enforcement: The INS, illegal travelers, and international airlines. *Law & Society Review, 31*(3), 505–530. doi:10.2307/3054044.
Guiraudon, V. (2003). Before the EU border: Remote control of the "huddled masses". In K. Groenendijk, E. Guild, & P. Minderhoud (Eds.), *Search of Europe's borders* (pp. 191–214). The Hague: Kluwer Law International.
Hardt, M., & Negri, A. (2000). *Empire*. Cambridge: Harvard University Press.
Heyman, J. M. C. (2004). Ports of entry as nodes in the world system. *Identities: Global Studies in Culture and Power, 11*(3), 303–327. doi:10.1080/10702890490493518.
Hindess, B. (2001). The liberal government of unfreedom. *Alternatives: Global, Local, Political, 26*(2), 93–111. doi:10.1177/030437540102600201.
Huysmans, J. (1995). Migrants as a security problem: Dangers of 'securitizing' societal issues. In R. Miles & D. Thränhardt (Eds.), *Migration and European integration: Dynamics of inclusion and exclusion* (pp. 53–72). London: Pinter Publishers.
IRU. (2001). *Round table on carriers' liability related to illegal immigration: Brussels, 30 November 2001*. Geneva: International Road Transport Union. http://www.iru.org/cms-filesystem-action?file=en_events_2001/Illegal2001.pdf
Isin, E. E. (2002). *Being political: Genealogies of citizenship*. Minneapolis: University of Minnesota Press.
Jessop, B. (1998). The rise of governance and the risks of failure: The case of economic development. *International Social Science Journal, 50*(155), 29–45. doi:10.1111/1468-2451.00107.
Lahav, G., & Guiraudon, V. (2000). Comparative perspectives on border control: Away from the border and outside the state. In P. Andreas & T. Snyder (Eds.), *The wall around the west: State borders and immigration controls in North America and Europe* (pp. 55–77). Lanham: Rowman & Littlefield.
Martin, P. L. (2004). The United States: The continuing immigration debate. In W. A. Cornelius, T. Takeyuki, P. Martin, & J. Hollifield (Eds.), *Controlling immigration: A global perspective* (pp. 51–85). Stanford: Stanford University Press.
Neocleous, M. (2003). *Imagining the state*. Maidenhead: Open University Press.
O'Malley, P. (1996). Risk and responsibility. In A. Barry, T. Osborne, & N. Rose (Eds.), *Foucault and political reason: Liberalism, neo-liberalism and rationalities of government* (pp. 189–208). Chicago: University of Chicago Press.
Rajchman, J. (1999). Diagram and diagnosis. In E. Grosz (Ed.), *Becomings: Explorations in time, memory, and futures* (pp. 42–54). Ithaca: Cornell University Press.
Rose, N. (1999). *Powers of freedom: Reframing political thought*. Cambridge/New York/ Melbourne: Cambridge University Press.
Salter, M. B. (2003). *Rights of passage: The passport in international relations*. Boulder: Lynne Rienner Publishers.
Salter, M. B. (2004). Passports, mobility, and security: How smart can the border be? *International Studies Perspectives, 5*(1), 71–91. doi:10.1111/j.1528-3577.2004.00158.x.
Sassen, S. (1999). *Guests and aliens*. New York: The New Press.
Simon, J. (1997). Governing through crime. In L. Friedman & G. Fisher (Eds.), *The crime conundrum: Essays on criminal justice* (pp. 171–184). Boulder: Westview Press.
Sparke, M. (2004). Belonging in the PACE lane: Fast border crossing and citizenship in the age of neoliberalism. In J. S. Migdal (Ed.), *Boundaries and belonging: States and societies in the struggle to shape identities and local practices* (pp. 251–283). Cambridge: Cambridge University Press.

UK Home Office (2004) Civil Penalty: Prevention of Clandestine Entrants. Vehicles. London: The Stationery Office. http://www.ebnlimited.co.uk/pdf/codeofpractice.pdf

Van der Ploeg, I. (1999). The illegal body: 'Eurodac' and the politics of biometric identification. *Ethics and Information Technology, 1*(4), 295–302. doi:10.1023/A:1010064613240.

Verstraete, G. (2001). Technological frontiers and the politics of mobilities. *New Formations, 43*, 26–43.

Veyne, P. (1997). Foucault revolutionizes history. In A. I. Davidson (Ed.), *Foucault and his interlocutors* (pp. 146–182). Chicago: University of Chicago Press.

Zolberg, A. R. (1999). Matters of state: Theorizing immigration policy. In C. Hirschman, P. Kasinitz, & J. DeWind (Eds.), *The handbook of international migration: The American experience* (pp. 71–93). New York: Russell Sage.

Chapter 11
Social Transformation, Subjectification, and Labour Migration: Theorizing the Heterogeneity of Migration Flows in the Current Italian Crisis

Gabriele Tomei

Contemporary social relations do offer great diversity, but it is diversity within increasingly universal relationships of power and inequality.

Castles (2010: 1575)

11.1 Introduction[1]

Using the example of Italy, this chapter focuses on the links and interdependencies between post-Fordist globalization and current migration flows and projects in Southern Europe. For many years it has been quite common in Italy, Greece, and Spain to find young Eritrean or Latin American girls working as housekeepers; women from Ukraine or Romania taking care of elderly members of upper- and middle-class families; and young men from Eastern Europe or North Africa working in agriculture or in the building sector. At the same time, the sons and daughters of the native middle class have generally avoided housekeeping, care taking, and other ancillary and low-status jobs, looking for better job opportunities.

Accordingly, the Italian labour market was highly segmented between a sector with rather high standards of employment protection (including protection from dismissal) and a big sector with largely temporary jobs. Before the recent economic crisis the opportunities in this segmented labour market tended to be distributed on the basis of class and nationality.

Beginning in the 1990s and especially following the economic crises since 2007, this constellation began to change. The countries of Southern Europe have been faced with a new and unexpected period of economic recession. On the one hand,

[1]A previous version of this chapter was presented at the 11th Conference of the European Sociological Association, Turin, August 28–31, 2013.

G. Tomei (✉)
Dipartimento di Scienze Politiche, Università di Pisa, Pisa, Italy
e-mail: gabriele.tomei@unipi.it

A. Amelina et al. (eds.), *An Anthology of Migration and Social Transformation*, IMISCOE Research Series, DOI 10.1007/978-3-319-23666-7_11

these countries have experienced considerable contraction of the regular (constant) labour markets and, consequently, a massive exclusion of many actual or potential workers from employment opportunities; on the other hand, the dismantling of many economic sectors and the expansion of the irregular and informal economy have led to 'social dumping' as a way to compensate for national industrial weaknesses. Although there continue to be migrant housekeepers, caretakers, and lower-class factory workers, almost all of them no longer have regular labour contracts, few have a regular permission to stay, and the majority must compete daily with an increasing number of native unemployed people claiming the same dirty, dangerous, and demanding jobs in some sectors of the labour market (i.e. construction). The careers of native middle-class sons and daughters have become more and more precarious, and today they must choose between lowering their expectations (i.e. accepting temporary contracts for less desirable jobs) or trying to meet their original aspirations by leaving their own countries (i.e. interpreting migration as their only option for achieving social mobility).

In the following, I argue for a specific theoretical perspective on these recent developments. The chapter hence does not present findings from a specific empirical study, but rather reads current developments through an analytical lens that is informed by Foucault's work on biopolitics (1978, 2008), on the one hand, and Emirbayer and Mische's (1998) conceptualization of agency. Section 11.2 discusses the paradigm of 'social transformation' (Castles 2001, 2010) to explain how developments in international migration are part of the same structural and long-term processes that lead to the worldwide division and displacement of manual as well as intellectual workforces, such as trends in the international flow of capital investments. This social transformation perspective provides a middle-range theoretical basis that enlightens both the historical-structural context in which recent migration flows are embedded and the reasons for their new heterogeneity in the post-2007 crisis in southern Europe.

Section 11.3 introduces Foucault's concept of 'biopolitics' (Foucault 1978, 2008) as a means to explore how the current global division of labour produces a specific system of knowledge that orients migrants' decisions and destinations and influences their personal beliefs and desires. In addition, Sect. 11.3 discusses some of the shortcomings of Foucault's framework experiments in explaining the process of migrants' subjectification.

Against this background, Sect. 11.4 then proposes one way to address these issues, starting from a specific concept of agency (Emirbayer and Mische 1998). This conceptual framework urges us to identify the main *keywords* that act as symbolic and moral devices for migrants.

Section 11.5 analyses the situation in Italy, arguing that the arrival of new immigrants and the departure of young native professionals during the post-2007 crisis have been two interdependent processes that must be interpreted in light of biopolitical migration management.

In essence, this chapter shows that social transformation affects the lives of old as well as new migrants, orienting the *keywords* of their mobility according to the tasks needed for global development. I propose to focus on these keywords of migrants' experiences as an analytical tool for a "biopolitical" theorization of how economic structures and personal decisions are intertwined; they are elements of the same type of knowledge – informing public discourse and administrative devices alike – that challenge migrant subjectivity into an entrepreneurial direction.

11.2 Social Transformation and Mobility

Paraphrasing Polanyi's definition of the 'great transformation' as the socioeconomic process that transformed Western economies in the nineteenth and twentieth centuries, Castles argues that globalization must be considered the new 'social transformation' because it has affected and radically modified the patterns of global development over the past two decades (Castles 2001). Castles notes that 'social transformation can be defined as a fundamental shift in the way society is organized that goes beyond the continual processes of incremental social change that are always at work. This implies a "step-change" in which all existing social patterns are questioned and many are reconfigured. Social transformations are closely linked to major shifts in dominant economic, political and strategic relationships' (Castles 2010: 1576).

After the Cold War era, the process of globalization significantly dismantled the existing economic and institutional systems. A radical shift occurred in the global geography of capital investments (Hirst and Thompson 1996) and in the international stratification of labour forces (Sassen 1998; Cohen 2006), moving financial and human resources from manufacturing industries to finance and high-technology sectors (Fumagalli 2007), deregulating the economy and the labour market, and improving the informal sector in the developed northern regions of Europe (Castles 2010; Reyneri 2003).

To provide the necessary workforce to meet the requirements of the changing economic dynamics, global markets selected people to migrate in the needed direction, producing new avenues of international mobility and stratification. Women in the lower socioeconomic classes moved to fill jobs in the domestic labour market, while the better-educated and well-to-do were recruited for more desirable, higher-paying jobs; people from the southern regions of Europe have been brought into the more demanding, labour-intensive sectors, and migrants who work intermittently have been drawn to less formal or even illegal occupations. According to Castles, all these examples suggest that we conceptualize 'migration not merely as a result of social transformation, nor as one of its causes, but as an integral and essential part of social transformation processes' (Castles 2010: 1578).

The new migratory flows that emerged into, from, and among the Southern European territories after the 2007 crisis may accordingly be seen as resulting from an interdependence between mobility and economic development. To understand this connection and shed light on the drivers of these new and heterogeneous dynamics, we must consider what is meant by 'social transformation'. One view might be to go beyond the possible deterministic interpretations of 'transformation' to analyse how economic globalization influences people's lives from the inside in terms of the cognitive and moral contexts that affect their agency in negotiating with and adapting to global economic needs (Tomei 2014).

11.3 Biopolitics and Subjectification in Migrants' Experience

The biopolitical approach offers an interesting perspective for an analysis of recent migrant flows in Europe, specifically in Italy. In the last several decades Foucault's reflections on 'power' have proved to be among the most enlightening and intriguing contributions to the study of this subject. Foucault contested the idea that 'structural constraints' are completely external and suggested that there is a need for theoretical investigation to focus attention more on the role of agency.[2] Foucault specifically argued that power does not have a transcendental status and does not drive people through external prescriptions and punishments, because it acts through 'a multiplicity of force relations immanent in the sphere in which they operate and which constitute their own organization' (Foucault 1978: 82).

Following this rationale, the power of economic globalization operates in an intentional but non-subjective way: problems and constraints are dealt with through a multitude of political, social, and economic agents, convincing people to comply with these solutions in order to be recognized as individuals who share the new rationale of economic calculation.

In Foucault's theorizing power is closely linked to knowledge that involves the individual and that individual's will in a discourse about the real nature and dynamics of people's lives. According to Foucault, 'one would have to speak of biopolitics to designate what brought life and its mechanisms into the realm of explicit calculations and made knowledge-power an agent of transformation of human life' (Foucault 1978: 126).

Human mobility provides an interesting opportunity to examine how these dynamics work (Geiger in Chap. 9 and Walters in Chap. 10 do demonstrate it). Recent studies discuss the interdependence of migration, power, and structural transformations in both the ascending and the declining phases of economic cycles (Raghuram 2009; Bailey 2013). From a Foucauldian perspective, the international mobility of the workforce also represents the result and the leverage of a form of knowledge that emphasizes 'growth', 'innovation', 'entrepreneurship', and 'mobility' as the four strategic keywords of personal compliance with market dynamics and capital needs. Under the discursive umbrella of 'neoliberalism' this specific form of knowledge-power forces migrants to face their public image as individuals who should act as personal investors and entrepreneurs in the global labour market (Foucault 2008: 190–191, 196). Even if never perfectly and completely, these processes affect their perceptions, sense-making and practices – with different out-

[2] For an overview of the most relevant contributions using a structure–agency approach in migration studies, see Bakewell (2010) and Tomei (2014).

comes depending on personal and collective capability for resistance (as discussed by Olivieri in Chap. 17).[3]

Biopolitics is the logic of governance that orients people's lives instead of controlling them from the outside. By means of devices and keywords embedded in public discourse, it contributes to mould people in line with requirements of the social-transformation agenda. In this sense the manner of such compliance and the forms it takes are not external but emerge as a constitutive process of the individuals in the form of their subjectification.

11.4 Keywords of Compliant Migration

Why is agency flexible enough to internalize generally the biopolitical orientations linked to the dominant political and economic patterns? On what is compliance with structural tasks based?

Unfortunately Foucault did not develop a theory of agency that could shed light on how, under what conditions, and why the knowledge- power of globalization influences and transforms migrants' cognitive and moral beliefs. This omission narrows the use of Foucault's framework for explaining processes of migrant subjectification.

One way to address this issue is by conceptualizing agency building on a phenomenological approach, according to which, the temporal-relational nature of subjectivity can shed some light on the capacity of the conscience to produce and make sense of its own will through its discursive relationship with the flow of time. Coming back to our main questions, this approach could unveil both the mechanisms through which public discourses may anchor a neo-liberal agenda in migrants' self-understanding and the ways in which they comply or resist to this very constellation.

A useful entry point for such an analysis is the recent debate on the stratified nature of agency. Emirbayer and Mische (1998) note that agency can be understood as the outcome of actualizing one's personal experience of time based on relevant systems that are relationally constructed. The specific ways in which people remember and make sense of past events and share meanings in the present, as well as the ways they imagine, talk about, negotiate, and make commitments to their future, 'influence their degree of freedom and manoeuvrability in relation to the existing structures' (Emirbayer and Mische 1998: 985).

According to this approach, three mechanisms can be said to reveal how time and consciousness matter when defining how present agency competence produces meanings that influence individual and collective actions. The first of these mecha-

[3] Compliance does not impede recognition of an irreducibility and critical resistance of the agency despite of its exposure to biopolitical exploitation. This point has been discussed in depth in the last few years by some critical post-Foucauldian thinkers. One of the main contributions on the topic is the work of Antonio Negri and Michael Hardt (2000, 2004, 2009).

nisms is *iteration*, that is, 'the selective reactivation by actors of past patterns of thought and action, as routinely incorporated in practical activity, thereby giving stability and order to social universes and helping to sustain identities, interactions, and institutions over time.' The second mechanism is *projectivity* (or imagination), which encompasses 'the imaginative generation by actors of possible future trajectories of action, in which received structures of thought and action may be creatively reconfigured in relation to actors' hopes, fears, and desires for the future'. The third mechanism is *practical evaluation*, which involves 'the capacity of actors to make practical and normative judgements among alternative possible trajectories of action in response to the emerging demands, dilemmas, and ambiguities of presently evolving situations' (Emirbayer and Mische 1998: 971).

The biopolitical regime of economic calculation animates migrants to behave, and even define themselves, as personal investors and entrepreneurs. This moulding of migrants' subjectivity operates through the three mechanisms identified by Emirbayer and Mische that re-define the strategic keywords that inform the cognitive, moral, and emotional orientation of migrants' practices.

The 'iteration' mechanism is centred on the new keyword of *responsibility*, which represents the way the migrants are asked to express their sense of belonging to their community via monetary remittances and periodic return visits, maintaining their self-representation as members (Carling 2008). That attitude operates as an orienting keyword for promoting the social-investment strategy of migrants as a way to minimize the risk of being excluded from their social networks (Lacroix 2013). Responsibility may operate in a biopolitical sense, combining the personal behaviours of migrants with the needs of the international economic network through monetizing personal emotions and inserting them into market dynamics.

The second mechanism, 'projectivity', becomes focused on *aspiration*, meaning the hypothetical desired future that migrants are asked to formulate in order to justify their decision to leave their home country according to the legitimate societal frame of reference (Appadurai 2004). This attitude represents the second orienting keyword in that it allows the migrants to detach 'good' and 'legitimate' aspirations from 'bad' ones and thus to distinguish between allowed and unacceptable directions of the migratory experience. In so doing, this attitude reveals its potential biopolitical role, giving moral and economic value to migratory projects based on their compliance with the 'imperative of economic growth' but condemning as immoral and wasteful those projects that explicitly reject the quest for a better economic position.

The third mechanism, practical evaluation, becomes organized around the *perception of risk*, that is the personal capacity to interpret and respond to the present situation in both the home country and the destination country. It operates as a keyword, firstly in suggesting that the decision to migrate is the only rational choice in the face of an intolerable situation and secondly in making the integration process endurable despite the difficulties it entails. The perception of risk may hence have a biopolitical meaning because its definition is linked to the need to mobilize people to adopt an exit strategy that includes expatriation and integration without conflict in the home country or the recipient country.

Theoretically, individuals can react to these constellation both positively (corresponding to it) and negatively (resisting it). In the next section our analysis will focus specifically on the way how present migratory flows correspond to neoliberal discourses on responsibility, aspiration, and perception of risk.[4] The Italian case will be used to explore the empirical strength of this hypothesis, comparing the effects of the three mechanisms on young, unskilled immigrants from Africa and Eastern Europe and young, skilled Italian emigrants in the wake of the post-2007 economic crisis.

11.5 The Case of Italy

After 2007 an increasing number of qualified young scholars and professionals began emigrating from Italy. Immigration started earlier – most immigrants arrived during the 1990s or in the first decade of the twenty-first century. Even though the ensuing economic recession caused many of these newcomers to be unemployed or underemployed, the majority of them did not abandon their new country but instead moved from the regular sector of economy to the informal one, where there was still a significant demand for labour.

A review of the situation in Italy provides us with a more holistic explanation of the observed phenomenon, with these two heterogeneous migration flows being seen as different parts of the same economic and political dynamics, linked by the broader contemporary process of social transformation.[5] The biopolitical approach, mediated by reflection on the keywords orienting the migrants' agency, reveals the discursive dimensions that persuade people to leave their home country and migrate to countries where the international labour market is in need of their workforce and their knowledge despite harsh living conditions, obvious exploitation, possible failure, and feelings of nostalgia.

The next two subsections describe how globalization transformed European national economies, resulting in a semi-peripheral status for some regions of the southern countries, linked to new and challenging trends in the dynamics, direction, and composition of migration flows. Focusing on the Italian case in particular, the third section discusses how the decision of young, skilled native people to emigrate and the decision of foreign immigrants to remain in the host country are both oriented according to the same form of biopolitical management that governs different migrants (with different effects) through the same theoretical keywords mentioned above.

[4] For reasons of space, I cannot discuss here ways in which similar mechanisms can support resistance against public discourse.

[5] For a broader discussion on the interplay between global economic trends and migration management patterns see Menz (Chap. 3) and Van Puymbroeck (Chap. 4, in this volume).

11.5.1 Becoming the Semi-periphery of Southern Europe

Over the past decades the process of neoliberal globalization has had different effects on different territories in Europe, producing divergent trends in gross domestic product (GDP), innovation, and employment growth rate and therefore creating new equilibria between the different economic sectors and areas that were developed, developing, or underdeveloped. In the decade after the introduction of the Euro (2001–2012), countries such as Luxemburg, Germany, Austria, and Sweden experienced a major growth in GDP per capita ranging from 5 % in Sweden to 37 % in Luxembourg. The GDP per capita in Germany grew by 6 % during this decade, increasing from 116 to 122 (EU-28 = 100); in contrast, Italy, Spain, Portugal, and Greece all experienced a decline in GDP per capita, ranging from 1 % in Spain to 20 % in Italy. In the case of Italy, one of the most industrialized countries of the world, GDP per capita dropped from 119 to 99, falling below the threshold of the EU-28 average.[6]

The Northern and Central European regions experienced a new concentration of financial capital, high-level technologies, and know-how that permitted the countries in these regions to maintain and even to strengthen their role as key players in the global knowledge-based economy. In this same period the southern areas of the European Union were pushed into a marginal role, focused on providing low-cost goods and services and seen as a potential field for investment by global funding companies interested in short-term acquisition (Fumagalli 2007).

Italy is rapidly shifting from being one of the most industrialized economies of the world to one of the prime losers of globalization, similar to Japan after the crisis of 1999.[7] Two major reasons for this change are the historically low level of expenditure on research and development (R&D) (1.25 % of GDP) and, since the early 1970s, the lack of strategic investments in R&D within the industrial sector (Gallino 2003). Both these trends increased the internal Italian divide that separates the southern regions from the developed central and northern ones into the country.[8] In the last few years the increasing cuts in public expenditure for higher education and research can be seen as a third reason.

Based on the analytical criteria of the world-systems theory (Wallerstein 1974, 1980, 1989, 2011), several Italian regions appear to have slid away from the 'centre'

[6] These data were obtained from the Eurostat online database (http://epp.eurostat.ec.europa.eu/portal/page/portal/statistics/search_database) on February 8, 2013 and have been analysed by the author.

[7] In 1975 Italy entered the G6, having achieved the distinction of being the sixth most industrialized country in the world; 38 years later, in the autumn of 2013, Italy left the G8 owing to the effects of deindustrialization.

[8] The structural difference between Italian regions stood at the origin of the specific intervention of EU structural funds in 7 Object 1 areas in the southern part of the country since the 1980s (Sicily, Sardinia, Campania, Basilicata, Puglia, Abruzzo, Molise). The 'Partnership Agreement 2014–2020' between the EU and the Italian Government (2014) registers an increasing difference between Italian southern and centre-nortern regions, arguing that in 2013 the former experienced a GDP downfall of 4 % (compared to −1.2 % of the latter).

of the world system of capitalist production to a marginal area defined by Wallerstein as the spatial and functional 'semi-periphery' of the world.[9] The centre, semi-periphery, and periphery are linked by the presence of structural differentials and exploitation mechanisms. The structural differentials that characterize Italy's relations with the more dynamic and the less dynamic economies of the world are both economic and juridical.

As has been described above, the economic differential that increasingly separates Italy from the more dynamic economies is caused by the country's structural differences and its continuing failure to invest in R&D. At the regional level, these differences have been exacerbated. These trends have affected the national labour market in two respects: (1) the unemployment level, which started to rise in 2007 and reached a peak in November 2013, did not improve, and those particularly affected were individuals under the age of 25 and the highly skilled[10]; (2) the informal sector gained prominence and work became much less secure[11] as a result of cost cutting to ensure international competition for the country's national and traditional products. Although these cuts created a grey area in which workers were not required to pay taxes or sign contracts, they also meant that the workers had to forgo labour rights, appropriate salaries, welfare assistance, and insurance coverage.

The migration push–pull mechanisms that resulted from the economic differential were enforced by the juridical differential—that is, the legal barriers that promote the migration of high-skilled labourers among the EU countries but prevent the same kind of migration from outside the EU, in keeping with the 'Fortress Europe' political approach. Whereas this differential drives skilled Italian youth to apply for special visas to work in countries such as the United States and Germany (Isaakyan and Triandafyllidou 2013), it forces migrants from outside the EU to surrender their competencies in order to enter the Italian labour market.

The economic and juridical differentials constitute the structural drivers of social transformation in Italy and represent the contextual conditions of the new dynamic and composition of the migration flows that will be examined in the next section.

[9] Wallerstein introduced the concept of 'semi-periphery' to identify the geographical areas that have been marginalized within the world production system even if they still play some strategic roles at medium and lower positions in the global value chain.

[10] It may be interesting to interpret this evidence in Marxian terms as the structural processes that create the equivalent of the 'industrial reserve army' in our time and that thus act as conditions for a new capital accumulation cycle.

[11] In 2008 the added value of the informal economy was 56.8 % of GDP in the hotel and catering sectors; 52.9 % in domestic services; 28.4 % in the construction industry; and 13.7 % in the textile, clothing, and footwear industries. In 2010 irregular workers constituted about 12 % of the workforce: 24.9 % in agriculture, 6.6 % in industry, and 13.5 % in services (Istat 2012b).

11.5.2 Evidence of Heterogeneity in Migration Flows

Since the beginning of the new millennium, Europe has experienced a decline in absolute terms, or at least a trend towards greater consolidation, in many of the migration patterns and paths from Southern and Eastern European non-EU countries. At the same time, the trend towards intra-European migration appears to have been renewed, correlating with the development of 'central' industrial sectors and regions.

In Italy young job seekers and refugees from Eastern Europe and North Africa have joined the current outflow of young skilled and educated workers who are migrating to the northern and more dynamic European economies, according to a sort of dynamic of substitution in the national composition of the workforce. Clearly the post-2007 economic crisis is seen as the most important cause of this shift, but it would not have had the effects it had without the action and the strength of the economic and juridical differentials, nor without the compliance of the migrants themselves, as will be discussed later.

The economic downturn in Italy had a direct, if differential, impact on various kinds of immigrants. The crisis forced resident immigrants with sufficient skills and human and social capital to return home or to move to other countries. In other cases, it decelerated new immigrations, except for student migrations and the reuniting of families. Although the unfavourable economic development led to a drastic reduction of the official number of irregular arrivals of labour migrants, it accentuated the overstaying of previously regular immigrants who lost their jobs[12] but stayed in the country because they hoped to compete for the new opportunities (i.e. dirty, dangerous, and demanding jobs) created by the recession. The material evidence of semi-legality (Kubal 2012)—that is, having no formal documents, no opportunity to act autonomously, and no formal access to economic resources—served as the basis for such conditions in the informal sector.

As noted earlier, the impact of the economic crisis on immigration is only one side of the coin. Italy, after having been an immigration country for decades and one of the new immigration countries since 1974, is suddenly becoming an official emigration country as well. After decades of low economic dynamism, Italian emigration grew by more than 9 % in 2011 as compared with 2010 and for the first time the number of Italian emigrants (50,057) exceeded the number of Italian citizens returning from abroad (31,466) (Istat 2012a: 4; Fondazione Migrantes 2013: 11). What is really new about this phase of Italian emigration is the enormous flow of young skilled and well-educated people who are leaving the country to explore the economic and social opportunities in the more prominent and more fascinating areas of post-industrial global growth.[13] Within a decade, the percentage of Italian emigrants

[12] The huge difference between the number of applications for work visas and the available annual quota reveals the high degree of migratory pressure and also possibly the large numbers of irregular jobs among the migrants who are already working in Italy (Ambrosetti 2009).

[13] Bilecen discusses aspects of student mobility in Europe in Chap. 15, of this volume.

who have graduated and are above the age of 25 increased from 11.9 % in 2002 to 27.6 % in 2011,[14] while the number of those with only average academic degrees declined from 51 % to 37.9 % within the same period (Istat 2012a: 6).[15] Both groups mainly emigrate to the United Kingdom (11.9 %), Switzerland (11.8 %), Germany (11 %),[16] France (9.5 %), and the United States (8.4 %) (Istat 2012a: 7).

Recent transformations in the Italian academic system may offer the clearest examples of how the economic and juridical differentials operate in a specific sector of the qualified labour market, and how they affect the comings and goings of highly skilled migrants. Since the beginning of the 1990s rules put forth by the universities and research centres have been progressively transformed so these institutions are less dependent on financial support from the Ministry of Education and are more attractive to private investors, are less reliant on researchers and professors with tenure, and are more willing to consider temporary fellowships. Instead of becoming a powerful form of leverage for innovation, these transformations have dismantled a consolidated system without providing resources to replace it with something new and better. Within less than two decades the research and teaching environment has changed completely, with a strangled labour market that impedes the recruitment of many young scholars and has no funds with which to promote the research projects of those who are already part of the system.

Owing to these transformations the majority of postgraduate students who wish to pursue opportunities in the R&D sector choose to migrate to other European countries such as Germany, the United Kingdom, and France, where the exploration of promising ideas can receive adequate funding and where temporariness does not necessarily mean precariousness. According to the OCSE report (2010), the emigration of Italian university students has resumed, with more and more Italian students getting enrolled at universities in the United Kingdom, Spain, and Germany. The 11 % of Italian students who attended postgraduate courses in their home country decided to emigrate to complete their academic training abroad (20 % in linguistics, engineering, and the naturals sciences) (Fondazione Migrantes 2013: 15).

Against this backdrop, very few researchers or professors from abroad have been recruited by the Italian universities, and are no longer being recruited by national companies operating in the R&D sectors, owing to national juridical barriers that,

[14] In the same year (2011) 22 % of Italian new emigrants had graduated, 28.7 % had a high school diploma, and 8.7 % had a high school diploma and were enrolled at universities (Fondazione Migrantes 2013: 12).

[15] The number of unskilled emigrants with only average school degrees increased steadily in the last few years, from 0.3 % of the total population of Italian emigrants in 2010 to 24.4 % in 2011. Some of them might be accounted for by the group of young people who emigrated mainly to Germany, France, and Switzerland (6,906 in 2010 and 8,617 in 2011) (Fondazione Migrantes 2013: 14).

[16] The institute for market research Iab Italia estimates that in the first half of 2013 Italians represented the third largest group of new foreign arrivals in Germany, after Poles and Romanians and before Hungarians and Spaniards. Members of the Iab Communication Office reported that in 2012 the migration balance of Italians in Germany was 369,000 and, on the basis of statistical evidence from first half of the year (+13 %), were expected to be 400,000 by 2013.

despite the most recent European rules, still resist recognizing qualifications obtained in non-EU countries and discourage scholars and professionals from outside the EU from entering the Italian skilled-labour market.

11.5.3 Devices and Keywords of Biopolitical Migration Management

Italy is experiencing a sort of 'workforce substitution' that reflects the U-turn in its development. The disinvestment of national and international capital in the industrial sector and the reorienting of the main economic players towards the financial sector has undoubtedly led to the expulsion of many workers and pushed those who were more skilled and educated to emigrate abroad. At the same time the progressive dismantling of the post-war welfare and workfare systems created conditions that promoted the growth of the informal labour market, which supported companies' competitiveness and provided an opportunity for them to drastically cut the labour cost of production. This shift also perpetuated immigration flows of people pulled by the demand for labour in the informal sectors—not in spite of the crisis but, absurdly, because of it.

The pivotal point for this analysis is that these processes were not just the result of external structural pressures. The highly skilled young people expatriated voluntarily to achieve their professional dreams and demonstrate the value of their competencies and attitudes. The immigrants became integrated into the informal sector, complying at the same time with their desires to earn money and with the needs of local employers for an additional low-cost and sometimes illegal labour force.[17]

The economic and juridical differentials that characterize the new international relations of the country as semi-peripheral do not force people to move but provide platforms for specific devices (e.g. visa regimes, criteria for recognizing status and qualifications, welfare systems, and labour market regulations) that orient people to migrate to express their entrepreneurship, fitting personal wishes to acceptable investments and concrete opportunities. It is here where the possibility of biopolitical migration management lies, in which the keywords discussed previously ('perception of risk', 'aspiration', and 'responsibility') assume specific, activating meanings.

Enhancing immigrants' and emigrants' perception of the crisis as a structural condition of risk is the best way to convince them that their country of origin might get worse and thus to instil in them the fear that there is no time to wait before moving abroad as a way to preserve their human and social capital. Official discourse about 'crisis' and 'emergency' fuels this mechanism for immigrants from outside the EU and for highly skilled Italian emigrants. The internalization of this kind of *perception of risk* is needed to set in motion both the aspirations and the

[17] Interactions between semi-legal migrants and employers fall along a spectrum between opportunism and exploitation (Kubal 2012: 18–19).

responsibilities of people with different degrees of freedom to decide to migrate and to choose where, how, and under what conditions to do so, depending on their position within the world patterns of social stratification.

Aspiration is the main driver of the biopolitical management of migratory projects. It directs the semi-legal migrants towards 'market-oriented' goals, such as earning money to start a family or a business activity at home, becoming a successful adult, and adopting a European consumer lifestyle. The same logic orients the young skilled and educated Italians, legitimating their goals to become successful adults, achieve the same lifestyle as previous generations, and be able to afford a lifestyle of conspicuous consumption.

By emphasizing personal *responsibility* in a context of crisis, the biopolitical discourse about entrepreneurship obliges the semi-legal migrants to accept the harshness of their situation and to join the available sector of the labour market, even if it is through informal or illegal arrangements, in order to compensate those who financed their voyage, to prove themselves to the relatives they left behind, and to maintain their self-image as 'heroes'. In the same way it encourages the young skilled and educated Italians to leave the country and seek their fortune abroad in order to pay back those who financed their education and professional training, to preserve their self-image as 'highly intelligent', and to conform to the neo-liberal ethic of merit.

11.6 Conclusion

In Italy the post-2007 economic crisis has led to the emergence of new forms of segmentation and segregation in the labour market. The country expelled young, better-educated, and more highly qualified people, convincing them to seek jobs abroad in the most knowledge-based economies. At the same time Italy began to retain regular migrants in low-wage and labour-intensive sectors, to invite family reunification to guarantee jobs for relatives who would accept any type of work, and to entice unemployed migrants to prolong their stay and new, irregular migrants to join them to fill jobs in informal, as well as illegal, markets, thereby providing a cheaper and more submissive labour force.

Without the inner stimulating action of the three keywords analysed in this chapter neither the economic and juridical differentials nor the associated devices for the selection and differentiation of migration flows would have produced their expected effects.

This chapter has indicated that there is a need to understand migration management as part of the repositioning of some of the Italian regions from the centre to the semi-periphery of the capitalist world system, through the dismantling of the knowledge-based economic sectors and the reinforcement of certain areas of the informal sectors in order to compete successfully in the global division of labour. A social transformation approach helps to unveil the systemic pattern of these dynamics but also the discursive dimensions that support the re-orientation of the perceptions, sense-making and practices of individuals. From a theoretical point of view, these developments served as an example to discuss possibilities to combine a social transformation perspective with the Foucauldian conceptual framework.

References

Ambrosetti, E. (2009). *The impact of the economic crisis on migration flows between Italy and North Africa* (CARIM analytic and synthetic notes 2009/36). San Domenico di Fiesole: European University Institute, Robert Schuman Centre for Advanced Studies. http://cadmus.eui.eu/bitstream/handle/1814/12991/CARIM_ASN_2009_36.pdf?sequence=1

Appadurai, A. (2004). The capacity to aspire: Culture and the terms of recognition. In V. Rao & M. Walton (Eds.), *Culture and public action* (pp. 59–84). Stanford: Stanford University Press.

Bailey, A. J. (2013). Migration, recession and an emerging transnational biopolitics across Europe. *Geoforum, 44*, 202–210. doi:10.1016/j.geoforum.2012.09.006.

Bakewell, O. (2010). Some reflections on structure and agency in migration theory. *Journal of Ethnic and Migration Studies, 36*(10), 1689–1708. doi:10.1080/1369183X.2010.489382.

Carling, J. (2008). The human dynamics of migrant transnationalism. *Ethnic and Racial Studies, 31*(8), 1452–1477. doi:10.1080/01419870701719097.

Castles, S. (2001). Studying social transformation. *International Political Science Review, 22*(1), 13–32. doi:10.1177/0192512101221002.

Castles, S. (2010). Understanding global migration: A social transformation perspective. *Journal of Ethnic and Migration Studies, 36*(10), 1565–1586. doi:10.1080/1369183X.2010.489381.

Cohen, R. (2006). *Migration and its enemies: Global capital, migrant labour and the nation-state*. Aldershot/Burlington: Ashgate.

Emirbayer, M., & Mische, A. (1998). What is agency? *American Journal of Sociology, 103*(4), 962–1023. doi:10.1086/231294.

Fondazione Migrantes. (2013). *Rapporto Italiani nel Mondo 2013*. http://www.chiesacattolica.it/pls/cci_new_v3/v3_s2ew_consultazione.mostra_pagina?id_pagina=49458

Foucault, M. (1978). *The history of sexuality: Volume 1: An introduction*. New York: Pantheon Books.

Foucault, M. (2008). *The birth of biopolitics: Lectures at the Collège de France: 1978–1979*. Basingstoke/New York: Palgrave Macmillan.

Fumagalli, A. (2007). *Bioeconomia e capitalismo cognitivo: Verso un nuovo paradigma di accumulazione*. Rome: Carocci.

Gallino, L. (2003). *La scomparsa dell'Italia industriale*. Turin: Einaudi.

Hardt, M., & Negri, A. (2000). *Empire*. Cambridge/London: Harvard University Press.

Hardt, M., & Negri, A. (2004). *Multitude: War and democracy in the age of empire*. New York: The Penguin Press.

Hardt, M., & Negri, A. (2009). *Commonwealth*. Cambridge: Belknap Press of Harvard University Press.

Hirst, P., & Thompson, G. (1996). *Globalization in question: The international economy and the possibilities of governance*. Cambridge/Malden: Polity Press.

Isaakyan, I., & Triandafyllidou, A. (2013). *High-skill mobility: Addressing the challenges of a knowledge-based economy at times of crisis* (RSCAS PP 2013/14). San Domenico di Fiesole: EUI, RSCAS Policy Paper 2013/14. European University Institute, Robert Schuman Centre for Advanced Studies. http://cadmus.eui.eu/bitstream/handle/1814/27706/RSCAS_PP_2013_14.pdf?sequence=1

Istat. (2012a). *Migrazioni internazionali e interne della popolazione residente: Anno 2011*. Rome: National Institute of Statistics.

Istat. (2012b). *Rapporto annuale 2010: La situazione del Paese*. Rome: National Institute of Statistics.

Kubal, A. (2012). *Socio-legal integration: Polish post-2004 EU enlargement migrants in the United Kingdom.*. Farnham/Burlington: Ashgate.

Lacroix, T. (2013). Collective remittances and integration: North African and North Indian comparative perspectives. *Journal of Ethnic and Migration Studies, 39*(6), 1019–1035. doi:10.1080/1369183X.2013.765667.

Raghuram, P. (2009). Which migration, what development? Unsettling the edifice of migration and development. *Population, Space and Place, 15*(2), 103–117. doi:10.1002/psp.536.

Reyneri, E. (2003). Immigration and the underground economy in new receiving South European countries: manifold negative effects, manifold deep-rooted causes. *International Review of Sociology–Revue Internationale de Sociologie, 13*(1), 117–143. doi:10.1080/0390670032000087023.

Sassen, S. (1998). *Globalization and its discontents: Essays on the new mobility of people and money*. New York: The New Press.

Tomei, G. (2014). Unveiling the mantra. The salience of network-based community belonging in understanding the structural and agentic conditions of the migration-development nexus. *International Review of Sociology/Revue Internationale de Sociologie, 24*(1), 145–163. doi:10.1080/03906701.2014.894336.

Wallerstein, I. (1974). *The modern world-system I: Capitalist agriculture and the origins of the European world-economy in the sixteenth century*. New York/London: Academic Press.

Wallerstein, I. (1980). *The modern world-system II: Mercantilism and the consolidation of the European world-economy: 1600–1750*. New York/London: Academic.

Wallerstein, I. (1989). *The modern world-system III: The second era of great expansion of the capitalist world-economy: 1730–1840s*. San Diego/New York: Academic.

Wallerstein, I. (2011). *The modern world-system IV: Centrist Liberalism Triumphant: 1789–1914*. Berkeley/Los Angeles/London: University of California Press.

Part III
Complexities of Mobilities: From One-Way Migration to Multiple Patterns

Bruno Meeus and Kenneth Horvath

Introduction to Part III

The entanglement of migration and mobility practices with the processes of broader societal transformations is the central theme of Part III. The focus is on migrants' sociospatial agency and the intersubjective framing of their practices. Envisioned in this part is the potential of the 'recalcitrant' mobile individual crossing national borders to challenge and eventually transform dominant frames of interpretation.

The five chapters included in this part provide insights into the diversification of mobility patterns. Furthermore, they investigate how these practices come into conflict with political regulations of migration and mobility. Hence, the chapters illustrate the institutional incorporation of specific mobility patterns—such as labour, student or retirement mobilities—into EU policies and discourses. In doing so, the chapters demonstrate a variety of methodological approaches.

The opening chapter of this part, Chap. 12 by Laura Wiesböck and her colleagues, analyses cross-border commuting as a key element of emerging transnational labour markets. Cross-border commuting occurs in various European regions and often builds on a long (trans)local history of cross-border movements. Examples include the former Iron Curtain borders, as well as other border areas where income differences or differing national tax regulations provide incentives for cross-border commuting. Using the Central European Region as an example, the authors illustrate how cross-border commuting is being captured by the EU's competitiveness agenda or, in other words, how the institutionalized promotion of intra-European mobility is becoming part of a politically driven social transformation project.

B. Meeus (✉)
Cosmopolis Centre for Urban Research, Vrije Universiteit Brussel, Brussels, Belgium
e-mail: bruno.meeus@vub.ac.be

K. Horvath
University of Education of Karlsruhe, Karlsruhe, Germany
e-mail: horvath@ph-karlsruhe.de

Cross-border commuting, as described in Chap. 12, eventually challenges the national scale of social-security provision. This issue is the central theme of Chap. 13 by Elaine Moriarty and her colleagues. Using the example of recent intra-EU labour mobility to Ireland, the chapter emphasizes the tension between the portability of social protection across national borders and the static conception of welfare entitlements in national welfare systems. The chapter draws on the example of migrant workers from the new accession states to analyse how nation states 'qualify' the European Union's commitment to the creation of a free movement zone, a zone in which all member state citizens—regardless of whether they cross national borders or not—should be treated equally. The authors highlight that, using the political rhetoric of 'welfare migration', Ireland has introduced several social-policy measures that restrict access to social protection for mobile EU-citizens from the new EU member states.

The problem of portability of social rights mirrors key contradictions of ongoing transformation processes in the context of the EU. In Chap. 14 Benno Herzog introduces international retirement migrants' mobility practices as an example of mobility that at first glance seems far less problematized. The chapter explains that there are different reasons for the framing of retirement migrants as 'tourists' and their self-segregation in well-off areas as 'unproblematic'. In practice, though, mobile retirees' transnational life-styles challenge national regulations of migration. Moreover, empirical research reveals that social isolation is a significant problem for retirement migrants, and that voluntary organizations cannot cope with their social needs on their own. In essence, Benno Herzog argues that the fact that retirees are not confronted with the political rhetoric of integration allows us to question static models of integration.

The European competitiveness agenda is further scrutinized in Başak Bilecen's contribution (Chap. 15), but from a very different angle. The author's starting point are mobility practices of doctoral students, who are envisioned as the future cosmopolitan elite in the European Union's knowledge-economy discourses. The chapter shows how cosmopolitanism is constituted through everyday practices of international doctoral students. Three dimensions are distinguished. Cosmopolitanism as a worldview emphasizes the openness towards the different Others as a result of studying abroad. Cosmopolitanism as multifocality denotes the competence to see things from different perspectives as a result of encountering other perspectives. Cosmopolitanism as 'being flexible' in a global market, finally, emphasizes students' acceptance of market-oriented career logics. The chapter thus underlines the important difference between emancipatory versions of cosmopolitanism and the neoliberal version, in which cosmopolitanism is stripped down to accepting the necessity of being geographically mobile.

In the last chapter of this part Helma Lutz (Chap. 16) analyses cross-border migration and mobility of Eastern European female care workers. Starting with a detailed description of two workers' labour and family experiences, the author unravels the dilemmas of motherhood that these women are confronted with. The efforts made by biological mothers to perform social mothering across wide geographical distances conflicts with ideologies of motherhood in the post-socialist and Western worlds: These notions of motherhood stipulate the primacy of the mother–child relationship and the impossibility of replacing a mother adequately with any other care-giving person. Potentially, these women's mobility practices could challenge the hegemonic, middle-class based ‘new maternalism’, which neglects the relevance of fatherhood practices. Instead, the ‘new maternalism’ discourse impinges strongly on the self-perception of migrant mothers. The resulting emotional distress is also co-determined by the denial of the right to family reunion by immigration states. Thus, Helma Lutz identifies how specific gendered narratives incorporated in practices of migration and mobility contribute to inequality experiences of migrant workers.

Chapter 12
Cross-Border Commuting and Transformational Dynamics in Europe: What Is the Link?

Laura Wiesböck, Christoph Reinprecht, Raimund Haindorfer and Roland Verwiebe

12.1 Introduction

This chapter considers cross-border commuting as a form of mobility that is linked to social-transformation processes in multiple ways. Building on an ongoing empirical study of the Central European Region, the chapter discusses (1) cross-border commuting as an institutionalized form of labour mobility, (2) cross-border regions as political complexes with diverse histories, and (3) economic outcomes and life satisfaction of cross-border commuters in comparison with the resident population. Beyond the (potential) role and function of geographical mobility both for social differentiation and for minimizing regional disparities, the chapter examines how new legal and institutional realities shape mobility and social inequality, and what the emerging types and patterns of cross-border commuting strategies imply for socially and symbolically integrated intra-European transnational labour markets. To address the effects on social transformation, it is crucial to understand commuting practices against the background of changing regional and border dynamics in which cultural, political, and economic asymmetries play a significant role. This is particularly relevant for circular East–West mobility in the current intra-European context, which is often marked by long-lasting regional disparities. The emergence of Euroregions as new forms of cross-border governance is a crucial element for the institutionalization of such stimulated regional cooperation along the national borders within the EU. The Central European Region (Centrope) is a notable example of this development: here the increasing cross-border commuting is framed in multiple ways by ongoing societal transformations resulting both from European enlargement processes and from the significant post-socialist reconfiguration of economic, political, and legal institutions.

L. Wiesböck (✉) • C. Reinprecht • R. Haindorfer • R. Verwiebe
Department of Sociology, University of Vienna, Vienna, Austria
e-mail: laura.wiesboeck@univie.ac.at

A. Amelina et al. (eds.), *An Anthology of Migration and Social Transformation*, IMISCOE Research Series, DOI 10.1007/978-3-319-23666-7_12

In the first part of the chapter we provide an overview of new patterns of labour circulation within the European Union. We will then introduce the promotion of intra-European mobility as a form of politically intended social transformation. The chapter proceeds with a discussion of Euroregions as institutionalized cross-border regions, showing how they contribute to the regional dimension of European integration. This is followed by some examples of borderlands in the EU, which are discussed on the basis of current empirical studies to illustrate our points, and an in-depth case study on Centrope. The chapter concludes with an outlook on further important research questions in this field.

12.2 Conceptualizing New Patterns of Temporary Movements Within Europe

There are a number of different conceptual tools available to describe current patterns of labour movements across EU borders. Traditional terminologies and distinctions used in studying these movement practices would not do justice to recent social changes, while the development of new vocabularies is still in its early stages (see e.g. Albert 1998: 56; Brettell and Hollifield 2008). First of all, we have to ask whether these types of movement are a form of *mobility* or a form of *migration*. According to Cresswell (2006), mobility can mean any type of territorial movement, migration just being one such type. While 'mobility' is predominantly conceptualized as a circular or temporary/short-term movement, 'migration' refers to permanent forms of settlement. However, empirical analysis of intra-EU movements shows that the old concept of migration, where individuals leave their country permanently, no longer applies (Mau et al. 2008). Rather, an increasing number of people go abroad for short periods of time to find seasonal employment or to commute across national borders on a regular basis (Mau and Büttner 2010). Given the predominance of short-term circulatory movement back and forth across borders as opposed to permanent one-way migration, it has been suggested that commuting is assigned to the concept of mobility rather than that of migration (Wallace 2002).

When it comes to the concepts covered by the umbrella term 'mobility', '*circular mobility*' and '*temporary mobility*' are often used interchangeably without regard to whether they refer to the same phenomenon or to different social and economic realities (Triandafyllidou 2013: 4). According to Vertovec (2007), circular mobility involves not only temporary stays and returns but repeated movement of the same person across borders. Newland et al. (2008) argue that circular mobility—as opposed to temporary mobility—involves both return and repetition, as well as continuous engagement in the sending and receiving countries. Vertovec (2007) also notes that in the early research on migration a wide range of terms was used to refer to mobility, including 'repeat', 'rotating', 'multiple', 'cyclical', and 'shuttle migration'. Van Houtum and Gielis (2006), for example, propose that the term '*elastic migration*' should be used to describe short-term transmigration across the Dutch–Belgian and the Dutch–German borders because the workplaces of the transmigrants under study were in the Netherlands, only a few kilometres from their homes in Belgium and Germany respectively. However, within the European Union '*circular mobility*' has become the accepted term to describe an intended and regulated form of labour movement. The current policy turn to circular-mobility policies stems in primarily from the relatively recent recognition of the significance of migrant transnational practices (Vertovec 2007, Chaps. 15 and 16, in this volume). Circular-movement practices are based on and establish further transnational social networks. However, the concept has been criticized for its neoclassical approach because circular movements of workers usually occur in response to the swings of the markets and the changing needs of employers, and not so much because the labourers want to be mobile.

12.3 Inner-European Labour Circulation as a Politically Stimulated Process of Social Transformation

Transnational labour markets and enhanced mobility within these markets are often promoted in EU policy as the way forward. A variety of policymakers advocate measures to facilitate the movement of migrants between their homelands and foreign workplaces primarily to generate a win-win-win situation which benefits receiving countries by meeting labour market shortages, sending countries by guaranteeing remittances for development, and migrants by offering employment and control over the use of their wages (Constant et al. 2012).

The EU has been strongly encouraging intra-European mobility through institutional and cultural programmes since the early 1990s. Relevant factors in fostering intra-European movements have included the implementation of the provisions of the Maastricht Treaty on freedom of movement, the recognition of foreign qualifications by EU member states, the Erasmus and Socrates programmes, and the development of a network of European employment offices (Findlay et al. 2006; King and Ruiz-Gelices 2003; Verwiebe et al. 2010). This new mode of migration management belongs to the flexibility paradigm that has prevailed in the European post-Fordist economies in the last few decades and is consistent with the idea that positions may be temporary both on the high and the low ends of the labour market (Venturini 2008). It appears to pose a limited-integration burden on destination countries while maximizing transnational transfers (Triandafyllidou 2013: 4).

The idea of European economic integration through mobility is also applied on a regional level. The European Commission strongly supports cross-border cooperation initiatives such as Euroregions. Euroregions are transnational administrative units that foster collaboration between subnational authorities in areas such as regional development, transport, local economy, cultural activities, and the environment. Although some of these initiatives date back to the 1950s, it was not until the

1990s that the number of cross-border regions in Europe increased significantly. Today there are virtually no local or regional authorities in border areas that are not involved in cross-border cooperation initiatives in some way or other (Perkmann 2003). Euroregions have started a new era in international politics as institutional entrepreneurs, as a model of international governance for regional actors contesting the nation state's traditional monopoly on foreign affairs and international politics (Perkmann 1999, 2002). The establishment of Euroregions is connected with several political visions such as a Europe without borders, a new regionalism, and a turn back to (imagined) common regional historical and regional cultural roots (Klatt and Herrmann 2011: 66). The 'integrationist' turn (Klatt and Herrmann 2011) in the academic research in this field has drawn attention to the rise of a new type of supranational governance that takes the forms of regional transnationalism (Perkmann 2003), border regions acting as pioneers and laboratories of European integration, and cross-border regions serving as a tier in today's system of multi-level government in the EU. Many Euroregions are active agents in the field of cross-border cooperation, which also includes enhanced labour mobility. In the following we will provide examples of major cross-border-commuting regions in Europe, some of which are political-institutional complexes with diverse histories or are constituted by multiple cross-border practices that are weakly institutionalized.

12.4 Some Examples of Major Cross-Border Regions in the European Union

The *Polish–German borderland* is a notable example of dynamic and consistent transnational movements of workers within the European Union. Miera (2008) notes that bilateral Polish–German migration regulations have had a crucial impact on the patterns of Polish migration to Germany: from long-term, legal settlement during the post-war era to an increase in commuter movements of legal and undocumented transmigrants after the 1990s. In 1993 the Pro Europa Viadrina Euroregion was founded. According to Miera, political-transformation processes in Eastern Europe have played an important role in shaping opportunity structures and different types of mobility for individual migrants. In his qualitative study on Polish domestic workers in Berlin, Cyrus (2008) shows that for most of the workers there is a functional separation between Berlin as territory of economic activity and Poland as their personal and emotional environment. However, in some cases friendships and relationships in Berlin are starting to develop. In the context of recent temporary labour migration from Poland to Germany, Kalter (2011) discusses the role of social capital as a relevant explanatory factor, making a strong argument that cross-border commuting in this region needs to be analysed as a social process in which social networks play a crucial part.

Another example of contemporary transnational labour markets within the EU is the *Danish–German border region* (van Houtum and Gielis 2006; Buch et al. 2009; Verwiebe et al. 2010; Strüver 2005a, b). The increase in cross-border commuting has been caused by labour market disparities in the region, which have led to significant differences between cross-border commuters on both sides of the border with respect to wages and main branches of employment (Buch et al. 2009). Most of the German commuters work in the construction and transportation sectors. In Denmark these branches pay much higher wages and generally have better working conditions than in the Northern German border region.

Yet another example is the border region between the *Netherlands* and *Germany*. Due to a housing shortage in the Netherlands, Dutch people began to move to German villages on the border while maintaining their jobs in the Netherlands (Strüver 2005b). The Belgian borderlands also attract Dutch transmigrants, mainly because of the fiscal climate in Belgium, which is more attractive than that in the Netherlands (van Houtum and Gielis 2006). Thus, what links both directions of short-distance migrations is first and foremost a cost-driven motivation. Yet the active and affective bond with the Netherlands remains very strong. If one considers the transformational effects of this cross-border region, one finds that there are challenges in urban planning on both sides of the border due to the increase in the number of Dutch people moving to Germany. The great demand for houses on the German side of the border has resulted in a rise of housing and land prices and a lack of affordable housing (van Houtum and Gielis 2006). German schools are confronted with an abundance of places for students, while Dutch schools are faced with a shortage of places.

The labour market of *Luxembourg* is a very interesting and instructive example of a transnational labour market (see Schmitz et al. 2012). As many as 50 % of those employed in Luxembourg's labour market are cross-border commuters, and for three decades their number has been on the rise (for example, in 1975 only 9 % were cross-border commuters), and now takes place in a labour market region that extends across four European countries (Schmitz et al. 2012: 6). While the Benelux-Middengebied Euroregion was founded as a transnational cooperation between Luxembourg, Belgium, and the Netherlands as far back as 1984, the Saar-Lorraine-Luxembourg-Rhin Euroregion was established in 1995 to collaborate with the border regions of Germany and France. Now, what can be said about the sociodemographic structure of commuters in this region? Transnational commuters come from a wide range of age groups (mostly 30–50-year-olds), occupations, and socioeconomic strata. Today nearly half of them are university graduates. The percentage of white-collar workers has risen sharply, while the percentage of those in skilled and unskilled manual occupations has decreased considerably. Interestingly, the rate of homeownership among commuters—described in de Gijsel and Janssen (2000) as a barrier to mobility—has risen.

The labour market of *Liechtenstein*, another rather small European country, is also characterized by a high number of commuters. About 46 % of those employed in Liechtenstein are cross-border commuters from neighbouring countries (Gottholmseder and Theurl 2007), and most of them are from the Austrian state of

Vorarlberg, one of the major regions of out-commuting in this part of Europe, not only to Liechtenstein but also to Switzerland, for example. Gottholmseder and Theurl (2007) ascribe these patterns to specific microeconomic characteristics of Liechtenstein's labour market, which include substantial differences in unemployment rates within the Bodensee region and the outstanding, extremely well-compensated employment positions for which Liechtenstein is known. Studer (2004) found that the average income in Liechtenstein is about twice as high as the average income in Vorarlberg, and Gottholmseder and Theurl (2007: 108) identified substantial differences in educational level—a large percentage of cross-border commuters are graduates of technical colleges.

Based on these brief descriptions of some major European borderlands, a number of factors that contribute to inner-European labour mobility patterns can be identified. First of all, institutional settings and restrictions have an influence on labour movements.[1] In addition, structural differences such as opportunity structures in the labour market, unemployment rates, and housing prices are push–pull factors in the mobility process. Historical patterns of cross-border cooperation and mobility also play an important role in fostering labour movements, and human, cultural, and social capital and sociodemographic characteristics can promote or limit processes of mobility. In the following section we will provide an in-depth look at the Central European Region (Centrope), an instructive example of a region with a specific historico-political context that has gone through a profound system change and (global) societal transformations.

12.5 Cross-Border Commuting and Transformational Perspectives in Centrope: A Case Study

The Central European Region is a distinct cultural area and political region consisting of eight federal provinces, regions, and counties with a total population of about 6.5 million. The largest city in Centrope is Vienna, which has a population of 1.8 million and, along with Bratislava, is one of the two national centres of power in the region. This is an exceptional situation in that most of the other inner-European border regions are located more peripherally Fig. 12.1.

Historically speaking, the dissolution of the Soviet Union, the EU enlargement, and the removal of the last barriers to the free movement of labour have brought about significant changes which in turn have led to new forms of interplay of economic, social, political and legal factors (Horvath 2012). Since May 1, 2011, when the final transitional arrangements were lifted at the end of the 7-year transitional

[1] However, it should be noted that there are no reliable data on non-documented forms of mobility, so analysis of the increase in cross-border movement must rely primarily on data on documented, 'legal' movement practices.

Fig. 12.1 The Central European region

period, citizens of the A8 countries have had full access to labour markets across the EU-27.[2]

Commuting within the Central European Union is not a recent phenomenon linked to the creation of a European common market (Terlouw 2012: 354). Formal and informal circularity between the countries has existed for many decades, although under specific conditions in the period of state socialism, and with a *longue durée* of cross-border mobility which began during the time of the Habsburg Monarchy. However, Centrope is one of many political projects in the European Union that foster enhanced mobility to strengthen competitiveness and the regional business location. Mobility of labour is one of the core aims of the Centrope Strategy 2013+, which emphasizes commitment to a collaboration that ranges from research and innovation to human-capital development and spatial integration to culture and tourism (Centrope Agency 2012). This reflects the differentiation of movement patterns within the European Union: from once-in-a-lifetime migration to mobility as a life strategy. This development is also due to the short distances between the places; for example, someone may commute between Bratislava and Vienna, the two most populous metropolitan areas in Centrope in 1 h.

In 2009 a slight but steady increase in the number of commuters from neighbouring countries began. This indicates that the unification of the region was already taking place as a result of a gradual opening of the labour market (Commuter Treaty, Professional Employee Regulation 2008, Substitute Workforce Procedure) before people from the non-EU countries even had unrestricted access to the EU labour market. The increase in cross border activities can be attributed to the gradual opening of the borders. However, the relatively high social inequality between the Austrian

[2]All citizens from A8 countries (Czech Republic, Estonia, Hungary, Latvia, Lithuania, Poland, Slovakia, Slovenia) were given the freedom to settle in other member states of the EU to seek employment according to their skills and qualifications.

Table 12.1 Regional statistics 2011

	Household income (€)	GDP per capita PPS (€)
Austria	19,800	32,300
Lower Austria	20,600	26,600
Vienna	19,800	41,300
Burgenland	19,400	21,700
Czech	10,200	20,300
Jihovýchod	9900	18,400
Slovakia	10,500	18,900
Bratislavský kraj	16,000	46,600
Západné Slovensko	10,700	18,100
Hungary	8600	16,900
Nyugat-Dunántúl	5600	17,100

Eurostat; household income: balance of primary income, net (uses), purchasing power standard based on final consumption per inhabitant; *GDP* Gross domestic product at current market prices, purchasing power standard per inhabitant

subregions and their neighbours continues to play an important role. Table 12.1 shows that there are still significant differences between household income and regional GDP levels.[3]

Very little comprehensive information is available on the integration of cross-border commuters from the Czech Republic, Slovakia, and Hungary into the Austrian labour market. The TRANSLAB research project of the University of Vienna was initiated to fill this gap in the research by building on the established 'ethnosurvey' methodology to collect data (see Massey 1987) and on associated, more recent applications adapted for the study of the European setting (see Kalter 2011; Wallace and Vincent 2007). Between October 2012 and June 2013 the Austrian branch of the consumer research group GfK and its Central European partner institutes conducted face-to-face interviews with 1345 commuters who worked in Austria and a reference group of 1334 non-commuters. Currently employed interviewees (at least 20 h a week) were aged 21–65 years and had their primary residence within regions bordering on Austria, such as South Moravia (Czech Republic), Bratislava and Trnava (Slovakia), and Győr-Moson-Sopron and Vas (Hungary). Due to a lack of compatible transnational sampling schemes, the subsample of commuters used here is the best approximation available; it was obtained through quota sampling, based on labour market statistics provided by the Public Employment Service Austria.

The TRANSLAB data allows for a detailed analysis of the sociodemographic structure and major labour market characteristics of the cross-border commuters from Hungary, Slovakia, and the Czech Republic and for a comparison of natives and migrants in Austria. We compare migrants with commuters because their types

[3] However, it should be noted that consumer good prices are relatively high compared with Austria.

of movement are very different from each other. Migrants have their main residence in Austria. Being a migrant does not necessarily imply long-term settlement, however, it indicates that the geographical and physical centre of one's life is in Austria. Cross-border commuters, by contrast, continue to live in their home country. Their main connection to Austria is their workplace, which is geographically separated from their personal lives. While most of the migrants in Austria live and work in urban areas, daily cross-border commuting mainly takes place in rural, peripheral territories.

The TRANSLAB study provides some interesting insights into the social composition of cross-border commuters in Centrope. Most of these commuters have *mid-level qualifications* (ISCED 3–4: 77 %). Low-skilled individuals make up a smaller percentage of cross-border commuters compared with migrant workers in Austria, and the percentage of academics among cross-border commuters is smaller than in all other comparison groups. The majority of cross-border commuters work in *service industries* (e.g. hospitality: 20 %, health care: 17 %) or in *construction* (17 %), with a very small group working in agriculture. The majority of cross-border commuters are *male* (57 % male, 43 % female), a finding consistent with the results of other recent studies (e.g. Drevon and Gerber 2012). Commuters are *relatively young*: 49 % are younger than 35, another 37 % are between 35 and 50 years of age, and only 14 % of the cross-border commuters are older than 50. This is consistent with the findings of Paci et al. (2010), who note that mobility in a cross-border labour market is a phenomenon characterized by young labour.

Due to the diverging forms of movement and different structural initial positions on the Austrian labour market, there are significant differences in real hourly wages and life satisfaction between commuters and migrants. Life Satisfaction has been an important issue in the recent research on the microconsequences of East–West migration/circular mobility in Europe. In particular, there has been considerable debate on whether migration or East–West circulation actually leads to improved quality of life as a result of more material resources being available to those who engage in it, given that occupational trajectories may not be optimal in all respects (Bălţătescu 2007: 65; Bartram 2013). Therefore, indicators of life satisfaction and wage differences are important factors when it comes to drawing conclusions about social inequality and the distribution of life chances.

Table 12.2 shows that *cross-border commuters receive medium-level wages*. They earn more than twice as much as non-mobile employees in Hungary, Slovakia, and the Czech Republic. However, their wages are much lower than those of natives and migrants who work in Austria. This may be due to the relatively strong segregation within the Austrian labour market. Wages are comparatively low in a number of branches, especially in hospitality, retail, health care, and other social services. For example, the average wage of Austrian natives is €9.30 in hospitality and €9.85 in social services (Authors' calculations based on EU SILC 2012). This is clearly below the national average, and the wages of migrant workers in these branches are even lower. Another reason for the wage difference may be that work experience gained in Hungary, Slovakia, and the Czech Republic is not given much credit in wage agreements.

Table 12.2 Wages and life satisfaction of natives, migrants (the 'foreign-born'), and commuters in Austria compared with non-commuters, 2012/13

	EU-SILC Statistik Austria Data		TRANSLAB Data	
	Natives	Migrants[a]	Commuters	Non-commuters
Real hourly wages (median)	14.58*	11.56*	7.77	3.45*
N	4,091	727	1,004	955
Life satisfaction (mean)[b]	5.33*	4.96*	4.77	4.18*
N	4,076	688	1,322	1,286

EU-SILC Statistik Austria Data 2012; TRANSLAB survey 2012/13; Authors' calculations based on data on workers between 21 and 65 years of age with a main job (minimum 20 hours/week) in Austria (without employers and family employees)

[a]The category 'migrants' comprises persons from the EU-27, former Yugoslavia (not including Slovenia), Turkey and all other countries

[b]1 = extremely dissatisfied, 6 = extremely satisfied. For an appropriate comparison with the EU-SILC measurement of life satisfaction, we transformed the ten-point scale of the TRANSLAB survey into a six-point scale. Statistical differences to the group of cross-border commuters were tested by using Mood's median-test (wages) and Games–Howell post-hoc-tests (life satisfaction); significance level: * $p < 0.05$

Cross-border commuters show a relatively high life satisfaction. Commuters in our study show a higher life satisfaction (4.77) than non-mobile employees in Hungary, Slovakia, and the Czech Republic (4.18). This is consistent with findings of Bartram (2013), who notes that East–West-migrants are happier on average than Eastern Europeans who stay in their home country. The level of life satisfaction of cross-border commuters is comparable with those of migrants residing in Austria. Our results also indicate that, on average, natives are more satisfied with their lives (5.33) than migrants (4.96).

This brief case study has illustrated that within the European context, and especially within the nascent European polity, national societies have been challenged and fundamentally transformed, and that they are no longer independent entities but rather are closely interwoven and connected (Mau and Verwiebe 2010). Increasing flows of commodities, people, capital, information, and knowledge have profoundly changed the functions and significance of borders (O'Dowd 2002). The intensification of cross-border relations and partnerships resulting from institutional relationships has been leading to a de-bordering of the European territory (Perkmann 2003). For this reason, 'methodological nationalism', which equates 'society' with 'nation state', has been subject to considerable criticism (see in particular Wimmer and Glick Schiller 2002). In the politically unified Europe the uniqueness of national reference systems is being replaced by the ambiguity of a variety of different membership zones and negotiable territorial spaces (Bös 2000; Bös and Zimmer 2006). The 'spatial connection of collective identities' (Bach 2008) formed through the binding of nations is becoming increasingly insecure. State borders are undergoing a major transformation: during the time of nation states they functioned as conflict and contact zones that separated territorial units, language, culture and identity borders. The abolition of Europe's internal borders since the implementation of the Schengen Agreement has transferred this exclusionary function to the EU's external borders (Eigmüller 2010).

12.6 Outlook

Recently, the new patterns of transnational commuting and their effects on socio-economic status, well-being, and emerging forms of transnational agency and belonging have been receiving increasing attention in migration research. From a sociological perspective, the conceptualization of new patterns of migration and mobility refers not only to the increasingly diversified practices of border crossing but also to the placement of migrants in the social stratification and cultural norm and value systems. Thus, key questions in sociological research include: Where are the newcomers placed in the dominant inequality system? What opportunities exist to leave socially assigned positions? How open is the dominant society to assimilate new conceptions of life and lifestyles? What can be done to let social conflicts result in social innovation rather than social aggression and exclusion? Traditionally, migration and integration processes have been explained by neoclassical economic theories (individual income maximization) and integration–assimilation theories. More recent approaches have defined migration as part of the linkages between societies, so migration research should be embedded in the study of globalization and social transformation to take into consideration the general (global) changes in social structures and social relationships (Castles 2010). Intra-European cross-border-mobility, particularly that along the line that used to separate the East and the West, is a prime example of such entanglement, and shows how useful it is to intersect migration theory and social theory. Therefore the contribution makes use of a politically driven social transformation perspective.

The question is whether institutionalization can help to transform the currently heterogeneous political and social area into a more homogeneous social, political, and legal space (see Bös and Zimmer 2006). However, analysis that focuses exclusively on processes of institutionalization and attempts at political control is not sufficient; instead, it is necessary to focus on the border regions themselves, considering that according to Mau (2006) the EU can best be understood in relation to its borders. Being the main places where the space of flows meets the space of places, border regions provide fertile ground to study the transformation of states in their struggle to control movements from transnational networks (O'Dowd 2002).

Future research should take different perspectives and focus on the effects on vulnerable groups in this process: mobile workers, but also certain groups of local residents. Until now, most of the research on migration and mobility has used the social-transformation perspective through the conceptual lens of development: the less developed sending region is being, and has to be, socially transformed, but no comprehensive analyses of the effects on local residents have been provided. The lives of local non-migrants are also being transformed even though they do not themselves move. This could also be a focus of further research. Specifically, it might be worthwhile to take a closer look at potential transformational effects within the local labour market. In addition, there is considerable need to explore research questions such as the following: To what extent do commuters act as agents in institutional development? How do commuters spend their money (improvement of living standards, daily household expenses, employment-generating activities)? Does cross-border commuting contribute to a new rift within the rural low-wage labour market sector (e.g. due to higher language proficiency requirements in the service sector)? How do new institutional realities influence social inequalities within the sending and receiving communities? How does the transformation of the function of physical inner-European borders lead to the creation of new symbolic borders? The body of academic literature in this field is still rudimentarily established and lacks a comprehensive understanding. Future studies dealing with these questions would contribute to a better understanding of social-transformational consequences of cross-border commuting in the European Union.

References

Albert, M. (1998). On boundaries, territory and postmodernity: An international relations perspective. *Geopolitics, 3*(1), 53–68. doi:10.1080/14650049808407607.

Bach, M. (2008). *Europa ohne Gesellschaft: Politische Soziologie der europäischen Integration.* Wiesbaden: VS Verlag für Sozialwissenschaft/GWV Fachverlage.

Bălţătescu, S. (2007). Central and Eastern Europeans migrants' subjective quality of life: A comparative study. *Journal of Identity and Migration Studies, 1*(2), 67–81.

Bartram, D. (2013). Migration, return, and happiness in Romania. *European Societies, 15*(3), 408–422. doi:10.1080/14616696.2012.726735.

Bös, M. (2000). Zur Kongruenz sozialer Grenzen: Das Spannungsfeld von Territorien, Bevölkerungen und Kulturen in Europa. In M. Bach (Ed.), *Die Europäisierung nationaler Gesellschaften: Sonderheft 40/2000: Kölner Zeitschrift für Soziologie und Sozialpsychologie* (pp. 429–455). Wiesbaden: Westdeutscher Verlag.

Bös, M., & Zimmer, K. (2006). Wenn Grenzen wandern: Zur Dynamik von Grenzverschiebungen im Osten Europas. In M. Eigmüller & G. Vobruba (Eds.), *Grenzsoziologie: Die politische Strukturierung des Raumes* (pp. 157–184). Wiesbaden: VS Verlag für Sozialwissenschaft/GWV Fachverlage.

Brettell, C. B., & Hollifield, J. F. (2008). *Migration theory: Talking across disciplines.* New York/Abingdon: Routledge.

Buch, T., Schmidt, T. D., & Niebuhr, A. K. (2009). Cross-border commuting in the Danish–German border region – Integration, institutions and cross-border interaction. *Borderlands, 24*(2), 38–54. doi:10.1080/08865655.2009.9695726.

Castles, S. (2010). Understanding global migration: A social transformation perspective. *Journal of Ethnic and Migration Studies, 36*(10), 1565–1586. doi:10.1080/1369183X.2010.489381.

Centrope Agency. (2012). *Centrope strategy 2013+: Centrope action plan.* Vienna: Europaforum Wien, ARGE Centrope.http://www.centrope.com/repository/centrope/downloads/centrope_Strategy_Action_Plan_2013_en.pdf

Constant, A. F., Nottmeyer, O., & Zimmermann, K. F. (2012). *The economics of circular migration.* Bonn: Discussion Paper No. 6940. http://www.iza.org/MigrationHandbook/03_Constant-Nottmeyer_Zimmermann_The_Economics_of_Circular_Migration.pdf

Cresswell, T. (2006). *On the move: Mobility in the modern Western world*. New York/Abingdon: Routledge.

Cyrus, N. (2008). Mobilität im Verborgenen: Plurilokale Mobilitätspraxen illegal beschäftigter polnischer Haushaltsarbeiterinnen in Berlin. In G. Hentges, V. Hinnenkamp, & A. Zwengel (Eds.), *Migrations- und Integrationsforschung in der Diskussion: Biografie, Sprache und Bildung als zentrale Bezugspunkte* (pp. 171–201). Wiesbaden: VS Verlag für Sozialwissenschaft/GWV Fachverlage.

De Gijsel, P., & Janssen, M. (2000). Understanding the Dutch–German cross-border labour market: Are highly educated workers unwilling to move? *Tijdschrift voor Economische en Sociale Geografie, 91*(1), 61–77. doi:10.1111/1467-9663.00093.

Drevon, G., & Gerber, P. (2012). Soziodemografische Profile, die starken Veränderungen unterworfen sind. In F. Schmitz, G. Drevon, & P. Gerber (Eds.), *Die Mobilität der in Luxemburg beschäftigten Grenzgänger: Dynamik und Perspektiven* (pp. 8–11). Esch-sur-Alzette: CEPS/INSTEAD.

Eigmüller, M. (2010). Räume und Grenzen in Europa: Der Mehrwert soziologischer Grenz- und Raumforschung für die Europasoziologie. In M. Eigemüller & S. Mau (Eds.), *Gesellschaftstheorie und Europapolitik: Sozialwissenschaftliche Ansätze zur Europaforschung* (pp. 133–141). Wiesbaden: VS Verlag für Sozialwissenschaft/GWV Fachverlage.

Findlay, A., King, R., Stam, A., & Ruiz-Gelices, E. (2006). Ever reluctant Europeans: The changing geographies of UK students studying and working abroad. *European Urban and Regional Studies, 13*(4), 291–318. doi:10.1177/0969776406065429.

Gottholmseder, G., & Theurl, E. (2007). Determinants of cross-border commuting: Do cross-border commuters within the household matter? *Journal of Borderlands Studies, 22*(2), 97–112. doi:10.1080/08865655.2007.9695679.

Horvath, K. (2012). National numbers for transnational relations? Challenges of integrating quantitative methods into research on transnational labour market relations. *Ethnic and Racial Studies, 35*(10), 1741–1757. doi:10.1080/01419870.2012.659270.

Kalter, F. (2011). Social capital and the dynamics of temporary labour migration from Poland to Germany. *European Sociological Review, 27*(5), 555–569. doi:10.1093/esr/jcq025.

King, R., & Ruiz-Gelices, E. (2003). International student migration and the European 'Year Abroad': Effects on European identity and subsequent migration behaviour. *International Journal of Population Geography, 9*(3), 229–252. doi:10.1002/ijpg.280.

Klatt, M., & Herrmann, H. (2011). Half empty or Half full? Over 30 years of regional cross-border cooperation within the EU: experiences at the Dutch–German and Danish–German border. *Journal of Borderlands Studies, 26*(1), 65–87. doi:10.1080/08865655.2011.590289.

Massey, D. S. (1987). The ethnosurvey in theory and practice. *International Migration Review, 21*(4), 1498–1522. doi:10.2307/2546522.

Mau, S. (2006). Die Politik der Grenze. Grenzziehung und politische Systembildung in der Europäischen Union. *Berliner Journal für Soziologie, 16*(1), 115–132. doi:10.1007/s11609-006-0008-2.

Mau, S., & Büttner, S. (2010). Transnationality. In S. Immerfall & G. Therborn (Eds.), *Handbook of European societies: Social transformations in the 21st century* (pp. 537–570). New York/Dordrecht/Heidelberg, London: Springer.

Mau, S., & Verwiebe, R. (2010). *European societies:Mapping structure and change*. Bristol: The Policy Press.

Mau, S., Mewes, J., & Zimmermann, A. (2008). Cosmopolitan attitudes through transnational social practices? *Global Networks, 8*(1), 1–24. doi:10.1111/j.1471-0374.2008.00183.x.

Miera, F. (2008). Long term residents and commuters: Change of patterns in migration from Poland to Germany. *Journal of Immigrant & Refugee Studies, 6*(3), 297–311. doi:10.1080/15362940802371028.

Newland, K., Agunias, D. R., & Terrazas, A. (2008). *Learning by doing: Experiences of circular migration*. Washington, DC: Migration Policy Institute. http://www.migrationpolicy.org/pubs/Insight-IGC-Sept08.pdf

O'Dowd, L. (2002). The changing significance of European borders. *Regional & Federal Studies, 12*(4), 13–36. doi:10.1080/714004774.

Paci, P., Tiongson, E. R., Walewski, M., & Liwiński, J. (2010). Internal labour mobility in Central Europe and the Baltic Region: Evidence from labour force surveys. In M. Walewski, F. E. Caroleo, & F. Pastore (Eds.), *The labour market impact of the EU enlargement: A new regional geography of Europe?* (pp. 197–225). Berlin/Heidelberg: Springer.

Perkmann, M. (1999). Building governance institutions across European borders. *Regional Studies, 33*(7), 657–667. doi:10.1080/00343409950078693.

Perkmann, M. (2002). Euroregions: Institutional entrepreneurship in the European Union. In M. Perkmann & N.-L. Sum (Eds.), *Globalization, regionalization and cross-border regions* (pp. 103–124). Basingstoke/New York: Palgrave Macmillan.

Perkmann, M. (2003). Cross-border regions in Europe: Significance and drivers of regional cross-border co-operation. *European Urban and Regional Studies, 10*(2), 153–171. doi:10.1177/0969776403010002004.

Schmitz, F., Drevon, G., & Gerber, P. (Eds.). (2012). *Die Mobilität der in Luxemburg beschäftigten Grenzgänger: Dynamik und Perspektiven*. Esch-sur-Alzette: CEPS/INSTEAD.

Strüver, A. (2005a). Spheres of transnationalism within the European Union: On open doors, thresholds and drawbridges along the Dutch–German border. *Journal of Ethnic and Migration Studies, 31*(2), 323–343. doi:10.1080/1369183042000339954.

Strüver, A. (2005b). *Stories of the 'Boring Border': The Dutch–German borderscape in people's minds*. Münster: LIT.

Studer, L. (2004). *Analyse der Arbeitsmärkte und Arbeitskräftewanderungen im Fürstentum Liechtenstein und in Vorarlberg*. Regensburg: Roderer.

Terlouw, K. (2012). Border surfers and Euroregions: Unplanned cross-border behaviour and planned territorial structures of cross-border governance. *Planning Practice & Research, 27*(3), 351–366. doi:10.1080/02697459.2012.670939.

Triandafyllidou, A. (2013). Circular migration: Introductory remarks. In A. Triandafyllidou (Ed.), *Circular migration between Europe and its neighbourhood: Choice or necessity?* (pp. 1–21). Oxford: Oxford University Press.

Van Houtum, H., & Gielis, R. (2006). Elastic migration: The case of Dutch short-distance transmigrants in Belgian and German Borderlands. *Tijdschrift voor Economische en Sociale Geografie, 97*(2), 195–202. doi:10.1111/j.1467-9663.2006.00512.x.

Venturini, A. (2008). *Circular migration as an employment strategy for Mediterranean countries: CARIM analytic and synthetic notes 2008/39*. San Domenico di Fiesole: European University Institute, Robert Schumann Centre for Advanced Studies. http://cadmus.eui.eu/bitstream/handle/1814/8390/CARIM_AS&N_2008_39.pdf?sequence=1

Vertovec, S. (2007). *Circular migration: The way forward in global policy? Year 2007: Paper 4*. Oxford: International Migration Institute, University of Oxford. http://www.imi.ox.ac.uk/pdfs/wp/wp4-circular-migration-policy.pdf

Verwiebe, R., Mau, S., Seidel, N., & Kathmann, T. (2010). Skilled German migrants and their motives for migration within Europe. *Journal of International Migration and Integration, 11*(3), 273–293. doi:10.1007/s12134-010-0141-9.

Wallace, C. (2002). Opening and closing borders: Migration and mobility in East-Central Europe. *Journal of Ethnic and Migration Studies, 28*(4), 603–625. doi:10.1080/1369183021000032227.

Wallace, C., & Vincent, K. (2007). Recent migration from the New European borderlands. *Review of Sociology of the Hungarian Sociological Association, 13*(2), 19–37. doi:10.1556/RevSoc.13.2007.2.2.

Wimmer, A., & Glick Schiller, N. (2002). Methodological nationalism and beyond: Nation-state building, migration and the social sciences. *Global Networks, 2*(4), 301–334. doi:10.1111/1471-0374.00043.

Chapter 13
Portability of Social Protection in the European Union

Transformation of National Welfare Systems?

Elaine Moriarty, James Wickham, Alicja Bobek and Sally Daly

13.1 Introduction[1]

This chapter explores the tensions between the European Union's commitment to a single European labour market in which all member state nationals are treated equally and the continuing national basis of welfare systems. In particular it highlights the dynamics between increasingly mobile European nationals who are accessing and moving their social welfare supports across the EU, EU directives guaranteeing equal protection among member state nationals, and national welfare implementation systems which have engaged in selective 'restriction' policies in response to EU enlargements during the 2000s. The chapter examines the topic using a case study of Polish migration to Ireland following Poland's accession to the EU in 2004.

It begins with a discussion of the context of intra-EU migration and increased cross-border mobility. In order to examine European mobilities and the portability[2] of social protection in the European Union, the results of a qualitative panel study (QPS) are presented which tracked a group of young Polish nationals in the Irish labour market (2008–2013), examining their experiences of employment, unemployment, welfare utilization, and mobility during a period of radically changing economic circumstances (see Krings et al. 2013). It also draws on stakeholder interviews with state and non-state actors, as well as on an analysis of the Irish

[1] The chapter has benefited from financial support of the Irish Research Council and from research assistance from Eleanor Russell.

[2] 'Portability' of social protection refers to the entitlement of EU citizens to move to live and work in another EU country and to be treated in the same way as the nationals in the new place of residence as regards their welfare benefits independent of nationality and country of residence (see Avato et al. 2010 for discussion).

E. Moriarty (✉) • J. Wickham • A. Bobek • S. Daly
Trinity College, University of Dublin, Dublin, Ireland
e-mail: emoriar@tcd.ie

A. Amelina et al. (eds.), *An Anthology of Migration and Social Transformation*,
IMISCOE Research Series, DOI 10.1007/978-3-319-23666-7_13

quarterly national household survey, Department of Social Protection records on social welfare transfers 2000–2010, and an analysis of Irish welfare policy adjustments since 2004.

The study reveals attempts to qualify EU social rights with the introduction of a series of social-policy adjustments based on residency during the 2000s. These measures served to reassert that people live in one place, accumulating benefits to be drawn down in that same place in the event of need. This static concept of welfare entitlement ignores the social transformation that has occurred as a result of new forms of mobility within Europe, particularly evidenced through the recent EU enlargements, and is contrary to the EU-wide policy, which advocates mobility with equality (for details on the concept of social transformation, see Chap. 2, in this volume).

13.2 Intra-EU Migration: A New European Mobility Space?

In recent decades migration flows in the European Union have been transformed, both quantitatively and qualitatively. Contemporary movements are often multidirectional and transient, covering a continuum of forms of mobility ranging from worker commuting (Wallace 2001) to lifestyle migration (O'Reilly 2007). While the number of EU citizens living abroad remains relatively low, it has steadily increased in the last two decades despite the economic crisis (OECD 2013). This is no longer an 'elite migration' of only the highly skilled but also appeals to individuals who seek to enhance their economic and cultural capital (Recchi 2006: 76; Kennedy 2010). Krings et al. (2013) use the concept of 'worklife pathways' to understand how, especially for the younger and more educated of these migrants, the move abroad not only is work-related but also involves lifestyle choices as part of a broader aspiration for self-development.

Much of this contemporary mobility is still work-related despite the constraints of the financial crisis because there is a continuous demand for migrant labour in the expanding service sectors of the advanced economies and also in lower-skilled manufacturing and construction sectors (OECD 2013). In addition, economic globalization and the associated labour market flexibilization have seen an increase in business travel, posted work, and frontier work, highlighting issues of multilocatedness (Ackers 2004). In this scenario workers' residences do not necessarily coincide with their location of employment. As cross-border mobility in the European Union has become more transient and circular, traditional concepts of integration and citizenship are less capable of capturing these movements. Furthermore, attempts to conceptualize intra-European migration have to go beyond the nation state and consider the evolving transnational social space (Faist and Özveren 2004) of the European Union in which these new mobilities occur. While some aspects of what this chapter describes as new mobilities are familiar, for example, transnational care practices (see Chap. 16, in this volume for a discussion of contemporary Eastern European female care worker migration) and circular migration were all common during the guest worker era (Krings et al. 2013) such migration was primarily governed at a bilateral level, with individuals often constrained by residence and work permits. This chapter emphasizes a far more complex supranational political framework that regulates contemporary mobilities in the European Union and has granted European nationals a form of agency and individualization that is new.

A significant facilitator of this individualized mobility is the role of social policy as a guarantor of cross-border mobility (Sainsbury 2006). The right to free movement in Europe—that is, the free movement of the four pillars of freedom: goods, capital, services, and labour—has been gradually extended since its founding, in 1957, as part of the Treaty establishing the European Economic Community. Early European regulations sought to reduce barriers to cross-border mobility for European workers by coordinating national social protection systems connected to working lives. For example, European Council Regulation 1408/71 provides that European member states may not discriminate against resident EU nationals from another member state as regards social security; EU migrant workers can receive their welfare benefits in a country other than the one where the right was earned; eligibility periods over different time periods can be aggregated; and benefits can be accumulated on the basis of the time spent in the respective countries. Another key regulation was Regulation 1612/68, which ensured that EU migrant workers have the same rights as nationals, that they enjoy the same social and tax advantages as national workers, and that they may not be discriminated against based on nationality.

The 2004 EU Directive on Free Movement extended the right to free movement and residence in the EU from the free movement of *workers* to the free movement of *persons*. Effectively, European 'migrant workers' have become 'EU movers' (Favell and Recchi 2009), which illustrates the dynamism associated with political integration at the European level. What distinguishes contemporary European movement is that EU nationals should no longer be bound by a residence or work permit, and that new mobility opportunities and lifestyle choices should be permitted (see Chap. 13, in this volume for a discussion of how institutionalised promotion of intra-European mobility facilitates cross-border commuting). Arguably, nationals of new member states increasingly resemble their West European peers in the pursuit of flexible worklife pathways in the new European mobility space.

In addition to European Council regulations, the European Court of Justice has played a major role in facilitating cross-border mobility, consistently interpreting these principles in a broad and favourable way towards migrants. Much of the initial testing of the applicability of such cross-border rights was related to health care. Obermaier (2009) demonstrates how the 1998 Kohll/Decker ECJ rulings, codified through the Directive on the Application of Patients' Rights in Cross-Border Healthcare, has enabled patients to seek health care in other European member states while the costs are covered by their national systems. While the threat to territorial principles of national governments was contested by individual nation states, the gradual incorporation of portable health care entitlements is seen by Obermaier as most significant. Interestingly, many of the cases taken to the ECJ to seek clarification on EU Directives emerge from cases taken to the courts by individual

European citizens (Eigmüller 2013). This shows that European political integration is being promoted at both the macrolevel, through European Council Directives and Regulations, and the microlevel, through individual citizen agency.

EU nationals are changing jobs more frequently than they did in the past, are more likely to go through periods of unemployment, and are more likely to work part time or to be self-employed (Holzmann and Koettl 2011: 2). Thus, the tension between the increasingly mobile European national who may choose to work, study, travel, and retire in various different European nation states in which they were not born and territorial nation states that continue to have a desire to control the 'legitimate means of movement' (Mau et al. 2012) becomes more pronounced. Individual member states are increasingly confronting the disconnect between the perceived legitimacy of the social-security system understood as based on solidarity with one's own community and the entitlement of mobile European nationals to social protection in their place of residence regardless of their sense of belonging. Indeed, the consequences of such tensions highlight an increasing focus by the political framework of the European Union on protecting the *individual* rights of European nationals in a unified labour market. Simultaneously, the national welfare systems attempt to 'adjust' access to what often continues to be deemed 'national' entitlements.

13.3 EU Enlargement, 'Free' Movement, and Social-Policy Adjustments

Since the European Union enlargement of May 1, 2004, the movement of European nationals has become a more contentious issue. Citizens of the Czech Republic, Estonia, Hungary, Latvia, Lithuania, Slovakia, Slovenia, Poland, Malta, and Cyprus were all granted the right of free movement across the European Union. However, the Treaty of Accession 2003 allowed existing member states to restrict the access of nationals of all the new member states (excluding Malta and Cyprus) to their labour markets for a transition period of up to 7 years. The aim of these transitional arrangements was to allow member states to gradually introduce free movement while also avoiding labour market disturbances the feared would occur as a result of a sudden inflow of workers following accession. There were three phases (2+3+2 years) in the 2003 transitional arrangements, during which member states could apply labour market restrictions to nationals of new member states. The key restriction mechanism applied by member states was work permit schemes (EC 2008).

Varying transitional arrangements were introduced in Phase 1 (2004–2006) by all countries except the United Kingdom, Ireland, and Sweden. During the course of the second phase (2006–2009) eight member states opened their labour markets (2006: Greece, Spain, Portugal, Finland, Italy; 2007: Netherlands, Luxembourg; 2008: France). From the beginning of the third phase (2009) Belgium and Denmark ended restrictions so that in the final 2 years of the transitional period only Germany and Austria continued to apply substantial restrictions on labour market access (EC 2011), which have since been lifted.

Transitional arrangements served to limit migrants' access not only to the labour market but also to the social-security systems of those member states. Jon Kvist (2004) examined these EU regulations in the context of EU accession and demonstrated how there was an intersection of labour market access and social-policy adjustment as a result of the EU enlargement in 2004. He found that EU-15 member states entered what he describes as strategic interactions on the assumption that welfare states with generous welfare benefits and accessible labour markets would 'become magnets' (Kvist 2004: 301) for welfare migration (see Borjas 1999 for discussion of welfare as a magent for migrants). He also showed how EU-15 countries with the fewest labour market restrictions were most active in social-policy adjustment coming up to accession in 2004. These adjustments were introduced to prevent 'welfare tourism', which was a much-discussed, and often ill-informed, public concern in 2004.

At the time of accession Ireland was one of only three countries, along with the UK and Sweden, which granted full free movement rights to citizens of new member states intending to work.[3] However, both the UK and Ireland changed their benefit regimes to prevent 'welfare tourism' from the new EU member states. The then UK Secretary of State for the Home Department, David Blunkett, told Parliament on February 23, 2004, that it was important to recognize that there was a potential risk of people from new member states abusing welfare, and that 'we have to make sure that any potential basis for the exploitation of any loopholes in rules is closed off' (Hansard 2004). This led the UK to impose a 2-year work requirement before migrants from new member states could access a range of British social-security benefits, social housing, and health care. In addition, nationals of new member states were required to register with a newly established Worker Registration Scheme that would monitor labour market developments and justify restrictions on migrant workers from new member states if deemed necessary.

On the same day the then Irish Taoiseach (Prime Minister), Bertie Ahern, announced that the Irish 'will put in place measures to prevent the abuse of the social welfare system' (Ahern 2004). This was followed by an announcement from the then Minister for Social and Family Affairs, Mary Coughlan, that she was 'concerned [...] that Ireland would remain the only country that had not put in place protection for its welfare system' and that she would propose 'changes to the social welfare code [...] no less robust than those in Britain' (Coughlan 2004). This bilateral strategic interaction shows signs of resistance to EU measures which had been introduced to ensure equal rights for all mobile EU citizens.

The primary measure Ireland introduced was the Habitual Residence Condition (HRC) mirroring the social-policy adjustments made in the UK. The HRC states that 'Since 1 May 2004, all applicants regardless of nationality are required to be

[3] Ireland did impose transitional arrangements for the 2007 accession of Romania and Bulgaria, though these have now been relaxed.

habitually resident in the State in order to qualify for' allowances including child benefit, carers allowance, and so on. The HRC applies in principle to both EU nationals (including returning Irish citizens) and non-EU nationals.[4] To qualify as habitually resident, applicants must provide evidence of residence over a continuous period of time (at least 2 years), the term 'habitually resident' being 'intended to convey a degree of permanence evidenced by a regular physical presence enduring for some time [...] and intended to continue [...] in the foreseeable future' (DSP 2013a). As early as 2004 the European Commission raised questions about this 2-year waiting period, noting that it may constitute a breach of the equality principle provided in Regulations 1408/71 and 1612/68. The European Commission was particularly concerned that the HRC conditions would have a greater negative impact on migrant workers than on workers of Irish nationality. A second key issue raised was that some social benefits such as child benefit and family payments should be available to all workers regardless of their nationality and outside of the HRC principle.

While this reminder from the European Commission was communicated across the Department of Social Protection in Ireland, with the onset of the recession the habitual residence condition was further adjusted. Since 2007, to be deemed habitually resident, applicants were required to prove that their 'centre of interest' was in Ireland.[5] In particular 'A person's main centre of interest would normally be in the country in which s/he has lived all his/her life and has his/her home and family. This may be maintained even where a person lives and works for a period of time in another country' (DSP 2013a). Two primary objectives were pursued. Firstly, there were concerns about the obstacles returning Irish migrants faced because of the HRC when trying to access social-welfare supports. New guidelines issued by the Department of Social Protection in 2011 clarified that 'returned [Irish] emigrants or retired missionaries who have chosen to resettle in Ireland should be considered to have their main centre of interest here' (Crosscare 2013). Secondly, it provided a means to undermine claims by nationals of new member states who, despite having lived in Ireland for the required time period, continued to have property or a family in another European country, which was thereby deemed to undermine their claim to centre of interest (Cairde 2013).

[4] Section 246 of the Social Welfare Consolidation Act 2005 provides that 'it shall be presumed, until the contrary is shown, that a person is not habitually resident in the State at the date of the making of the application concerned unless he has been present in the State or any other part of the Common Travel Area for a continuous period of 2 years ending on that date.'

[5] Section 30 of the Social Welfare and Pensions Act 2007 provides that, 'a deciding officer or the Executive, when determining whether a person is habitually resident in the State, shall take into consideration all the circumstances of the case including, in particular, the following: (*a*) the length and continuity of residence in the State or in any other particular country; (*b*) the length and purpose of any absence from the State; (*c*) the nature and pattern of the person's employment; (*d*) the person's main centre of interest, and (*e*) the future intentions of the person concerned as they appear from all the circumstances.'

Thus, despite the gradual transfer of social-policy competences from national levels to the European level, the fact that the core functions of national welfare systems remain within the remit of the nation state shows the power of the state to intervene in the transposition and application of such European instruments.

13.4 Ireland, Migration, and the Welfare State in an Enlarged Union

Ireland was a major recipient of migrant flows from the new EU member states. An economic boom in conjunction with a flexible and open labour market facilitated large-scale inward migration from the accession states. Since 2004 almost 500,000 nationals of new member states have arrived in Ireland. With over 300,000 arrivals, Polish nationals account by far for the largest nationality group of all migrants from new member states. As can be seen in Fig. 13.1, inflows from the new member states peaked in 2006.

A qualitative panel study (QPS) (2008–2013) was designed to track a group of young Polish nationals active in the Irish labour market and in particular their experiences of employment, unemployment, welfare utilization, and mobility during a period of radically changing economic circumstances (Krings et al. 2013). The QPS is comprised of 10 women and 12 men aged between 22 and 38 years, almost all of whom arrived in Ireland after the enlargement of 2004. While some were educated to secondary level, the majority held a third-level degree. They were found in a variety of occupations ranging from general operatives and less-skilled service sector positions to managerial and professional positions in four employment sectors: construction, hospitality, software, and financial services.

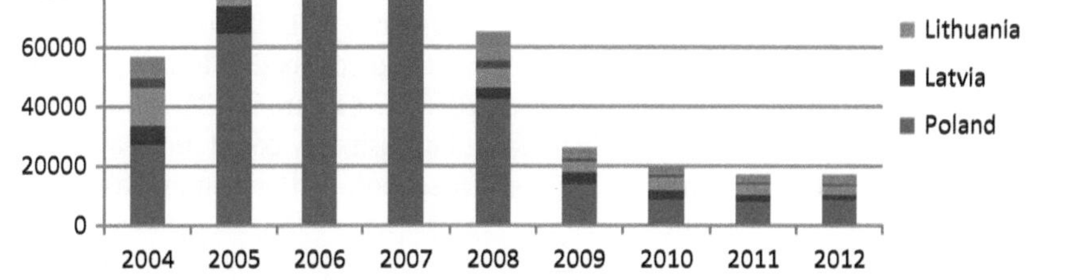

Fig. 13.1 Allocation of Personal Public Service numbers for migrants from new member states by year and country (DSP 2013b)

The QPS found that their motivation for moving to Ireland included better employment opportunities, higher wages, and an opportunity to learn the English language. Others cited the spirit of adventure, opportunity to travel, and a desire to escape the 'dull reality' of daily life in Poland. When studying the participants' mobility, we noted frequent travel to Poland to visit the hairdresser, the dentist, the doctor, and other service providers. This frequent mobility prompted an examination of what strategies and tactics migrants were engaging in to either invest in their welfare futures or deal with contemporary challenges.

After almost two decades of unprecedented growth during the Celtic Tiger years Ireland was severely hit by a recession. A dramatic decline in the housing market in conjunction with the global financial crisis dramatically altered the economic fortunes of the country. GDP growth in Ireland reached 6 % in 2007, only to be replaced by a 3-per-cent contraction in 2008. The unemployment rate, once among the lowest in the European Union, reached 14.4 % in 2013. An increase in unemployment was particularly noticeable among nationals of new member states, with unemployment rates almost trebling from 6.4 to 18 % (CSO 2011a). In the context of the recession and unemployment, social welfare protection became very important. As more migrants lost their jobs, they increasingly utilized their welfare entitlements as a 'survival' strategy to cushion the impact of unemployment (Krings et al. 2009).

The study shows that welfare considerations did not influence the initial decision to move to Ireland. However, changes in employment opportunities do raise questions about social-welfare activity. EU-15 to EU-25 state nationals experienced the greatest change in social welfare activity between 2006 and 2011. Those arriving in 2006 had a social-welfare activity rate of 8 % in that year, but the rate had risen to 32 % by 2011, illustrating that those on social welfare tended to be longer-term migrants who had been active in the labour market but had lost their jobs (CSO 2011b). In other words, the data shows that this group of migrants does not engage in 'welfare tourism', confirming previous research on intra-European migration that found little evidence to suggest that welfare provisions in the host country are a migration incentive (Kvist 2004; Barrett and McCarthy 2008).

While there were conflicting reports by participants on experiences of engaging with the social-welfare system in Ireland, some participants reported being pleasantly surprised by how smoothly the application process worked in the country. However, some of the representatives of the stakeholders interviewed[6] mentioned severe delays in accessing entitlements and also claims of 'inconsistent interpretation' (Crosscare 2011) of the Habitual Residency Condition guidelines by social-welfare officers. Issues included difficulties encountered by both young and single individuals seeking to prove their centre of interest and connection to Ireland when applying for social-welfare assistance (Cairde 2013; Crosscare 2013). Some single individuals were deemed not habitually resident because they could not prove links with Ireland, did not have family or children in school, and/or continued to have

[6]Stakeholders interviewed included Cairde (Challenging Ethnic Minority Health Inequalities), Focus Ireland (an organization providing support for homeless people), and Crosscare (a social-support agency that helps marginalized people in Dublin).

family in Poland (Focus Ireland 2013). Pressurizing European nationals to return 'home' if they cannot prove a 'connection' to Ireland reinforces a static concept of migration.

While most of the participants did not report difficulties in accessing social-welfare benefits in Ireland, those who had accessed social protection felt some considerable shame and embarrassment. For some participants this translated into only applying for what was absolutely necessary but also what was perceived by those participants as their having *a right to*, such as unemployment benefits. But decisions were made not to apply for rent allowance (housing cost assistance) or medical cards, which would have had an element of means testing and discretion. This attitude of Polish nationals reflects attitudes found by Delaney (2007) among Irish nationals living in post-war Britain who were hesitant to apply for council housing despite having lived there for decades, deeming British nationals to have that *right* but not regarding themselves as migrants. This raises questions about discourse and practice around legitimacy. There is a growing division being reinforced between insurance-based contributions, which are considered individually earned and mobile, and universal, location-based entitlements, which are considered 'national' and to which some residents should not be entitled.

One crucial aspect of changing encounters with welfare provision is the rise of individualized and privatized social provision. The study of Polish nationals in Ireland found that many participants who remain resident in Ireland have chosen to purchase property or buy private life insurance and pension schemes in Poland, the main reason put forward being that it was a form of investment in the future. But, contrary to what the literature on migrant remittances has suggested, this was an individualized investment by young European nationals for their own personal benefit (Krings et al. 2013).

For many Polish nationals the Irish welfare system offered the opportunity to stay and search for new employment. However, the possibility of transferring welfare rights also raises a fundamental issue of cross-border entitlements and protection.

13.5 Portability of Welfare Rights between Ireland and Poland

A significant finding from the QPS study was the European dimension of migration and social protection, and in particular European nationals' awareness of the right to transfer welfare benefits from one EU country to another. However, there has also been a growing tension between the enjoyment by migrants of such cross-border social protection rights and national welfare states' nationalizing and restricting discourses and practices.

The social-security rights of people moving around the European Union are governed by EU Regulations 83/2004 and 987/2009 (DSP 2013a). Under such regulations a person who is getting jobseeker's benefit for at least 4 weeks in Ireland can

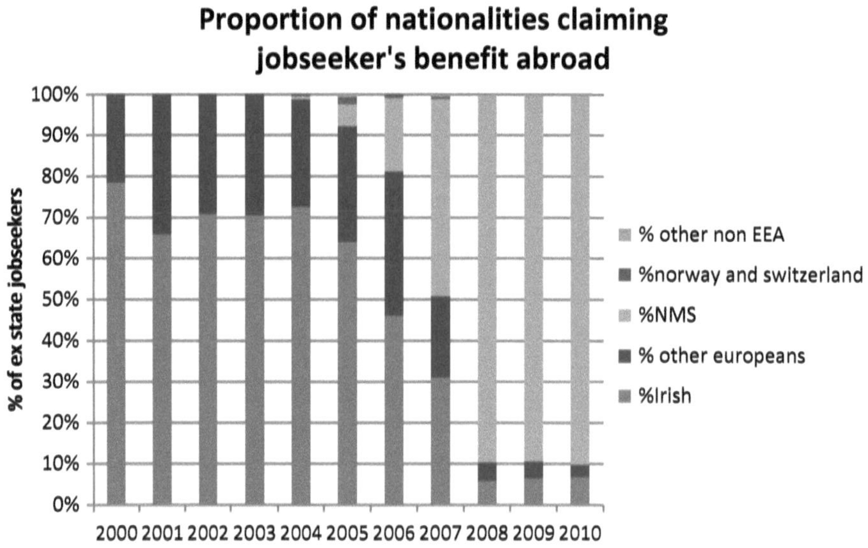

Fig. 13.2 Proportion of nationalities claiming jobseeker's benefit abroad, 2000–2010 (DSP 2013c)

transfer their claim to another member state for up to 13 weeks in order to look for work in that country. These new EU regulations have had a significant impact on the portability of social insurance–based benefits. In particular the replacement of the paper-based system with electronic data exchange has seen the introduction of direct payments between the competent state and the individual claiming.

Since the 2004 accession social-protection mobility has become increasingly significant for European nationals, as demonstrated by the analysis of the 'recipients receiving jobseeker's benefit from Ireland abroad'[7] presented in Fig. 13.2. This also shows a significant decrease in Irish nationals claiming jobseekers benefit abroad from 79 % in 2000 to 7 % in 2010 while NMS national claims have increased from 0 % in 2000 to 90 % of all claims abroad in 2010.

There is also increasing evidence of European nationals seeking to move more diverse types of benefits and supports. Stakeholders interviewed reported that EU nationals are provided with assistance in accessing illness benefit, invalidity pensions, carers benefit, and medical treatment (Cairde 2013; Crosscare 2013). The number of individuals accessing these diverse benefits abroad has increased though the number of these claims remain low. Recipients were primarily located in the 'old' European Community (UK, Italy) until 2006; since then, most claims have been filed by nationals of new member states (Czech Republic, Lithuania, Latvia, Estonia) (DSP 2013c).

[7] The figures presented in this section were accessed through a Freedom of Information request (DSP 2013c).

However, the issue that has most absorbed the energies of the Irish government are the implications of the EU's principle of equal treatment for eligibility to child benefit, namely that eligibility to benefits cannot be made dependent on nationality. Successive governments have expressed concerns about a threat to the legitimacy of the national welfare system, such as 'EU rules on benefits affecting the integrity of national social security systems in the wider union' (Smyth 2011a). As Table 13.1 shows, the cost of paying child benefit to the parents of non-resident children increased from €720,000 in 2005 to €20.9 million in 2008, although by 2012 this figure was reduced to €13.3 million spent supporting 7871 children (DSP 2013d). However, what is most apparent is how small this cost is relative to overall child benefit expenditure.

Early discourse focused on the importance of 'people in Ireland [having] confidence that particularly in times of scarce resources, benefits are paid to people who need them', as the Minister for Social Protection, Joan Burton, put it in 2011. This discourse questions the legitimacy of entitlements, particularly of the entitlement to family benefits for those not resident in Ireland, despite EU policy guarantees. In this context, Minister Burton sought to raise the issue at the EU level by requesting an 'impact assessment on how EU regulations on benefit payments are affecting national social welfare systems' (Smyth 2011b). European Commissioner for Employment, Social Affairs, and Inclusion László Andor did not support the Irish

Table 13.1 Child benefit expenditure

Child benefit	Total programme expenditure on child benefit[1]	Expenditure on child benefit claims going abroad[a2]	% of child benefit expenditure claimed abroad
2000	€637,543,000	Information not given	–
2001	€964,847,000	Information not given	–
2002	€1,462,793,000	Information not given	–
2003	€1,666,530,000	Information not given	–
2004	€1,765,117,000	Information not given	–
2005	€1,899,936,000	€720,000	0.04 %
2006	€2,056,925,000	€2,200,000	0.11 %
2007	€2,232,974,000	€4,770,000	0.21 %
2008	€2,453,957,000	€20,900,000	0.85 %
2009	€2,495,304,000	€19,700,000	0.79 %
2010	€2,213,429,000	€15,400,000	0.70 %
2011	€2,076,338,000	€13,100,000	0.63 %
2012	€2,046,955,000	€13,300,000	0.65 %

DSP (2013d)

[a]This expenditure reflects payments going to any country outside of Ireland, not just EU destinations

[1]Source: Department of Social Protection's ' Statistical Information on social welfare services', various years (http://www.welfare.ie/en/Pages/Statistical-Information-Reports---Archive.aspx accessed 19th November 2013)

[2]Source: Email correspondence with EU section of the child benefit office in the Department of Social Protection, November 2013

move to change EU rules governing entitlements to benefits. 'For us the question is about social security coordination and what I can say is that we have not been thinking about changing the rules here and especially not about restrictions'. He also confirmed that 'the free movement of workers is a fundamental right in the EU' (Collins 2011). Some European Union states such as Denmark and the UK have continued their attempts to raise the need for an impact assessment on how EU regulations on benefit payments are affecting national social-welfare systems (Lynch 2013).

By October 2012 Minister Burton had conceded that the 'implementation of change in this area [child benefit] is unlikely' (Minihan 2012). However, the unease and concern about 'welfare tourism' continues, with issues now being raised about the amount of revenue that is being lost as a consequence of transferring social benefits out of Ireland. The Fianna Fáil spokesman on Social Protection and Social Equality, Willie O'Dea, expressed 'concern at the "enormous" sum that was being taken out of the Irish economy and called on the department [of Social Protection] to examine how it can reduce the cost of paying benefits to up to 60,000 claimants in 93 different countries' (McQuinn and Hutton 2013). What is neglected in this national concern is the issue of Irish workers living in countries such as the UK and Germany. In addition, Warnes (2002) estimates that up to 20 % of the then Irish population aged over 65 were in receipt of a British old-age pension.

Importantly, the tension between nationality and residence requirements and European mobility has shown the lack of equality of social-rights access due to renewed emphasis on temporality of residence and by nationalizing discourses focusing on issues of legitimacy.

13.6 Conclusion

This chapter suggests that a rise in various forms of mobility has implications for national welfare systems and individual wellbeing. The examination of the Irish context shows that there is clear evidence of increased mobility across the European Union and a pronounced increase in the portability of social protection across borders as European nationals are exercising their right to be mobile. Attempts by the Irish state to qualify EU social rights and to adjust its obligations have been presented. In the first instance the Irish state introduced a qualified acceptance of entitlement with the use of HRC and centre of interest. These measures served to reassert the assumption that people live in one place, accumulating benefits to be drawn down in that same place in the event of need. These barriers were challenged at the macrolevel by interventions by the European Commission and also from a microlevel, whereby individuals, often with the support of NGOs, took cases against the Department of Social Protection in Ireland.

Ultimately, European mobility is likely to continue to transform in size, form, and complexity over the coming decades. Strategies to resist cross-border portability, the entitlement to, and portability of, social protection in the European Union have been transformed despite national welfare implementation systems. This static concept of welfare entitlement is being challenged through the social transformation that has occurred as a result of new forms of mobility within Europe, particularly evidenced through the recent EU enlargements. Further work is required to examine the extent to which the Irish experience of increased mobility and increased transferability of social protection is applicable in the wider European Union. With the ending of transitional arrangements for the new accession countries Bulgaria and Romania, public and political discourse have again ignited fears about 'welfare tourism' and the 'integrity' of national welfare systems across the European Union.

Given the territorially bound fiscal basis of contributions, the potential of a hierarchical social-protection system is emerging, with a clear political preference for contribution-based rather than general taxation–based welfare supports. Contemporary forms of mobility, particularly transnational types, could serve to undermine universal, non-contribution-based welfare supports and contribute to the expansion of private and contribution-based forms of welfare.

References

Ackers, L. (2004). Managing relationships in peripatetic careers: Scientific mobility in the European Union. *Women's Studies International Forum, 27*(3), 189–201. doi:10.1016/j.wsif.2004.03.001.

Ahern, B. (2004, February 23). *Ahern speaks of possible impact of enlargement on Irish Labour market.* Government of Ireland press.

Avato, J., Koettl, J., & Sabates-Wheeler, R. (2010). Social security regimes, global estimates and good practices: The status of social protection for international migrants. *World Development, 38*(4), 455–466. doi:10.1016/j.worlddev.2009.10.003.

Barrett, A., & McCarthy, Y. (2008). Immigrants and welfare programmes: Exploring the interactions between immigrant characteristics, immigrant welfare dependence and welfare policy. *Oxford Review of Economic Policy, 24*(3), 542–559. doi:10.1093/oxrep/grn026.

Borjas, G. (1999). Immigration and welfare magnets. *Journal of Labor Economics, 17*(4), 607–637.

Cairde. (2013, May 17). *Interview with representative.*

Collins, S. (2011, June 18). EU resists bid to cut cash for children not living here. *Irish Independent.* http://www.independent.ie/irish-news/eu-resists-bid-to-cut-cash-for-children-not-living-here-26743596.html

Coughlan, M. (2004, February 24). *Minister for social and family affairs, Mary Coughlan, to announce new social welfare code restrictions for Ireland.* Government of Ireland press.

Crosscare. (2011, March 9). *Interview with representative.*

Crosscare. (2013, May 17). *Interview with representative.*

CSO. (2011a). *Quarterly national household survey, 2004–2010.* Cork: Central Statistics Office.

CSO. (2011b). *Social welfare activity of New Member State migrants (2006–2011) by year of arrival.* Cork: Central Statistics Office.

Delaney, E. (2007). *The Irish in post-war Britain.* Oxford/New York: Oxford University Press.

DSP. (2013a). *Habitual residence condition.* Dublin: Department of Social Protection.

DSP. (2013b). *Personal Public Service Statistics (PPSN).* Dublin: Department of Social Protection.

DSP. (2013c). *Freedom of Information request: Statistics for welfare schemes (unemployment, carers, illness, child benefit) claimed abroad. November 2013.* Dublin: Department of Social Protection.

DSP. (2013d). *Statistical Information on social welfare services, various years*. Dublin: Department of Social Protection.
EC. (2008). *Commission report on transitional arrangements regarding free movement of workers* (MEMO/08/718). Brussels: European Commission. http://europa.eu/rapid/press-release_MEMO-08-718_en.htm?locale=en
EC. (2011). *Report from the commission to the council on the functioning of the transitional arrangements on free movement of workers from Bulgaria and Romania*. Press release IP-08-1729. Brussels: European Commission. http://europa.eu/rapid/press-release_IP-08-1729_en.htm
Eigmüller, M. (2013). Europeanization from below: The influence of individual actors on the EU integration of social policies. *Journal of European Social Policy, 23*(4), 363–375. doi:10.1177/0958928713507467.
Faist, T., & Özveren, E. (2004). *Transnational social spaces: Agents, networks and institutions.*. Aldershot/Burlington: Ashgate.
Favell, A., & Recchi, E. (2009). Pioneers of European integration: An introduction. In E. Recchi & A. Favell (Eds.), *Pioneers of European integration: Citizenship and mobility in the EU* (pp. 1–25). Cheltenham/Northampton: Edward Elgar.
Focus Ireland. (2013, November 6). *Interview with representative*.
Hansard. (2004, February 23). *EU enlargement: Free movement of workers. House of commons debates*. House of Commons Harsard.
Holzmann, R., & Koettl, J. (2011). *Portability of pension, health, and other social benefits: Facts, concepts, issues* (IZA DP No. 5715). Bonn: Institute for the Study of Labor. http://ftp.iza.org/dp5715.pdf
Kennedy, P. (2010). Mobility, flexible lifestyles and cosmopolitanism: EU postgraduates in Manchester. *Journal of Ethnic and Migration Studies, 36*(3), 465–482. doi:10.1080/13691830903426838.
Krings T., Bobek, A., Moriarty, E., Salamońska, J., & Wickham, J. (2009). Migration and recession: Polish migrants in Post-Celtic Tiger Ireland. *Sociological Research Online*, 14(2). doi:10.5153/sro.1927. http://www.socresonline.org.uk/14/2/9.html
Krings, T., Bobek, A., Moriarty, E., Salamońska, J., & Wickham, J. (2013). Polish migration to Ireland: 'Free Movers' in the new European mobility space. *Journal of Ethnic and Migration Studies, 39*(1), 87–103. doi:10.1080/1369183X.2012.723250.
Kvist, J. (2004). Does EU enlargement start a race to the bottom? Strategic interaction among EU member states in social policy. *Journal of European Social Policy, 14*(3), 301–318. doi:10.1177/0958928704044625.
Lynch, S. (2013, April 26). EU member states raise immigration concerns with Irish presidency. *The Irish Times*.
Mau, S., Brabandt, H., Laube, L., & Roos, C. (2012). *Liberal states and the freedom of movement: Selective borders, unequal mobility*. Basingstoke/New York: Palgrave Macmillan.
McQuinn, C., & Hutton, B. (2013, September 22). €300 m worth of State benefits paid to claimants abroad. *Irish Independent*. http://www.independent.ie/irish-news/300m-worth-of-state-benefits-paid-to-claimants-abroad-29401795.html
Minihan, M. (2012, October 12). Efforts to save money on child benefit going abroad shelved. *The Irish Times*.
O'Reilly, K. (2007). Intra-European migration and the enclosure–mobility dialectic. *Sociology, 41*(2), 277–293. doi:10.1177/0038038507074974.
Obermaier, A. (2009). *The end of territoriality? The impact of ECJ rulings on British, German and French social policy*. Farnham/Burlington: Ashgate.
OECD. (2013). *OECD skills outlook 2013: First results from the survey of adult skills*. OECD Publishing. http://dx.doi.org/10.1787/9789264204256-en
Recchi, E. (2006). From migrants to movers: Citizenship and mobility in the European Union. In M. P. Smith & A. Favell (Eds.), *The human face of global mobility: International highly skilled migration in Europe, North America and the Asia-Pacific* (pp. 53–80). New Brunswick: Transaction.

Sainsbury, D. (2006). Immigrants' social rights in comparative perspective: Welfare regimes, forms in immigration and immigration policy regimes. *Journal of European Social Policy, 16*(3), 229–244. doi:10.1177/0958928706065594.

Smyth, J. (2011a, March 21). State seeks to change EU child benefit rule. *The Irish Times.*

Smyth, J. (2011b, June 20) Burton to pursue reform of benefit despite resistance. *The Irish Times.*

Wallace, C. (2001). Conceptual challenges from the new migration space. In C. Wallace & D. Stola (Eds.), *Patterns of migration in Central Europe* (pp. 45–71). Basingstoke/New York: Palgrave Macmillan.

Warnes, A. M. (2002). The challenge of intra-Union and in-migration to 'social Europe'. *Journal of Ethnic and Migration Studies, 28*(1), 135–152. doi:10.1080/13691830120103976.

Chapter 14
International Retirement Migration: Transforming Societies Through Purchasing Power?

Benno Herzog

14.1 Introduction

International retirement migration (IRM) is a growing phenomenon in the globalized world. Like individuals engaged in more traditional forms of migration, international retirement migrants challenge the national boundaries and institutional organizations of immigration societies, but unlike traditional forms of migration, IRM appears to be quite unaffected by labour market, integration, or social-welfare politics. Their relatively high purchasing power enables these migrants to organize their lives apart from that of the host society. Being a result of social, legal, and economic transformation in Europe, IRM also fosters social change (see Chap. 2 for more details on the social-transformation perspective). It forces host societies and societies of origin, as well as the institutions of the European Union, to respond to their diverse needs. The tension between a high level of wellbeing apart from society and the—at least partial—need for integration could be understood as a core dilemma of IRM.

The term 'IRM' refers to the migration of retired—and often early retired—individuals to traditional tourist regions because of the climate of the host countries and the relatively higher purchasing power that retirement migrants enjoy there. Many of these migrants acquire a house or an apartment in the host region, and they are characterized by a high level of wellbeing when they migrate. Despite a tradition of IRM in Europe that is more than 40 years old, relatively little *social* research has been conducted in this field. Retired European migrants have not been considered politically controversial (Simó Noguera and Herzog 2005), meaning they are not believed to be the cause of social problems, and they are not perceived as needy, poor, or deprived. However, their transnational lifestyles, the dialectics of their

B. Herzog (✉)
Department of Sociology and Social Anthropology, University of Valencia, Valencia, Spain
e-mail: benno.herzog@uv.es

A. Amelina et al. (eds.), *An Anthology of Migration and Social Transformation*, IMISCOE Research Series, DOI 10.1007/978-3-319-23666-7_14

detachment from national boundaries, and their dependence on social-welfare structures are changing the societies of their countries of origin and those of their countries of destination. Particularly in Europe, where the political will is clearly to harmonize welfare structures and to guarantee the wellbeing of European citizens across borders, IRM poses important policy challenges.

14.2 Who Are the International Retirement Migrants?

The different theoretical ways of framing IRM that have been employed in studies over the last decade indicate the diversity in the different lines of research. Many of the terms used in the 1980s and early 1990s to describe this population were linked to the ideal type of 'tourist' rather than that of 'migrant'. Instead of addressing migration, the terms that were used, such as '*real-estate tourism*' (Mazón Martinez et al. 1996), '*residential tourism*' (Mazón Martinez and Aledo Tur 2005), and '*second-home tourism*' (Breuer 2005), seemed more appropriate to conceptualize this phenomenon. Consequently, the focus of this type of research was more on the economic effects of these social groups, on their impacts on the natural environment, and on their effects on urban planning, but understandings based on tourism typically emphasize the effect on the host society and disregard the complex transnational realities of migrants' lives. With the emergence of the concept of IRM and its connotations of long-term migration and residence, research has shifted its emphasis to the migrants themselves and to their migration experiences, social situation, culture, and quality of life, among other things (Casado-Díaz et al. 2004; Gustafson 2001; Warnes et al. 1999). However, the concept of IRM limits the focus to the most numerous group: retired migrants. When discussing the issue of political and social rights and participation in Europe, the terms '*European residents*' and '*mobile EU citizens*' (Collett 2013) have been used occasionally to underline the fact that this type of retirement migration occurs in a common political space, namely the European Union (Simó Noguera and Herzog 2005). Although logically these terms include citizens from a country of destination, they are commonly used by the host society to distinguish *foreign* EU residents from citizens of the host countries. Furthermore, the common social connotation of these terms is migrants from rich European countries (mostly retired people), not migrant workers from poorer EU countries. Thus, the terms typically refer to migrants of the EU-15 (and to Norwegian and Swiss nationals who, despite their countries' non-membership in the EU, have comparable international rights and privileges in member states under special treaties[1]). However, the concepts of European residents and international retirement migrants have shifted the focus; researchers are realizing that these mobile pensioners stay longer, thus permitting more social investigations (García Andreu 2005; Mazón Martinez and Aledo Tur 2005). Another recent term is '*lifestyle migration*' (Benson 2010; Benson and O'Reilly 2009; Huete et al. 2013).

[1] Examples are the Agreement on the European Economic Area (EEA) of 1994 and the bilateral treaties between the EU and Switzerland on the free movement of people of the year 2000.

Although this concept illuminates important and unique features of this migration type, it also includes migrants of working age who seek increased levels of wellbeing frequently related to the idea of a more 'authentic' life or a 'slower pace of life'.

Although the term 'IRM' can denote all types of retired migrants, it does not tend to mean all of the types of retirement migrants identified by Ackers and Dwyer (2004: 455). When discussing IRM, researchers do not refer to 'retirement migrant community workers', that is, people who migrate for work and subsequently retire in the new country. Furthermore, IRM does not denote return migration following retirement or the migration of retired individuals who accompany their working migrant children (Ackers and Dwyer 2004: 455). IRM, as used in the literature, denotes post-retirement migrants who retired in their home country and who have moved to another nation, but often, such as in the case of UK retirees who migrate to Tuscany or Malta, previous work relations with the destination country were established prior to migration (King et al. 2000). Still, most retired migrants are familiar with their new country only because they had visited it as tourists. It could be said that the term 'IRM', as used in the scientific literature, refers only to the intersection between retired migrants and lifestyle migration.

However, drawing a line between international retirement migrants and tourists is not always easy. A comparative study demonstrated that in six of nine destination areas fewer than 25 % of international retirement migrants still maintained a house in their country of origin, whereas in Torrevieja, the Canary Islands, and Majorca 38 %, 51 %, and 68 % of international retirement migrants, respectively, owned a house in their home countries (Casado-Díaz et al. 2004).[2] The data indicate that it is difficult to distinguish clearly between long-term tourists, seasonal—or 'snowbird'—migrants, and those who reside in their country of destination full time, so the line between identities and social perceptions of the social models of 'tourist' and 'migrant' is blurred.

IRM grew into an influential phenomenon in the 1970s, and it appears to be continuing to grow. Although IRM is not exclusively a European phenomenon,[3] the main flows travel from Northern and Central Europe to the European part of the Mediterranean coast and to the Canary Islands. There are political reasons for the general increase in IRM. Less bureaucracy, at least for people immigrating from wealthy regions of the world, and the process of political unification within Europe may be important facilitator of IRM. Other reasons include an increase in infrastructure, a simultaneous drop in prices for medium-distance and long-distance travel, and the retirement of the baby boomers.

Although research on IRM is expanding, trying to find reliable data on stocks, flows, and sociodemographic aspects of IRM is still a challenge. With the EU no longer requiring European citizens to hold residence permits, official statistics,

[2] These data should be interpreted with caution because they are highly sensitive to the sampling methods used (see Casado-Díaz et al. 2004: 361).

[3] Other major flows extend from the United States to the Pacific Coast of Mexico. The United States is the only Western country that has an important *national* alternative for retirement migrants: Florida and California (Sunil et al. 2007). Flows to South America or Southeast Asia are increasing but are not as significant in volume as flows to the areas previously mentioned.

which are typically based on municipal registers, have often underrepresented IRM. Many retirement migrants, particularly those who spend a large part of the year in their home countries, are not officially registered. Quantitative data from questionnaires often yield inconclusive results due to insufficient sample size and, particularly, ill-suited sampling methods. Because there is no official register of international retirement migrants, researchers usually contact associations or use snowball sampling (for an overview of the methods used in nine studies on IRM, see Casado-Díaz et al. 2004: 358). These data probably overrepresent young, healthy migrants integrated into the national (or linguistic) migrant community.

When examining individual reasons for migration, research often describe international retirement migrants as amenity seekers (Sunil et al. 2007). The main reasons cited in responses to various questionnaires are the climate and the cost of living, both of which are related to ideas of health and healthier (i.e. more active and more sociable) lifestyles (Casado-Díaz et al. 2004; Warnes et al. 1999). The Mediterranean way of life and, more generally, a 'slower pace of life' have also been reported as reasons to migrate.[4]

Other reasons explain the unequal distribution of IRM across the European islands and coasts and the creation of designated areas for retirement migrants. Important housing development plans such as those in Torrevieja on the Costa Blanca in the 1990s and infrastructure projects such as the construction of new airports can be decisive in determining the appeal of particular regions. Some authors assert that having relatives or friends in a particular region is an important reason for choosing to live there (Casado-Díaz et al. 2004; O'Reilly 2000; Rodriguez et al. 1998). All these factors might be considered self-increasing tendencies that produce a critical mass that facilitates the emergence of infrastructures that in turn enhance the appeal of a region.

In terms of class structure, European retirement migrants represent mostly middle and upper income classes (Casado-Díaz et al. 2004), and typically maintain above-average cultural capital. Some notable differences are evident throughout Europe. British retirees with the lowest educational levels and of the lowest socioeconomic classes appear to reside in Malta, whereas those in Tuscany have achieved the highest relative educational level and class affiliation (Braun and Arsene 2009; Casado-Díaz et al. 2004; King et al. 2000). Oliver and O'Reilly (2010) note that other class-related aspects, such as taste and cultural capital, reflect this regional differentiation.

With regard to age structure, it has been suggested that the average age of a retired migrant is lower than that of a retired non-migrant. This age difference stems mainly from the fact that some migrants return home when their partner passes away or when they experience significant health issues (Simó Noguera et al. 2013; Warnes et al. 1999). Some evidence suggests a slight male predominance in retirees (Casado-Díaz et al. 2004). Casado-Díaz et al. (2004) suggests two categories of international retirement migrants with different migration patterns: migrants who

[4] Similar reasons are reported by Sunil et al. (2007) on the United States policy on international retirement migration to Mexico.

reside in their country of destination for a long time and have little contact with the home country, and migrants who stay in the destination country for a relatively short period of time and have more contact with their home country, where many of them continue to own property. However, in practice there are many cases that fall between these categories, and the line between them is blurred. Generally speaking, there is a high seasonal mobility in winter, when more migrants reside in Southern Europe, whereas during the hot summer months migrants tend to stay in their home countries.

Spain is the most important recipient of IRM in Europe, and official data show that more than 725,000 foreigners aged 55 or older are officially registered in the country (INE 2013). Most foreigners who unambiguously match the profile of retirement migrants are from the EU-15 (mainly the UK and Germany),[5] Norway, and Switzerland. According to unofficial reports, there are an estimated 1.5 million EU citizens living along the Spanish coast alone (Bahar et al. 2009). The most important region with respect to IRM is the Costa Blanca, a stretch of coastline in the Province of Alicante in the autonomous community of Valencia, where more than 28 % of the population aged 55 and older are foreign citizens (36 % are in the age range 65–74). In 24 municipalities across the Costa Blanca the number of foreigners aged 55 and older is greater than the number of native Spaniards of the same age, and in 12 of these municipalities the number is twice as large.

14.3 Wellbeing and Not-So-Wellbeing

Generally speaking, individuals migrate to improve their wellbeing, and international retirement migrants are no different in this respect. What distinguishes these migrants from most other types of migrants is the lack of a force that compels them to abandon their home countries and a wide range of possibilities to decide where and how to live. Retirement migrants can consciously and deliberately decide how to spend a relatively long stage in their lives (Benson and O'Reilly 2009; Huber and O'Reilly 2004). Consequently, what these migrants expect of retirement in another country are greater wellbeing and greater life satisfaction, and often the reality they experience is in line with these expectations. Furthermore, their legal status, their freedom to choose between destinations, and particularly their high purchasing power enable them to create the social structures they need to ensure their wellbeing, which makes them active agents in transforming European host societies.

Measuring improvements in wellbeing and life satisfaction is difficult. However, these concepts are typically related to subjective happiness or fulfilment, enjoyment of a healthy and active lifestyle, integration into family and wider social communities, economic aspects such as purchasing power or housing, and status or power in

[5] Romanians represent an important nationality when it comes to older migrants. Nevertheless, most belong to the category of 'joiners', that is, people who 'move in order to accompany or join their Community migrant children' (Ackers and Dwyer 2004: 455).

relation to others (for an overview, see Huber and O'Reilly 2004: 721f). Quantitative and qualitative research has found that all these factors contribute to expectations with respect to migration and to the 'new life in the sun' (see e.g. Alaminos and Santacreu 2009; Casado-Díaz et al. 2004; Huber and O'Reilly 2004; Warnes et al. 1999). All of these studies indicate that retired migrants enjoy a relatively high degree of wellbeing. The climate in the destination countries was described as a factor that improves retirees' health, particularly because it allows them a more active lifestyle. A relatively high number of social contacts and integration into the national, language, and/or IRM community has also been reported to contribute to overall wellbeing.[6] Some studies have reported that on average visits in the destination country from relatives and friends were longer and more frequent than the visits of the retired migrants in their home country. Economic factors such as lower cost of living were also mentioned as having positive effects on wellbeing.

Aspects with negative effects on the retirees' wellbeing have been reported as well. Poor command of the local language is a key problem, particularly for non-English-speaking retirees; in most destinations a wide range of services and activities are offered in English (Huber and O'Reilly 2004). Having to deal with the local bureaucratic structure has been found to be another pressing issue. A poor command of the language, combined with unfamiliarity with the bureaucratic structure, can present significant problems for property owners and people in need (Warnes et al. 1999). Both issues are connected to another set of difficulties, which are related to medical and nursing services. In addition, some studies have shown that separation from family and friends left behind in the home country was more of an issue than expected.

As indicated, wellbeing is strongly related to the possibility of a fulfilling social life. International retirement migrants lose their traditional support networks when they embark on a new life in another country, and social contact with society in the host country may be more difficult than expected. O'Reilly (2001) explains this by the way these migrants are perceived by their host society. Because they are not clearly socially distinguishable from tourists who occupy the same social spaces, retired migrants are not considered individuals with whom one should try to build long-term meaningful relationships. Other authors stress the absence of urgent necessities and structural relationships, such as those typically fostered by work relations or between retired migrants and retired or non-retired locals (see Simó Noguera and Herzog 2005; Simó Noguera et al. 2013). Consequently, retired migrants have been observed to exhibit a tendency to be isolated in residential areas (O'Reilly 2000).

But, unlike the segregation of other migrant groups, the isolation of international retirement migrants is seldom perceived as problematic because of the relatively high levels of wellbeing and life satisfaction they enjoy. Despite the lack of integration into the Spanish society, for example, international retired migrants typically

[6] It is important to note that the survey methods used have their limitations because they are usually based on contact established through IRM organizations and snowball sampling, which favours answers from retirees with a richer social life.

feel well-integrated in their diaspora group. Mobile EU pensioners tend to create a community of *Heimat* or *Gemeinschaft* within their host societies (Alaminos and Santacreu 2009; Huber and O'Reilly 2004; Simó Noguera and Herzog 2005). An extremely rich associational life appears to replace traditional social networks, and clubs increase the wellbeing of their members by offering a wide range of activities (Warnes et al. 1999). While conducting research on associational life in the autonomous community of Valencia Simó Noguera and Herzog (2005) found more than 700 associations of European residents, predominantly along the Costa Blanca in the Province of Alicante. These associations have different objectives, the most important being the promotion of general sociability and specific cultural and leisure activities. Other important objectives of such clubs include providing mutual support, solidarity, neighbourhood security, animal protection, religious and spiritual assistance, political participation, and property ownership protection. These associations, which cater almost exclusively for international retirement migrants, represent a new form of social capital for their members in the form of an important source of information, advice, and assistance (O'Reilly 2000; Simó Noguera et al. 2013).

Social and associational life also create and express transnational linkages and new identities (see also Chaps. 12, 15, and 16, in this volume). The definition of transnationalism as 'a process by which migrants, through their daily life activities and social, economic, and political relations, create social fields that cross national boundaries' (Basch et al. 1994: 22) is supported by many of the practices of international retirement migrants. The most obvious of these is probably the substantial degree of mobility between home and destination countries (see also Gustafson 2008: 457f). The most important conditions are the excellent transportation infrastructure (low airfares), the relatively high purchasing power, the lack of work obligations, and a relatively intense level of contact with family and friends in other localities (Gustafson 2008; Simó Noguera et al. 2013). Identity and belonging are another important issue when it comes to transnational relationships. Whereas Gustafson (2008) highlights a wide variety of senses of belonging that are reflected in a more or less strong attachment to both the country of origin and the country of destination, Simó Noguera et al. (2013) report the emergence of substantially *new* identities that are different from the migrants' original sense of identity and belonging. In diasporic life language can lead to the creation of cross-national boundaries (for example, Germans, Swiss, and Austrians may form German-speaking communities). In addition, most participants interviewed by Simó Noguera and Herzog (2005) described themselves as 'European residents', an identity clearly distinct from that of being a Spaniard or a 'normal' migrant.

As we have seen, international retirement migrants generally experience relatively high levels of wellbeing. However, life in the sun also has a largely unacknowledged dark side. Most problems begin as a result of the particular way the European residents integrate, namely the relatively close contact with fellow expatriates and (leisure) clubs that provide some of the high quality of life for these retired migrants. This type of wellbeing is the other side of the limited degree of integration into the local institutional structures. Many retired migrants have little knowledge of the local language and some of them have problems learning it because of their advanced age (see e.g. Legido-Quigley and McKee 2012). Many of them also have little knowledge of local institutions and seldom attend special integration courses the local authorities offer for all migrants (Collett 2013).

Expatriate communities often help the retired migrants to meet their individual social and health requirements or to deal with local authorities in case of administrative issues. But being dependent on intermediaries can lead to a situation where bridges to the host society may disappear as well if serious health issues suddenly make active participation in community activities impossible (Legido-Quigley and McKee 2012). For those who become ill, disabled, or isolated because of old age and/or their partner's death, social and health issues can have serious consequences (Huber 2003; Simó Noguera and Herzog 2005). For this reason, some of the retired migrants remigrate back to their home countries when they face major health issues. With insufficient knowledge of the local language and local institutions and a lack of family support, retirees frequently face difficulties that exacerbate their individual social or health issues. The social and health systems of many host societies also depend significantly more on family support than do those in the countries of origin.

The helplessness and dependence of some of the older migrants has led criminals to seek to exploit disoriented retirees. The larger the nationalcommunity and the greater the volunteering tradition, the larger the number of charity groups, self-help groups, or religious communities that try to help retirees cope with their situation. However, volunteers alone are usually unable to meet these increasingly stringent social requirements (Simó Noguera and Herzog 2005).

For host societies and their institutions there are two major obstacles to coping with older migrants' social and health problems. Socially, international retirement migrants are considered to be more like tourists than like citizens (Simó Noguera et al. 2013), which is why the host society does not believe it is responsible for this group, and the retirement migrants are not regarded as a particularly vulnerable group because of their relative wealth and wellbeing. The second obstacle is that social and health services are often distributed according to the number of citizens living in municipalities. The fact that large segments of the retirement migrant population are not officially registered not only makes it difficult for them to access social and health services, but it also makes it difficult for institutions to plan the distribution of such services. Official statistics tend to underrepresent IRM. Planning to determine and address health needs becomes particularly complicated in municipalities with a high percentage of unregistered international retirement migrants (Collett 2013). Because retired migrants are socially and politically perceived as a group with few social needs, and because a large portion of the population of retired migrants is statistically invisible, there is no coherent approach to address this population's social and health needs.

It has been observed that there are major differences in the way social and medical institutions are perceived by retired migrants from different countries. People from the UK have reported a high level of satisfaction with the Spanish health system (Legido-Quigley and McKee 2012; Legido-Quigley et al. 2012), citing good nursing practice, clean hospitals, excellent medical instruments, and the proximity of primary-care clinics that are open 24 h a day. These migrants considered Spain's public health system more favourably overall than hospitals in the UK. The retired migrants' lack of Spanish language skills appeared to be no issue because most of those working in the Spanish health system speak English. Simó Noguera and Herzog (2005) reported that some members of the German-speaking community have more significant problems because the linguistic barrier made it impossible for them to communicate with health professionals without an interpreter present. Religious communities were able to assist in some severe cases but not with everyday communication between patients and professionals. In many cases these groups did not attempt to bridge the gap between the patients and the local services but rather attempted (yet often failed) to mobilize resources from the home country.

In Spain, the most important destination country, a general problem reported by citizens of all nationalities interviewed was that nurses are not supposed to perform menial tasks, and that personal care in hospitals is typically provided by family members. Individuals who are unaware of this fact or do not have family members who can provide an appropriate level of care might experience significant problems. The importance of family care for the elderly in Southern Europe is also a problem when it comes to home care because the official structures for those without a family are often insufficient (Legido-Quigley and McKee 2012).

In the case of Spain, other public services such as the police and council services were described clearly in much more negative terms than were the health services (Legido-Quigley and McKee 2012; Legido-Quigley et al. 2012). Long queues, a heavy load of bureaucratic paperwork, unhelpful and impolite workers, and an ineffectively coordinated public administration were the main points of criticism by many of the retired migrants. Property owners in particular often feel impotent when confronted with an unfamiliar bureaucracy.

14.4 Social Transformation

Retirement migration in Europe has an international and intercultural dimension (Božić 2006), and it is profoundly changing national and international cultures, societies, and legal systems. International retirement migrants usually depend on a combination of national laws, bilateral agreements (on taxation, residence permits, etc.), and international rules. European international retirement migrants are the first large group to use and therefore to test European[7]welfare arrangements (for more details on mobility and welfare in Europe, see also Chap. 13, in this volume). IRM is thus exerting a certain amount of pressure on local, national, and supranational institutions to harmonize their legal schemes (Božić 2006). The pressure stems from the challenge of guaranteeing social welfare and health care for mobile

[7] Here the term 'European' refers mainly to the European Union but in most cases it applies equally to the European Economic Area (including Iceland, Norway, and Lichtenstein) and to Switzerland.

European citizens, but there are also problems related to the possibilities of 'gaming the system' (Collett 2013), which in the case of IRM refers primarily to medical tourism and tax evasion.

The lifestyle of international retirement migrants is typically not only related to the sending and receiving countries; it also changes European bureaucracies and challenges national boundaries, thus justifying the use of the term 'transnational' in this context (Bauböck 1994) and creating a 'critical mass' of EU migrants that must be addressed by a common political framework. Presently, the European Union is not a welfare state, and its mobile citizens enjoy very different degrees of wellbeing. Entitlements depend on a variety of factors and contributions in and from the country of origin and in the country of destination. It is for this reason that Ackers and Dwyer (2004) discuss important status differences among retirement migrants in the European Union.

IRM is not just transforming political and legal frameworks; it also has major economic and social effects. Retirement migration often starts with purchasing property and involving transnational property agents (Božić 2006). It continues with the creation of an important market targeting the expatriate population with shops, bars, restaurants, and all types of services and commerce, such as local services provided by expatriate personnel or by linguistically competent workers and transnational services and commerce. Examples of the last-mentioned range from commerce specializing in importing commodities from home countries, such as food and books, to offices, banks, and insurance companies that cater for migrants. Gustafson (2008) relates the exceptional but nevertheless noteworthy and possibly ground-breaking case of a Norwegian hospital on the Costa Blanca that was paid for by Norwegian municipalities and private health insurances and that was dedicated to Norwegian patients living in Spain and to Norwegians in Spain whose main residence is in Norway.

Migration can also lead to major social changes. While it may appear that international retirement migrants live their lives separate from their host society, Triandafyllidou (2008) notes that immigrant civic activism often becomes a lever for transcultural capital and transcultural community building. With its relative independence from social and labour policies as main instruments of integration, IRM can spur a rethinking of integration and, ultimately, of new modes of social cohesion. Models of integration that combine organizational life, social participation, inclusion, and migration are highly influenced by models of working immigrants with urgent social needs, which is why many of these models disregard migrant groups with dissimilar sociodemographic qualities. Socioeconomic-status models relate the possibilities for successful integration and social participation directly to an individual's or a group's standard of living (see e.g. Ramakrishnan and Espenshade 2001) and note that social groups that have resources such as education, money, and time also have a better chance of integration. However, in the case of international retirement migrants none of these resources automatically promotes integration and participation (or recognition or European citizens' rights) as long as 'integration' is understood in a static sense as integration *into* the host society. Moreover, although integration is often considered a political ideal, it is not deemed an explicit goal by international retirement migrants (Huber and O'Reilly 2004; Simó Noguera and Herzog 2005).

The fact that a large part of the IRM community does not think it necessary for them to integrate calls the normative imperative of integration into question and challenges static models of integration in general. Thus it is necessary to rethink integration models in highly individualized, transnational frameworks, in which there are types of migrants who convert non-integration into a virtue and prefer to maintain a lifestyle that in some respects is as similar as possible to the one they were used to back in their home countries (Gustafson 2001). However, increasing dependence on local community services can lead to serious social, psychological, and health problems for international retirement migrants, particularly in old age. With their transnational lifestyles and diasporic organizations, these migrants are challenging the legitimacy of national boundaries (Božić 2006) and questioning concepts of integration that are based on the nation state. What integration means when migrants are faced with these actual realities of transnational life is something that must be investigated. Solutions are required that transcend national or regional administrations, because a collective, even one traditionally identified with a high standard of living, has extensive social needs. The emerging research on IRM could substantially contribute to addressing this future challenge.

The need for research on IRM is closely related to the challenge of coping with serious social problems. The guarantees of social welfare, health care, and access to goods and services across national borders have reached a level that would have been unthinkable half a century ago. Nevertheless, the need to improve and harmonize legal frameworks and policy backgrounds persists. Further action is required to help the most vulnerable members of the population: people of old age, particularly those with few economic resources who are in poor health. The administrative and social invisibility of these individuals impedes the development of coherent and effective social policies.

In addition to those directly involved in IRM, migration research can also benefit from studies on IRM. Comparative research that includes different migration types can be a powerful tool to test hypotheses, synthesize common social structures, and identify particularities. It can help shape the theoretical and conceptual knowledge about migration. For example, we could rethink the use of the concept of integration in relation to IRM and pose questions such as: Is integration necessary? Why would it be required if the socially less integrated enjoy a relatively high degree of wellbeing? What might integration mean for social groups with transnational social ties? In addition, the corollary question is: integration into what: into a certain (national) community of a limited size, into a broader society, or even into several broader societies?

Similar questions might be posed regarding the normative imperative of the creation of a common identity to ensure social solidarity and cohesion. Is this identity necessary or possible—is it even progressive? Other aspects that require reconsideration vis-à-vis IRM are social participation (Who participates where? What are the challenges for transnational social participation?) and, more generally, the idea of living together. What does it take to live together peacefully, and what does it imply? IRM may stimulate the debate about these topics. Moreover, socially deprived retired migrants can be considered an embedded polarity in IRM. Consideration of this specific minority could help us sharpen our intellectual tools for thinking about theoretical concepts and social models. IRM can thus be regarded as a promising practical and intellectually challenging area.

References

Ackers, L., & Dwyer, P. J. (2004). Fixed laws, fluid lives: The citizenship status of post-retirement migrants in the European Union. *Ageing and Society, 24*(3), 451–475. doi:10.1017/S0144686X0300165X.

Alaminos, A., & Santacreu, O. (2009). Living across cultures in a transnational Europe. In E. Recchi & A. Favell (Eds.), *Pioneers of European integration: Citizenship and mobility in the EU* (pp. 98–119). Cheltenham/Northampton: Edward Elgar Publishing.

Bahar, H. I., Laçiner, S., Bal, I., & Özcan, M. (2009). Older migrants to the Mediterranean: The Turkish example. *Population, Space and Place, 15*(6), 509–522. doi:10.1002/psp.528.

Basch, L., Glick Schiller, N., & Szanton Blanc, C. (1994). *Nations unbound: Transnational projects, postcolonial predicaments, and deterritorialized nation-states*. Langhorne: Gordon and Breach.

Bauböck, R. (1994). *Transnational citizenship: Membership rights in international migration*. Aldershot/Brookfield: Edward Elgar.

Benson, M. (2010). The context and trajectory of lifestyle migration: The case of the British residents of Southwest France. *European Societies, 12*(1), 45–64. doi:10.1080/14616690802592605.

Benson, M., & O'Reilly, K. (2009). Migration and the search for a better way of life: A critical exploration of lifestyle migration. *The Sociological Review, 57*(4), 608–625. doi:10.1111/j.1467-954X.2009.01864.x.

Božić, S. (2006). The achievement and potential of international retirement migration research: The need for disciplinary exchange. *Journal of Ethnic and Migration Studies, 32*(8), 1415–1427. doi:10.1080/13691830600928805.

Braun, M., & Arsene, C. (2009). The demographics of movers and stayers in the European Union. In E. Recchi & A. Favell (Eds.), *Pioneers of European integration: Citizenship and mobility in the EU* (pp. 26–51). Cheltenham/Northampton: Edward Elgar Publishing.

Breuer, T. (2005). Retirement migration or rather second-home tourism? German senior citizens on the Canary Islands. *Die Erde, 136*(3), 313–333.

Casado-Díaz, M., Kaiser, C., & Warnes, A. M. (2004). Northern European retired residents in nine southern European areas: Characteristics, motivations and adjustment. *Ageing and Society, 24*(3), 353–381. doi:10.1017/S0144686X04001898.

Collett, E. (2013). *The integration needs of mobile EU citizens: Impediments and opportunities*. Brussels: Migration Policy Institute Europe.

García Andreu, H. (2005). Un acercamiento al concepto de turismo residencial. In T. M. M. Mazón Martinez & A. Aledo Tur (Eds.), *Turismo residencial y cambio social: Nuevas perspectivas teóricas y empíricas* (pp. 55–70). Alicante: CAM, Obras Sociales.

Gustafson, P. (2001). Retirement migration and transnational lifestyles. *Ageing and Society, 21*(4), 371–394. doi:10.1017/S0144686X01008327.

Gustafson, P. (2008). Transnationalism in retirement migration: The case of North European retirees in Spain. *Ethnic and Racial Studies, 31*(3), 451–475. doi:10.1080/01419870701492000.

Huber, A. (2003). *Sog des Südens. Altersmigration von der Schweiz nach Spanien am Beispiel Costa Blanca*. Zurich: SeismoVerlag.

Huber, A., & O'Reilly, K. (2004). The construction of *Heimat* under conditions of individualised modernity: Swiss and British elderly migrants in Spain. *Ageing and Society, 24*(3), 327–351. doi:10.1017/S0144686X03001478.

Huete, R., Mantecón, A., & Estévez, J. (2013). Challenges in lifestyle migration research: Reflections and findings about the Spanish crisis. *Mobilities, 8*(3), 331–348. doi:10.1080/17450101.2013.814236.

INE. (2013). *Explotación estadística del Padrón: Revisión del Padrón Municipal 2013: Datos a nivel nacional, comunidad autónoma y provincia.* Madrid: National Statistics Institute. http://www.ine.es

King, R., Warnes, A. M., & Williams, A. M. (2000). *Sunset lives: British retirement migration to the Mediterranean.* Oxford: Berg Publishers.

Legido-Quigley, H., & McKee, M. (2012). Health and social fields in the context of lifestyle migration. *Health & Place, 18*(6), 1209–1216. doi:10.1016/j.healthplace.2012.08.005.

Legido-Quigley, H., Nolte, E., Green, J., la Parra, D., & McKee, M. (2012). The health care experiences of British pensioners migrating to Spain: A qualitative study. *Health Policy, 105*(1), 46–54. doi:10.1016/j.healthpol.2012.02.002.

Mazón Martinez, T. M. M., & Aledo Tur, A. (2005). El dilema del turismo residencial: ¿turismo o desarrollo inmobiliario? In T. M. M. Mazón Martinez & A. Aledo Tur (Eds.), *Turismo residencial y cambio social: Nuevas perspectivas teóricas y empíricas* (pp. 13–30). Alicante: CAM, Obras Sociales.

Mazón Martinez, T., Aledo Tur, A., Martínez, E., & Arrocha, A. (1996). *El turismo inmobiliario en la provincia de Alicante: análisis y propuestas.* Alicante: Provincial Tourism Council of Alicante.

O'Reilly, K. (2000). *The British on the Costa del Sol: Transnational identities and local communities.* London/New York: Routledge.

O'Reilly, K. (2001). Blackpool in the sun: Images of the British on the Costa del Sol. In R. King & N. Wood (Eds.), *Media and migration: Constructions of mobility and difference* (pp. 173–188). London/New York: Routledge.

Oliver, C., & O'Reilly, K. (2010). A Bourdieusian analysis of class and migration: Habitus and the individualizing process. *Sociology, 44*(1), 49–66. doi:10.1177/0038038509351627.

Ramakrishnan, S. K., & Espenshade, T. J. (2001). Immigrant incorporation and political participation in the United States. *International Migration Review, 35*(3), 870–909. doi:10.1111/j.1747-7379.2001.tb00044.x.

Rodriguez, V., Fernández-Mayoralas, G., & Rojo, F. (1998). European retirees on the Costa del Sol: A cross-national comparison. *International Journal of Population Geography, 4*(2), 183–200. doi:10.1002/(SICI)1099-1220(199806)4:2<183::AID-IJPG101>3.0.CO;2-8.

Simó Noguera, C., & Herzog, B. (2005). El asociacionismo de los residentes europeos en la Comunidad Valenciana. In T. M. M. Mazón Martinez & A. Aledo Tur (Eds.), *Turismo residencial y cambio social: Nuevas perspectivas teóricas y empíricas* (pp. 427–454). Alicante: CAM, Obras Sociales.

Simó Noguera, C., Herzog, B., & Fleerackers, J. (2013). Forms of social capital among European retirement migrants in the Valencian Community. *Migraciones internacionales, 7*(1), 131–163.

Sunil, T. S., Rojas, V., & Bradley, D. E. (2007). United State's international retirement migration: The reasons for retiring to the environs of Lake Chapala, Mexico. *Ageing and Society, 27*(4), 489–510. doi:10.1017/S0144686X07005934.

Triandafyllidou, A. (2008). Sub-Saharan African immigrant activists in Europe: Transcultural capital and transcultural community building. *Ethnic and Racial Studies, 32*(1), 93–116. doi:10.1080/01419870802196021.

Warnes, A. M., King, R., Williams, A. M., & Patterson, G. (1999). The well-being of British expatriate retirees in southern Europe. *Ageing and Society, 19*(6), 717–740. doi:10.1017/S0144686X9900759X.

Chapter 15
International Students and Cosmopolitanisms: Educational Mobility in a Global Age

Başak Bilecen

15.1 Introduction

Increase in the free movement of capital and persons caused by globalization and neoliberal economic restructuring is reflected in the ways societies live today. Migration and mobility are prominent functions and creations of societal transformation worldwide. Social transformation is fundamentally linked with economic and political relationships, representing a fundamental shift in the ways in which societies are organized (see for an extensive discussion Chap. 2, in this volume). According to the new-mobilities paradigm (see Sheller and Urry 2006), advances in travel and communication technologies enable the proliferation of connections at a distance. The social is constituted by a set of ties among individuals in a variety of locales, which is indicative of increasing transnationalization at various scales. In addition to the technological advances, over the past few decades, global economic and political systems have transformed along with global media (see Chap. 21, in this volume), have fostered mobility. This is particularly true of Europe, with its single market and the related freedom of movements within the EU and associated countries. In this age of globalization and transnationalization, individuals are thus connected more than ever before. Migration, then, cannot be conceptualized as a unidirectional, one-time, single project of individuals, but rather as a variety of different forms, directions, motivations, timeframes, and persons involved in migratory processes, which are embedded in broader patterns of social transformation. International students represent an overlooked category of mobile persons, with neoliberal ideology framing the competition for advantage to advance the economies—usually in the developed regions of the world—derived from knowledge and expertocracy. In other words, knowledge is considered to be the new electricity of

B. Bilecen (✉)
Faculty of Sociology, Bielefeld University, Bielefeld, Germany
e-mail: basak.bilecen@uni-bielefeld.de

A. Amelina et al. (eds.), *An Anthology of Migration and Social Transformation*, IMISCOE Research Series, DOI 10.1007/978-3-319-23666-7_15

the global economy, in which universities are dynamic entities (Castells 2001). The internationalization of higher education systems, as well as the emphasis on knowledge and skills at the nexus between labour market recruitment and resources, reflect a transformation of economic theories into models that focus more on human capital (Romer 1994). Furthermore, one can observe new migratory trends that tend to favour the migration of a skilled or highly skilled workforce, particularly in Europe (see also Chap. 8, in this volume). International doctoral students, who are both consumers and producers of knowledge, are at the nexus between education and mobility, thus constituting an interesting population that is in a stage of transition to become the future elite. After all, not everyone has the means, ties, and motivations to study in other countries.

Until recently, international student mobility was generally neglected by the disciplines concerned with migration. Compared with other types of migrants and mobility schemes, students are younger and supposedly have better language skills that allow them to gain educational, intercultural, and valuable social experiences. There is a growing percentage of mobile students that cannot be ignored, not only at higher education institutions, but also in societies and labour markets in general. The result has been an increase in academic, economic, and political interests. 'During the 2000–2011 period, the number of foreign tertiary students enrolled worldwide more than doubled […]. Europe is the top destination for students at the tertiary level of education enrolled outside their country of origin, hosting 48 % of these students' (OECD 2013: 305). The high percentage of international students in Europe is linked to current societal transformation processes, which are caused not only by demographic shifts but also by the ongoing debate surrounding the crucial role of knowledge in global capitalist economies. The recent policy changes in favour of international students (such as post-study schemes) and other highly skilled professionals in most European countries, are primarily the result of projected labour market shortages related to ageing demographies and increasing competitiveness within perceived knowledge economies (see e.g. Favell 2008). At this conjuncture, cosmopolitanism, which is considered to have a crucial transformative influence on individuals' everyday consciousness and identities (Beck 2002), is a useful lens to analyse international students' experiences.

According to Craig Thompson and Siok Kuan Tambyah, who studied expatriates working in Singapore, 'consumer experiences are situated in a collectively shared identity project (i.e., trying to be cosmopolitan) […]. Through this identity project, they inscribe their life narratives, career goals, and outlooks toward travel and the consumption of cultural differences in a complex ideological system whose discourses are integral to the dominant cultural logic of post-Fordist, globalizing capitalism' (Thompson and Tambyah 1999: 214). In this global and transnational age the elite (which includes businesspeople, professionals, and academics) are usually regarded as cosmopolitan because they are highly educated; have social, cultural, economic, and intellectual capital; and access to social networks that make it easy for them to move across territorial and symbolic borders.[1] International students are

[1] This is not to take for granted, however, that there is a debate on whether only members of elites can have a cosmopolitan outlook (see Nowicka and Rovisco 2009).

usually seen as highly skilled, young and 'easier' to integrate into host societies. From the perspective of countries providing education, this makes them potentially perfect elite migrants for the ageing Western populations. Students, on the other hand, might regard studying in another country as a way of migration. Doctoral students in particular represent a group that is in a stage of transition from being consumers of knowledge to being producers of knowledge and thus innovation, which makes them an important group for further investigation (see Bilecen 2014; Bilecen and Faist 2015). The main aim of this chapter is to provide examples to show that educational mobility is a 'new' form of migration trajectory, and to discuss how international students experience cosmopolitanism at the intersections of social, economic, political, and cultural global flows.

The chapter begins with a review of the literature on cosmopolitanism and student mobility in Europe, and then proceeds to discuss what experiences international doctoral students have while pursuing their studies. Drawing on 35 qualitative interviews conducted in Germany, the analysis presented in this chapter focuses on three dimensions: (1) experiencing difference and becoming more tolerant, (2) multifocality, and (3) flexibility. The chapter concludes with a discussion of the main findings with regard to social inequalities.

15.2 Cosmopolitanisms and Educational Mobility

In recent years, the number of international students has grown across the globe. Europe is no exception in this regard. According to OECD (2012), the number of international students in Europe increased by around 114 % between the year 2000 and 2012, and Europe was identified as among the most desired study destinations worldwide. The number of international students in Europe, as well as the number of migration-related studies of this group, have been increasing. However, statistics on students in Europe that would lend themselves to comparative research are still not easy to come by. Moreover, although national statistical offices and organizations such as UNESCO, OECD, and EUROSTAT have been collecting data on student mobility, there is much work to be done (Kelo et al. 2005). Citizenship status is usually used as an indicator to identify incoming student mobility. In this globalizing era, however, the normative assumption that someone's citizenship corresponds with their place of residence is becoming less and less viable. In the German context, for example, the term '*Bildungsinländer*', meaning 'educational natives' in the sense of 'immobile foreign students', indicates that these students received their pre-university education in Germany because either they or their parents were born in Germany; whereas the term '*Bildungsausländer*', meaning 'educational foreigners' in the sense of 'mobile foreign students', is used to denote students with non-German citizenship who did not receive their pre-university education in Germany. In statistics for a number of other countries such as Ireland and the United Kingdom, permanent residence, rather than citizenship, is used to determine whether a student is regarded as a foreign or native student.

The promotion of the internationalization of higher education in general, and of the international mobility of students in particular, has come to be regarded as an important element of higher education policy, which seeks to improve economic competitiveness among countries and to help students to pursue their personal biographies and their future careers. Although student mobility in Europe dates back to the time of wandering scholars, it did not become a particularly important realm of cooperation until the 1950s, when it was seen as a way to overcome mistrust within Western Europe and promote the political integration of Eastern Europe (Teichler 2009). In 1987, the Erasmus programme was developed, not only for economic purposes, but also to create a shared sense of European identity (King and Ruiz-Gelices 2003) and consolidate European citizenship (Papatsiba 2006). In 1999, the Bologna Declaration was signed, primarily as a means to structurally converge European higher education systems and to facilitate temporary intra-European mobility of students. Erasmus has become the largest student exchange programme in the world, with 2.2 million students having moved within Europe between 1987 and 2010 (van Mol 2013).

The Erasmus programme involves student mobility that is commonly referred to as '*credit mobility*'. This term is used to denote student mobility of less than 1 year, which is highly regulated by institutions. Students typically complete their studies upon return to institutions in their countries of origin. Another type of student mobility is *degree mobility*; which describes students who study in a country other than their country of origin to complete their degree. The third type is summer schools and field trips, which involve less institutionalization and voluntary or mandatory schemes. Other important factors that can be used to distinguish different types of student investigating student mobility in addition to timeframes include *level of study* and *subject of study* (King and Raghuram 2013). In the European context, all types of student mobility can be observed, and at an ever increasing rate. Recent developments such as the Erasmus + programme, which started in January 2014, are expected to increase student mobility not only within Europe as planned in the original Erasmus programme, but also to other countries. This makes Erasmus + a prime example of institutional support for student mobility beyond European territories.

The concept of cosmopolitanism is widely used in literature covering the experiences of international students. Fazal Rizvi (2005) has argued that international education perpetuates a strategic cosmopolitan imaginary identity, which sees the world from more of an instrumentalist perspective than a moral one, and leads to cosmopolitan solidarity. Rizvi has also suggested that the identities of international doctoral students continue to be involved in national and global discourses of power and class, systems of history, and social interactions, all of which are embedded in transnational social spaces that shape the students' being, belonging, and becoming (Rizvi 2010). In a similar vein, this chapter explores the narratives of international doctoral students on what it feels like to be cosmopolitan, what 'cosmopolitan' means to them, and how they experience identifying themselves as cosmopolitan.

Much of the existing research on cosmopolitanism involves a high level of abstraction and does not explain in any detail what the theoretical concepts used may mean in particular empirical settings (Carens 2000). According to Matthews and Sidhu (2005: 53), 'a cosmopolitan orientation is associated with an intellectual and aesthetic sense of openness towards peoples, places and experiences from different cultures, especially those from different nations'. Similarly, Hannerz (1996: 243) notes that the core idea of cosmopolitanism is 'an orientation, a willingness to engage with the Other. It entails an intellectual and aesthetic openness toward divergent cultural experiences'. However, the question is what form such openness might take and how it can advance our understanding. According to Urry (2000), it is materialized in intellectual and aesthetic spheres, as an aspiration to and gratitude for cultural diversity. Skrbis et al. (2004) state that it also includes moral and emotional engagement in the form of empathy for and the interest in other cultures. This involves firm ethical commitments to universal values and ideas that are anticipated to go beyond the local experience. We can thus think of cosmopolitanism as a worldview of individuals (Vertovec and Cohen 2002). As such, cosmopolitanism lays the groundwork for investigating personal outlook or identity that stimulates people to become world citizens and thus form a community, which is morally bound to shared values.

In addition to being regarded as a worldview, cosmopolitanism is conceptualized as a mode of practice or competence (see e.g. Vertovec and Cohen 2002).[2] According to Vertovec and Cohen (2002), this way of conceptualizing cosmopolitanism is associated with consumption and a shared taste for music, food, fashion, art, and literature from all parts of the world. This type coincides with what Skrbis et al. (2004: 130) call 'mundane or "unreflexive" forms of cosmopolitanism'. However, in this chapter I argue that cosmopolitanism, as a competence, refers to a set of skills that are devised through constant interaction with 'the Other', and that international students constantly have to (re)contextualize themselves in different environments, that change depending on timeframe and context.

In addition, cosmopolitanism can also be a strategy for locating the self within local, global, and transnational formations. It thus extends beyond the competences or skills that individuals possess insofar that it intersects with a neoliberal perspective whereby 'the Other' is motivated by 'global competitiveness' in labour markets. In order to be competitive and have better life chances, individuals strategically customize their biographies according to personal and national contexts (Mitchell 2003). Likewise, Rizvi (2005) argues that strategic interests of the global economy frame international students' cosmopolitan outlooks. Strategies relate to what individuals do or envision, and they can be found in everyday life practices as well as future trajectories that are embedded in macro-opportunity structures, interpersonal networks, and personal goals.

---

[2] Vertovec and Cohen (2002) consider cosmopolitanism in six ways, namely as (1) a socio-cultural condition; (2) a kind of philosophy or world view; (3) a political project towards building transnational institutions; (4) a political project for recognizing multiple identities; (5) an attitudinal or dispositional orientation; and/or (6) a mode of practice or competence.

15.3 Research Design, Methods, and Sample

Semi-structured interviews with 21 female and 14 male international doctoral students at two universities in Germany provide the empirical basis of this chapter.[3] With 20 different nationalities, the interviews cover a wide range of ethnic and religious backgrounds.[4] The interviewees were between 25 and 41 years old. All of them had previous international experience, including participation in exchange programmes, work as interns at international organizations, attendance in language courses, or work and study in another country at some point in their lives. The participants were chosen from students of two graduate schools in two cities which receive funding under the Excellence Initiative programme.[5] The interview questions revolved around the students' experiences while studying in another country, belonging, their reasons for choosing Germany as the country of education, their friendship ties, their supportive roles, and their daily cross-border practices.

15.4 Experiencing the Difference: Ways to Become Tolerant

When the students talked about their experiences while studying abroad, the word 'different' was used very frequently in relation to culture, lifestyle, working environment, and academic culture. Their experiences revolved around difference, which included seeing different places and cultures, meeting different people and colleagues, different ways of being, and tasting different cuisines. The exact content of difference can be very diverse, and may include different geographical features, tangible things, traditions, customs, daily life practices, attitudes, and views. In the participants' narratives, comparisons were visible and important. National difference was assumed almost automatically. For example identifying that 'this is the German way', shows how nationality can be decisive in delineating boundaries. Although the content of difference appears to be ambiguous, the perception of its existence in various settings—not only in relation to the home and host countries,

---

[3] The data used in this chapter were collected for my doctoral project, which I concluded in 2012 and which was funded by the ZEIT Foundation's Settling Into Motion programme and also presented in Bilecen 2013, 2014.

[4] The nationality distribution was as follows: Belarus (1), Benin (1), Bulgaria (1), China (4), India (2), Israel (1), Jamaica (1), Japan (1), Kazakhstan (1), Kyrgyzstan (2), Macedonia (2), Malawi (1), Mexico (4), Netherlands (2), Nigeria (1), Philippines (1), Russia (3), Taiwan (2), Turkey (3), and Ukraine (1).

[5] The main aim of this programme is to promote outstanding research, to transform graduate schools into internationally competitive centres of science, and to advance the German academic and scientific environment. (For more information, see the website of the German Research Council at www.excellence-initiative.com. On attracting international postgraduate students, see the website of the central information platform of the initiative to "Promote Innovation and Research in Germany" by the Federal Ministry of Education and Research at www.research-in-germany.de).

but also in relation to other places—is fundamental and quite remarkable. This is because, along with the difference, it makes their experience unique and causes them to create various ways of identification. When asked how studying in other countries (and, more specifically, in Germany and Europe) was beneficial for the participants, responses along the lines of 'seeing difference', 'enjoying to meet different people', 'different contacts', 'exploring different cities', and 'my life here is different', led students to become aware of and appreciate their being transformed into more tolerant persons.

All of the respondents spoke about the positive learning experiences they had in Germany and how they benefited from their studies because they were 'learning to interact with a whole different' culture (Dulani).[6] One interviewee stated,

> I think living abroad, it's definitely a cliché, but it does broaden your horizon [laughs], gives you a different perspective, and you learn a lot just having a different environment and a different focus, yeah, I know, just little things, just the differences, you learn more about yourself and about your involvement (Saskia).

There clearly is perception, awareness, and appreciation of difference, which makes the students become more understanding, accepting, and tolerant (Bilecen 2013). Difference is something to be seen and enjoyed. For instance, it can come in the form of new tastes:

> I learned about different cuisines here [...]. One can buy different types of wine at the supermarkets here, such as Italian and Spanish, and enjoy them (Natasha).

Seeing and enjoying difference also goes hand in hand with experiencing new places, cities, and countries. The respondents appreciated being in Europe, going to see various different countries, or simply walking around their city with open eyes as a way of enjoying difference. The following statement illustrates how one student enjoyed her free time:

> My life here is simply different. Saturdays are shopping days—in Russia it doesn't matter because the shops there are always open. On Saturdays I go to the market, shopping; there is a local vendor on the open market in the neighbourhood [...]. On Sundays we always go outside with my husband, we walk around in the parks, or we take the train, go somewhere. We look around, saying, 'That's an interesting city,' so we go out and walk around [...]. Riding a bike is much more relaxing than in Russia. Seeing something beautiful, simply going out—you can go for a walk in the forest on your own without fear (Natasha).

Similarly, another doctoral student told how he liked to take short trips within Europe, emphasizing that for him, sightseeing was a form of learning about different cultures:

> I try to travel once a month, try to visit one different country. I mean, it's not expensive in Germany because you can find a lot of good offers, for example with Ryanair. Now you can fly to a lot of countries, and try to do that. Tomorrow I'm going to fly to Stockholm, and I really enjoy that: being able to see different places, different cultures, not only the German one but others as well (Alvarez).

---

[6] All names used in this chapter have been changed to protect the interviewees' identities.

What Natasha's and the other narratives on practices of consumption show is that although the respondents do compare Germany with their countries of origin, they emphasize not their otherness but rather their feeling of connection to a new place and the local way of life. Natasha described how she incorporated certain aspects of the lifestyle in Germany into her own, such as going shopping on Saturdays and relaxing on Sundays. To her it was not so much about what was consumed, but about how she related to it. She showed a sense of familiarity with and belonging to a place and interacted with the locals. It was not just about keeping a distance from her context and consuming; rather, there was interaction, and the students incorporated the local ways of life into their own. This behaviour is consistent with Ulf Hannerz's concept of cosmopolitanism. According to him, cosmopolitanism is the willingness and capability to engage with the cultural Other through face-to-face interactions experienced in the 'round of everyday life in a community' (Hannerz 1990: 240). As the student Alvarez pointed out, the respondents not only appreciated being in a different place as such, they particularly appreciated being in Europe. Thus, one could argue that studying in Europe causes students to develop a tolerant cosmopolitan outlook.

In the next sections I will investigate the substance and understanding of cosmopolitan experiences as conveyed by the participants, and develop other principles of cosmopolitanism in more detail.

15.5 Multifocality

The respondents stated that they developed the ability to consider things from different points of view. This has been referred to in previous research 'bifocality', that is, 'a capacity to see the world alternatively through quite different kinds of lenses' (Rouse 1992: 41). Migrants are bifocal if they feel at home in both their country of origin and in the host country (Rouse 1992), and if the boundary between the local and the far-away is blurred (Mahler 1998). In the case of international doctoral students, however, it would be more appropriate to speak of 'multifocality' because 'bifocality' implies a dichotomy. Multifocality, by contrast, involves a multiplicity of perspectives which students employ. They are exposed to more than two different living and studying environments, and furthermore, they move back and forth among them and incorporate some of their aspects into their own identities. This is a process that leads to what Ulrich Beck coined the '*internalized* Other' (Beck 2002: 18, emphasis in the original). When asked about the advantages of studying in another country, one of the students explained how studying in Germany had changed him and how he had gained a new perspective:

> I can see more sides now, not just one (Huang).

The development of multiple perspectives was mentioned often during the interviews, regardless of the specific topic addressed. All respondents who, prior to their doctoral studies, already had experience studying in a country other than their country of origin, were travelling a lot to attend conferences and had travelled as tourists or for other reasons. They used comparative perspectives in their responses, and when talking about a specific subject they always compared their previous experiences with those they had at the time of the interview. The ability to have and compare multiple views can be understood as an acceptance of one's own perspective or as the ability to do things in one of several possible ways, as the following statement illustrates:

> I'm learning about another culture, it's about daily life, it's about academic life, it's about everything in general. Every semester I meet many people from different countries, it makes me curious about the world, but more importantly, it shows me that the way I do things is unique (and maybe sometimes not so unique). I know it's such a cliché, but this intercultural thing I get to experience teaches me a lot; I really enjoy being an international person (Fang).

In addition to leading to the behavioural transformations, such as becoming more accepting and tolerant, international PhD students' multifocality, in the sense of being able to perceive things from various angles, is about how they do things. What is learned during the process of studying in another country is translated into action. The transformation of the students' views is also reflected in transformed behaviour. When asked what she had learned at various stages in her life while studying in another country, Elena stated the following:

> First of all, I saw a different culture, and Germans are totally different from Asian people, who are very open and very welcoming, so it's very nice to see the contrast. In addition, when I came to Germany I came to an international university [to pursue her Master's studies], and I saw students from other countries because there are students from 90 or more countries studying there, so it was very diverse, and I was able to interact with students from different cultures, and I learned many interesting facts: okay, now I know this nationality behaves like this and has this type of social ways, and this one does it like that. But, I also think my point of view has changed in a way that... For example, when I have a problem, sometimes I can be [like] a German or an Asian, so I use something from every country to deal with it (Elena).

The three examples above show that interaction with other cultures plays a very important role in the lives of international doctoral students. However, it is crucial to note that these students combine aspects of the various different perspectives they encounter, thus developing a perspective of their own which makes them flexible and allows them to navigate a variety of different cultures. This 'built-up skill of manoeuvring through systems of meaning' (Vertovec and Cohen 2002: 13) could also be called 'cosmopolitan competence', which is regarded as one gained while pursuing their studies in another country rather than as a disposition. As the next section will show, it is a skill and a strategy international PhD students develop and use to be able to live and study in a new environment.

15.6 Cosmopolitanism as Flexibility in a Global Market

Participants stressed their ability to be flexible and adapt to new environments. Flexibility—that is, abilities resulting from various types of mobilities: the ability to live anywhere, and the sense of being at home anywhere in the world—is crucial. This is particularly true for international students who have had previous international experience, be it while pursuing another degree, doing an internship, gaining work experience, or attending language courses. This flexibility to be able to live anywhere and the feeling of being highly mobile become ways of being, as the following narrative helps illustrate:

> I like to be cosmopolitan, you know. I like the fact that I know Europe, that I know the world, that I know people from abroad. [...] The ties with my country of origin aren't really firm enough to make it impossible for me to feel at home and live in Germany, or in Turkey, or anywhere else if I'm content (Damjan).

When asked about his plans to stay in Germany after graduation, Nadir clearly showed a cosmopolitan affiliation based on a similar understanding. He stated that he was flexible enough to be able to live in any country, even if he went the next day. He was, in other words, flexible in terms of place and time:

> I think my life is different somehow [...]. I see my career options, my life options more from the perspective of a world citizen. I could be anywhere in the world tomorrow. If I got a job in Africa, I would go there; if I got a job in America, I would go there; so I don't know how much longer I will stay in Germany; if I had the prospect of getting a better job in Germany, I might stay in Germany, but if I had the prospect of getting a better job in India, or in Africa, or in Australia, I would go there [...]. I feel at home anywhere in the world (Nadir).

Interestingly, what makes Nadir's response different from some of the others is that his experience of cosmopolitanism is very much in relation to job opportunities across the globe. This is evidence that 'international education is indeed a site where cosmopolitanidentities are produced, but that the meaning that the students attach to cosmopolitanism is highly contradictory and is linked more to their strategic interests within the emergent global economy and culture' (Rizvi 2005: 79). This sort of flexibility is required and produced by the global neoliberal market and the fluid environment to which the students are exposed. Their sense of flexibility in terms of home and workplace, or in terms of continuing mobility, became apparent when asking about their career plans. Generally speaking, the participants had no idea where they would be after graduation, but they did have certain aspirations and motivations with regard to the future. They also stated that they would be flexible enough to move to another place depending on their employment prospects. The following were typical responses regarding their plans for the future:

> I'm very flexible in the sense that I can stay in Germany or move on to another country—it depends where I find a good job. Now, I don't think I will go back [to the country of origin], but that would be another option if nothing else worked out, of course (Fang).
>
> It will depend on a lot of factors, so I can't make any specific plans right now; it will also depend on what plans I will have, what types of career I want to pursue. For example, if I

> decided to pursue an academic career, it wouldn't really make much sense to go back to Saint Petersburg because we wouldn't have any opportunities at the moment to earn enough money in this area. You always have to have something else as well, and it's extremely difficult. So I will consider every option anywhere in the world, as long as it's not Russia (Irina).

As these examples illustrate, there was a general tendency among international doctoral students to consider various career options in various places. It appears as if the employment prospects themselves were more important to them than the place where those employment opportunities are provided. All respondents agreed that studying in Europe had increased their career chances and thus their life chances. In that sense, they would consider all possible job opportunities regardless of geographical location—, they were highly mobile. Writing about those successful in the global economy, Richard Sennett, , notes that 'many of their achievements they owe to the practice of flexibility' (Sennett 1998: 61). As a strategy, cosmopolitanism is thus not only fostered by the students' experiences of mobility and education in other countries—cosmopolitanism is also required by the global market. In order to be successful on the global neoliberal market, international PhD students develop a strategy which connects their intercultural, international, educational, and personal competences to the cultural values of the global economy, which in turn shapes their own competences (Ong 1992).

15.7 Conclusion

Cosmopolitanism is a concept used to study elite groups such as professionals, businesspeople, and academics. Although its conceptual basis is rather extensive and inclusive, the ways in which it is experienced by elites tend to differ. As this chapter has illustrated, international doctoral students are significant actors in neoliberal economies of today's world because of their knowledge base, which allows them to develop into members of the 'wanted' workforce. The fine-grained analysis of the cosmopolitanisms of international doctoral students presented contributes to the existing literature on this subject. These students' experiences have been broadly categorized as various cosmopolitanisms. The students interviewed for this study valued and enjoyed the differences they saw, learned from, and enjoyed, and these differences caused them to develop a more tolerant—in other words, a cosmopolitan—outlook. Multifocality has been discussed here as a cosmopolitan competence that international students develop during their studies through their encounters with individuals from their country of education and beyond. Flexibility has been shown to be one of the major competences and strategies with regard to international doctoral students' cosmopolitanisms. The prospect of being offered employment opportunities is considered to be more important than the country in which the job is offered. This sort of flexibility is required and produced by the global market and the fluid environment to which the students are exposed. In a way, the experiences of international doctoral students are similar to those of expatriates who have a sense of cosmopolitanism. However, it is not so much in a moral understanding, but more in relation to global markets and employment opportunities, which requires them to be flexible and adaptive enough to live and work anywhere and with anyone. As Ong (1999) and others have shown, international doctoral students, as cosmopolitan elites, have adopted a strategy of flexibility in order to be able to navigate the global economy for their own benefit. By using the lens of cosmopolitanism, this chapter has illustrated how they experience studying in another country. Future studies of social inequalities should further contextualize knowledge, skills, and intercultural encounters.

As the interconnections among nation states intensify, so do the interconnections among labour markets, where education is crucial. New skills, knowledge, and having studied in another country, are increasingly becoming decisive factors in the selection of employees and, to some extent, migrants. International mobility has become a new standard of our transforming societies today and is even expected, particularly of elite members such as businesspeople and academics. International doctoral students possess social, human, and cultural capital that is not available to many other categories of mobile and non-mobile populations. As a result of the intensified unequal distribution of a variety of capitals through outcomes of globalization, the relatively affluent classes of the global economy can consume and commodify them (Thompson and Tambyah 1999). However, while encouraging as regards international experience and a cosmopolitan outlook, the discourse on the nexus of knowledge economy and education is also susceptible to challenges posed to internationalizing higher education institutions. Such developments have clearly transformed higher education institutions, not only through international student exchange but also through collaboration and academic mobility. These expand educational opportunities (selectively), and are reflected in the labour markets and in societies at large. Relative social inequalities rooted in the class and family background of students appear to persist globally as well as within Europe. While moving within Europe may be 'easier' for those enrolled in participating institutions or for EU citizens, going to third countries such as Canada and Japan may not be quite so easy. Many students from 'richer' or privileged countries find it easy to enter Europe, while students from other countries do not. In addition, the possibility of inequalities has increased because students are classified into 'more desirable' and 'less desirable' by universities, as are employees in the labour market. This represents a process of dichotomization between 'the haves' and 'the have-nots' that shapes their biographies. Inequalities do not develop in a vacuum; rather, they are the product of power and knowledge imbalances caused by globalization and neoliberalideology which are reflected in the higher education sector. It is highly likely that unequal knowledge distribution and thus social positioning within Europe and across countries will continue to exist. Future studies should reflect on the processes and mechanisms of hierarchization within and across societies, which are in part a result of disparities in knowledge and study experience in other countries.

References

Beck, U. (2002). The cosmopolitan society and its enemies. *Theory, Culture & Society, 19*(1–2), 17–44. doi:10.1177/026327640201900101.

Bilecen, B. (2013). Negotiating differences: Cosmopolitan experiences of international doctoral students. *Compare: A Journal of International and Comparative Education, 43*(5), 667–688. doi:10.1080/03057925.2013.821329.

Bilecen, B. (2014). *International student mobility and transnational friendships*. Basingstoke: Palgrave Macmillan.

Bilecen, B., & Faist, T. (2015). International doctoral students as knowledge brokers: Reciprocity, trust and solidarity in transnational networks. *Global Networks, 15*(2), 217–235. doi:10.1111/glob.12069.

Carens, J. H. (2000). *Culture, citizenship, and community: A contextual exploration of justice as evenhandedness*. Oxford/New York: Oxford University Press.

Castells, M. (2001). *The internet galaxy*. Oxford: Oxford University Press.

Favell, A. (2008). *Eurostars and Eurocities: Free movement and mobility in an integrating Europe*. Malden/Oxford/Carlton: Blackwell Publishing.

Hannerz, U. (1990). Cosmopolitans and locals in world culture. In M. Featherstone (Ed.), *Global culture, nationalism, globalization and modernity* (pp. 237–252). London/Thousand Oaks/New Delhi: SAGE.

Hannerz, U. (1996). *Transnational connections: Culture, people, places*. London/New York: Routledge.

Kelo, M., Teichler, U., & Wächter, B. (Eds.). (2005). *EURODATA: Student mobility in European higher education*. Bonn: Lemmens.

King, R., & Raghuram, P. (2013). International student migration: Mapping the field and new research agendas. *Population, Space and Place, 19*(2), 127–137. doi:10.1002/psp.1746.

King, R., & Ruiz-Gelices, E. (2003). International student migration and the European 'Year Abroad': Effects on European identity and subsequent migration behaviour. *International Journal of Population Geography, 9*(3), 229–252. doi:10.1002/ijpg.280.

Mahler, S. J. (1998). Theoretical and empirical contributions: Toward a research agenda for transnationalism. In M. P. Smith & L. E. Guarnizo (Eds.), *Transnationalism from below* (pp. 64–100). New Brunswick: Transaction Publishers.

Matthews, J., & Sidhu, R. (2005). Desperately seeking the global subject: International education, citizenship and cosmopolitanism. *Globalisation, Societies and Education, 3*(1), 49–66. doi:10.1080/14767720500046179.

Mitchell, K. (2003). Educating the national citizen in neoliberal times: From the multicultural self to the strategic cosmopolitan. *Transactions of the Institute of British Geographers, 28*(4), 387–403. doi:10.1111/j.0020-2754.2003.00100.x.

Nowicka, M., & Rovisco, M. (Eds.). (2009). *Cosmopolitanism in practice*. Farnham/Burlington: Ashgate.

OECD. (2012). *Education at a glance 2012: OECD indicators*. OECD Publishing. http://www.oecd.org/edu/EAG%202012_e-book_EN_200912.pdf

OECD. (2013). *Education at a glance 2013: OECD indicators*. OECD Publishing. http://dx.doi.org/10.1787/eag-2013-en

Ong, A. (1992). Limits to cultural accumulation: Chinese capitalists on the American Pacific Rim. In N. Glick Schiller, L. G. Basch, & C. Blanc-Szanton (Eds.), *Towards a transnational perspective on migration: Race, class, ethnicity, and nationalism reconsidered* (pp. 125–143). New York: New York Academy of Sciences.

Ong, A. (1999). *Flexible citizenship: The cultural logics of transnationality*. Durham: Duke University Press.

Papatsiba, V. (2006). Making higher education more European through student mobility? Revisiting EU initiatives in the context of the Bologna process. *Comparative Education, 42*(1), 93–111. doi:10.1080/03050060500515785.
Rizvi, F. (2005). *International education and the production of cosmopolitan identities*. Paper presented at the March 4th, 2005 transnational seminar series at the University of Illinois, Urbana-Champaign. https://www.ideals.illinois.edu/handle/2142/3516
Rizvi, F. (2010). International students and doctoral studies in transnational spaces. In M. Walker & P. Thompson (Eds.), *The Routledge doctoral supervisor's companion: Supporting effective research in education and the social sciences* (pp. 158–170). Oxon/New York: Routledge.
Romer, P. M. (1994). The origins of endogenous growth. *Journal of Economic Perspectives, 8*(1), 3–22. doi:10.1257/jep.8.1.3.
Rouse, R. (1992). Making sense of settlement: Class transformation, cultural struggle, and transnationalism among Mexican migrants in the United States. In N. Glick Schiller, L. G. Basch, & C. Blanc-Szanton (Eds.), *Towards a transnational perspective on migration: Race, class, ethnicity, and nationalism reconsidered* (pp. 25–52). New York: New York Academy of Sciences.
Sennett, R. (1998). *The corrosion of character: The personal consequences of work in the new capitalism*. New York: W.W. Norton.
Sheller, M., & Urry, J. (2006). The new mobilities paradigm. *Environment and Planning A, 38*(2), 207–226. doi:10.1068/a37268.
Skrbis, Z., Kendall, G., & Woodward, I. (2004). Locating cosmopolitanism. *Theory, Culture & Society, 21*(6), 115–136. doi:10.1177/0263276404047418.
Teichler, U. (2009). Internationalisation of higher education: European experiences. *Asia Pacific Education Review, 10*(1), 93–106. doi:10.1007/s12564-009-9002-7.
Thompson, C. J., & Tambyah, S. K. (1999). Trying to be cosmopolitan. *Journal of Consumer Research, 26*(3), 214–241. doi:10.1086/209560.
Urry, J. (2000). *Sociology beyond societies: Mobilities for the twenty-first century*. London/New York: Routledge.
Van Mol, C. (2013). Intra-European student mobility and European identity: A successful marriage? *Population, Space, and Place, 19*(2), 209–222. doi:10.1002/psp.1752.
Vertovec, S., & Cohen, R. (Eds.). (2002). *Conceiving cosmopolitanism: Theory, context, and practice*. Oxford: Oxford University Press.

Chapter 16
'Good Motherhood' – A Dilemma for Migrant Women from Eastern Europe

Helma Lutz

16.1 Introduction

> Deep down, I wanted to go home. I wanted to be able to spend time with my children in the last few years that they are likely to live at home, crucial years for their development into responsible, productive, happy, and caring adults, but also irreplaceable years for me to enjoy the simple pleasures of parenting—baseball games, piano recitals, waffle breakfasts, family trips, and goofy rituals (Slaughter 2012).
>
> I was sad the whole time. The relationship [with the employers] was very good, but I was in a foreign country, it was a foreign family, and you know that you've left your own child; although, of course, I knew my mother was there and would never let any harm come to him. And yet you want to be there yourself and see how your child is growing up, so [you're in] *that* mental state. [...] The mental state was the hardest thing for me (Myroslava 2009, a Ukrainian mother of a three-year-old boy, on working as a nanny in Poland).

These quotes are from two mothers living worlds apart in different parts of the geo-political spectrum. Yet, as I will show in the course of this chapter, they have a great deal in common. Myroslava, born in the Western part of Ukraine in 1976, is in her late teens when the Soviet Union breaks down and Ukraine becomes an independent state; in 1999, unemployed in spite of her university degrees, she leaves her husband, her 2-year-old son, and her parents behind to work as a nanny in Poland. On a circular-migration scheme, she returns to her own family every 6–8 weeks for a period of about the same length, during which a friend replaces her in her employer's household. For taking care of a baby girl and two young boys twenty-four hours a day, seven days a week she earns $150 a month. After 2 years she has paid back her student loans and returns home for good. Eventually, she finds a position as a teacher in her village.

Anne-Marie Slaughter, a Princeton-tenured law professor, and the first female Director of Policy Planning for the U.S. State Department (under then Secretary of State Hillary Clinton), made public her 'choice' to leave her job in the summer of

H. Lutz (✉)
Goethe-University Frankfurt am Main, Frankfurt, Germany
e-mail: lutz@soz.uni-frankfurt.de

A. Amelina et al. (eds.), *An Anthology of Migration and Social Transformation*, IMISCOE Research Series, DOI 10.1007/978-3-319-23666-7_16

2012 after 18 months' employment. In an article titled 'Why women still can't have it all' Slaughter, announced that she had made her decision for the benefit of her son, who needed her more than the State Department. Although, she writes, she still believes that women—like men—can have it all at the same time, she does not see this materializing in 'the way America's economy and society are currently structured' (Slaughter 2012).

Slaughter's article became a heated subject for feminists all over the world; her article appeared to resonate with many women's feeling that they have to choose between good motherhood and a career.[1]

In her announcement Slaughter articulates a widespread (white) middle-class maternalist ideology of 'good motherhood' which reinforces universal standards for good motherhood by proclaiming that it is the mother—and only the mother—who should be the primary caregiver responsible for bringing up healthy children and quality citizens. This modern image of motherhood has been referred to as 'romanticized maternalism' by the feminist historian Sonya Michel (Michel 2012: 24); it functions as a normative standard and denotes any other style of mothering (such as single motherhood, single and co-fatherhood, grandparent caring, etc.) as nonconformant and defiant (Michel 2012: 24; see also Collins 1990; Boris 1993: 104).

In this chapter I argue that 'romanticized maternalism' is noticeably gaining traction, even in those parts of the world where it was unknown in this form before. The avocation of 'good motherhood', and—where caretaking of old and frail parents is concerned—of 'good daughterhood', is key to the social framing of the middle classes 'doing family' in the twenty-first century.

I will first introduce some key information for the understanding of European care migration—much of which is circular—from Central and Eastern Europe westward into the European Union. This will be followed by a presentation of migrant women's voices on motherhood. I draw on biographical interviews with Ukrainian and Polish female migrant care workers from the Landscapes of Care Drain: Care Provision and Care Chains from Ukraine to Poland and from Poland to Germany research project (see Lutz and Palenga-Möllenbeck 2010, 2011, 2012), in which we focused on Polish migrant women working in Germany and Ukrainian care migrants working in Poland, analysed how they managed the care gap, and interviewed their family members, their relatives, and their friends who take on the caring tasks when the women are away. Finally, I will come back to the debate about 'modern motherhood ideals' and middle-class standards, and analyse commonalities and differences between Myroslava and Anne-Marie, and between the worlds for which they stand.

[1] There were about one million reactions from all over the globe within the first month.

16.2 Care Migration

Although the Iron Curtain was lifted 25 years ago, it is now clear that the system transformation has caused enormous hardship and strains for many countries in the region (for the analysis of postsocialism and migration, see also Chap. 6, in this volume). Millions of people lost their work, and in most of the countries unemployment is skyrocketing—in some regions around 50 % of the workforce population are unemployed. Migration was and is one of the few possible routes out of poverty, corruption, and other daily pains induced by the combination of reckless capitalism and Soviet-style nomenclature which has replaced state socialism since 1989 (see also Ghodsee 2011). Coinciding with the liberalization of the border regimes after 1989 was a strong demand for care workers in many EU member countries as an effect of women's growing employment rates.[2] Care work can be defined as 'multifaceted labor that produces the daily living conditions that make basic human health and well-being possible' (Zimmerman et al. 2006: 3–4); it is work mainly performed for dependent others. In addition to practical, physical duties, care work involves emotional work (the expression of affection, kindness, enthusiasm, love, etc.), and like no other activity it is a personalized relationship characterized by intimacy, trust, and responsibility. Caregivers and the receivers of care are involved in a special relationship. This is particularly so when the work is performed in a private household because in this setting care receivers are also employers and caregivers are employees. While in the majority of the OECD countries the massive entry of women into paid labour is a recent development, in the post-socialist/post-communist world a trend in the opposite direction can be observed: most countries in Eastern Europe had full-time employment for women as a rule, and the employment rate before the system transformation was even higher than it presently is in most countries of the 'Western' world. However, after the breakdown of state socialism women were the first to lose their employment and were literally 'sent home'; for many highly educated as well as for many less well-educated women unemployment is now the new rule (Saxonberg and Szelewa 2007; Plomien 2009).

When women from Central and Eastern Europe started to fill the care deficit in the 'old Europe' they initiated what was then a new phenomenon in the region: 'feminized migration', which is characterized by transnational (circular) migration (see Lutz 2011), and which started as a rotation system between pairs of neighbouring countries that was organized by the migrants themselves. Now these transnational

[2] Data on domestic and care work migration is very poor. The International Labour Organization's conservative estimate suggests a total of at least 53 million people worldwide employed in private households, of which 83 % are women (ILO 2013: 19). The estimation for Europe is 3,6 million whereby workers from Eastern Europe constitute the majority of employees in Southern and Western Europe (ibid.). However, as between 35 and 70 % of the employment in the receiving countries is reported to be undocumented, and the sending countries prefer to characterize transnational workers as temporarily absent citizens which are not reported as migrants, realistic data are still sparse.

migrants no longer take their families with them to where they work; instead they commute at intervals ranging from 1 week to several months.

Given the income gap between Eastern and Western Europe, the wages they can earn as care and domestic workers in Western Europe are attractive to Eastern European women, notwithstanding the lack of regulation in this sector. The circular migration pattern they have developed allows them to keep their main residence in their home country, while leaving children, elderly family members (in need of care), and partners/husbands behind. The pattern works efficiently because it is driven by female workers' loyalty and sense of responsibility to uphold care obligations at home, as well as their desire to maintain this home with their earnings. The emerging scheme, then, is one of a transnational care commitment, albeit one that women must balance individually with the help of personal networks because the sending states do not provide any support in the form of special social programmes designed to compensate for the caring labour of women absent from their home country. Indeed, in many places women are denounced for producing 'Euro orphans' (Lutz and Palenga-Möllenbeck 2012).

16.3 Migrant Women's Motherhood[3]

I have chosen two case studies for their generic representation of typical biographies. They show some of the many variations in and important differences between the biographies of migrant mothers. One of the women is a Ukrainian mother working for a Polish family, the other a Polish woman providing care for elderly people in private households in Germany; both of them are highly educated, but they are from different age groups.

16.3.1 Myroslava

At the age of 24 the Ukrainian woman Myroslava (Myra) leaves her home, which she shares with her husband, their 3-year-old child, and her parents, for the first time and travels across the border to work for a Polish family. On her first day the family's 1-year-old daughter is handed to her, and Myra is introduced to her duties as a nanny:

> When I arrived at the house the woman employer told me straight away: 'Always imagine it's your child you are holding in your arms.'

Although she sees herself as 'part of the family' and gives the impression of an idyllic family life, no rest periods have been agreed on, and she cannot distance herself mentally or physically in her situation, which requires her to share the infant Maria's bedroom. Myra accepts what is expected of her. She does not ask for any

[3]Data from this case study were also used in my article 'Myra's Predicament: Motherhood Dilemmas for Migrant Care Workers, Social Politics, 3, 2015.

time off, holidays, or rest breaks; apparently it makes her happy to be considered a 'family member'. At her remote place of work on the edge of town she has few opportunities to find friends and acquaintances outside the family. Moreover, her full-time responsibility for the children and the household makes it difficult to leave the workplace.

Isolated from her familiar context, and because she has no contact with other women in a similar position, she does not complain about the scandalously low wage of $150 a month. Rather, she idealizes the job in retrospect and, astonishingly, draws a positive conclusion:

> Actually, I was doing the same things I do at home, except that at home I don't get paid for the work, and nor is it appreciated.

Nevertheless, for all the recognition that she receives for her work, she also has to put up with a series of intense conflicts in this household, such as when the second-oldest boy refers to her in derogatory terms as 'the maid' and she feels deeply hurt. Myra's most important conflict in these 2 years is her struggle with herself. In keeping with what is expected of her, she invests her maternal feelings in the little daughter as if she were her own child, although she finds it almost impossible to be separated from her 3-year-old son:

> It was a huge inner battle; [...] the first two weeks were very difficult. After that you buckle under, you get used to it, you know that there's no other way and, as people say, like a soldier you count the days until the end of military service.

Two metaphors are of interest here. First, the statement that she accepts her inevitable fate and 'buckles under' characterizes the adjustment process as one of symbolic violence; second, she uses the term 'military service'. She apparently views her work as the fulfilment of an obligation towards her fatherland—and not just in the metaphorical sense, because after all she is paying off her student debt to the Ukrainian state. This metaphor also manages to convey the unduly immense strain of being separated from her son. However, this analogy only makes sense retrospectively because the length of her 'military' service was by no means certain from the outset. What is striking about Myroslava's narrative is the implication that this separation is 'a trauma', not so much for her son but mainly for herself as a mother. What pains her most is the instruction to drop the normal distinction between her own children and a stranger's, and to lavish her love and affection on a child that is not her own. Arlie Hochschild (2003) refers to this process, which is essential to the work of nannies, as the supply of 'emotional surplus'. Although this is precisely what Myroslava is doing, deep inside she resists it. Her dilemma is not just that she is expected to transform private motherhood into professional motherhood as described by Hochschild, but rather that she is not emotionally capable of viewing *the stranger's child entrusted to her care* as a *surrogate* for her own.

This conflict is made even worse when she learns that her son back home is doing well without her, because, while the physical distance torments her, she realizes that she is far from irreplaceable and that her son has in fact come to terms with the situation and accepted it.

During her absence, her son is taken care of by her mother, Olesja, and her husband, Oleksij. Olesja, who grew up as an orphan and wanted her two daughters 'to be spared such hardship', introduces the term 'trauma' to describe what her daughter goes through; she herself is evidently caught up in her suffering:

> I saw what a terrible mood she was in every time she drove away. And [...] and I knew it wasn't easy for her there, getting up during the night for someone else's child, putting up with all the foibles of a stranger's child for 100 or 150 dollars.

Olesja also underscores her disgust with the employer's family und the discrepancies between the two parties in terms of educational and social class status: in comparison to the employer's family, Olesja and Myroslava's family have much higher educational degrees, which in 'normal' times meant better social standing. In post-socialism, however, an educated woman must hire herself out as a 'nanny' and come to terms with the fact that employers, while they may have bad habits and badly brought-up children, also have the financial resources at their disposal to afford servants. Every member of Myroslava's family has a higher-level education degree, and the Polish family's lifestyle is alien to her. The fact that she strongly resists being called a 'maid' and presents herself as the 'nanny' instead can be seen as an attempt to upgrade herself using the profession of the traditional 'governess'. This case is a typical example of the distortion of class relations in post-socialist Europe: the old hierarchies erode and new ones, dominated by economic capital and inequality, emerge.

Myroslava finally terminates her employment with the Polish family when the male employer makes sexual advances to her. At the time of the interview, it has been 8 years since Myroslava returned. Since then she has been working as a biology and chemistry teacher in her home town, earning about $100 a month. She has had a second child and would like to have a third. Although she is very satisfied with her work and has no further migration plans for the time being, money is still very tight in the household, and the family has to manage without many consumer goods already found in other households. Myroslava and Olesja estimate, based on the observations of their pupils' families, that between one in three families in the town have at least one parent who has (temporarily) migrated; also in Myroslava's family the next migration is already impending: Oleksij wants to set up a business, but has no start-up capital; he decides to go to Russia to earn the money as he speaks Russian and knows his way around. Obviously, the couple's choices of destination country are influenced by their language skills and the perceived cultural and linguistic affinity with the two neighbouring post-socialist states.

In our sample[4] this is a typical case of members of the younger, well-educated generation who only experienced the era of state socialism in their childhood, and taking a more or less pragmatic approach to deal with the system transformation. Most of these families are two-parent families who see the new opportunities for geographical mobility that have presented themselves since the opening of the

[4] We conducted 22 narrative biographical interviews with Ukrainian and Polish migrant women and 41 in-depth interviews with their family members in the home countries.

borders as a chance to improve their financial situation, in return for which they will temporarily accept constraints on traditional family life. In none of these families are the gender relations radically altered during the period of the mothers' absence. As a rule, the grandmothers take charge of the children, while the fathers do a (small) share of the housework for some time and get somewhat more closely involved with the children. As Oleksij's explains,

> I also had to cook for myself at times and figure out what still had be done for lunch, breakfast, or supper. I basically had to *adapt* and remind myself how I coped in my student days.

The period spent as a student is seen here as the frame of reference for the housework and the caring responsibilities to be performed, which means that this is the only phase in life in which many men have autonomous responsibility for doing housework.

In contrast to Myra's case, the majority of our interviewees take their migration decision in the context of family fragmentation: they are either widowed or divorced and are forced to earn a living to support themselves and their children.

16.3.2 Halina

When Halina goes abroad to Germany for the first time in 2003 she is already 42 years old. Born in 1961, she finishes her university entry exams in 1978 but misses the deadline for enrolment. She then starts working as a bookkeeper in a factory, where she meets her husband. Between 1982 and 1997 she gives birth to three children. While working in the human resources departments of various firms, she would still like to study but is held back by her husband; still she does not leave him in order to realize her aspirations. After the fall of the Iron Curtain her husband and a friend open a bar, for which Halina takes out a loan. At his request she also gives up her job. Their business goes well at first, but after financial disputes it has to go into liquidation. Her husband flees the country to escape his creditors and works on building sites in Germany and Austria. When he dies in a car accident in 1996 Halina is already pregnant with Iga. She then goes back to her old job at a porcelain factory.

As if all that were not enough, she finds out that her husband had not paid any insurance premiums for the family and that she is liable for the debts he left, which causes massive financial difficulties for her. However, somehow this is the moment she has been waiting for: immediately after his death Halina takes a correspondence course in European Administrative Law. She continues to pursue the degree even after Iga's birth, and her employer grants her leave to attend the face-to-face blocks of tuition. Her financial situation is desperate; she has to sell her jewellery and the apartment; her parents help her maintain the most basic standard of living for herself and the children. Despite the hardship, she continues her studies and in 2000 graduates with a Master's degree. Unfortunately, she then realizes that this degree does not help her to find better-paid jobs as easily as she had hoped. She stays at the factory until 2002 when it becomes insolvent and closes down. Her eldest daughter, who is 20 years old by now and leaves school with excellent grades, starts working in the service sector, initially in Poland and later in the Netherlands.

When Halina goes to Germany for the first time her youngest daughter, Iga, is 5 years old. Initially the elder daughter takes charge of her care, but once she goes abroad, Halina has to find a new solution: various female friends whom she pays symbolically by bringing them gifts take care of her child. Iga is repeatedly sent to stay with Halina's sister for a while when there are problems. The relationship between Iga and Lucyna, the friend of her mother's who currently cares for her, is not good: Iga complains about the fact that her care taker loves watching soap operas all day (which she abhors) and Lucyna laments the 'outspokenness and boldness of Iga. Halina tries to manage these problems from afar:

> 'I say, 'Iga, watch that soap opera and do your homework afterwards, turn the TV off then, that's a deal.'

Evidently, Iga, 11 years old at the time of the interview, has clear preferences which probably echo her mother's tastes, so 'soaps' are seen as low-culture and incompatible with the family's habitus. Halina has recently acquired a computer for her daughter on which she can download films, with her older brother's help. Iga and her mother talk to each other on the telephone every day, and Halina has a very close relationship with her daughter.

In the 4 years between 2003 and 2007 Halina works as a 24-h-a-day caregiver for elderly and sick people in German households on a 2–3-month cycle, at first illegally, but from 2006 as a nominally 'self-employed' worker. During those years she has to change households and employers seven times because her clients are seriously ill (cancer, Alzheimer's) and either die or are transferred to a care home at their relatives' wish. In some cases Halina takes responsibility for end-of-life care, although she is not trained for it and her German language skills are not really up to the task. Several times she tries to bring Iga with her to Germany, but the employer is against it and the plan comes to nothing. Halina's free time is limited to five hours twice a week; her monthly pay is a little over €1,000. Because the pay scale is influenced more by language skills than by occupation and work experience, and Halina's command of German is poor, she is unable to negotiate better pay to improve her income; her 'willingness' to accept difficult working conditions without complaint, citing her Christian faith and her strong sense of humanitarianism, obviously leaves her open to exploitation by employers.[5]

In August 2007 she gives up her job, returns to Poland, and begins working as a bookkeeper and manager for a care agency in Poland.

Halina's story contains all the characteristics of a single mother who lacks support. Her family has been through a succession of bereavements (car accidents, cancer), the parents are either dead or no longer in a position to care for the children, and the older children are unable or unwilling to ease their mother's load. The eldest

[5] A German care service would charge €6,000 to €8,000 per month for this work.

daughter is a migrant worker herself and the son is unemployed and lives with Halina but is unwilling to support his mother, nor does she expect him to.

Although Halina has educational aspirations for her children and although what pains her most is that her daughter has shunned a university education, she has no means to put any such ambition into practice. This is a bitter insight for her, because apart from the necessity to repay her husband's debts, the attempt to give her children the chance of a better life was the most important stimulus that made her migrate in the first place. Just like Myra, she finds it particularly difficult to be separated from her family, most of all from Iga:

> In the evening when I go to my room these terrible thoughts come over me. What am I doing here? How did this happen? I try to find an explanation. Could I not have taken my life in a different direction? Could I have done this or that? That's when those thoughts come.

In this situation, simply choosing to go home and do without the money is a luxury that she does not have. She manages motherhood from a distance to a certain extent by maintaining constant telephone contact with her children, but time and again crisis situations flare up which can only be handled with great difficulty from afar. She lacks the family resources that are apparent in Myra's case. She regrets having told Iga at every parting that she would stop 'going abroad' yet is constantly breaking that promise:

> I say: 'You know how hard it is, look what people earn in our country, how hard life is, how poor the people are.' And that's how I try to .... yes, it's bribery.[6]

Halina's story also makes it clear that, far from being a choice, 'mothering at a distance' is the only way she can do mothering at all in her situation, while she actually condemns this form of motherhood because it is contrary to her own ideals and principles of motherhood.

16.4 The Pervasiveness of Maternalism

There is remarkably little difference between the motherhood ideals cherished by the migrants presented here and those described in Anne-Marie Slaughter's essay. Despite the stark contrast between these Eastern European women migrant's living and working conditions and the daily life of a woman professor in the United States, there are numerous overlaps with regard to ideologies of idealized motherhood. They share a common belief that the mother–child relationship has primacy over all others and that no other care person, neither fathers nor 'other mothers', can replace a mother adequately; that the emotional relationship with one's own child has a special quality which is not substitutable; and that the wellbeing of children comes first and thus takes priority over maternal employment and career ambitions.

[6] Meaning that deceives the child.

The overlaps are almost inexplicable at first glance, particularly considering the system-based differences. On one side is the United States' post-industrial capitalist society in which the provision of care for children and elderly people is primarily the family's and the market's responsibility rather than the state's (Koven and Michel 1990; Michel 2012), but which still relies on female employment. On the other side are the post-socialist states that have developed since 1990, which have withdrawn from their previous role of providing comprehensive cradle-to-grave care in the form of day care centres, all-day schools, and old people's homes and watching over the population, and in which a radical privatization of care provision has led to the closure of many institutions and to high co-payments as the only viable way of financing them. Before the system transformation motherhood and employment were expected to be 'citizenship obligations' for women, whereas in post-socialism pronatalist policies are gaining ground with the support of the Catholic and the Russian Orthodox Churches, manifesting themselves in the form of abortion bans and extended maternal leave, so that motherhood is now considered to be the 'primary obligation of female citizens'. Idealization of the mother is a central element of the nationalistic symbolism of the 'new' Eastern European nation states (Skocpol 1992; Kis 2007; Solari 2010), and it is key to family and employment policy reforms heralding the re-familialization of social policy. The socialist ideal of equality, which may have been realized in working life but not in the private sphere (Kalwa 2008), has been replaced by a 'new' understanding of femininity that idealizes and propagates the role of the housewife and mother, along with certain ideals of beauty (Michoń 2009). 'Having a child means having a real, useful, purposeful and dignified femininity' (Trzebiatowska 2013: 208). Trzebiatowska also argues convincingly that the changes in the political system have brought about a cultural change that has led to new forms and hierarchies of femininity and social performances in which the key features are compliance, nurturance, and empathy, an investment in what Raewyn Connell calls 'emphasized femininities' (Connell 1987: 188). Such 'emphasized femininity' can be seen in Myra's strong belief in the biological bond between mother and child, which impedes the transformation of 'private motherhood' into 'professional motherhood', and in Halina's normative script, which emphasizes her motherly instincts and nurturing behaviour. The fact that both women underscore their dedication to their children's needs can be interpreted as a fear of deviating from the general maternalism ideal.

But evidence of fear of being labelled as a 'bad mother' can also be found in Anne-Marie Slaughter's account; she also cannot believe that her children are taken care of adequately during her times of absence, although she acknowledges that her husband takes care of all the necessary tasks. She feels not only that the children need her but that she also needs the children, and this needing the children has become a pivotal element of 'modern motherhood': becoming a mother is no longer a fate but a choice, no longer a sacrifice for the sake of the child but pleasure and fulfilment for the mother.

In *The Conflict: How Overzealous Motherhood Undermines the Status of Women*, her book on the new maternalism, Elisabeth Badinter shows that since the 1970s when the wide availability of contraceptive pills meant that the majority of women in industrialized countries could *choose* to have children, women have been confronted with a myriad of new demands concerning the performance of 'good motherhood'. Badinter provides various examples of ideological battles over *becoming a good mother*, f.e. she demonstrates that the 'ideological crusade' in favour of breastfeeding, which would have the 'good mother naturally [put] her child's needs before everything else' and feed it as long as possible, as well as the advice to co-sleep with a child until the age of four (Badinter 2013: 69ff., 101ff.), all reintroduce a biological-nurturing model which impedes and even forestalls balancing motherhood with a working career.

New maternalism was inspired by John Bowlby's 1958 article 'The Nature of the Child's Tie to His Mother', which laid the ground for the global influence of 'attachment theory', but, as Badinter shows, feminists have embraced this theory of 'natural motherhood' and 'motherly instincts' in various ways since the 1980s. In general, the wisdom that the bond between mother and child has no equal has become a dominant ideology of post-modernity. However, I would add that this 'wisdom' is not confined to the 'Western' world described by Badinter, but that it finds its equivalent in post-socialism. Post-socialist societies put more emphasis on the importance of the mother–child bond than the predecessor system did, but emphasis on bonding and fatherhood was as absent in the socialist world as in 'the West'. During state socialism women's emancipation was equated with (compulsory) participation in the labour market, while the distribution of care tasks in the private sphere was unequal, with women taking charge of the lion's share of the work.

Obviously, gender relations in the post–state socialist world *and* in the capitalist post-industrial countries have converged to a greater extent than is usually acknowledged: expecting women to be 'good mothers' as well as 'ideal workers' increasingly appears to be a paradox that resembles the squaring of a circle.[7]

For women in Eastern Europe this means that at a time when their money is needed more than ever—particularly to ensure the education and well-being of their children—and working abroad looks like an alternative to staying at home unemployed, their reputation as a 'caring mother' is at stake. I have shown in my earlier work how migrant women become pioneers of transnational family life by 'mothering from a distance' (see Lutz 2011). Transnational mothering is not exactly a new phenomenon considering that it has been practised in the Caribbean for decades (see Chamberlain 1997; Olwig 1999, 2002, 2012). Patricia Hill Collins (1990) has demonstrated that black women in the U.S. who were employed as servants and domestic workers left their children in the care of 'other mothers' (female kin or friends). There are also many examples in the European history of care work of servants, wet nurses and nannies who had to leave their own children in the care of minders so as not to jeopardize their jobs. Servanthood and motherhood were considered irreconcilable. As we have seen in the stories of Myroslava and Halina, this view is shared by their modern (Polish and German) employers.

[7] On the interplay of gender, sexuality and race in the context of migration processes, see Chap. 19, in this volume.

Authors writing on the context of slavery and its aftermath and on the Caribbean case emphasize that what is meant by motherhood is not just associated with direct *care for* the child, where the biological mother is responsible for the child's day-to-day care and upbringing, but that it is also perceived as *care about* the child in the form of financial contributions. In the absence of the biological mother, 'other mothers' are entrusted with the tasks involved in the children's care and upbringing, with motherhood going hand in hand with a collective sense of family in which the collective of the mothers shares in the decision-making about the children's development.

As has been demonstrated, in the case of migrant women from Eastern Europe transnational motherhood as a circular absence and presence from the family left behind has become the rule. It can be defined as an effort by biological mothers to perform social mothering across long geographical distances by using the latest telecommunication technologies in order to get in touch every day (e.g. through 'Skype mothering' and texting). Despite all the constraints this entails, these mothers combine *caring for* their children with *caring about* them.

In my last book (i.e. Lutz 2011) I did not deny that transnational mothers are torn by feelings of tremendous guilt, but given that this form of mothering is a daily practice of millions of migrant women, I was optimistic that the mother-blaming discourse would be counteracted by the reality of everyday life and eventually fade away. However, this is far from what is actually happening. On the contrary, the 'good meotherhood' discourse has a strong negative effect on the self-perception of migrant mothers, and there is nothing on the horizon to suggest that change may be on the way. The human right to family life may be widely acknowledged, but receiving states still deny many migrant women the right to family reunion, particularly those who work undocumented, while the sending regions have no interest in losing their citizens, but encourage them to send remittances home instead.

In conclusion, the dilemmas of maternalism become a pivotal aspect for female migrants. Their migration trajectories show that, due to difficult living conditions, they do not return to homemaking but rather leave their home country to seek employment elsewhere. Not unlike their 'sisters' in the wealthy and high-income countries, they more often than not share the idealized perceptions of good and decent mothering practices. Myra and Halina may not have a desire to go to their children's baseball games or prepare a waffle breakfast for them, as Anne-Marie Slaughter does, but they would love to practice their own 'goofy rituals' with their kids just as much.

Their obvious dilemma, therefore, is that their ideals cannot be reconciled with the forced temporal and spatial separation caused by migration. Consequently, these women and their families are caught up in the dilemmas of transnational motherhood. However, one of the most striking commonalities in the concepts of motherhood debates worldwide is that little, if any, attention is paid to fatherhood.

References

Badinter, E. (2013). *The conflict: How overzealous motherhood undermines the status of women*. New York: Picador.

Boris, E. (1993). What about the working of the working mother? *Journal of Women's History, 5*(2), 104–109. doi:10.1353/jowh.2010.0400.

Bowlby, J. (1958). The nature of the child's tie to his mother. *International Journal of Psycho-Analysis, 39*, 350–373.

Chamberlain, M. (1997). *Narratives of exile and return*. London: Macmillan.

Collins, P. H. (1990). *Black feminist thought: Knowledge, consciousness, and the politics of empowerment*. New York: Routledge.

Connell, R. W. (1987). *Gender and power: Society, the person and sexual politics*. Cambridge: Polity Press.

Ghodsee, K. (2011). *Lost in transition: Ethnographies of everyday life after communism*. Durham: Duke University Press.

Hochschild, A. R. (2003). *The commercialization of intimate life: Notes from home and work*. San Francisco: University of California Press.

ILO – International Labour Organization. (2013). *Domestic workers across the world: Global and regional statistics and the extent of legal protection*. Geneva: ILO.

Kalwa, D. (2008). Commuting between private lives. In S. Metz-Göckel, M. Morokvasic, & S. Münst (Eds.), *Migration and mobility in an enlarged Europe: A gender perspective* (pp. 121–140). Opldaden/Farmington Hills: Barbara Budrich.

Kis, O. (2007). "Beauty will save the world!": Feminine strategies in Ukrainian politics and the case of Yulia Tymoshenko. *Spacesofidentity*, *7.2*, 31–75. http://pi.library.yorku.ca/ojs/index.php/soi/article/viewFile/7970/7102

Koven, S., & Michel, S. (1990). Womanly duties: Maternalist politics and the origins of welfare states in France, Germany, Great Britain, and the United States, 1880–1920. *The American Historical Review, 95*(4), 1076–1108. doi:10.2307/2163479.

Lutz, H. (2011). *The new maids: Transnational women and the care economy*. London/New York: Zed Books.

Lutz, H., & Palenga-Möllenbeck, E. (2010). Care work migration in Germany: Semi-compliance and complicity. *Social Policy and Society, 9*(3), 419–430. doi:10.1017/S1474746410000138.

Lutz, H., & Palenga-Möllenbeck, E. (2011). Care, gender and migration: Towards a theory of transnational domestic work migration in Europe. *Journal of Contemporary European Studies, 19*(3), 349–364. doi:10.1080/14782804.2011.610605.

Lutz, H., & Palenga-Möllenbeck, E. (2012). Care workers, care drain, and care chains: Reflections on care, migration, and citizenship. *Social Politics, 19*(1), 15–37. doi:10.1093/sp/jxr026.

Michel, S. (2012). Maternalism and beyond. In M. van der Klein, R. J. Plant, N. Sanders, & L. R. Weintrob (Eds.), *Maternalism reconsidered: Motherhood, welfare and social policy in the twentieth century* (pp. 22–37). New York: Berghahn Books.

Michoń, P. (2009). "Bleib zu Hause, Liebling" – Mütter, Arbeitsmärkte und staatliche Politik in Polen und den baltischen Ländern. In C. Klenner & S. Leiber (Eds.), *Wohlfahrtsstaaten und Geschlechterungleichheit in Mittel- und Osteuropa* (pp. 163–191). Wiesbaden: VS Verlag für Sozialwissenschaften.

Olwig, K. F. (1999). Narratives of the children left behind. *Journal of Ethnic and Migration Studies, 25*(2), 267–284. doi:10.1080/1369183X.1999.9976685.

Olwig, K. F. (2002). A 'respectable' livelihood: Mobility and identity in a Caribbean family. In N. N. Sørensen & K. F. Olwig (Eds.), *Work and migration: Life and livelihoods in a globalizing world* (pp. 85–105). London/New York: Routledge.

Olwig, K. F. (2012). The care chain, children's mobility and the Caribbean migration tradition. *Journal of Ethnic and Migration Studies, 38*(6), 933–952. doi:10.1080/1369183X.2012.677175.

Plomien, A. (2009). Welfare state, gender, and reconciliation of work and family in Poland. Policy developments and practice in a new EU member. *Social Policy & Administration, 43*(2), 136–151. doi:10.1111/j.1467-9515.2009.00652.x.

Saxonberg, S., & Szelewa, D. (2007). The continuing legacy of the communist legacy? The development of family policies in Poland and the Czech Republic. *Social Politics, 14*(3), 351–379. doi:10.1093/sp/jxm014.

Skocpol, T. (1992). *Protecting soldiers and mothers: The political origins of social policy in the United States*. Cambridge: Harvard University Press.

Slaughter, A.-M. (2012, July/August). Why women still can't have it all. *Atlantic Magazine*. http://www.theatlantic.com/magazine/archive/2012/07/why-women-still-cant-have-it-all/309020/?single_page=true

Solari, C. (2010). Resource drain vs. constitutive circularity: Comparing the gendered effects of post-soviet migration patterns in Ukraine. *Anthropology of East Europe Review, 28*(1), 215–238.

Trzebiatowska, M. (2013). Beyond compliance and resistance: Polish Catholic nuns negotiating femininity. *European Journal of Women's Studies, 20*(2), 204–218. doi:10.1177/1350506812455985.

Zimmerman, M. K., Litt, J. S., & Bose, C. E. (2006). *Global dimensions of gender and carework*. Stanford: Stanford University Press.

Part IV
Shifting Politics of Belonging

Bruno Meeus and Kenneth Horvath

Introduction to Part IV

Symbolic struggles over belonging that accompany the political regulation of migration on the one hand and the practices of migration on the other are the subject of Part IV. From a social-transformation perspective, it is essential to analyse these struggles over belonging in their interplay with changing forms of political representation as well as in relation to social inequalities. In essence, the arguments of the chapters of this part implicitly refer to two prominent concepts. The first, the politics-of-belonging approach (Yuval-Davis 2011), highlights the contested nature of demands for equality. It points to a variety of (institutionalized) gendered, ethnicized/racialized and class-related discourses which are engendered in struggles for rights and equality. The second approach that is relevant in this context is Nancy Fraser's justice-theoretic concept. In her book *Justice Interruptus* (1997) Fraser describes a shift in the grammar of political claims-making that occurred in the last few decades of the twentieth century. According to Fraser, emancipatory politics are differentiated along the dimensions of recognition, redistribution and representation (Fraser 2009, 2011). All three dimensions are necessary conditions for what she calls 'participatory parity'. Without explicitly using Nancy Fraser's terms, the five chapters of this part relate to such struggles for redistribution, recognition, and representation that have been on the rise in Europe.

The first chapter of this part, Chap. 17 by Federico Oliveri, argues that migrants' political struggles align against a key mechanism of neoliberal citizenship that

B. Meeus (✉)
Cosmopolis Centre for Urban Research, Vrije Universiteit Brussel
Brussels, Belgium
e-mail: bruno.meeus@vub.ac.be

K. Horvath
University of Education of Karlsruhe, Karlsruhe, Germany
e-mail: horvath@ph-karlsruhe.de

currently prevails at the European level. The author provides evidence for migrant activism in Europe, which is analysed as a response to the rise of highly selective, security- and market-driven regulations of migration on the one hand and the maldistribution, misrecognition, and misrepresentation of migrants' rights by the responsible political authorities on the other. Federico Oliveri emphasizes that these migrant struggles anticipate potential new citizenship patterns.

The culturalization of maldistribution is studied in greater detail in Chap. 18 by Ayhan Kaya, who shows how 'Islamophobism' acts as a form of cultural racism in current neoliberal Europe. This cultural-religious discourse operates as an ideology, Kaya argues, and frames social, political, and economic injustice in terms of religious difference. Islamophobism thus masks the maldistributional injustices of poverty and unemployment and the injustices caused by the lack of political participation by employing references to 'Islamic background', which is believed to clash with Western secular norms and values.

The ethnicized and racialized politics of belonging are further scrutinized by Paul Scheibelhofer (Chap. 19), who investigates the ways in which seemingly emancipatory politics of recognition, such as those proposed by women's and sexual-minorities' movements, may in practice reinforce Eurocentric imageries of difference. These Eurocentric recognitional politics tend to draw on a 'historical archive of knowledge about racialized and gendered sexualities' that already appeared in colonial narratives when imperialist disappropriation was reframed as adventures into sexualized spaces where aberration and excess reigned. Legal measures such as integration tests that serve to foster migrant women's and sexual-minorities' rights therefore actually have detrimental effects. They become part of a domopolitics that is based on the premise that migration is an eminent threat to national communities.

The next chapter, by Nina Glick-Schiller and Ayşe Çağlar (Chap. 20), moves away from the supranational European scale and draws attention to the significance of urban localities in struggles over belonging. Introducing the concept of migrant emplacement, the authors focus on how the economic, cultural, and political positioning of different cities generates different social opportunities for migrants. To illustrate their point, the authors use the example of migrant businesses. The cultural recognition of 'ethnic entrepreneurs' masks the diverse social and economic roles of migrant businesses. Depending on the urban opportunity structure, migrant businesses can be part of the survival infrastructure of a city, as well as of neoliberal urbanization projects. Through their activities migrant businesses can advocate and strengthen neoliberal discourses that legitimate growing social and economic inequalities—or they may join movements for justice and against forms of structural adjustment.

The final chapter of this part, Chap. 21 by Ricarda Drüeke, analyses the role of the public sphere in the political struggles for redistribution, recognition, and representation. Drüeke argues that research on media and migration has mainly drawn attention to mainstream national media, focusing on how migrants and migration are covered, to what extent migrants have access to the production site of these media, and which mainstream national media they consume. Such studies imply a single national audience. The chapter, therefore, calls for the analysis of plural publics and counter-public spheres that are co-produced by migrants across the plurality of media spaces.

References

Fraser, N. (1997). *Justice interruptus: Critical reflections on the "Postsocialist" condition*. New York/London: Routledge.

Fraser, N. (2009). *Scales of justice: Reimagining political space in a globalizing world*. New York: Columbia University Press.

Fraser, N. (2011). Marketization, social protection, emancipation: Toward a neo-Polanyian conception of capitalist crisis. In C. Calhoun & G. Derluguian (Eds.), *Business as usual: The roots of the global financial meltdown* (pp. 137–156). New York: New York University Press.

Yuval-Davis, N. (2011). *The politics of belonging: Intersectional contestations*. London/Thousand Oaks/New Delhi/Singapore: SAGE.

Chapter 17
Struggles at the Boundaries of Neoliberal Citizenship: Theorizing Immigrant-Led Movements in Contemporary Europe

Federico Oliveri

17.1 Introduction

Our present time is not only marked by the 'proliferation of borders', the main purpose of which is to manage human mobility in line with the demands for flexible labour power by global markets, thereby differentiating life opportunities of people according to characteristics such as class, 'race', national origin, and legal status (Mezzadra and Neilson 2013). It is also a time of multiple struggles on and against these borders, which are being contested as a key mechanism of neoliberal migration governance and the related neoliberal citizenship regime that currently prevail in the global North and West. Currently dominant migration and citizenship regimes can be characterised as *neoliberal* essentially because their logic corresponds to the political rationality of neoliberalism, they are functional for the current politico-economic model, and they reproduce existing unequal social relations (Horvath 2014). On the one hand, neoliberal migration governance allows public authorities to subordinate the rights of migrants to their conditions of entry and stay, *i.e.* to their *usefulness* as determined by labour and electoral markets. On the other hand, neoliberal citizenship regimes stratify the population according to their supposed *competitiveness* and *deservingness*, managing insecurity mainly through the criminalization of marginal categories such as non-citizens and failed citizens (Anderson 2013).

Migrant struggles which contest these mechanisms should be distinguished from other forms of activism, at least for the following reasons. They are autonomously enacted and directed by people with personal or familial migration experiences, affirming themselves as rights-bearing subjects in a rather unprecedented way. They largely rest on practices of self-organization and self-representation. They express

F. Oliveri (✉)
Sciences for Peace Interdisciplinary Centre, University of Pisa, Pisa, Italy
e-mail: federico.oliveri@cisp.unipi.it

A. Amelina et al. (eds.), *An Anthology of Migration and Social Transformation*,
IMISCOE Research Series, DOI 10.1007/978-3-319-23666-7_17

controversial and often anti-institutional political claims. They have a repertoire of collective action based on protest, including civil disobedience. With regards to the first point, migrant-led mobilizations differ from autochthonous no border and anti-racist movements; regarding the other aspects, they differ from established community migrant associations (Oliveri 2015a). There can be overlap and cooperation between these forms of activism; the essential point is how far supporting organizations respect the autonomous voice and agency of the people directly involved in mobilizations.

This chapter aims to explore from a theoretical point of view the potential for social transformation entailed by migrant struggles directed against the neoliberal-citizenship regime in contemporary Europe. There are, at least, two elements which confer on those movements such a potential for change. On the one hand, migrant struggles express a strong dissent from the dominant politics of immigration control, trying to counterbalance the popular consensus enjoyed in all European States by restrictive border policies despite their failures. On the other hand, migrant struggles generally anticipate alternative regimes of free circulation and post-national citizenship, related to a radically universalist and anti-essentialist approach to human rights and belonging. Ongoing trends towards the Europeanization of dissent and alternatives in this field should be taken into account, as they express the potentiality of migrant struggles for social change at different levels, and their capacity to take advantage of the ambivalences of current European migration governance, highlighted also by Leila Hadj-Abdou in Chap. 7 of this volume.

17.2 Migrant Struggles and Social Transformation: Theoretical and Methodological Issues

In order to carve out the specific transformation potential of migrant struggles, I suggest to stress in particular the processes of political subjectivization through which marginalized groups of immigrants construct themselves as autonomous subjects to whom *the right to have rights* is due by co-citizens and institutions.

Instead of considering legal status, membership and rights as fixed and already given (Marshall 1950), we need to conceive of the boundaries of any 'community' as a battlefield. By using new concepts such as 'acts of citizenship' (Isin 2008) it is possible, for example, to explore ruptures and innovations in the political field which enable migrants, including undocumented ones, to become visible and audible in the public sphere and to construe themselves as equal rights-bearing subjects.

From this perspective, struggling migrants may contest and reframe dominant regimes of 'justice' and 'legality': they eventually violate laws which they consider unjust, ask for the full implementation of the existing human rights legal framework, or demand an entirely new paradigm for regulating mobility, residence, belonging, and access to full social rights. In order to support their normative claims, struggling migrants may produce counter-discourses on migrations and receiving societies which allow to uncover the hidden interests supporting their systematic discrimination, in terms of labour exploitation, electoral gains, or need of scapegoats especially in time of crisis and austerity. At the same time, they may try to overcome racialized identities which produce divisions and competition among themselves and with the rest of the population, building instead new solidarity and social alliances based on shared needs and class issues (Oliveri 2012).

Against this background, existing social movement and migration studies should be criticized in so far as they fail to appreciate the autonomous, non-conventional and conflictual activism of certain groups of migrants. Despite the recognition of migrant workers as an emergent political force in Europe (Miller 1981), some scholars still maintain a more or less hidden 'nationalist' point of view, focusing, for example, exclusively on the political behavior of 'ethnic minorities' in the elections of receiving countries, on the participation of migrants in ethnicity-based associations, national political parties, and national trade unions, or on the involvement of immigrants in political movements in their countries of origin.

In this following, I will present a basic theoretical classification of migrant struggles inspired by the protest events which took place in Europe since the 1990s, with a special focus on those that occurred more recently in connection with the global economic crisis. I decided to adopt as classification criteria the *claims* raised by migrants in their mobilizations against the different mechanisms which enact, from their critical point of view, neoliberal migration governance and citizenship regimes. As a result, three main fields of contention emerge that are interconnected with one another: freedom of movement against bordering mechanisms; the right to stay and to choose where to live against irregularization and precarization mechanisms; the right to free and decent work against exploitation mechanisms. These three fields are not an exhaustive list of all the political issues raised in migrant-led mobilizations, which may also include recognition of cultural identity and diversity, fair access to nationality, respect and access to equal rights for so-called 'second' and 'third generations' (Oliveri 2015a).

Within the three main categories of migrant struggles presented here, I will draw further distinctions according to the specific nature of the power mechanisms that are the target of migrants' criticism. For each kind of struggle, I will focus on a specific, exemplary case of mobilization. This 'exemplariness' is obviously disputable, but it is not arbitrary as it rests on reasonable criteria in each case: the presented struggle has either been generally recognised as symbolic of the issue (see border crossings in Ceuta and Melilla), has been innovative (see the border crossing of Tunisian migrants in Ventimiglia in 2011), has spread widely, up to the national level (see protests on administrative detention in Italy), has given rise to collective action at the European level (see the recent German movement against compulsory residence), has used new strategies such as strikes and occupations of workplaces for demanding residence permits (see *sans-papiers* workers in France between 2008 and 2010), has endured repression for many years (see the collective 'Lampedusa in Hamburg' asking for the right to stay since 2011), or has produced an extension of rights for all workers (see strikes in the logistics sector in Northern Italy).

I will briefly analyse each struggle drawing on three kinds of sources, where available: documents produced by migrants themselves, press coverages of the events, and studies on the mobilization, possibly including interviews with those directly involved. It is essential to focus on the *voices* of the people who are mobilizing in order to recognize the role of migrant agency in social change, even if those who are engaged in such struggles are a minority. Moreover, we may thereby avoid the risk that studying migrant struggles might in the end legitimize abstract discourses which idealize migrants as *ipso facto* avant-guards of anti-capitalist or new working-class movements.

17.3 The Neoliberal Turn in European Migration Governance and Citizenship Regime

Migrant struggles in contemporary Europe are generally a response to precarious living and working conditions which continue to affect many groups of immigrants, especially but not exclusively newcomers and undocumented ones, who face limited room for improvements, and have often been hit severely by the economic crisis in terms of social downgrading and growing exploitation rates (Oliveri 2015b).

Historically, these conditions started to spread in the 1970s, in connection with the neoliberal restructuring of the European economy under the constraints of internal and global competition. As Stephen Castles affirms in the Chap. 2 of this volume, labour forces in developed countries have been restructured 'through increased use of employment practices such as subcontracting, spurious self-employment, temporary employment, and casual work': international migration has been crucial to their diffusion also because 'migrants are more likely than natives to find themselves in situations of precarious employment'.

Not surprisingly, these trends have been supported by the rise of an increasingly selective form of migration governance based on market and security concerns. This new approach to mobility has been gradually implemented by the European Union and its members states since the 1990s, when the abolition of internal border checks was accompanied by a strengthening of the EU's external borders according to Schengen rules, and when the harmonization of asylum policies started according to the Dublin rules (Balzacq and Carrera 2006). Seen from this angle, the right to circulate freely into a space of security, freedom ad justice for EU citizens has always had as corollary the restriction to exercise this right for non-EU citizens (Rodier 2003).

The three main aims of this new approach to migration governance have been to manage incoming mobility from non-EU or new EU member States in order to attract 'the best and the brightest' migrant workers, to produce a cheap and adaptable labour force to be largely confined in low-cost, ethnicized labour market sectors, and to reduce as far as possible the number of refugees and family reunifications. All forms of mobility that go against these three aims have been the target of restrictive and repressive measures, culminating in the increasingly intense criminalization of unauthorized entry and stay in the territory.

This form of migration governance warrants the label 'neoliberal' because migrants' rights are inexorably linked to their conditions of entry and stay in a country, which in turn are linked to their usefulness and deservingness as determined by immigration rules. Employers play a key role within this frame, as they become *de facto* the main gatekeepers in the access of migrant workers to legal status, to human rights and thus, more generally, to full social existence. The key tool of their power is the link between visa, working contracts and residence permits, which exist in different versions in almost all European migration policies. This tool is supported by a panoply of selection mechanisms such as entry quotas, points-based systems, labour market tests based on skill shortages and national or EU labour force preferences, temporary residence permits, access to rights depending on length of stay, administrative and penal detention, expulsion, and readmission agreements with countries of origin.

Under this neoliberal migration governance, irregularization, and thus precarization and social exclusion, are systematically produced by migration and labour laws, increasing the risk of exploitation and unfair competition among all workers. Many non-EU migrants are *de facto* required to go through periods of irregularity: only those who accept to be subject to highly de-regulated, flexible, and segmented labour markets, to live in uncertain conditions and with no or few rights will be admitted to the rank of regular migrants. To help migrants who entered illegally or overstayed after their residence permits have expired, a variety of legalization programmes have been launched in many countries over the last 20 years (Brick 2011). Moreover, as criteria for accessing and renewing residence permits are often very strict and arbitrary, 'deportability' (De Genova 2002) becomes a general condition and an everyday risk for all migrants.

This kind of 'differential inclusion' produces general effects on receiving societies, in terms of a 'civic stratification' (Morris 2002) and of a racialized opposition between 'us' and 'them' (Anderson 2013). These phenomena are crucial for what I theorize as '*neoliberal citizenship*' (Oliveri 2015c). As soon as market-based competition becomes the benchmark of any political and social action, there is little room for taking care of the population as a whole (Foucault 2008): inclusive, egalitarian, and democratic citizenship tends to be substituted by an exclusionary, stratified, and post-democratic citizenship, designed by, and in aid of, a purely economic logic. The neoliberal state promotes freedom and security at the top and fosters punishment and insecurity at the bottom (Wacquant 2009).

On the one hand, neoliberal citizenship legitimizes inequalities in accessing rights on the base of individual merits and failures: 'the neoliberal subject is therefore not a citizen with claims on the State, but a self-enterprising citizen-subject who is obligated to become an entrepreneur of himself or herself' (Ong 2006, 15). On the other side, as this marketization tends to produce social insecurity, anomy and conflicts instead of social cohesion, neoliberal citizenship is linked to the criminalization and racialization of marginal groups, the 'securitization' (Wæver 1998) of social problems, and to the 'communitarization' (Bauman 2001) of ethical issues.

These mechanisms have been extensively experimented with in Europe, especially with regards to migrants and their descendants, as part of the construction of the current neoliberal citizenship regime. Through the criminalization of 'illegal' migrants, or the stigmatization of would-be refugees as 'bogus asylum seekers', citizens accept growing rates of discrimination and exploitation of migrants, according to class, 'race', national origin, and legal status (De Giorgi 2010). Respect for the law, including immigration and penal laws, functions as a more politically-correct mechanism that racializes membership, stunting social solidarity towards those who do not respect *our* rules. Through the securitization of migration, citizens apprehend social problems related to human mobility as a threat, and tend to consider crime control, repression, incarceration, and expulsion as the main solutions. Through the communitarization of ethical issues, isolated and scared citizens are embedded in presumed homogenous 'communities of value', constituted by 'good citizens' essentially opposed to 'failed citizens' and 'non-citizens', stigmatized as importing backward traditions and habits (Anderson 2013).

17.4 Freedom of Movement Against Bordering Mechanisms

Bordering mechanisms are sets of norms, practices, and discourses that extend border functions to society as a whole. As William Walters explains in Chap. 10 of this volume, we have experienced in the last decades the disaggregation of border functions away from the borders, which have become a grid ranging over the social, political and economic space rather than a distinct line separating it from the outside. These mechanisms are fundamental in the enforcement of current neoliberal migration governance and in the structuring of the connected neoliberal citizenship regime. They have multiple aims, such as deterring 'unwanted' people from moving; stopping them once they are on the move; deporting them back from where they arrived; differentiating, selecting, and controlling them according to their status and the needs of receiving societies; and legitimizing discriminatory access to rights, membership, working and living opportunities. Interestingly, these mechanisms are not only about immobilization and expulsion; they also operate on a temporal level, decelerating the *speed* of migrants (Karakayali and Rigo 2010) to filter and stratify them according to changing economic and political interests.

Bordering mechanisms in the Euro-Mediterranean region are the target of a growing wave of struggles, promoted directly by migrants in the name of *freedom of movement*. This concept involves a plurality of claims, including the right to escape from one's own country because of a lack of living and working opportunities; the right to choose freely where to live; the right not to be detained and not to be deprived of personal freedom merely because of a lack of a valid visa or residence permit; and the right to circulate freely in the country of arrival. These claims challenge not only the dominant neoliberal migration governance but also the modern conception of sovereignty as an almost absolute right of the states to control mobility across their borders and residence in their territory.

In the following I will distinguish and reconstruct struggles for freedom of movement according to different types of bordering mechanisms, which may be *external*, such as the fences around the EU exclaves of Ceuta and Melilla; *internal*, such as the controls at the Italian–French border; *national*, such as mandatory residence for asylum seekers in Germany; or *local*, such as administrative detention.

17.4.1 Struggles on the EU-External Border at Ceuta and Melilla

Ceuta and Melilla are two Spanish exclaves on the North African coast of the Mediterranean Sea which each share a border with Morocco. When Spain joined the Schengen Agreement in 1991 fortification of the two exclaves started, producing one of the most heavily guarded EU borders against unauthorized migrations. Most of the migrants who try to enter Ceuta and Melilla are sub-Saharan Africans; they camp out in the coastal forest around the two cities, and late at night try to scale the metal border fences or to enter from the sea.

On September 27, 2005, some 1,000 male migrants tried to climb over Melilla's perimeter fences; about 300 of them made it. On September 28 another 220 crossed the border to Ceuta in one night; 5 of them died during the attempt, and 200 were injured, 30 of them seriously. According to the reconstructions of a survivor, migrants had walked for days, and in some cases weeks, to reach the metal fences. The operation was prearranged, given that it had all the trappings of a well-coordinated initiative, not least aided by the use of mobile phones. Moreover, migrants came with ladders, gloves, and protective clothing to ensure that they would be able to scale the fences, which are topped with razor wire. At the appointed time they all climbed the fence simultaneously. They were entirely self-organized (Kein 2006).

Similar mass attempts to climb over the by now heavily militarized fences at Ceuta and Melilla have been made since then regularly, especially in April and August 2013 and in February 2014. Moreover, in Summer 2015 during the so-called 'refugee crisis', intense migrant struggles took place at other sites of the EU-external border, namely between Turkey and Greece, or Serbia and Hungary, revealing worldwide the failures of the current European asylum regime. They should be considered as a particular form of 'civil disobedience' enforced by the representatives of an emergent 'global citizenship' (Cabrera 2010). They are openly directed against the current 'global hierarchy of mobility' (Bauman 1998) enforced by receiving countries, with the collaboration of transit and sending countries: controls and punishment affect mainly 'the margins of current global mobility, while the top and centre enjoy increased security of residence and mobility rights' (Horvath 2014).

17.4.2 Struggles on the EU-Internal Border between Italy and France

France has been the preferred destination of most of the young Tunisians who have left their country by boat since the 'Revolution' of 2011. The majority of those who transited from Lampedusa were headed to Ventimiglia, the Italian town closest to the French border, because they wanted to benefit from the fact that there are no internal controls within the Schengen Area.

After the Italian government decided to issue residence permits to those who had arrived from North Africa between January 1 and April 5, 2011, the French government tightened internal border controls, calling for an even stricter respect of the entry conditions under the Schengen Borders Code. The tensions escalated on April 17, when French authorities suspended trains arriving from Italy for several hours, citing public-order concerns after some 300 Tunisian migrants and no-border activists had announced that they wanted to board a 'Train for Dignity' from Italy to France (Oliveri 2013). The group's idea was to cross the border openly and publicly rather than secretly. The title of the petition announcing the special train was 'Our Europe has no borders', a public denunciation of the race and class biases of European border controls. Migrants and activists saw evidence of these biases in the fact that some of the internal European borders that had been abolished by the Schengen Agreement were suddenly rebuilt as soon as the right to free circulation was enacted by unwanted migrants from Tunisia: 'Whereas it is generally acceptable that migrants cross borders in any way, with the possible risk of falling into clandestinity, undeclared work and blackmail, today Europe cannot accept that borders are crossed under the sunlight, with your head held high, and the dignified look typical of [one] who rejects domination' (Welcome 2011, translation mine, F. O.).

Similar collective attempts to cross the Italian-French border, accompanied by the construction of a permanent sit-it at Ventimiglia, have been repeated in Summer 2015 by hundreds of asylum seekers, especially from Eritrea and Somalia, trying to reach Northern Europe through Italy.

17.4.3 Struggles Against Mandatory Residence in Germany

The section of the Asylum Procedure Act on compulsory residence, which was passed in Western Germany in 1982, introduced the obligation for asylum seekers to live within certain territorial boundaries. Violations are punished with a fine or, for repeat offenders, imprisonment for up to 1 year and deportation. The first nationwide mobilization against this provision took place between May 17 and 19, 2001, in the form of a march, culminating in a demonstration in Berlin. Protests of asylum seekers and pro-migrant groups have regularly taken place in Germany since then.

A recent turning point was March 19, 2012, when a group of Iranian refugees in Würzburg went on hunger strike to protest their living conditions. Their hunger strike was in response to the suicide of Mohammad Rahsepar, a 30-year-old Iranian asylum seeker who had been held in the local refugee camp after having arrived in Germany 7 months earlier. Nationwide initiatives, in the form of 'tent actions', took place in March 2012: 'It is only in the streets where one can reach out for one's rights, therefore we shall leave our rooms in the camps and unite in the streets' (Berlin Refugee Strike 2012). Hundreds of asylum seekers occupied public squares in German cities such as Berlin, Regensburg, Düsseldorf, and Bamberg, referring to themselves as 'refugees on strike' and consciously violating the law in the name of dignity, freedom, and access to work.

Berlin-based 'refugees on strike' were also among the first promoters of the European March for Freedom started on May 17 2014, just before the European Union Parliament elections. Migrants marched together an average of 45 km a day from Strasbourg to Brussels, crossing borders without papers, and stopping at towns along the route to raise awareness. They developed a comprehensive agenda for alternative EU migration governance that would ensure that everyone has the freedom to move and live in dignity.

17.4.4 Struggles for Personal Freedom against Administrative Detention in Italy

According to the latest map published by Migreurop (2013), there are currently about 390 closed camps detaining non-EU citizens in the European Union, in countries which have applied for membership in the EU, and in countries that qualify for the European Neighbourhood Policy. Their typology varies in relation to their basic functions as pre-admittance detention centres, reception or processing centres, and deportation centres (Guild 2005). Since their general introduction in Europe during the 1990s migrant detention facilities have been met with harsh criticism. They have also evoked protests, hunger strikes, and attempts to escape by 'detainees' moved by 'the sense of injustice, the uncertainty about when or whether they will be released and whether or not they will finally be deported' (Hayter 2000: 126).

Since their introduction in 1998, migrant administrative detention facilities in Italy have been the scene of intense and repeated protests, both inside and outside the buildings themselves. Complaints have been many from the start, including concerning the very idea of a closed structure 'detaining' people for a significant period just because of their legal status, the absence of a general law detailing the conditions of stay, or particularly harsh living conditions coupled with very thin legal guarantees (Di Martino et al. 2013).

In the Summer of 2009, as the Parliament was debating the extension of the detention period from 60 to 180 days, hunger strikes and occupations took place almost at the same time in different centres, such as in Milan, Gorizia, Turin, Modena, and Rome. They were accompanied or followed by collective escapes. In the aftermath of these revolts the voices of the detained migrants became increasingly public and audible, mostly in the form of open letters. 'We are tired of not living well. We live like rats. Food sucks. We live as convicts but we are not. Detention time is extraordinary long: six months for identifying someone is too much. There are people here who made their lives in Italy, have children, went to school and grew up here. It's not fair. We're not criminals. (…). Here is worse than prison. We come in here healthy and go out crazy' (Oliveri 2014).

Hunger strikes and occupations of the roofs of detention centres aimed to produce a rupture in the invisibility and the inaudibility of undocumented migrants. This extreme and spontaneous form of protest denotes the difficulty in having access to other, more usual forms of political mobilization. Migrants politicized their 'bare bodies' as a form of revolt against the kind of 'suspended life' or 'no-life' imposed on them by the present system of border controls. Protests of this kind continue to be frequent in Italy and produced, in the last years, the temporary or the definitive closure of many migrant detention facilities.

17.5 The Right to Stay Against Irregularization Mechanisms

Mechanisms of irregularization are crucial to neoliberal migration governance, as much as criminalization mechanisms are crucial to the neoliberal citizenship regime. Under threat of losing regular status and being deported, all migrants are turned into precarious non-citizens and thus are forced to accept exploitation and discrimination with regard to access to rights. In addition, the wholesale stigmatization of migrants as a threat for public security unifies unequal and fragmented European societies against this new external/internal enemy, and prevents solidarity among workers and people of different origin.

Many struggles in Europe during the last 20 years have been carried out by unauthorized migrants, usually for the *right to stay*, which includes at least three fundamental claims: the right to be legalized through general and fair regularization procedures, under the slogan '*papers for all*'; the right not to be deported; and the right to free establishment. Legal residence is also the key to access to other fundamental rights, namely the rights to regular and decent work, housing, and welfare. More radically, the right to stay has regularly been evoked in order to contest the distinction between 'legal' and 'illegal' migrants as one produced by migration laws and entailing the violation of the very right to have rights (Balibar 2000). Because of the innovations in respect to the struggles of the *sans-papiers* that occurred in the 1990s (Cissé 1999), I will in the following concentrate on the strikes of undocumented migrant workers in France between 2008 and 2010, and on the struggle of the asylum seekers collective 'Lampedusa in Hamburg' that began in 2012.

17.5.1 The Struggles of the Sans-Papiers Workers in France

Between April 2008 and June 2010 thousands of undocumented migrant workers, mostly men from Francophone Africa aged between 20 and 35, organized a series of strikes in the Greater Paris region, with the support of the CGT trade union confederation. They claimed the regularization of their status, forcing employers to take up their responsibility for having let them work without residence permit. The protest reached its peak in October 2009, when some 6,800 workers occupied enterprises, employer federations and temporary work agencies. It ended with the occupation of the staircase of the Bastille Opera, and the partial acceptance of the demands of the strikers and their supporters by the government (Barron et al. 2011).

The mobilization started in a context of shrinking opportunities for traditional amnesties, due to the new turn taken by the government, which abrogated in 2006 the right to obtain a residence card after 10 years of continuous irregular stay, and introduced in 2007 the possibility of undocumented workers to be exceptionally regularized by their employers.

Strikes and occupations of workplaces represented a significant turning point in the mobilizations of undocumented migrants for the right to be regularized. Traditionally, these struggles adopted a repertoire of protest based on the occupation of public sites or religious buildings, and on hunger strikes. Under the slogan 'We work here, we live here, we stay here!', undocumented migrants claimed now their legal status as workers, and as such they seek full recognition of their rights and equal treatment with other workers.

Connecting strikes with occupations has proven as a powerful vehicle of political subjectivization. First, by occupying their workplace or, in case of part-time or agency workers, the siege of their labour intermediators, undocumented workers made their formal right to strike effective. Second, by asking their employers to undertake the necessary steps for their regularization, they openly revealed their situation: on the one hand, this put them in an extremely vulnerable position under the immigration law; on the other side, when on strike, undocumented workers became immunized against unfair dismissal under the labour law. Third, undocumented workers made themselves visible and audible during the occupations: as they highlighted their economic contribution as cooks, cleaners, construction workers, security agents, etc. and explained they almost had working contracts and payed social security, they reversed the common idea of 'illegal migrants' as living in the shadow, taking advantage of undeclared or even criminal economies. Fourth, through occupations they gained autonomous spaces for collective discussion and organization (Isidro 2011).

17.5.2 The Struggle of the Collective 'Lampedusa in Hamburg'

Most of the sub-Saharan people who founded the groups Lampedusa in Hamburg were working in Libya when they had to leave the country on boats in the Spring of 2011, fleeing unrest and the war against Gaddafi. After having passed through the asylum seeker hosting centre on Lampedusa, which inspired the name of their collectives, they were housed in temporary camps and facilities throughout Italy. After the closure of the Italian programme for the refugees in March 2013 they were turned out on the street with €500 each, and it was suggested to them that they move to Northern Europe, benefiting from free circulation within the Schengen Area.

About 300 of these refugees from Libya arrived in Hamburg in April 2013. Later that year they stated in a press release that 'we are the innocent civilians that Germany pretended to protect when it participated in the war in Libya. We never had intention to come to Europe. Before the NATO-bombs forced us to leave we had a good life in Libya.' With regard to the circumstances that had motivated the claims they were making, they asked, 'Do the European governments think they can bomb any country on our continent Africa at will, that they can destroy our lives and then hide from their responsibility?' (Lampedusa in Hamburg 2013, translation mine, F. O.).

Since the beginning the conflict between German authorities and Lampedusa in Hamburg was concerned with the legal situation of the group's members and their access to residence permits. The position of the city council was in line with the Dublin Regulation: asylum seekers had to go back to Italy because that was their first safe country of entry. The humanitarian permits most refugees received from Italian authorities did not allow them to stay abroad beyond the 90-day-period allowed by their tourist visas, or to find work or have access to fundamental social services (Meret and Della Corte 2014). This is why struggling migrants gradually expressed their clear opposition also to the European system of asylum, and drew parallels to the opposition to Germany's legal provisions on compulsory residence, emphasizing that in both cases the right of the refugees to choose where they want to live was denied.

The strategy Lampedusa in Hamburg used, with the support of a pool of lawyers, was to demand to be granted residence as a group—namely refugees—in accordance with Section 23 of the German Residence Act. To counter this demand, the Senate of Hamburg offered to support individual applications for residence permits on humanitarian grounds and to grant the migrants a temporary status for as long as their applications would be under review. Lampedusa in Hamburg rejected this offer. Between October 2013 and May 2015 demonstrations called by the group or by their supporters took place regularly, often ending in clashes with police.

17.6 Labour Rights Against Exploitation

Labour exploitation concerns regular as well as irregular migrant workers throughout Europe. It encompasses phenomena of different gravity that are often interrelated, including violations of national laws and international standards with regard to minimum wage and maximum working hours, unlawful gang-master activities, lack of official contracts of employment, lack of safety and health protection measures, forced labour, debt bondage, and new forms of slavery. There are many factors that make migrants vulnerable to exploitation, and they are generally connected with neoliberal migration governance and the related neoliberal citizenship regime. Vulnerability of migrants derives in particular from their highly precarious status under the law, their weak negotiation position, their being represented in the mainstream media as legitimate only if they are 'useful' to the national economy, and their difficulties in accessing courts and law enforcement agencies to have their rights recognized, especially if they are undocumented or work in the underground economy.

Migrants in Europe struggle against these phenomena, claiming the *right to free and decent work*, and access to *equal labour rights*. This includes a number of claims, such as the rights to have a regular employment contract, to have workdays/workweeks of reasonable length, to receive equal pay for equal work, to work in healthy working conditions, to have access to social security and to social and medical assistance, to organize and to strike, and, more fundamentally, the right to choose employment freely and to work free from discrimination, restrictions, or menaces. These struggles are important because they allow migrants to act as workers with equal rights and thus, at least potentially, as equal fellow citizens, and because they promote new forms of class solidarity among workers across national lines. The analysis provided in this section will focus on the series of strikes initiated in 2011 by migrant workers of the logistics sector in Northern Italy, which are still ongoing at the time of writing.

17.6.1 Strikes in the Logistics Sector in Northern Italy

Piacenza in Northern Italy is host to one of the largest logistics hubs in Europe. Since July 2011 the city, the entire Emilia-Romagna region, and the Padua area in Veneto have become sites of a series of struggles in which non-EU migrant workers with regular residence permits played a key role. Blockades and strikes started at TNT, the express distribution company, then spread to General Logistics Systems and IKEA, and finally concerned also the food company Granarolo and the furniture company Artoni. The primary claims were almost the same everywhere: respect for the national collective agreement adopted by cooperatives providing logistic services for the multinationals mentioned; wages and working hours equal to those of workers directly employed by the multinationals; safe working conditions; no discriminatory treatment; no wrongful dismissals; and the abolition of Italian immigration law, which connects permits to stay with regular working contracts, thus giving employers enormous power, especially in times of economic crisis. Supervisors often intimidated migrant workers—who had to have a valid working contract to have their permit to stay in Italy renewed—and tried to create a 'slavery-like system of work' (Curcio and Roggero 2012): they decided on a day-to-day basis who would or would not be allowed to work, and for how many hours; they silenced people who asked for a pay raise or demanded compliance with regulations on maximum working hours; and they declared only a part of the paid salaries to evade taxes.

Many migrant workers who tried to improve their working conditions through strikes and blockades did so successfully. The role of grass-roots trade union, such as SI Cobas and ADL Cobas, were also crucial in supporting the claims of migrant workers and organizing them across ethnic and national divides. In particular, after a year of mobilizations, in February 2015 they obtained significant amendments in the national collective agreement for the logistics sector, which now incorporates some of their demands in terms of guarantees against arbitrary dismissals, reduction and delay of pay, and other forms of violations of their rights they had suffered before, especially in the case of subcontracting. This lead to a general improvement of the working conditions in the sector, both for migrants and national workers. Another success was that many of those who had been fired for participating in the mobilization, over the last years, were allowed to go back to work.

These successes were possible because migrant workers themselves overcame internal divisions, developed a form of class unity and solidarity, and made alliances with national workers and other social movements to fight against austerity measures and labour exploitation. The example of the Arab revolutions, specifically that in Egypt, played a key role in mobilizing immigrant workers, especially in the case of the mobilization against TNT. 'After thirty years Mubarak has been driven out, something unimaginable for all of us. Nobody was expecting what then happened in our company (TNT), neither, thanks to our struggle. This is why we didn't call it a strike, but a revolution. For us, it was like in Egypt: the strike was our revolution' (Curcio and Roggero 2012).

17.7 Conclusion

So far studies on migrant struggles have concentrated on single mobilizations by particular categories of people with specific claims, most of them undocumented and thus primarily interested in demanding their 'papers' (e.g. McNevin 2006; Varela 2009; Karyotis and Skleparis 2013). Comparative studies have addressed different cities (Chimienti 2011; Monforte and Dufour 2013) or different countries (Laubenthal 2007), eventually leading to the perspective of an Europeanization of mobilizations (Monforte 2014), but they have regularly maintained a focus on a single category of people and struggles. With this background in mind, I tried to develop in this chapter a different approach, namely a theoretical one, aimed at exploring the potential for social transformation of migrant struggles by classifying the claims that they raise against the dominant neoliberal migration governance and citizenship regime.

Along with no-border and grass-roots anti-racist movements, migrants in contemporary Europe are engaged in autonomous struggles against what they directly experience as repressive, utilitarian and emergency-based immigration policies, which have been gradually implemented in the EU since the 1990s within a general neoliberal turn in the economy and the society. Even if the number of people involved represents a minority of the whole migrant population, these struggles entail a significant potential for social transformation, which deserves recognition and closer scrutiny, and which may aggregate and mobilize all those who suffer under the exclusionary logics of neoliberal citizenship regimes.

First, migrant struggles open the opportunity for processes of political subjectivization through which previously silenced and invisible people occupy the public scene, and affirm themselves as rights-bearing subjects, contesting the current rules and boundaries of neoliberal citizenship.

Second, these struggles spell out in the public sphere the dangerousness of the current politics of immigration control. On the one hand, drawing on their direct experience, they denounce the mechanisms of bordering, irregularization and exploitation which produce them as marginal and disposable subjects in allegedly democratic European societies. On the other hand, they show the general negative effects of those mechanisms, in terms of degrading political and legal culture, growing social inequalities, civic stratification in the access to rights, divisions and competition along 'racialized' differences of origin, legal status, culture, etc. especially with regard to labour market, welfare provisions, values, and sense of belonging.

Third, the claims addressed by struggling migrants to local, national and European authorities, especially concerning free movement, the right to stay and to choose where to live, and the right to free and decent work, anticipate an alternative and eventually more sustainable idea of society. This idea is based, among others, on a cosmopolitan, *i.e.* truly universal access to membership and rights essentially linked to residence rather than to nationality or legal status, within an exploitation-free model of economic development, and a real democratic and pluralistic conception of the political community.

References

Anderson, B. (2013). *Us & them? The dangerous politics of immigration control*. Oxford: Oxford University Press.

Balibar, É. (2000). What we owe to the Sans-Papiers. In L. Guenther & C. Heesters (Eds.), *Social insecurity: Alphabet city no. 7* (pp. 42–43). Toronto: House of Anansi Press.

Balzacq, T., & Carrera, S. (Eds.). (2006). *Security versus freedom: A challenge for Europe's future?* Hampshire: Ashgate Publishing.

Barron, P., Bory, A., Chauvin, S., Jounin, N., & Tourette, L. (2011). *On bosse ici, on vie ici. La grève des sans papiers: une aventure inédite*. Paris: La Découverte.

Bauman, Z. (1998). *Globalization: The human consequences*. Cambridge: Polity Press.

Bauman, Z. (2001). *Community: Seeking safety in an insecure world*. Cambridge: Polity Press.

Berlin Refugee Strike. (2012). *First declaration of striking asylum seekers in Berlin*. http://asylstrikeberlin.files.wordpress.com/2012/08/first_declaration_english.pdf

Brick, K. (2011). *Regularizations in the European Union: The contentious policy tool*. Washington, DC: Migration Policy Institute. http://www.migrationpolicy.org/sites/default/files/publications/EURegularization-Insight.pdf

Cabrera, L. (2010). *The Practice of Global Citizenship*. Cambridge: Cambridge University Press.

Chimienti, M. (2011). Mobilization of irregular migrants in Europe: A comparative analysis. *Ethnic and Racial Studies, 34*(8), 1338–1356.

Cissé, M. (1999). *Parole de sans-papiers*. Paris: La dispute.

Curcio, A., & Roggero, G. (2012, December 11). The revolution in logistics. *UniNomade 2.0*. http://www.uninomade.org/the-revolution-in-logistics

De Genova, N. (2002). Migrant 'illegality' and deportability in everyday life. *Annual Review of Anthropology, 31*, 419–447.

De Giorgi, A. (2010). Immigration control, post-Fordism, and less eligibility: A materialist critique of the criminalization of immigration across Europe. *Punishment & Society, 12*, 147–167.

Di Martino, A., Biondi Dal Monte, F., Boiano, I., & Raffaelli, R. (2013). *The criminalization of irregular immigration: Law and practice in Italy*. Pisa: Pisa University Press.

Foucault, M. (2008). *The birth of biopolitics: Lectures at the Collège de France: 1978–1979*. Basingstoke/New York: Palgrave Macmillan.

Guild, E. (2005). *A typology of different types of centres in Europe: Report for the European parliament: Directorate-general internal policies of the Union*. http://www.libertysecurity.org/article1181.html

Hayter, T. (2000). *Open borders: The case against immigration controls*. London: Pluto Press.

Horvath, K. (2014). Policing the borders of the 'Centaur State': Deportation, detention, and neoliberal transformation processes – The case of Austria. *Social Inclusion, 2*(3), 113–123.

Isidro, L. (2011). La grève des travailleurs sans-papiers. Réflexions sur l'occupation. *Revue du droit du travail, 6*, 363–369.

Isin, E. F. (2008). Theorizing acts of citizenship. In E. F. Isin & G. M. Nielsen (Eds.), *Acts of citizenship* (pp. 15–43). London: Zed Books.
Karakayali, S., & Rigo, E. (2010). Mapping the European space of circulation. In N. De Genova & N. Peutz (Eds.), *The deportation regime: Sovereignty, space, and the freedom of movement* (pp. 123–146). Durham/London: Duke University Press.
Karyotis, G., & Skleparis, D. (2013). Migrant mobilisation during the economic crisis: Identity formation and dilemmas. In M. Tsilimpounidi & A. Walsh (Eds.), *Remapping crisis: A guide to Athens* (pp. 124–143). Alresford: Zero Books.
Kein. (2006, May 8). *"We are all a collective combination something …": Interview with M.K. who succeeded in the collective storm in Ceuta.* http://www.kein.org/node/71
Lampedusa in Hamburg. (2013, October 1). *Senate escalates situation and relies on inhuman blackmail.* Hamburg: Lampedusa in Hamburg. http://thevoiceforum.org/node/3346
Laubenthal, B. (2007). *Der Kampf um Legalisierung: Soziale Bewegungen illegaler Migranten in Frankreich, Spanien und der Schweiz.* Frankfurt am Main/New York: Campus.
Marshall, T. H. (1950). *Citizenship and social class, and other essays.* Cambridge: Cambridge University Press.
McNevin, A. (2006). Political belonging in a neoliberal era: The struggle of the Sans-Papiers. *Citizenship Studies, 10*(2), 135–151. doi:10.1080/13621020600633051.
Meret, S., & Della Corte, E. (2014, January 22). Between exit and voice: Refugees' stories from Lampedusa to Hamburg. *Opendemocracy.* https://www.opendemocracy.net/can-europe-make-it/susi-meret-elisabetta-della-corte/between-exit-and-voice-refugees-stories-from-la
Mezzadra, S., & Neilson, B. (2013). *Border as method, or, the multiplication of labor.* Durham: Duke University Press.
Migreurop. (2013). *Close the camps: Mapping of migrant camps.* http://www.aedh.eu/Close-the-camps-mapping-of-migrant.html
Miller, M. (1981). *Foreign workers in Western Europe: An emerging political force.* New York: Praeger.
Monforte, P. (2014). *Europeanizing contention. The protest against 'Fortress Europe' in France and Germany.* New York/Oxford: Berghahn.
Monforte, P., & Dufour, P. (2013). Comparing the protests of undocumented migrants beyond contexts: Collective actions as acts of emancipation. *European Political Science Review, 5*(1), 83–104. doi:10.1017/S1755773912000045.
Morris, L. (2002). *Managing migration: Civic stratification and migrants' rights.* London/New York: Routledge.
Oliveri, F. (2012). Migrants as activist citizens in Italy: Understanding the new cycle of struggles. *Citizenship Studies, 16*(5/6), 793–806. doi:10.1080/13621025.2012.698509.
Oliveri, F. (2013, September 11). "Our Europe has no borders". Young Tunisians acting as European Citizens. *Acts: The Archives Project.* http://www.enginfisin.eu/cms/our-europe-has-no-borders
Oliveri, F. (2014). Acts of citizenship against neoliberalism: The new cycle of migrant struggles in Italy. In N.-K. Kim (Ed.), *Multicultural challenges and sustainable democracy in Europe and East Asia* (pp. 221–242). London/New York: Palgrave.
Oliveri, F. (2015a). Lotte dei migranti ai confini della cittadinanza: una proposta teorico-metodologica. In M. Omizzolo & P. Sodano (Eds.), *Migranti e territori* (pp. 133–158). Rome: Ediesse.
Oliveri, F. (2015b). Migrant struggles in Italy within and against the economic crisis. In A. Borghini & E. Campo (Eds.), *Exploring the crisis.* Pisa: Pisa University Press.
Oliveri, F. (2015c). Subverting neoliberal citizenship. Migrant struggles for the right to stay in contemporary Italy. *ACME: An International E-Journal for Critical Geographies, 14*(2), 492–503.
Ong, A. (2006). *Neoliberalism as exception: Mutations in citizenship and sovereignty.* Durham: Duke University Press.

Rodier, C. (2003). Les camps d'étrangers, nouvel outil de la politique migratoire de l'Europe. *Mouvement, 30*, 102–107.

Varela, A. (2009). Residency documents for all! Notes to understand the movement of migrants in Barcelona. *Refuge, 26*(2), 121–132.

Wacquant, L. (2009). *Punishing the poor. The neoliberal government of social insecurity*. Durham/ London: Duke University Press.

Wæver, O. (1998). Security, insecurity and asecurity in the West-European non-war community. In E. Adler & M. Barnett (Eds.), *Security communities* (pp. 69–118). Cambridge: Cambridge University Press.

Welcome. (2011, April 17). *Trains de la dignité: La dignité n'a pas de frontières. Global Project*. http://www.globalproject.info/it/in_movimento/17-aprile-2011-genes-vintimille-marseille-trains-de-la-dignite/8162

Chapter 18
'Islamophobism' as an Ideology in the West: Scapegoating Migrants of Muslim Origin

Ayhan Kaya

18.1 Introduction[1]

The construction of a contemporary European identity is built in part on anti-Muslim racism, just as other forms of racist ideology played a role in constructing European identity during the late nineteenth and early twentieth centuries. Use of the term 'Islamophobia' assumes that fear of Islam is natural and can be taken for granted, whereas use of the term 'Islamophobism' presumes that this fear has been fabricated by those with a vested interest in producing and reproducing such a state of fear, or phobia. By describing Islamophobia as a form of *ideology*, I argue that Islamophobia operates as a form of *cultural racism* in Europe which has become apparent along with the process of *securitizing* and *stigmatizing* migration and migrants in the age of neoliberalism.

This chapter delineates the ways in which the neoliberal states in Europe have used Islamophobism based on recent survey findings and the results of fieldwork I conducted over the past decade, particularly in Germany, France, Belgium, and the Netherlands. In addition, I trace the genealogy of the ideology of Islamophobism since the 1973 Arab–Israeli War. So far, events ranging from this Arab–Israeli conflict and the oil crisis of 1974 to the broadcasting of the fake film trailer *Innocence of Muslims* in 2012 have led to questions about the significance of Muslims' collective presence in Europe and to the radicalization of European Islamic identity. The escalation of events such as these and their effect on Islamophobic discourse among some political figures and public intellectuals has separated the European population

[1] I would like to express my gratitude to Anna Amelina, Kenneth Horvath and Bruno Meeus as well as to the anonymous reviewers for their valuable and constructive suggestions and for their critique of the manuscript.

A. Kaya (✉)
Department of International Relations and Political Science,
Istanbul Bilgi University, Istanbul, Turkey
e-mail: ayhan.kaya@bilgi.edu.tr

A. Amelina et al. (eds.), *An Anthology of Migration and Social Transformation*,
IMISCOE Research Series, DOI 10.1007/978-3-319-23666-7_18

into two worlds: *Muslims* and *non-Muslims*. It is certain that Islam has become politicized by various groups with a Muslim background as well as by some non-Muslims. Those Muslims who politicize Islam have been in search of an ideology to protect themselves against detrimental forces of globalization such as injustice, inequality, poverty, unemployment, exclusion, racism, and discrimination.[2] Some Western political leaders and public intellectuals, on the other hand, have also politicized Islam as a way to mobilize the majority to serve their own interests, as well as inculcating fear of 'an enemy within' or 'an external enemy'.

In one way or another, the events mentioned above and several others have shaped the ways in which the public in the West perceives Muslims, as well as the ways in which Muslims have regarded the Western world. In truth, both groups are extremely heterogeneous. Yet such perceptions explain, for example, why immigrants of Muslim origin and their descendants have often been considered guilty until proved innocent in times of turmoil, such as after the mass murder that took place in Norway on July 22, 2011,[3] when the Muslims were the first to be blamed for the atrocity.

Based on a review of the recent literature on Islamophobia in Europe through the lens of immigration studies, this chapter examines the political and public discourses in more detail to show how Islamophobia has been used as a form of *ideology*. In addition to presenting current thinking and the debate about Islamophobia, I also seek to address the most recent data available from public surveys and discourses regarding the current state of Islamophobia within the European context.

18.2 Islamophobia, or What?

The term 'Islamophobia' is much used but little understood. It is believed to have become popular in the wake of the report by The Runnymede Trust's Commission on British Muslims and Islamophobia (CBMI), entitled *Islamophobia: A Challenge for Us All* (Runnymede Trust 1997). This report asserts that the term 'Islamophobia' was first used by an American newspaper reporter in 1991. CBMI defined Islamophobia as 'an unfounded hostility towards Islam, and therefore fear or dislike of all or most Muslims'.[4] There are also a number of other possible terms to refer to negative feelings about and attitudes towards Islam and Muslims, such as 'anti-Muslimism', 'anti-Muslim racism', 'cultural racism', 'intolerance against Muslims',

[2] Islamic references used in various acts of opposition tend to express the need to belong to a legitimate, counter-hegemonic global discourse, such as that concerning Islam, and to derive symbolic power from that. It seems that religion is now replacing the Left in the absence of a global leftist movement. Michel de Certeau (1984: 183) reminds us of the discursive similarities between religion and the Left, with religion offering a *different world* and the Left offering a *different future*—and both offering solidarity.

[3] The myth that Muslim immigrants are taking over Europe and multiculturalism is harmful led to the murder of 77 individuals by the right-wing extremist Anders Behring Breivik in Norway.

[4] For a more detailed analysis of the terminology of Islamophobia, anti-Muslim sentiments, and cultural racism, see Allen (2010), Meer and Modood (2009), Werbner (2005), and Halliday (1999).

'anti-Muslim prejudice', 'anti-Muslim bigotry', 'hatred of Muslims', 'anti-Islamism', 'Muslimophobia', 'demonization of Islam', and 'demonization of Muslims' (Richardson 2012).

Today the term most commonly used is probably 'Islamophobia'. Richardson (2012) also reminds us that a similar range of contested terms exists in other languages as well, not only in English. For instance, in German there is a dispute between *Islamophobie* (fear) and *Islamfeindlichkeit* (hostility). In French the dispute is in part between *islamophobie* and *racisme anti-arabe* (or *racisme anti-maghrébin*), the latter indicating that the phenomenon is mainly seen as a form of anti-immigrant racism devoid of theological and cultural connotations. The Scandinavian term *Muslimhat* literally means 'hatred of Muslims'. Such terminological differences may reflect a set of differences in understanding and focus. These different terms may be used to distinguish between various manifestations of the phenomena under discussion. For instance, as Sivanandan (2010) rightfully states, the term '*anti-Muslim racism*' is used to refer to hate crimes and to harassment, rudeness, and verbal abuse in public spaces, whereas the term '*Islamophobia*' refers to discourse and mind-sets in the media, which include the broadsheets as well as the tabloids.

Since Fred Halliday put 'Islamophobia' in inverted commas in the title of his 1999 article "'Islamophobia' Reconsidered", the term has also been discussed by scholars. Some criticisms refer to the unintended consequences the term might have or to its possible political and ideological exploitation. Halliday himself furnishes an example, arguing that the term 'reproduces the distortion [...] that there is one Islam' and that this serves to 'play into the hands' of individuals or groups in Muslim communities who seek to promote a more conservative agenda and to arrogate to themselves the authority to speak for the tradition and culture, whether it be on the status of women, the right to free speech, or violence (Halliday 1999: 898). He also posits an objection on the grounds that the term is a misnomer. According to Halliday, once upon a time, 'the enemy' was the religion of Islam, and it was attacked during the time of the Crusades and the Reconquista. But today the target is a different one: it is no longer Islam as a faith that is attacked but rather Muslims as a people, which is why he prefers the term 'anti-Muslimism' (Halliday 1996: Chap. 6).

There is currently no legally agreed upon definition of 'Islamophobia', nor have the social sciences developed a common definition, policy, and programme of action that could be used to combat it. However, Islamophobia is discussed in relation to the broad concepts of 'racism' and 'racial discrimination', which are universally accepted by governments and international organizations. Therefore, the United Nations,[5] the Council of Europe,[6] the Organization for Security and Co-operation in

[5] For the UN's definition of racial discrimination, see the "International Convention on the Elimination of All Forms of Racial Discrimination," which was adopted and opened for signature and ratification by General Assembly Resolution 2106 (XX) of December 21, 1965, and which entered into force on January 4, 1969.

[6] See the European Commission against Racism and Intolerance (ECRI) general policy recommendation No. 7 on national legislation to combat racism and racial discrimination, adopted on December 13, 2002.

Europe (OSCE),[7] and the European Union Monitoring Centre on Racism and Xenophobia (EUMC 2006)[8] base their approaches to identifying the phenomenon and its manifestations on internationally accepted standard definitions of 'racism'. In 2005 a Council of Europe publication entitled 'Islamophobia and Its Consequences on Young People' referred to Islamophobia as

> the fear of or prejudiced viewpoint towards Islam, Muslims and matters pertaining to them. Whether it takes the shape of daily forms of racism and discrimination or more violent forms, Islamophobia is a violation of human rights and a threat to social cohesion (CoE 2004).

In this regard, paraphrasing Edward Said, Semati (2010: 266–267) also eloquently defines what Islamophobia refers to:

> Islamophobia is a cultural–ideological outlook that seeks to explain ills of the (global) social order by attributing them to Islam. It is a way of thinking that conflates histories, politics, societies and cultures of the Middle East into a single unified and negative conception of Islam. It is an ideology in which the 'backwardness' of the other is established through an essentialized Islam. It is, as a form of racism, an essentialist view of peoples whose culture it deems 'different' in an eternal, fixed, and immutable fashion.

Andrew O'Hagan (2008) also observed that Islamophobia is one of the big questions of our day, presenting a problem that is most often answered with ignorance or common hysteria and almost never with fresh thinking. The damage this brings to bear on the European public is 'making a monster where it shouldn't exist, a monster made from the mania of our own fear' (Evans 2010: 3). Similarly, Cesari et al. 2006: 8) argues that Islamophobia actually conceals different forms of discrimination resulting from structural inequalities:

> This phenomenon cannot simply be subsumed into the term Islamophobia. Indeed, the term can be misleading, as it presupposes the pre-eminence of religious discrimination when other forms of discrimination (such as racial or class) may be more relevant. We therefore intend to use the term Islamophobia as a starting point for analyzing the different dimensions that define the political situation of Muslim minorities in Europe.

Presumably, the 'monster made from the mania of our own fear' derives from a '*glocal*' context (a portmanteau of 'global' and 'local') which is shaped by a growing feeling of insecurity that makes individuals more and more heteronomous in a way that essentializes communal, ethnic, cultural, linguistic, and religious boundaries. It is this feeling of insecurity that makes individuals rely on what is cultural, religious, and communal in an age of prudentialism. Nostalgia, the past, ethnicity, culture, and religion turn out to be a kind of lighthouse beckoning even the members of the majority societies back to the shore—the one point on the landscape that gives hope of direction in a time characterized by prudentialism, post-social state, insecurity, fear, loneliness, distrustfulness, and aimlessness (Miller and Rose

[7] See consolidated summary of the OSCE Meeting on the Relationship between Racist, Xenophobic and Anti-Semitic Propaganda on the Internet and Hate Crimes, Conference in Paris, June 16/17, 2004, available at http://www.osce.org/cio/37720

[8] EUMC later became the European Union Agency for Fundamental Rights (FRA) on 1 March 2007.

2008). This is actually the way the neoliberal state operates through securitizing and stigmatizing those who are ethnoculturally and religiously different from the majority societies—a point to be discussed later in this chapter.

18.3 Islamophobism as an Ideology

The term 'Islamophobia' assumes that the fear directed toward Islam is innate and taken for granted. Recently, however, a growing scientific literature has been arguing that this fear is in fact constructed and fabricated by those who have a vested interest in producing and reproducing such a phobia. Hence, I want to offer an alternative term, '*Islamophobism*', likening it to 'anti-Semitism' in terms of its genesis and development[9] Islamophobia as an ideology, or Islamophobism, is being manufactured in parallel with the growing stream of ethnicization, racialization, and culturalization that has characterized social and political trends in the West since the early 1990s (Brown 2006).[10] This stream is advocated by several politicians and public servants, the bureaucracy, the judiciary, the police, and the media in order to hold socioeconomically and politically deprived migrants and their descendants responsible for their isolation, exclusion, poverty, unemployment, lack of schooling, and any kind of failure in everyday life (Balibar 2004: 37–38). The process of ethnicizing, racializing, and culturalizing that which is social and political is shaped not only by dominant political discourses that are considerably conservative in tone but also by the enormous demographic changes led by the dissolution of the Eastern Bloc in the late 1980s and early 1990s (Brubaker 1991; Kaya 2009). One could also argue that contemporary European identity is in part built on what I call Islamophobism, or anti-Muslim racism, in a fashion similar to the construction of

[9] Despite the fact that Islamophobism and anti-Semitism cannot be categorically compared due to the historical resonance of the latter during the Holocaust, I am inclined to argue that the structure and function of anti-Muslim racism and anti-Semitism are actually similar in terms of the ways in which they operate especially in times of social-economic and political turmoil. Accordingly, my assumption is very similar to that of Maleiha Malik (2010), who argues that Jews and now Muslims have been the targets of cultural racism. Hence, differences arising from their religious cultures are pathologized and systematically excluded from definitions of 'being European' or 'being Western'. Both anti-Semitism and anti-Muslim racism focus on belief in religious law to render Jews and Muslims as threats to the nation. Anti-Semitism refers to a set of opinions, stereotypes, and prejudices, racializing Jews as an assimilated threat to national interests emerging at moments of crisis. Similarly, Muslims are now being represented as a different kind of *folk devil*, a social group that is openly and aggressively trying to impose its religion on national culture.

[10] One should note here that the process of ethnicizing, racializing, and culturalizing what is social and political is not necessarily a top-down process (see also Chaps. 17 and 18, in this volume); it may be a relational, dialectical, and dialogical process as well. It is manufactured not only by the neoliberal states as a way to reduce structural problems such as poverty, exclusion, inequality, injustice, violence, and unemployment to a culturalist explanation; social and cultural minorities also contribute to this process in that they tend to reify their culture, community, purity, authenticity, and religion as a way to protect themselves from the detrimental effects of globalization, deindustrialization, and structural exclusion.

the European identity of the late nineteenth and early twentieth centuries, which was in part built on anti-Semitism.

A brief history of the term 'ideology' may help us understand what the concept of Islamophobism actually denotes. The term was first used by the French philosopher Destutt de Tracy (1754–1836) in 1796 to refer to a 'new science of ideas' (literally an *idea-ology*) that set out to uncover the origins of conscious thought and ideas. In coining this science as a separate discipline, his expectation was that ideology would eventually enjoy the same status as established sciences such as biology and zoology. However, in the mid-nineteenth century Karl Marx gave a more enduring meaning to the term, defining it as a set of beliefs and ideas leading the masses to *false consciousness*. Marx went even further, redefining the function of ideology as a way to naturalize the status quo by persuading oppressed social classes to accept the dominant regimes of truth, or dominant descriptions of reality, which render 'subordination' natural. Marx actually meant that ideology amounted to the ideas of the 'ruling class'; that is, ideas that thus uphold the class system and perpetuate exploitation. Marx and Engels wrote the following in their early work *The German Ideology*:

> The ideas of the ruling class are in every epoch the ruling ideas, i.e. the class which is the ruling material force in society is at the same time the ruling intellectual force. The class which has the means of material production at its disposal has control at the same time over the means of mental production (Marx and Engels [1846] 1970: 64).

As far as capitalist production is concerned, the ideology of the property-owning bourgeoisie fosters *delusion*, or *false consciousness*, among the exploited social groups, preventing them from recognizing the fact of their own subordination and exploitation. Nevertheless, Marx did not believe that all political views had an ideological character. He held that his own work, which attempted to reveal the processes of class exploitation and oppression, was scientific. In his view, a clear-cut distinction could be drawn between science and ideology, between *truth* and *falsehood*. Subsequently, however, Vladimir Ilyich Lenin (1988) and Antonio Gramsci (1971) redirected this distinction by referring not only to 'bourgeois ideology' but also to 'socialist ideology' or 'proletarian ideology'—terms that Marx would have considered absurd.

The emergence of totalitarian dictatorships in the period between the two world wars prompted writers such as Karl Popper ([1945] 1966) and Hannah Arendt (1951) to view ideology as *an instrument of social control to ensure compliance and subordination*. Such Cold War liberal usage of the term treated ideology as a 'closed' system of thought, one that refused to tolerate opposing ideas and rival beliefs by claiming a monopoly of truth. Eventually, Louis Althusser moved away from the earlier Marxist understanding of the concept of ideology, which was believed to create what was termed a 'false consciousness', or an incorrect understanding of the way the world functioned. According to Althusser (2001), it is impossible to access the 'real conditions of existence' owing to our reliance on *language*, which shapes what we think, imagine, and believe. However, through a rigorous 'scientific' approach to society, economics, and history, we can come close to perceiving, if not those 'real conditions', at least the methods by which we are indoctrinated with a certain ideology by complex processes of recognition.

Althusser also made a distinction between conventional state apparatuses (government, administration, army, police, courts, and prisons) and ideological state apparatuses (education, family, media, church, culture, and means of communication). In contrast to the conventional state apparatuses, the ideological state apparatuses are less coercive, less centralized, and more heterogeneous; they are also believed to access the private rather than the public realm of existence. The main thing that distinguishes ideological state apparatuses from state apparatuses is ideology: 'the repressive state apparatus functions by violence, whereas the ideological state apparatuses function by ideology' (Althusser 2001: 97). Althusser's understanding of ideology has in turn influenced a number of important Marxist thinkers, including Chantal Mouffe, Ernesto Laclau, Slavoj Žižek, and Fredric Jameson.

One could thus argue that Islamophobism as an ideology is being constructed by ruling political groups to foster a kind of false consciousness, or delusion, within the majority society as a way of covering up their own failure to manage social, political, economic, and legal forces and consequently the rise of inequality, injustice, poverty, unemployment, insecurity, and alienation. In other words, Islamophobism turns out to be a practical instrument of social control used by the conservative political elite to ensure compliance and subordination in this age of neoliberalism, essentializing ethnocultural and religious boundaries. Muslims have become global 'scapegoats', blamed for all negative social phenomena such as illegality, crime, violence, drug abuse, radicalism, fundamentalism, conflict, and financial burdens. One could argue that Muslims are now being perceived by some individuals and communities in the West as having greater social power. There is a growing fear in the United States, Europe, and even in Russia and the post-Soviet countries that Muslims will demographically take over sooner or later.[11]

Accordingly, Mehdi Semati (2010) finds a correlation between the rise of Islamophobic discourse that prevails in the West and the ongoing political crisis in the Middle East. With a special focus on the United States, he states that the current discourse on Islam and Muslims is inextricably bound with issues such as terrorism and the protection of national security, which tend to frame all other issues that concern the Middle East.[12] The major thrust of U.S. foreign policy in the 1980s was formulated in response to (perceived) aggression by the Soviet Union. The threat of terrorism as 'Russia's secret weapon' then became a major theme in the new Cold War. During the Presidency of George W. Bush (2001–2009), U.S. foreign policy became more engaged in the war against the 'axis of evil', which symbolized mainly the (perceived) 'terrorist' Islamic countries (Semati 2010: 259–260).

---

[11] A good example of those prejudicial interpretations made in the West about Muslims is Greenfield (2013), who expresses his fear about the Muslims demographically taking over the United States, Europe, and Asia in the next couple of decades.

[12] For further discussions about the securitization of migration see Chaps. 10, 17 and 22, in this volume as well as Bigo (2002), Huysmans (2006), Cesari et al. (2006), Kaya (2009), and Cesari (2013).

Hence, as Chris Allen (2010: 195) eloquently revealed, Islamophobia is not really a 'phobia'; rather, it is a form of ideology,

> similar in theory, function and purpose to racism and other similar phenomena, that sustains and perpetuates negatively evaluated meaning about Muslims and Islam in the contemporary setting in similar ways [...] that inform and construct thinking about Muslims and Islam as Other.

The aim of Islamophobia as an ideology is to make the majorities of a society believe that Muslims and Islam represent an 'enemy within' in the European context and an 'external enemy' in the U.S. context, so that the unity of the nation in question can be protected against the national, societal, and cultural security challenges posed from inside or outside (Robin 2004; Huysmans 2006; Kaya 2009; Allen 2010).

As this type of discourse travels among states, civil societies, and citizens, produces and organizes these subjects, and is then used by these subjects to govern themselves, Islamophobia could also be seen to embody what Foucault formulated as a distinctive feature of modern *governmentality*.[13] An analysis of modern 'government' needs to pay particular attention to the role accorded to 'indirect' mechanisms for aligning economic, social, and personal conduct with sociopolitical objectives. Today political power is exercised through a set of multiple agencies and techniques, some of which are only loosely associated with the executives and bureaucracies of the formal organs of state (Miller and Rose 2008: 26). The state is not the source or agent of all governing power, nor does it monopolize political power; rather, the powers and rationalities governing individual subjects and the population as a whole operate through a range of formally nonpolitical knowledge and institutions. The ensemble of legal and nonlegal, pedagogical, cultural, religious, nationalist, and social discourses on Islamophobia together produce what Foucault regards the signature of modern governmentality.

18.4 Public Surveys: Islamophobia Has Become Mainstream!

Islamophobic discourse has recently become mainstream in the West. It seems that social groups belonging to the majority nation in a given territory are more inclined to express their distress resulting from insecurity and socioeconomic deprivation, through the language of Islamophobia even in cases unrelated to the actual threat of Islam. Certainly Islamophobic discourse has resonated substantially within the last decade, so users of this discourse can be heard by both local and international

[13] Michel Foucault (1979) defines 'governmentality' as the ensemble formed by the institutions, procedures, analyses, reflections, calculations, and tactics that allow this very specific, albeit complex, form of power, which has the population as its target, political economy as its principal form of knowledge, and apparatuses of security as its essential technical means. For further discussion on the notion of governmentality see Chap. 10, in this volume.

communities, although their distress did not really result from anything related to Muslims in general. In other words, in many parts of the world Muslims have become popular scapegoats, being seen as responsible for any troubling situation. For a little over a decade primarily European societies have viewed migrants of Muslim origin and their descendants as a financial burden and virtually never as an opportunity for the country. These groups tend to be associated with illegality, crime, violence, drug, radicalism, fundamentalism, and conflict, and are in many other respects represented in negative ways.

A public poll taken by the Pew Research Center in the United States in August 2010 revealed that favourable opinions of Islam among the American public had declined since 2005. As many as 35 % of the public believed that Islam more than other religions encourages violence.[14] Similarly, the British Social Attitudes Survey conducted in 2009 showed that 45 % of the UK population do not like Muslims much, and do not really believe in free speech at all. It was revealed that the dislike of Muslims is related to the belief that the UK is too diverse, and that religious diversity is harming Britain, a view that was also expressed by Prime Minister David Cameron in February 2011.[15] Islamophobia has also become evident in countries such as Sweden that are known to be nonreligious and highly secular. Sweden received harsh criticism from the Swedish United Nations Association in 2009 for failing to abide by a number of UN conventions. The report stated that hate crimes in Sweden increased as a result of Islamophobia, anti-Semitism, and homophobic sentiments.

The growing distance between the life-worlds of the majority societies and their allochthonous Muslim-origin minorities has also become evident. Detlef Pollack, a sociologist from Münster, conducted an extensive survey in Germany, France, Denmark, Portugal, and the Netherlands in late 2010. The survey revealed that the German society, as compared with the French, Dutch, and Danish, has recently developed a less tolerant perspective on Islam. His findings also disprove the statement made by the then President of Germany, Christian Wulff, on October 19, 2010, that 'Islam is part of Germany'.[16] In fact, the survey findings reaffirmed a comment made by the then German Minister of the Interior, Hans-Peter Friedrich, who announced that Islam may not belong in Germany.[17] The study also revealed that fewer than 5 % of Germans, as compared with more than 20 % of Danish, French, and Dutch citizens, consider Islam to be a tolerant religion.

These findings were confirmed by a survey conducted by the German Marshall Fund in 2010 (GMF 2010). The participants in several different countries were asked about their perception of the level of integration of Muslim immigrants and

---

[14] For more details, see http://people-press.org/files/legacy-pdf/647.pdf

[15] For more on the British Social Attitudes Survey see http://www.uk.sagepub.com/books/Book234304?siteId=sage-uk&prodTypes=any&q=british+social+attitudes&fs=1. For David Cameron's speech, see http://www.bbc.co.uk/news/uk-politics-12415597

[16] For the President's speech, see http://www.bbc.co.uk/news/world-europe-11578657

[17] For the Interior Minister's speech, see http://www.guardian.co.uk/world/2011/mar/04/germany-muslim-integration-row

their descendants into their societies. Canadians were split evenly, with 45 % believing Muslim immigrants were integrating well and 44 % thinking they were integrating poorly. Americans were the most optimistic about Muslim integration: 45 % thought these immigrants were integrating well, 40 % believed they were not integrating well, and 14 % stated that they did not know, probably because the number of Muslim immigrants residing in the United States is comparatively low. Respondents in Spain and Germany were remarkably pessimistic about the degree of integration of Muslim immigrants and their descendants, and large majorities stated that Muslims were integrating poorly (70 % and 67 % respectively). They were followed by the Dutch (56 %), the British (53 %), the French (51 %), and a plurality of Italians (49 %) who also thought that Muslim immigrants were integrating poorly (GMF 2010).

A survey conducted in 2011 by the Friedrich Ebert Foundation in various countries of the European Union revealed that in most of the countries a majority of the respondents believe that *Islam is a religion of intolerance*, with agreement just below 50 % only in the United Kingdom and the Netherlands (Table 18.1). In almost all the countries more than half the respondents said that *Muslims make too many demands*; Portugal was the only exception, with about one third stating this. The statement that there are *too many Muslims in the country* was affirmed by just over one fourth of respondents in Portugal and by about one third of the respondents in France; in Germany, the United Kingdom, Italy, and the Netherlands more than 40 % of respondents made this complaint, and in Hungary this figure was about 60 %. The figures for those who said that *Muslim culture is compatible with their own* ranged from 17 % in Germany and 19 % in Poland to about 50 % in Portugal and France. A majority of more than 70 % of European respondents found *Muslim attitudes towards women* incompatible with their own values. One third of respondents in the surveyed countries believed that *Muslims treat Islamist terrorists as heroes*, although somewhat fewer believed that *terrorism finds moral support in the Muslim community* (ranging from under 20 % in Germany and the Netherlands to nearly 30 % in Hungary). It is obvious that Europeans are largely united in their rejection of Muslims and Islam. The most widespread anti-Muslim attitudes are found in Germany, Hungary, Italy, and Poland, closely followed by France, the United Kingdom, and the Netherlands. Anti-Muslim attitudes are least popular in Portugal (Zick et al. 2011: 60–63).

From the opposite point of view, migrants of Muslim origin and their descendants are greatly concerned about how they are being treated by the majority societies in the West. For instance, a survey conducted by the European Monitoring Centre on Racism and Xenophobia (EUMC 2006) reveals that Islamophobia, discrimination, and socioeconomic marginalization play a primary role in generating disaffection and alienation among migrants of Muslim origin and their descendants who reside in countries within the European Union. Muslims feel that their acceptance by society is increasingly based on their ability to 'assimilate', and on the assumption that they are willing to give up their Muslim identity. This sense of exclusion is particularly relevant considering the challenges posed by terrorism,

Table 18.1 Anti-Muslim statements (agreement in percent)

Anti-Muslim statement	Germany	United Kingdom	France	The Netherlands	Italy	Portugal	Poland	Hungary
There are too many Muslims in [country].	46.1	44.7	36.2	41.5	49.7	27.1	47.1	60.7
Muslims are too demanding.	54.1	50.0	52.8	51.8	64.7	34.4	62.3	60.0
Islam is a religion of intolerance. [France: Islam is a religion of tolerance.]	52.5	47.2	52.3	46.7	60.4	62.2	61.5	53.4
The Muslim culture fits well into [country/Europe].	16.6	39.0	49.8	38.7	27.4	50.1	19.0	30.2
Muslims' attitudes towards women contradict our values.	76.1	81.5	78.8	78.2	82.2	72.1	72.1	76.8
Many Muslims perceive terrorists as heroes. [France: Question not asked].	27.9	37.6	–	29.2	28.5	30.3	30.2	39.3
The majority of Muslims find terrorism justifiable. [France: Not justifiable]	17.1	26.3	23.3	19.9	21.5	22.4	26.0	29.6

Source: Zick et al. (2011)

particularly in the aftermath of 9/11, which has led to a general suspicion that they are likely to be terrorists (Cesari 2009).

All the public surveys conducted in Europe and America confirm the prevalence of negative opinions about Islam. In the European countries the negative perception of Islam probably springs mainly from the presence of migrants of Muslim origin and their descendants who reside in the respective countries, whereas in the United States it is more likely to derive from foreign-policy challenges posed by Islam in general. The increase in negative attitudes towards Muslims in Europe has been confirmed by opinion polls carried out by various researchers, as detailed above. In some European countries the percentage of those interviewed who have either a 'somewhat unfavourable' or a 'very unfavourable' opinion of Muslims increased substantially between 2005 and 2014 or, in specific cases, has remained at a high level, sometimes close to 50 %. Many Europeans even perceive Islam as a major threat to Europe because they feel that the Muslim minority is growing, and that Islam is incompatible with 'modern European life'. Discrimination has been greatest in the areas of employment and services provided by the private sector.[18] In addition, the results of other surveys cited above indicated increasing numbers of attacks and instances of discrimination against Muslims, as well as rallies and public gatherings touting anti-Muslim messages.

18.5 Conclusion

The supremacy of cultural–religious discourse in the West is likely to frame many of the social, political, and economic conflicts within the range of societies' religious differences. Many of the ills faced by migrants and their descendants, such as poverty, exclusion, unemployment, illiteracy, lack of political participation, and unwillingness to integrate, are attributed to their Islamic background, believed stereotypically to clash with Western secular norms and values. Accordingly, this article has just argued that "Islamophobism" is a key ideological form in which social and political contradictions of the neoliberal age are dealt with, and that this form of culturalisation is embedded in migration-related inequalities as well as geopolitical orders. Culturalization of political, social, and economic conflicts has become a popular sport in a way that reduces all sorts of structural problems to cultural and religious factors. The solution, therefore, would be to generate a post-culturalist, post-religious, and post-civilizational approach to understanding the main sources of the conflicts that exist in the European countries. The question is, how can we develop such an approach?

[18]The European Union Minorities and Discrimination Survey (EU-MIDIS) conducted in 2009 very clearly showed that individuals of Muslim origin residing in the European space complain primarily about discrimination in the labour market. For instance, the Pew Global Attitudes Survey of 2006 found that 78 % of Muslims in the United Kingdom, 84 % in France, 81 % in Germany, and 83 % in Spain stated unemployment as a serious or somewhat serious worry.

Majority nations could begin to refrain from contributing to the essentialization of ethnocultural and religious borders, while the community members of immigrant origin could try to obtain citizenship in the countries in which they have settled, which may serve as a protective shield against the destabilizing forces of globalization. Furthermore, the term 'phobia', which actually means an irrational, uncontrollable fear (and in many cases is a form of mental illness), should not be used in political or social contexts, including 'Islamophobia'.

I have argued in this chapter that Islamophobia is actually an ideology constructed by neoliberal political and societal forces to cover up the failures committed by contemporary Western nation states to provide justice, fairness, equality, prosperity, and employment for all. I have also revealed that most of the public surveys conducted in the West do not perceive Islam itself as the main stumbling block; rather, the respondents tended to blame extremists and certain politicians who deploy religion in support of narrow agendas. Majorities of the respondents appear to believe that the relationship with minorities of Muslim origin as well as with nations that are predominantly Muslim can improve over time. Pessimism about initiating dialogue at present and in the immediate future may eventually prove to be compatible with cautious optimism over the long term.

One should not underestimate the fact that European Muslims have become even more politically active since the rise of Islamophobic tendencies in the aftermath of 9/11. The growing interest and success of candidates of Muslim origin in local, general, and European elections indicate that the time of crisis characterized by Islamophobia has brought about its own windows of opportunity for the European public in general. All in all, the tragic incident in Norway on July 22, 2011, demonstrates that Islamophobism as an ideology is no longer sustainable.

References

Allen, C. (2010). *Islamophobia*. Farnham/Burlington: Ashgate.

Althusser, L. (2001). *Lenin and philosophy and other essays*. New York: Monthly Review Press.

Arendt, H. (1951). *The origins of totalitarianism*. New York: Schocken Books.

Balibar, É. (2004). *We, the people of Europe? Reflections on transnational citizenship*. Princeton/Woodstock: Princeton University Press.

Bigo, D. (2002). *To reassure and protect, after September 11*. New York: Social Science Research Council. http://www.ssrc.org/sept11/essays/bigo.htm

Brown, W. (2006). *Regulating aversion: Tolerance in the age of identity and empire*. Princeton: Princeton University Press.

Brubaker, R. (1991). International migration: A challenge for humanity. *International Migration Review, 25*(4), 946–957. doi:10.2307/2546853.

Cesari, J. (Ed.). (2009). *Muslims in the West after 9/11: Religion, politics and law*. London/New York: Routledge.

Cesari, J. (2013). *Why the West fears Islam: An exploration of Muslims in liberal societies*. New York: Palgrave Macmillan.

Cesari, J. et al. (2006). *Securitization and religious divides in Europe: Muslims in Western Europe after 9/11: Why the term Islamophobia is more a predicament than an explanation*. http://www.libertysecurity.org/IMG/pdf_Challenge_Project_report.pdf

CoE. (2004). *Islamophobia and its consequences on Young People. European Youth Centre Budapest: 1–6 June 2004* (Seminar report). Ingrid Ramberg. http://www.coe.int/t/dg4/youth/Source/Resources/Publications/Islamophobia_consequences_young_people_en.pdf

De Certeau, M. (1984). *The practice of everyday life*. Berkeley: University of California Press.

EUMC. (2006). *Muslims in the European Union: Discrimination and Islamophobia*. Vienna: European Monitoring Centre on Racism and Xenophobia. http://fra.europa.eu/sites/default/files/fra_uploads/156-Manifestations_EN.pdf

Evans, T. (2010). The limits of tolerance: Islam as counter-hegemony? *Review of International Studies, 37*(4), 1751–1773. doi:10.1017/S0260210510000185.

Foucault, M. (1979). On governmentality. *Ideology and Consciousness, 6*, 5–21.

GMF. (2010). *Transatlantic trends: Immigration 2010: Key findings*. Washington, DC: German Marshall Fund of the United States.

Gramsci, A. (1971). *Selection from the prison notebooks*. London: Lawrence & Wishart.

Greenfield, D. (2013, October 30). Islamerica, Eurabia and Eurasia. *Frontpage Mag*. http://www.frontpagemag.com/2013/dgreenfield/islamerica-eurabia-and-eurasia

Halliday, F. (1996). *Islam and the myth of confrontation: Religion and politics in the middle East*. London/New York: I.B. Tauris.

Halliday, F. (1999). 'Islamophobia' reconsidered. *Ethnic and Racial Studies, 22*(5), 892–902. doi:10.1080/014198799329305.

Huysmans, J. (2006). *The politics of insecurity: Fear, migration and asylum in the EU*. London/New York: Routledge.

Kaya, A. (2009). *Islam, migration and integration: The age of securitization*. Basingstoke/New York: Palgrave Macmillan.

Lenin, V. I. (1988). *What is to be done?* London/New York: Penguin.

Malik, M. (Ed.). (2010). *Anti-Muslim prejudice in the West: Past and present*. London: Routledge.

Marx, K., & Engels, F. ([1846] 1970). *The German ideology*. London: Lawrence & Wishart.

Meer, N., & Modood, T. (2009). Refutations of racism in the 'Muslim question'. *Patterns of Prejudice, 43*(3-4), 335–354. doi:10.1080/00313220903109250.

Miller, P., & Rose, N. (2008). *Governing the present: Administering economic, social and personal life*. Cambridge/Malden: Polity Press.

O'Hagan, A. (2008, April 8). Fear of Islam is ruining our chance for peace. *The Telegraph*. http://www.telegraph.co.uk/comment/columnists/andrewo_hagan/3557031/Fear-of-Islam-is-ruining-our-chance-for-peace.html

Popper, K. ([1945] 1966). *The open society and its enemies: Vol. 1: The spell of Plato* (5th ed.). Princeton: Princeton University Press.

Richardson, R. (2012). *Countering intolerance against Muslims through education*. Paris: UNESCO. http://www.insted.co.uk/countering-intolerance.pdf

Robin, C. (2004). *Fear: The history of a political idea*. Oxford/New York: Oxford University Press.

Semati, M. (2010). Islamophobia, culture and race in the age of empire. *Cultural Studies, 24*(2), 256–275. doi:10.1080/09502380903541696.

Sivanandan, A. (2010, March 15). *Fighting anti-Muslim racism: An interview with A. Sivanandan*. London: Institute of Race Relations. http://www.irr.org.uk/news/fighting-anti-muslim-racism-an-interview-with-a-sivanandan

Trust, R. (1997). *Islamophobia: A challenge for us all*. London: The Runnymede Trust.

Werbner, P. (2005). Islamophobia: Incitement to religious hatred: Legislating for a new fear? *Anthropology Today, 21*(1), 5–9. doi:10.1111/j.0268-540X.2005.00323.x.

Zick, A., Küpper, B., & Hövermann, A. (2011). *Intolerance, prejudice and discrimination: A European report*. Berlin: Friedrich Ebert Foundation. http://library.fes.de/pdf-files/do/07908-20110311.pdf

Chapter 19
'How Would You React If You Learned That Your Son Was Gay?' Racialized Sexualities and the Production of Migrant Others in Europe

Paul Scheibelhofer

19.1 Introduction

Issues of gender equality figure prominently in contemporary debates about migration and integration in Europe. This is certainly a positive development in that it opens the possibility to broaden feminist agendas to include the struggles and interests of migrant women. But a closer look shows that many of the current discourses and politics aimed at encouraging gender equality among migrants ultimately work to re-establish hierarchies of migrant and non-migrant populations. The aim of this chapter is to show that focusing on the role of *sexuality* can advance our critical understanding of these processes and help unravel contemporary 'paradoxes of integration' (Anthias et al. 2013). In the following, historical trajectories of racializing others through particular ideas of 'foreign' sexualities are retraced. In this context, a peculiar archive of knowledge about racialized and gendered sexualities has been established.

Throughout Europe this archive of knowledge informs contemporary discourses about migrants and reappears in modernized forms. The analysis highlights, that contemporary politics of belonging (Yuval-Davis 2011) are informed and transformed by notions about sexuality. Discourses about dangerous Muslim traditions, oppressed migrant women and homophobic migrant men aim to solve complex questions regarding the shifting boundaries of 'us' and 'them' by drawing a clearly defined boundary between a sexually liberated Europe and repressed, backward migrant others.

P. Scheibelhofer (✉)
Department of Sociology, University of Vienna, Vienna, Austria
e-mail: paul.scheibelhofer@univie.ac.at

A. Amelina et al. (eds.), *An Anthology of Migration and Social Transformation*, IMISCOE Research Series, DOI 10.1007/978-3-319-23666-7_19

19.2 Of Savages, Victims, and Saviours

Post-colonial studies has proven central to a critical understanding of the legacy and the continuing relevance of Eurocentric imageries of difference. Scholars have convincingly shown that imperial conquest not only established the old metropolises at the top of a global hierarchy of power and wealth but was also a site where modernist imageries of human progress and Western superiority were created (Said 1978; Chakrabarty 2000). In addition, feminist post-colonial scholars have shown that this process of colonial and imperial conquest was a deeply gendered endeavour. In her analysis Anne McClintock (1995) shows how colonial exploitation and conquest was legitimized and made intelligible within a racialized, masculinist framework. This framework established an archive of knowledge about otherness that is still being invoked and re-articulated to the present day. Colonial narratives reframed imperialist disappropriation into adventures of 'discovering' uncharted territory, and alluded to imageries of penetrating virgin female bodies. Irvin Schick (1999: 110) argues that 'the masculinized colonizer and the feminized colony were depicted in a sexual, that is, natural/biological encounter, establishing a sense of necessity, of harmony, that justified Western domination'.

Narratives of the 'foreign land' and of its people were quite contradictory, and imageries of peaceful spaces were populated by childlike inhabitants stood side by side with 'European porno-tropics' (McClintock 1995: 22). Time and again colonized areas were described as sexualized spaces where deviance and excess reigned. Local women were portrayed as passively waiting to be taken while also being endowed with monstrous genitals and insatiable lust, leading to contradictory 'fantasies of conquest and fear of engulfment' (McClintock 1995: 27). Colonial narratives also reported about foreign men, and these narratives were marked by contradicting imageries as well. On the one hand, the entire narrative of colonialism was one of feminizing the non-European other vis-à-vis a masculinized self-image. This also manifested itself in imageries of degenerated black men with a merely childlike masculinity (McClintock 1995: 240). Similar imageries of emasculation could be found in British colonial discourses about 'effeminate Bengali men', who supposedly lacked virility and autonomy (Sinha 1995). But colonialist narratives also produced very different ideas of othered masculinities. In line with the evolutionist assumption that colonized people represented an earlier stage of human development, native men were often described as vicious brutes whose masculinity was not restricted by the morals of civilization. This idea was most explicitly propagated in discourses of rape committed by colonialized men. There were numerous reports, narratives, and novels about indigenous women, as well as white women, who were subjected to rape. Colonizing powers made use of this trope to legitimize repressive measures against colonized people as necessary actions not only to defend the honour and safety of white women but also to save indigenous women from their men (Sharpe 1993). Gayatri Spivak's (1988: 297) often-cited phrase of 'white men saving brown women from brown men' refers to this strategy of legitimizing colonial intervention in the name of doing good.

As we will see, many of the imageries of racialized sexualities that were established and propagated during this time reappear in today's discourses about migrant otherness in Europe, and they are once again employed to legitimize measures that target migrant populations. It is thus important to understand that the 'post' in 'postcolonial' does not mark a distant and concluded historical phase. Rather, this phase, which was so important for the political, economic, and philosophical consolidation of European nations, established power relations and discursive archives that inform modes of producing others to the present day. In this relation of dominance the concept of 'social transformation' itself becomes part of an imagined geopolitical map of the world in which a European self is understood as the site of enlightenment, emancipation, and progress as opposed to non-European others who embody backwardness and stagnation.

19.3 The Crisis of Multiculturalism and Integrationist Interventions

A central frame of reference for many recent developments in European migration politics is the discourse about the—supposed—failure of multiculturalism (Vertovec and Wessendorf 2010). In past years politicians throughout Europe have blamed multiculturalism for a wide range of social problems, calling for a change in migration and integration politics. In late 2010 German Chancellor Angela Merkel publicly denounced the political project of multiculturalism as a failure. Only a few months later two of her colleagues, the Prime Minister of the UK, David Cameron, and the then French President, Nicolas Sarkozy, joined in the criticism. The arguments they presented were roughly similar: that multiculturalism promoted tolerance of intolerable beliefs and practices; that it encouraged migrant communities to live separate lives; and—with particular reference to Muslim migrants—that it ultimately fosters violence and terrorism. This observation was then used by politicians to call for a less naïve and more vigilant stance on migrants (Lentin and Titley 2011). One example of this is the concept of 'muscular liberalism', as propagated by UK Prime Minister David Cameron. According to Cameron, this new approach would specifically tackle Muslim communities and combine measures to prevent fundamentalist radicalization and foster gender equality in these communities (BBC News 2011).

But a closer look shows that this critical stance on multiculturalism does not actually mark a fundamental shift because, as Ann Phillips and Sawitri Saharso remind us, multiculturalism was under attack almost from its inception. Also, the calls for *ending* multiculturalism in Europe is like tilting at windmills, for multiculturalism

> was never adopted as official policy in any part of Europe [...] in France, however, multiculturalism was rejected pretty much out of hand as at odds with republican principles; in Germany, as at odds with a predominantly ethnicized conception of citizenship; while in Italy and Spain, multiculturalism barely figured in either popular or political discourse until

> the last few years. In those countries most commonly cited as exemplars of multicultural policy—the UK, the Netherlands, Sweden—practices varied and were rarely codified in any explicit way (Phillips and Saharso 2008: 292).

But even without multiculturalist state politics in place the discourse of failure could successfully be employed throughout Europe to argue for new, stricter migration and integration laws.

This happened in a context in which EU institutions and think tanks throughout Europe propagated an increased 'Europeanization' of migration policies and a shift towards approaches of 'managing migration' (McGauran 2010: 126). According to the idea of managing migration, rather than merely restricting migration, new economic and population challenges require policies that actively shape it in profitable ways. In search of policies that could reconcile a more liberal approach with the assertion of continuing political control over migration, the concept of *integration* entered debates and led to a multiplicity of political measures (see Hess and Moser 2009). In the eyes of many, integration measures offered opportunities to support migrants as well as to provide means of monitoring migrants' integration progress, backed up by disciplinary measures (Kontos 2014). Furthermore, the economistic logic of diversity politics was adopted in state and municipal politics as an approach to embrace migration realities in profitable ways (e.g. by marking out cities as particularly modern and *colourful* and thus attracting creative businesses; see Neuhold and Scheibelhofer 2010).

From a critical point of view however, it would be wrong to regard the turn to integration and diversity politics as merely a modernization of migration politics; rather, this new politics should be understood in the context of a most recent re-articulation of racism under neoliberal conditions (Lentin and Titley 2011).

Lentin and Titley's analysis builds on Etienne Balibar's idea of racism as a historically shifting 'total social phenomenon' that articulates itself in practices, discourses, and representations. As Balibar famously argued, there is a 'new' racism which

> is a racism of the era of 'decolonization', of the reversal of population movements between the old colonies and the old metropolises, and the division of humanity within a single political space. Ideologically, current racism [...] fits into a framework of 'racism without races' [...]. It is a racism whose dominant theme is not biological heredity but the insurmountability of cultural differences, a racism which, at first sight, does not postulate the superiority of certain groups or peoples in relation to others but 'only' the harmfulness of abolishing frontiers, the incompatibility of life-styles and traditions (Balibar 1991: 21).

According to Lentin and Titley, many of the current integration measures primarily serve to define and discipline migrant others within the borders of nation states. In line with a dominant view that in Europe (biological) racism is a thing of the past, these integration measures are not called for on the basis of perceived biological differences but because of the supposed problems that arise from *religiocultural* differences between a European self and a migrant other. But this line of argument should itself be understood as a new articulation of a 'new' racism. In this context, which Lentin and Titley call 'racial neoliberalism', racial stigmatization is increasingly affecting those who are seen as a burden to the modern nation and its economic wellbeing. Racial neoliberalism does not simply draw on national insider–outsider distinctions but 'increasingly [focuses on] the boundaries between the rational, self-managing citizen-subject and the wilful, dependent, resource-heavy subject (Lentin and Titley 2011: 178). In the same vein, positive and negative qualities are ascribed to different migrant populations, creating ideas of 'good' and 'bad' diversity (Lentin and Titley 2011: 176). While 'good diversity' is hailed as an asset for the modern nation, those deemed to represent 'bad diversity' become the target of political measures that range from pedagogical intervention to disciplinary measures such as the cancellation of social benefits to the threat of deportation.

As in the case of 'muscular liberalism', Muslim communities in countries throughout Europe are portrayed as representatives of 'bad diversity' and find themselves at the centre of debates about the alleged problems caused by multiculturalist naiveté. The image of the suppressed Muslim woman serves as proof of the backwardness of Muslim migrant communities. With a logic that Liz Fekete (2006) criticized as 'enlightened fundamentalism', disciplinary integration politics are touted as being able to modernize these communities, which are seemingly so behind the times.

The veil debate in France is an example of this logic. 'The casting of veiled Muslim women in the role of the subjugated female pushes familiar orientalist buttons. However, it is also complicit in the image of the "good" autonomous subject versus the "bad" dependent one mediated in neoliberal formations' (Lentin and Titley 2011: 190).

In Germany this economistic logic became all too obvious when Thilo Sarrazin's 2010 book *Deutschland schafft sich ab* ('Germany Is Abolishing Itself') sold over 1.5 million copies, making it the bestselling non-fiction book in Germany's post-war history. In it, Sarrazin combines biologistic, culturalizing, and economistic racist arguments to warn of the dangers that Muslim populations pose to Germany:

> Demographically, the enormous fertility of Muslim migrants constitutes a threat to the cultural and civilization balance in an ageing Europe. [...] In all European countries Muslim migrants, due to their low labour market participation and the large number of recipients of social benefits among them, cost the state more than they generate in economic value (Sarrazin 2010: 267, transl. mine, P.S.).

The above quote is a good example of the role that awkward imageries of foreign sexuality can play in contemporary discourses about 'bad diversity'. Concerning questions of 'old' and 'new' racism, the success of Sarrazin's book is also a reminder that discourses of racism may have shifted over past decades, but that it would be wrong to believe that earlier racisms (e.g. biologistic racism) simply vanished and have been replaced. Rather, they inform each other and can be resurrected to form new articulations to fit, in this case, a neoliberal ideology of the *Leistungsgesellschaft* (Friedrich 2011). Being a 'total social phenomenon', racist discourses are not static but shift and adapt to wider societal transformations in Europe.

19.4 Islam vs. 'Sexularism'?

While changes in migration law generally affect migrants from many different countries and religious backgrounds, it is often arguments about Muslim migrants in particular that are used to call for new restrictive legislation (see e.g. Bunzl 2005; Erdem 2009; Keskinen 2012, see also Chap. 18, in this volume). Issues of gender and sexuality have gained increasing prominence within these discourses on Islam and Muslim migrant communities.

The idea of 'imperilled Muslim women and dangerous Muslim men' (Razack 2004) became a standard argument in political discourse, thus reviving the long-established logic of indigenous women who must be saved by white men. The above-mentioned headscarf debates in countries across Europe have been one site where this logic was particularly prominent (for an overview, see Rosenberger and Sauer 2012). Although these debates apparently focused on issues of women's attire, much broader issues of community and difference were negotiated in the debates about veils. In her analysis of the ban on headscarves in French schools Leora Auslander (2000) argues that this ban actually articulates political anxieties around national community in times of globalization, with Muslim migrants' religiosity, visibly symbolized by headscarves, coming to represent a threat from within. In these debates a dividing line is drawn between a religious other and a modern secular self, with the result that once again the age-old evolutionist idea of Europe as the pinnacle of human advancement is employed.

All narratives of progress need markers that symbolize the state of development a given community is thought to inhabit. In the debates on headscarves, and on Islam more broadly, religiosity has come to figure as the yardstick of advancement, with secularism as the imagined end point of development. As with colonialist discourses, conceptions of *time* play a crucial role in these debates. These conceptions of progress

> define themselves over and against a pre-modern temporality that they produce for the purposes of their own self-legitimation. Politically, the questions, what time are we in? are all of us in the same time? and specifically, who has arrived in modernity and who has not? are all raised in the midst of very serious political contestations (Butler 2008: 1).

These are thoroughly gendered and sexualized discourses, as Joan Scott, among others, has pointed out. Based on her research on the headscarf debates in France, she coined the term '*sexularism*' (Scott 2009) to highlight how in contemporary debates about Islam ideas of secularism are infused with ideas about sexuality and gender equality. Sexularist discourses assume a direct link between secularization processes and the advancement of gender quality and sexual liberation. Whereas Islam comes to represent a state of archaic gender inequality, Western societies are understood to have evolved beyond such inequalities.

Interestingly, feminist arguments have become increasingly important in these discourses, and some feminists have actively participated in the debates. In Germany, for example, the widely known feminist Alice Schwarzer has repeatedly warned of Islam. In her feminist journal, *EMMA*, as well as in her book *Die große*

Verschleierung ('The Big Veiling'), she argued that headscarves were actually the flag of Islamism, and that the proliferation of covered women threatened to undermine the political victories of past feminist struggles and turn back time. Feminists in other European countries, such as Élisabeth Badinter in France and Cisca Dresselhuys in the Netherlands, have raised similar arguments.

Sara Farris (2012) proposed to term such instances in which feminist arguments fuse into nationalist discourses in debates about Islam 'femonationalism'. A productive discourse, femonationalism was employed beyond veil controversies and was used to legitimize the introduction of restrictive policies across Europe in the name of 'saving Muslim girls and women'. For example, after the Danish general election of 2001 the minimum age for transnational marriages was set to 24 years, and a number of other laws restricting family reunification were passed, based on the argument that these were measures to prevent forced marriage (Siim and Skjeie 2008). With a similar rationale, the Parliament of the UK set the sponsorship age on a spousal or fiancé visa to 21 years of age in 2008 (Lenon 2012).

These political measures employ a women's-rights discourse but situate it in a clash-of-culture logic, thus creating highly problematic solutions. In this logic migrant women are not seen as part of the matrix of structural inequalities that affects *all* women and that can affect their freedom to make choices, such as about marriage and child-bearing. Rather, 'a racist descent into arguments of cultural deficit occurs when coercion is treated as a salient feature of racialized communities represented as overtly patriarchal and inherently uncivilized' (Lenon 2012: 279). The culturalist, quasi-feminist arguments help divert attention from uncomfortable questions we need to ask, such as how the precarious social and legal situation of many migrant women makes them socially vulnerable, or how the closing of ever more migration channels pushes people into spousal migration. Instead, the imperilled 'Muslim woman emerges and is discursively represented as the always already formed, singular and monolithic victim-subject, inviting measures of stigmatization, surveillance and control' (Lenon 2012: 279).

These discourses and political measures build upon what Uma Narayan termed the 'package picture of culture', which understands cultures as distinct entities with clear boundaries and sharply differing content. This package picture homogenizes cultures by disregarding issues of internal diversity and contradiction, as well as the political practice of defining the boundaries between cultures (Narayan 2000: 1084). This goes along with essentialized understandings of *traditional practices*:

> The package picture of cultures mistakenly sees the centrality of particular values, traditions, or practices to any particular culture as a given and thus eclipses the historical and political processes by which particular values or practices have come to be deemed central components of a particular culture (Narayan 2000: 1085).

Narayan admits that women are often still the ones whose life is most negatively affected by what is called tradition, but she urges feminists to get involved in the ongoing struggles and social changes in any community, and to critically engage in practices of 'selective labelling [...] whereby those with social power conveniently designate certain changes in values and practices as consonant with cultural preservation and others as cultural loss or betrayal' (Narayan 2000: 1085).

But the package picture of culture prevailed, and all across Europe the past decade has seen a rise in measures aimed to emancipate migrants—especially women and children—from the stranglehold of their culture.

19.5 Integrating the Homophobic Other?

Recently another marker of backwardness was added to the arsenal of resources used in the discourse on Muslim migrants in Europe: their alleged homophobia. Against the backdrop of reports of the maltreatment of homosexuals in Iran, Iraq, and other countries of the 'axis of evil', Muslim migrant communities have also come to be viewed with suspicion because of their stance on homosexuals (Haritaworn et al. 2008).

A variety of integration measures have started to address the question of whether migrants live up to an alleged European norm of appreciating homosexuality and gay rights. A video for immigrants in the Netherlands included pictures of two men kissing and of bare-breasted women to test migrants' tolerance. In 2006 the German state government of Baden-Württemberg introduced a test exclusively for immigrants from countries that the German authorities listed as 'Muslim countries'. In the course of this 'Muslim test', as it was soon called (see Erdem 2009: 189), migrants were asked not only whether they saw the 9/11 attacks as terrorist or heroic acts but also about their ideas about gender and sexuality, such as whether it would be a problem for them to work for a female boss, or how they would react if they learned that their son was gay.

Framing the problem of homophobia as a problem of certain individuals and/or certain cultures makes it possible to describe European societies as inherently *gay-friendly* and leave out the institutional heteronormativity that still exists in European countries and still is an important feature of the dominant European religion, Christianity (Haritaworn et al. 2008).

Again, post-colonial theory can help to understand the discursive dynamics at work. In orientalist discourses conceptions of time and human advancement were often conflated with ideas of space, creating images that McClintock (1995: 40) described as 'anachronistic spaces'. These anachronistic spaces are represented not only as geographically distant but also as still living in a time that the European centre has long since passed. The image of the homophobic 'Turk' or 'Arab' builds on this logic in that migrants' homophobia is seen as a hazardous good imported from a backward country or culture. As a result, the question of who is the victim and who needs to be saved shifts: while in the past it was 'their women' who had to be saved from Muslim men, now 'our people' are entering the stage in the migrant homophobia discourse. In this discourse white homosexuals become part of the group of imperilled victims of violent migrant masculinity and the backward sexuality that accompanies it (Scheibelhofer 2012).

Interestingly, some gay and lesbian rights groups in countries such as Germany and the UK have actively participated in the discourse about Muslim homophobia (Petzen 2012). Rather than criticizing this latest development in the long history of racializing Muslim sexuality, activist groups and prominent spokespeople have engaged in problematizing Muslim culture as a culture that is prone to homophobia, and became actors in drafting new integration measures aimed to tackle homophobia among migrants and their (male) children.

To make sense of this peculiar development, we need to reflect upon the shifting politics around homosexuality within neoliberal state politics. According to Lisa Duggan, these politics are shaped by what she terms 'homonormativity', 'a politics that does not contest dominant heteronormative assumptions and institutions, but upholds and sustains them, while promising the possibility of a demobilized gay constituency and a privatized, depoliticized gay culture anchored in domesticity and consumption' (Duggan 2003: 50). Adherence to homonormative discourses and lifestyles opened up possibilities of participation and of recognizing some of the concerns of the gay and lesbian rights movement. In a context of thorough neoliberal political and economic reconstruction homonormativity paved the way for legal amendments that de-criminalized some aspects of non-heterosexuality, inclusion into anti-discrimination legislation, and heightened visibility of (a particular conception of) 'gay life and culture' on the street and in the media. But these gains are bought dearly, as Duggan's critique makes clear, because the mainstreaming politics that has been adopted is based on the exclusion or marginalization of radical groups and demands for sexual rights. Building on and extending Duggan's analysis, Jasbir Puar coined the term 'homonationalism' to grasp the intricate relationship of homonormativity and nationalism today, arguing that this relationship has recently shifted fundamentally, so that we now experience 'a cultural moment of national inclusion for homosexuality, alluding to a particular kind of parallel possibility for the liberated nation and the liberated queer' (Puar 2007: 1).

Homosexuals, who have historically been constructed as standing outside the norms of the community and even as *destructive* to the national population—from discourses of 'decadence' a century ago to their stigmatization as carriers of the HIV/AIDS virus—have become figures 'tied to ideas of life and productivity' (Puar 2007: xii) and have thus come to symbolize another instance of 'good diversity'. Homonormativity fundamentally questions neither the rules of the heteronormative dichotomous gender order nor the workings of neoliberal exploitation, and can thus be incorporated into the modern diverse nation as yet another minority.

As the cases of the Dutch video and the 'Muslim test' show, the act of incorporating and 'recognizing' homosexuality could itself be framed as yet another sign of European progressiveness. Along the line of the analysis developed here, it is important to note that, while integration tests may seem simply to investigate attitudes towards homosexuality, they actually mean a particular—that is, a homonormative—version of homosexuality which does not fundamentally challenge heteronormative structures. As some have argued, *sexuality* may thus have replaced *gender* as an important marker of modernization and civility in contemporary discourses of otherness (Haritaworn et al. 2008; Sona and Rieske 2011).

The gendered and sexualized construction of otherness is not timeless and fixed but changes as power dynamics and actors participating in the construction of selves and others change. As certain groups (e.g. homosexual rights groups) gain visibility and power, hegemonies within the field of gender and sexuality are rearranged to include parts of previously marginalized groups and new outsiders are created. While the image of the homophobic Turkish/Muslim man is a recent development, it reinstates the anything-but-recent strategy of sexualizing the other as part of racialization processes.

19.6 Conclusion

Critical scholars have highlighted the problematic aspects of new migration and integration legislation in Europe that seeks to protect social cohesion through testing the norms and values of migrant populations. This politics is driven by what has been termed 'domopolitics' (Walters 2004, see also Chap. 10, in this volume), a politics based on the premise that migration is an eminent threat to national communities that must be contained through selection, monitoring, and surveillance. In this context, integration should be understood as more than a set of pedagogical measures what Manuela Bojadžijev (2008: 288) termed an 'integration imperative'. Integration, in this view, is not something that migrants can actually 'attain' but rather a flexible discourse that marks migrants as defective. According to the logic of the integration imperative, migrants can demand full citizenship rights only if they accomplish all integration-related tasks. In effect this imperative permanently prevents migrants' equal participation as citizens.

This chapter has shown that negotiations around migrant sexuality contribute to the transformation of contemporary politics of belonging. To grasp these interconnections we need to expand our critical analyses of migration discourses and politics to include the gendered and sexualized script of *domopolitics*, the *integration imperative*, and other contemporary ways of governing migration and integration. This will help us to understand the manifold ways in which representations of racialized sexualities are used to legitimize restrictive migration laws. If we take a critical look, as proposed in this chapter, we realize that many legal measures that supposedly serve to promote the rights of migrant women and members of sexual minorities actually have detrimental effects. This perspective leads us to reflect on how these discourses legitimize new exclusions and produce new outsiders, and hopefully this perspective can help us develop new ways of conceiving of communities of difference based on solidarity rather than on gendered and sexualized boundary making.

References

Anthias, F., Kontos, M., & Morokvasic-Müller, M. (Eds.). (2013). *Paradoxes of integration: Female migrants in Europe*. Dordrecht/Heidelberg/New York/London: Springer.

Auslander, L. (2000). Bavarian crucifixes and French headscarves: Religious signs and the post-modern European state. *Cultural Dynamics, 12*(3), 283–309. doi:10.1177/092137400001200302.

Balibar, É. (1991). Is there a 'neo-racism'? In É. Balibar & I. Wallerstein (Eds.), *Race, nation, class: Ambiguous identities* (pp. 17–28). London/New York: Verso.

BBC News. (2011, February 5). *State multiculturalism has failed, says David Cameron*. http://www.bbc.co.uk/news/uk-politics-12371994

Bojadžijev, M. (2008). *Die windige Internationale: Rassismus und Kämpfe der Migration*. Münster: Westfälisches Dampfboot.

Bunzl, M. (2005). Between anti-Semitism and Islamophobia: Some thoughts on the new Europe. *American Anthropologist, 32*(4), 499–508. doi:10.1525/ae.2005.32.4.499.

Butler, J. (2008). Sexual politics, torture, and secular time. *The British Journal of Sociology, 59*(1), 1–23. doi:10.1111/j.1468-4446.2007.00176.x.

Chakrabarty, D. (2000). *Provincializing Europe: Postcolonial thought and historical difference*. Princeton/Woodstock: Princeton University Press.

Duggan, L. (2003). *The twilight of equality? Neoliberalism, cultural politics, and the attack on democracy*. Boston: Beacon.

Erdem, E. (2009). In der Falle einer Politik des Ressentiments: Feminismus und die Integrationsdebatte. In S. Hess, J. Binder, & J. Moser (Eds.), *No integration?! Kulturwissenschaftliche Beiträge zur Integrationsdebatte in Europa* (pp. 187–206). Bielefeld: Transcript.

Farris, S. R. (2012). Femonationalism and the "Regular" army of labor called migrant women. *History of the Present, 2*(2), 184–199. doi:10.5406/historypresent.2.2.0184.

Fekete, L. (2006). Enlightened fundamentalism? Immigration, feminism and the right. *Race & Class, 48*(2), 1–22. doi:10.1177/0306396806069519.

Friedrich, S. (Ed.). (2011). *Rassismus in der Leistungsgesellschaft: Analysen und kritische Perspektiven zu den rassistischen Normalisierungsprozessen der "Sarrazindebatte"*. Münster: Edition Assemblage.

Haritaworn, J., Tauquir, T., & Erdem, E. (2008). Gay imperialism: Gender and sexuality discourse in the 'War on Terror'. In A. Kuntsman & E. Miyake (Eds.), *Out of place: Interrogating silences in queerness/raciality* (pp. 71–95). York: Raw Nerve Books.

Hess, S., & Moser, J. (2009). Jenseits der Integration: Kulturwissenschaftliche Betrachtungen einer Debatte. In S. Hess, J. Binder, & J. Moser (Eds.), *No integration?! Kulturwissenschaftliche Beiträge zur Integrationsdebatte in Europa* (pp. 11–26). Bielefeld: Transcript.

Keskinen, S. (2012). Limits to speech? The racialised politics of gendered violence in Denmark and Finland. *Journal of Intercultural Studies, 33*(3), 261–274. doi:10.1080/07256868.2012.673470.

Kontos, M. (2014). Restrictive integration policies and the construction of the migrant as 'Unwilling to Integrate': The case of Germany. In F. Anthias & M. Pajnik (Eds.), *Contesting integration, engendering migration: Theory and practice* (pp. 125–142). Basingstoke: Palgrave Macmillan.

Lenon, S. (2012). Hidden hegemonies of the rainbow: The racialised scaffolding of forced marriage and civil partnership in the UK. *Journal of Intercultural Studies, 33*(3), 275–287. doi:10.1080/07256868.2012.673471.

Lentin, A., & Titley, G. (2011). *The crises of multiculturalism: Racism in a neoliberal age*. London/New York: Zed Books.

McClintock, A. (1995). *Imperial leather: Race, gender and sexuality in the colonial contest*. New York/London: Routledge.

McGauran, K. (2010). Managing migration: The development of EU migration politics from 1975 to 2005. In V. Bakondy, S. Ferfoglia, & J. Janković (Eds.), *Viel Glück! Migration Heute: Wien, Belgrad, Zagreb, Istanbul* (pp. 106–141). Vienna: Mandelbaum.
Narayan, U. (2000). Undoing the "Package Picture" of cultures. *Signs: Journal of Women in Culture and Society, 25*(4), 1083–1086. doi:10.1086/495524.
Neuhold, P., & Scheibelhofer, P. (2010). Provincialising Multiculturalism: Postkoloniale Perspektiven auf Multikulturalismus, Diversität und Emanzipation. *PROKLA – Zeitschrift für kritische Sozialwissenschaft, 40*(1), 85–100.
Petzen, J. (2012). Queer trouble: Centring race in queer and feminist politics. *Journal of Intercultural Studies, 33*(3), 289–302. doi:10.1080/07256868.2012.673472.
Phillips, A., & Saharso, S. (2008). Guest editorial: The rights of women and the crisis of multiculturalism. *Ethnicities, 8*(3), 291–301. doi:10.1177/1468796808092443.
Puar, J. K. (2007). *Terrorist assemblages: Homonationalism in queer times*. Durham: Duke University Press.
Razack, S. H. (2004). Imperilled Muslim women, dangerous Muslim men and civilised Europeans: Legal and social responses to forced marriages. *Feminist Legal Studies, 12*(2), 129–174. doi:10.1023/B:FEST.0000043305.66172.92.
Rosenberger, S., & Sauer, B. (Eds.). (2012). *Politics, religion and gender: Framing and regulating the veil*. Oxon/New York: Routledge.
Said, E. W. (1978). *Orientalism*. New York: Vintage Books.
Sarrazin, T. (2010). *Deutschland schafft sich ab: Wie wir unser Land aufs Spiel setzen*. Munich: Deutsche Verlags-Anstalt.
Scheibelhofer, P. (2012). From health check to Muslim test: The shifting politics of governing migrant masculinity. *Journal of Intercultural Studies, 33*(3), 319–332. doi:10.1080/07256868.2012.673474.
Schick, I. C. (1999). *The erotic margin: Sexuality and spatiality in alterist discourse*. London/New York: Verso.
Scott, J. W. (2009). *Sexularism*. Florence: European University Institute. http://cadmus.eui.eu/bitstream/handle/1814/11553/RSCAS_DL_2009_01.pdf?sequence=1
Sharpe, J. (1993). *Allegories of empire: The figure of woman in the colonial text*. Minneapolis: University of Minnesota Press.
Siim, B., & Skjeie, H. (2008). Tracks, intersections and dead ends: Multicultural challenges to state feminism in Denmark and Norway. *Ethnicities, 8*(3), 322–344. doi:10.1177/1468796808092446.
Sinha, M. (1995). *Colonial masculinity: The 'manly Englishman' and the 'effeminate Bengali' in the late nineteenth century*. Manchester/New York: Manchester University Press.
Sona, R., & Rieske, T. M. (2011). Homophobic others: A case study in the culturalization of homonegativity within social research. In M. Groneberg & C. Funke (Eds.), *Combatting homophobia: Experiences and analyses pertinent to education* (pp. 137–158). Münster: LIT.
Spivak, G. C. (1988). Can the subaltern speak? In C. Nelson & L. Grossberg (Eds.), *Marxism and the interpretation of culture* (pp. 271–313). Urbana/Chicago: University of Illinois Press.
Vertovec, S., & Wessendorf, S. (Eds.). (2010). *The multiculturalism backlash: European discourses, policies, and practices*. Oxon: Routledge.
Walters, W. (2004). Secure borders, safe haven, domopolitics. *Citizenship Studies, 8*(3), 237–260. doi:10.1080/1362102042000256989.
Yuval-Davis, N. (2011). *The politics of belonging: Intersectional contestations*. London/Thousand Oaks/New Delhi/Singapore: SAGE Publications.

Chapter 20
Locating Migrant Pathways of Economic Emplacement: Thinking Beyond the Ethnic Lens

Nina Glick Schiller and Ayşe Çağlar

20.1 Introduction

Beginning in the 1980s, urban areas in many countries experiencing new migration were transformed by the growth of migrant businesses.[1] If you were a middle-class New Yorker, you began to experience more food choices in the form of a new array of ethnic restaurants or fruit, vegetable, and flower markets with extensive Korean-owned carryout buffets open day and night. If you lived in New York's or Los Angeles' inner-city neighbourhoods, you found that Hispanic bodegas were replaced or supplemented by Chinese food takeaways. At market 'stalls' in the towns surrounding Manchester, England, Pakistani vendors sold inexpensive jumpers produced locally in a garment production that had recently passed from Jewish manufacturers to South Asian, whilst throughout the UK 'off-licence' shops and fish and chip restaurants became migrant-owned or migrant-operated. Migrant businesses and vendors become an important part of gateway cities such as Paris, Berlin, and Toronto. By the 1990s new migrant businesses also thrived in less globally connected cities. In the wake of the capitalist transformation of Eastern Europe migrant

This chapter originally appeared in the *Ethnicities*, 13(4), 494–514, 2013.

[1] In the literature on entrepreneurs people of migrant backgrounds are referred to as immigrants. This causes difficulties since many others without permission to legally remain are also important actors in city-making processes. We use the term 'migrant' to refer to all those who cross international borders. We also recognize that this usage is highly problematic since it renders invisible and unproblematic the mobility of all those who move within the nation state.

N.G. Schiller (✉)
Department of Social Anthropology, University of Manchester, Manchester, UK
e-mail: nina.glickschiller@manchester.ac.uk

A. Çağlar
Department of Social and Cultural Anthropology, University of Vienna, Vienna, Austria

A. Amelina et al. (eds.), *An Anthology of Migration and Social Transformation*, IMISCOE Research Series, DOI 10.1007/978-3-319-23666-7_20

businesses proliferated so that you could easily buy Chinese takeaway food in Budapest, Prague, Warsaw, and Sofia.

Scholars, noting this transformation, began a spirited discussion of what they termed 'ethnic enterprises', echoing Light (1972), a pioneer of studies of migrant businesses. The majority of researchers assumed without any further reflection that there were real differences between 'ethnic entrepreneurs' and all other business-people, and sought explanations for migrant entrepreneurial behaviour in ethnocultural traditions, ethnic moral frameworks, behavioural patterns, loyalties, and markets.

This chapter offers an alternative approach to the study of migrant businesses by exploring urban-based entrepreneurial activities as a mode of emplacement. Emplacement is understood as a relationship between the continuing restructuring of a city within networks of power and migrants' efforts to settle and build networks of connection within the constraints and opportunities of a specific locality. It focuses analytic attention on the conjunction of time and place. In this approach migrants' local and transnational networks of connection are considered in relation to local institutions, structures, and narratives, as they emerge at particular moments in the historical trajectory of specific cities.

In offering this approach, we argue that analysts need to move 'beyond the ethnic lens' (Glick Schiller et al. 2006; Glick Schiller and Çağlar 2008, 2011a). To take this stance is to reject methodologies and analyses that begin with the assumption that ethnic or ethnoreligious identities, beliefs, practices, and networks are central to the lives of people of migrant background. As Fox and Jones (2013: 386) state, 'ethnicity is naturalized as a taken-for-granted fixture of the migration and post-immigration landscape', which obscures the ways in which 'diverse forms of belonging are enacted.' We agree and stress that to critique the ethnic lens is to neither neglect nor privilege ethnic identities. It is only by rejecting the unquestioning use of the ethnic group as the primary or exclusive unit of study and analysis in migration research that scholars obtain the analytical distance to investigate when, why, and how ethnic identities become salient for people of migrant background and for the institutions of governance. At the same time, by rejecting the ethnic lens scholars can explore the ways in which all people, including people of migrant background, deploy multiple frames of action and forms of belonging.

Jon E. Fox and Demelza Jones, the editors of the special issue of *Ethnicity* in which this chapter was originally printed addressed the methodological and analytical challenges that accompany a critique of the ethnic lens by suggesting the saliency of the 'everyday' (see Fox and Jones 2013). In this chapter we respond to their challenge by examining the identities, practices, and relationships of migrant entrepreneurs, as they are constituted within specific cities and points of time. We emphasize that we are not using the spatialization of the 'everyday' life within a specific neighbourhood, institution, or form of activity as an entry point to the study of the relationships between cities and migrants. This is because we believe that more is needed than to 'specify the actual practices and processes through which ethnicity and other modalities of belonging are negotiated and reproduced, or undermined, resisted, rejected and rendered irrelevant' (Fox and Jones 2013: 394). To confine our discussion to such a perspective is to assume that whatever 'other modalities' of belonging or frames of action are in process, ethnicity is always relevant. In contrast, we argue that to analyse migrant businesses scholars must examine the changing opportunity structures and barriers to entrepreneurial activity as they are configured by the continuing regeneration of urban space, governance, and structures of capital accumulation. Descriptions of everyday practice must be extended to encompass the ways all residents of a city participate in multiple hierarchical networks and institutions of unequal power. From such an analysis we can see how all residents of a city mutually constitute and are constituted by the local, the national, and the global in processes that change over time.

20.2 Locating the Problem

Most of the literature about migrants' local and transnational economic integration has been shaped by methodological nationalism that equates society and culture with the nation state, and sees national borders and the boundaries of belonging generated by the nation state as the unit of analysis (Amelina et al. 2012; Beck 2002; Wimmer and Glick Schiller 2003). This perspective on culture and membership is a product of twentieth- and twenty-first-century nation state–building processes. These processes legitimate a political ideology that portrays individuals as having only one country and one identity.

When assessing the implications of migration across state borders, researchers have come to see differences in national origin as the most significant social and cultural division within the population of a particular nation state. Through a single discursive act those who are native to the territory of a nation state are transformed into participants in a shared and homogenous culture; those departing from one national territory to settle in another are likewise seen as sharing identity and culture so that they become identified by the nationality of their homeland. It is this foundational binary of difference that leads scholars to approach all people of the same national or ethno-religious migrant background as homogenous in terms of their values, culture, achievement, and identity. When migration researchers adopt a transnational perspective on migration but retain an ethnic lens, they assume that migrants who share an ethnic identity form a transnational or diasporic community that links their homeland and new lands of settlement (Cohen 1997).

Shaped by a methodological nationalism, migration scholars concerned with migrant economic incorporation generally have either: (1) compared migrant workers to natives within a specific nation state using 'migrant' and 'native' as comparative categories (Borjas 1994) or (2) studied migrants grouped by nationality, conceptualizing economic incorporation as an outcome of the cultural attributes or human-capital attainments of a specific ethnic group (Aldridge and Waldinger 1990; Light 1972; Waldinger 1986). In the first analytical strategy the optic is the 'foreign'–'native' divide, which rests on the underlying assumption that cultural differences or differences in human capital substantively separate the 'native' workers, who belong within a nation state, from the newcomers. In this approach 'natives' who differ in educational background, skills, and income are conflated to a single national indicator of economic outcome against which migrant success can be measured. When structural factors have been addressed, scholars have generally examined them on a national level (Borjas 1994).

In the second approach the unit of analysis for the study of economic integration is the ethnic group, and the analyst highlights the cultural repertoire, skills, beliefs, and practices of a population assumed to share similarities that structure their abilities to obtain employment and their subsequent economic performance (Bonacich and Modell 1980). The role of local urban-based institutional structures has typically not been addressed (Pécoud 2000). In adopting and popularizing these approaches within discourses about social cohesion, researchers seriously diminish their ability to examine non-ethnic forms of social relations and conflate migrants' ancestral origins, practices, and identity (Laurence 2011).

By the 1990s some scholars began to explore class variations within and between migrant groups, arguing that it was the degree of capital, education, and prior business experience of the 'immigrant entrepreneur' rather than cultural traits or ethnic solidarity that produced success in small business ventures (Bates 1994; Min and Bozorgmehr 2000). There was some recognition that an array of factors led to the growth of such businesses. These factors ranged from high unemployment, lack of qualifications, and discrimination to the willingness of some migrants to open or purchase businesses in neighbourhoods where customers were poor and racialized as dangerous. Moreover, many studies of 'ethnic' entrepreneurs and 'enclaves' noted that manufacturers and small-business people organized their economic activity, sought workers, and built a customer base with people of diverse ethnic backgrounds (Light et al. 1999; Portes 1995; Rath and Kloosterman 2000). Other scholars described a progression from businesses that 'once catered mostly to co-ethnic customers [...] [to those that] rely largely on a non-immigrant clientele' (Pécoud 2004a: 19). To move beyond the concentration on co-ethnic social capital, Kloosterman et al. (1999) offered a concept of 'mixed embeddedness' that included non-ethnic networks and highlighted the significance of varying urban opportunity structures in explaining the trajectories of migrant businesses. Pécoud (2004a) in turn spoke of 'cosmopolitan businesses'.

In the light of this research, one would have expected an emerging consensus that 'ethnic entrepreneur' is often a misnomer (Pieterse 2003: 3), and that businesspeople of migrant background are first and foremost entrepreneurs seeking a viable supply network and customer base. Yet the concept of the ethnic entrepreneur has assumed a life of its own in the literature on migration. As Rath and Klosterman (2000: 663) have noted, even critiques of the ethnic niche literature equate 'immigrant businesses' with 'ethnic businesses', and assume that they are marked by 'ethnic loyalties and ethnic markets' and cultural difference. Consequently, decades after the conflation of the business activities of persons of migrant background and the concept of 'ethnic business' the concept of ethnic entrepreneurs continues to structure research, policy proposals, and remains prominent in the public imagination (Constant et al. 2007; Deakins et al. 2009; Kitching et al. 2009; Masurel et al. 2004).

Nonetheless, at the beginning of the twenty-first century policy-makers in a wide range of European countries began to examine variations in the structural factors that shape migrant integration on the level of cities (CLIP 2010). Organizations and research networks in the European Union have fostered an interest in the role of cities in the development and implementation of public policy, regulatory regimes, programmes of support, and anti-discriminatory policies, all of which shape migrant emplacement. The National League of Cities (2011), an organization of U.S. cities, has articulated a similar understanding of the synergies that develop between migrant businesses and migrant-friendly policies and urban growth.

At the same time it is important to note that, as they highlight variations in local factors that shape the relationships of migrant businesses to urban development, urban policy initiatives have continued to frame migrant businesses in ethnic terms. Thus, the CLIP Network, a coalition of research centres and local authorities, discussed businesspeople of migrant background as 'ethnic entrepreneurs', while noting 'the increasing importance of ethnic entrepreneurship for local economies'. They differentiated and culturalized the contributions of these businesspeople, while proclaiming that these entrepreneurs 'have long remained 'unsung heroes'[...] [who are] active agents, shaping their own destinies as well as revitalizing economic sectors especially in neoliberal times' (CLIP 2010: 5).[2]

20.3 Alternative Starting Points for Migration and Policy Studies

In sum, researchers might consider joining ethnographies of migrant everyday practice to a structural locational approach. Such an approach could examine the relationship between migrants' local emplacement through small businesses and the positioning of a city within time and within spatially differentiated global networks of power. Researchers would then be able to theorize urban variation and its relationship to the possibilities and pathways of migrant emplacement through entrepreneurial activities. Rather than assuming that the unit of analysis is an ethnic group within the boundaries of a nation state, scholars of migrant businesses might find it more productive to deploy a concept of multiple embeddedness.

Multiple embeddedness would highlight the processes through which individual migrants in their everyday entrepreneurial practices form networks of social relations and multiple social fields. Social fields are networks of uneven power that may be locally situated or extend nationally or transnationally and link individuals to economic, political, social, and cultural institutions (Glick Schiller 2003). Social fields are the aspect of social relations through which broader social forces enable, shape, and constrain individual migrants and their networks. States are significant actors within the constitution of these fields of differential power. Through their

[2]The use of the phrase 'unsung heroes' by CLIP responds to and reinforces this description of migrant businesspeople by *Business Week* in 2000 (see Business Week 2000).

institutions states impose territorial and legal borders; however, an analysis of the forces that shape migrants' emplacement cannot be restricted to or contained within state institutions and actors.

This conceptualization of emplacement emphasizes that all individuals live within, as they create, a social nexus composed of all to whom they are connected by various forms of interaction (Giddens 1984). In order to study how migrant entrepreneurs actually establish and maintain their businesses, migration scholars must explore the linkages of the entrepreneurs' business-related everyday local activities to urban institutions, as well as broader fields of power. Differences in national and local jurisdictions and shared cross-border regulations such as those of the EU and WTO affect the economic insertion of migrants, the availability of employment, the degree to which wages can be locally modified, and the regulations that confront small entrepreneurs. At the same time, as they are differentially reconstituted as actors in these varying networks and hierarchies, cities matter.

As Rath (2011) has noted, local policies, histories, demographics, and the relative cultural and political power of a specific locality structure the business and employment possibilities for everyone living in a specific place. Analysts must describe and analyse the role of structural factors reflected in spatial variation in accounting for the particular trajectories, successes, or failures of migrant entrepreneurs. All capital—economic, human, social, cultural—is in fact a socially based form of unequal emplacement, for migrant emplacement is 'the product of the interaction of structural factors such as migration history and processes of social, economic and political incorporation in the mainstream, as well as their spatial variations' (Rath 2006: 5).

However, it is insufficient to examine urban variations that affect migrants and their businesses without an analysis of the global reach and power of the processes and actors that restructure various forms of capital, including urban real estate. Scholars of neoliberal urban restructuring and regeneration have made it clear that cities are not bounded units but contribute to and are shaped by the ongoing reconstitution of capital (Brenner and Theodore 2002; Harvey 2006). These processes through which cities, nation states, and globe-spanning institutions are continually mutually constituted are simultaneously economic, political, and cultural and occur within networks of differential power that are substantiated within specific places and periods of time.

Cities are therefore useful entry points because they have the coherence of a specific institutional structure of governance, including taxation and regulation; a territorialized opportunity structure as a result of historical and contemporary conjunctions of economic and political power and geographic positioning; and institutions that create, brand, and market local cultural configurations and identities. Consequently, the relative positioning of cities within hierarchies of uneven power can enable or impede the pathways of emplacement for all those—migrants and non-migrants alike—who reside in a particular place in a specific period of time.

20.4 Cities as Entry Points for the Study of Migrant Emplacement Through Entrepreneurship: A Processual Example

To make these arguments more concrete, we draw on ethnographic research we conducted with co-researchers between 2000 and 2007 in Halle (Saale), Saxony-Anhalt, in Eastern Germany. This research, preliminary and ethnographic in nature, is insufficient to constitute a fully developed exploration of the relationships among urban economic opportunity structure, local narratives about migrants, and migrant businesses as pathways of settlement. However, this example concretizes our argument for an alternative approach by illustrating a way to study the intersection of three fields of interest: (1) specific urban restructuring and rebranding projects and policies; (2) urban leaders' narratives about migrants that reflect their restructuring agendas; and (3) migrant emplacement. In addition, by using an ethnographic account of a migrant pathway of emplacement in a relatively powerless city, we move the current conceptualization of migrant economic emplacement beyond the limits of data collected in global and gateway cities.[3] Our hope is to alert researchers to the need to link specific pathways of emplacement to the varying opportunity structures of different localities, noting that both the localities and these pathways develop with global networks of power.

When we speak of Halle as a relatively powerless city, we refer to its positioning within the economic, political, and cultural networks that connect this city within larger fields of power. We mean by cultural positioning the reputation of the city, which is a factor in each city's efforts to attract and maintain capital investment, new-economy industries, and other forms of local economy such as tourism. The research we conducted in Halle was not confined to the migrant population. It included open-ended interviews with city leaders and more than 60 interviews with migrants—migrants, refugees, asylum seekers, undocumented workers, and students. We also collected and reviewed relevant city statistics, policies, and pronouncements that touched on the political economy and on city leaders' approach to urban regeneration, rebranding, and migrant 'integration'. In addition, we participated, together with our co-researchers, in formal and informal events and activities organized for or by migrants or by local political or cultural activists (see Glick Schiller and Çağlar 2011a).

20.4.1 *Urban Restructuring and Rebranding Projects and Policies*

Historically and within the German Democratic Republic, Halle had been a centre of science and of the petroleum and chemical industries. These gave the city, its university, and scientists international prominence. However, after German

[3] Without comparative material from other cities it is not possible to specify the various factors within local processes of incorporation and transnational connection (Glick Schiller and Çağlar 2009, 2011b).

unification in 1989 Halle experienced dramatic deindustrialization, massive unemployment. and out-migration. In the reorganization that followed unification Halle lost out politically to neighbouring Magdeburg, which became the capital of the newly formed state of Saxony-Anhalt, and economically to Leipzig, where the regional airport was located. The population of the metropolitan area had shrunk to 237,000 people by 2005 (half its former size), while the city itself contained 135,000 people (City Population 2011; Geohive 2012; International Building Exhibition Urban Redevelopment Saxony-Anhalt 2010).[4] In 2004 the city's unemployment rate stood at just under 20 %, the youth unemployment was much higher, and there was stiff competition among local residents for even low-paid employment. Halle had few opportunities for employment or social mobility for either those seen as natives or those described as 'foreigners' or 'of migrant background'. Consequently, and in rather dramatic contrast to German cities with more economic, political, or cultural resources, Halle attracted few migrants.

Although the size of the migrant population doubled in the 15 years following German unification, in 2005 it was only 4 % of the population of Halle, with the largest number of migrants coming from other countries of the European Union.[5] Within this population migrants from several different countries of Africa and the Middle East, as well as those from Vietnam made up a small but visible minority.[6] Few of these migrants voluntarily came to Halle, and those who did often sought to leave and settle in Western Germany, where there were much greater possibilities for employment. The narrative of Halle as a shrinking city that was unfriendly to migrants contributed to the outward flow of migrants. The migrants who remained included asylum seekers, whose mobility in Germany was legally limited; students; migrants who were married to, or had children with, members of the local German population; and the elderly, who came as either refugees, Jewish settlers, or 'ethnic Germans' and who did not believe they would be employable elsewhere in Germany. Although city leaders often portrayed the migrants as uneducated, rather than desirable technologically skilled newcomers who could help rebuild the city, relatively few migrants were without some education, and the migrant population included multilingual people with professional degrees and university students who wanted to settle in Halle because they had local ties.

Between 2000 and 2007 the European Union and the German state's efforts to revitalize the city and the region contributed to a refurbishment of Halle's historic centre, but this influx of capital did not immediately revitalize the city's overall economy or lower unemployment. The former massive petrochemical complex was

[4]Estimates of Halle's shrinkage are complicated by the fact that after unification the city of Halle incorporated nearby Halle-Neustadt.

[5]The statistics in Halle did not record people from the former Soviet Union who either claimed German ancestry or who were Jewish (and migrated under a special immigration provision) as 'foreigners'. It also did not count asylum seekers or the undocumented. Consequently, the 4 % figure is an estimate based on taking these other migrant streams into consideration.

[6]These are pre-accession numbers, and those from the EU were primarily from Italy and Greece. Bosnians and Poles were among the non-EU migrants.

privatized and converted into one of the world's most modern chemical production facilities (CeChemNet 2008). Impressive international capital investment provided a relatively small number of high-tech jobs and made this region of Halle a 'leading industrial site in central Germany', according to local promoters (Barjak 2001; CeChemNet 2008: 18). There were also major public investments in research facilities, and these began to rejuvenate Halle's research and technological facilities.

20.4.2 Responses to Restructuring: City Leaders' Narratives About Migrants

In the context of the high-tech jobs that were being generated—3000 by 2008—city developers and local corporate representatives faced the challenge of attracting professionals and skilled technicians necessary to maintain and build these industries. City leaders sought ways to refurbish the city's prestige and reputation so as to provide the cosmopolitan ambience necessary to attract global talent and further corporate investment. However, they found that the relatively weak economic, political, and cultural positioning of the city affected their redevelopment strategies and marketing. They could not boast of global or regional corporate headquarters, nor did they have the power or resources to brand the city as a financial or intellectual centre. City promoters sought tourists, but Halle's reputation as a deindustrialized, impoverished, and racist city did not make it a desirable tourist destination.

The city leaders we interviewed in 2001—city officials and members of political, economic, religious, and social service organizations from very different political affiliations—spoke about migrants through the lens of the city's positioning. When speaking about the relationship between Halle and its migrants, these respondents shared certain assumptions. They were committed to changing the public image of the city, not only in Germany but worldwide. They saw their city as down but not out, and sought ways for Halle to regain its former prestige and prominence. In this task they faced numerous obstacles, including the fact that the city had gained a reputation as racist following several attacks on migrants by angry neo-Nazi youth, who were a very small but dangerous sector of the population. Publicity surrounding these attacks proved detrimental to efforts to attract investment, industry, and 'global talent.'[7]

In the context of Halle's competition with other cities, city leaders created a narrative that, in different contexts, depicted some or all migrants to the city as belonging to Halle. Facing an economic positioning of the city that yielded few possibilities of employment for most inhabitants, city leaders became convinced that migrants could contribute to positively repositioning the city. They subscribed to a common narrative and policies that contributed to migrant emplacement in Halle through domains of commonality rather than difference. In these narratives migrants, rather

[7] In point of fact, unlike many of its neighbouring cities, Halle also had a vibrant antiracist music scene and a coalition of mainstream organizations committed to standing up to racism.

than being seen as ethnic actors, were hailed as small-business people who were particularly important to the city. Even when they used the term 'foreigner', these leaders included these foreigners as part of the locality and emphasized how the provincialism of natives could be overcome with the help of those from elsewhere.

It is true that in some instances city institutions and leaders participated in events that profiled the cultural variation of migrants. Interestingly, these were often initiated and funded by foundations and religious organizations based elsewhere than in Halle. The Heinrich Böll Foundation, linked to the German Green Party, funded some multicultural activities, including an African week, and city leaders such as the vice mayor spoke at an official ceremony that was part of the celebration. City leaders also participated in a celebration of a Week of the Foreign Citizens initiated by a national religious network, although activities were locally organized.

However—and this point is crucial if we are to develop an analytical framework that can encompass the relationship between the varying and relative positioning of different cities and migrant emplacement in those cities—Halle's weak positioning within various powerful networks meant that ethnic difference was not a central aspect of its urban restructuring and branding efforts. In this dimension Halle differed from cities with greater degrees of cultural, political, or financial capital where city leaders and developers have approached migrant businesses as ethnic businesses (Pécoud 2004a, b). In those cities there was a synergy between the funding by city authorities of ethnic organizations and activities and the celebration of migrant ethnic difference as part of the successful branding and marketing of their city as innovative, diverse, and cosmopolitan (Binnie et al. 2006; Florida 2003; Rath 2011). Ethnic and cultural industries provided opportunities for social, cultural, and political mobility for people identified as ethnic leaders. None of this happened in Halle.

In the first stages of their restructuring activities Halle's leaders rather saw migrant businesspeople as economic actors who were agents of the city's redevelopment. In discussing Halle's efforts to revive its small-business sector, most city leaders included migrant entrepreneurs as part of the city. They acknowledged that after reunification the rebuilt city centre would have been replete with empty shopfronts without the shops and restaurants opened by migrants. A representative of the Employment Bureau explained, 'foreigners who want to open a shop here [...] help the employment situation if they come here and also employ people who already live in Halle'. A city councillor stated that he was 'comfortable with migrants who had made a place in the city through the establishment of small businesses'. These leaders tended to emphasize migrants' common humanity rather than their exotic marketable difference.

City leaders also embraced migrants as an indication of the city's openness, which was badly needed to improve its competitive positioning. Responding to the need for city leaders to combat Halle's image as a racist, unwelcoming city, they tried to link openness to learning about the world via migrants. As local people recognized the humanity of migrants, they would learn about the world from them, and so migrants were key to connecting Halle to the world. A city councillor from a minority party commented that 'there are too few foreigners living here'.

20.5 Migrant Economic Emplacement

Migrant economic pathways of emplacement in Halle were not confined to small businesses. People of migrant background participated in many other forms of city-making, including the forging of local and transnational familial, religious, social, and cultural ties not confined to ethnic relations (Glick Schiller and Çağlar 2008; Glick Schiller et al. 2006). However, migrant small businesses were visible as well as significant in the city centre space in the 15 years after German reunification. Migrants from Vietnam, Nigeria, Ghana, Turkey, Greece, India, Bosnia, Iraq, Sudan, and Azerbaijan initiated or were employed in these businesses. In all cases we observed the networks upon which these businesses were built were composed of people from multiple backgrounds, both migrant and non-migrant. Often spouses native to Germany became partners in a business.

Migrant-owned businesses were significant within the specific period of the research for several reasons. As we have indicated, city leaders publicly recognized migrant entrepreneurs as contributors to Halle's regeneration. Migrant businesses filled city centre shop fronts that otherwise would have been empty. Our 2001 survey identified 75 businesses that had migrant workers or owners within several city centre streets. Although only 4 % of the population of the city had migrant backgrounds, 12 % of the businesses in the sample were owned or operated by migrants.

Migrant businesses provided affordable, needed goods to local residents. They provided a significant proportion of the inexpensive fast food and fresh produce available in the city for at least 15 years after reunification. Migrant businesses supplied low-cost fruit, vegetables, and staples such as milk, bread, and salt; and inexpensive clothing and household items. These goods were particularly welcome in a period in which local Germans faced job losses and displacement from managerial positions and skilled work. Local people were confronted with lowered living standards, the diminution of savings accounts when the West German Deutsche Mark replaced the currency of the German Democratic Republic, and later rising prices when the euro replaced the Deutsche Mark.

At the time of unification and the reintroduction of a local capitalist economy migrants were able to compete with natives, who did not have much commercial experience or access to wholesale networks. Moreover, German policy in the region at that time allowed migrants to obtain permanent residency if they opened a business. This was true in other Eastern German cities, but Halle had its own specific opportunity structures, including a politically progressive leadership that sponsored migrant-friendly policies such as city centre housing for asylum seekers and free German lessons. As a result, Halle attracted Kurdish refugees without entrepreneurial backgrounds but with access to commercial networks (mostly in nearby Berlin), former guest workers from Vietnam with professional education, and migrants from West Africa with some history of small-scale trading in Africa.

20.6 Living Economic Embeddedness in a Globally Restructuring City

We offer several ethnographic examples to illustrate the ways that changing opportunity structures, which are produced by restructuring and urban narratives, are significant for an analysis of entrepreneurial emplacement as a form of daily practices of network building and sociality that are not configured by the ethnic background of the actors. We begin with a brief description of Madame Flora's Emporium and two other businesses that in Germany are often labelled 'Afro-shops', because of all the migrant businesses, at first glance, these seem to be the most ethnic. However, an examination of the histories and customer base of these shops makes it clear that, though commonly labelled 'Afro-shops' in Europe, these businesses cannot be understood as ethnic enterprises. Their owners drew on both ethnic and non-ethnic ties to build their businesses, as did the other migrant entrepreneurs in our research.

Arriving from Ghana as an asylum seeker, Flora was able to gain permanent legal status through opening the first 'Afro-shop' in Halle. In finding her way through the bureaucratic procedures necessary to open a legal business Flora was assisted by her 'best friend', a women migrant from Russia who spoke German. Flora soon expanded her multilingual competencies to include some German. Her business was located on the periphery of the city's redeveloped area and in the vicinity of run-down housing blocks and the sites of abandoned or demolished factories. From conversations with Madame Flora, as well as participant observation in the shop, it soon became clear that her business served not only African asylum seekers and refugees but also local residents of the neighbourhood.

Flora skilfully marketed to her various clienteles. Although there were virtually no other Ghanaians in Halle, she sold food products, frozen fish, male and female beauty products, and telephone calling cards that were familiar to customers from a range of other African countries including Nigeria, the Congo, and Mozambique. Madame Flora served the needs of her impoverished German customers for beer, soft drinks, cigarettes, and snacks, having situated her shop in an area where there were no other outlets for such products. In the front part of the shop a migrant from Nigeria sold hip-hop fashions produced in Asia. The backroom of her shop served as a meeting place where young men from various African countries could purchase cooked food and exchange information about how to settle in the city and further develop their network connections to cities throughout Europe and North America.

The second 'Afro-shop' we visited was a telephone-calling shop owned by a migrant from Nigeria and his wife from Halle. They identified their business as Christian rather than African. The third business owned by migrants from Africa followed the business strategy adopted by Madame Flora of supplying cooked food to African migrants and beverages and cigarettes to customers of various backgrounds in the local neighbourhood. This shop owner was less successful than Flora in this strategy because there were more sources of food and drink close at hand until late in the evening.

Most migrant businesses in Halle provided products needed by natives and migrants alike. Their supply chains made use of regional wholesale suppliers, often accessed through connections with people of multiple migrant backgrounds.

Entrepreneurial concerns rather than ethnicity regulated their relations to and with suppliers. For example, the shops and restaurants owned by migrants of Vietnamese background had access to Vietnamese wholesale sources in Leipzig 20 miles away. However, clothing and inexpensive manufactured goods in their shops were also part of commodity and distribution chains that extended to China. This supply chain was also used by the African migrant who sold clothing from Flora's shop, and another African migrant who opened a branch of his Berlin-based business in the city centre, where he sold baggy jeans and shorts, sweatshirts, and other African-American men's fashions to local youth.

In general, shops selling inexpensive clothing and household goods, as well as fast-food restaurants, carryouts, and *imbiss* (kiosks), which were set up in mobile trailers on empty lots or unused land, were often identified with ethnic labels by the city's inhabitants even though they were organized to utilize the most expedient supply chains and as broad a customer base as possible. Fruit and vegetable and döner kebab businesses were publicly identified in Halle as 'Kurdish' (although in German cities such as Berlin they might be identified as 'Turkish'), and in at least one instance included workers from Azerbaijan. Shops labelled 'Vietnamese' included fruit and vegetable stores, as well as 'textile' shops that sold inexpensive clothing and gift items.

It is noteworthy that these restaurants and food shops were not of the type highlighted in discussions of the cosmopolitan city and its broad array of ethnic culinary treats and exotic items of clothing and décor. These were shops that had become part of the provision of inexpensive foods and clothing to the unemployed or poorly paid local German population.

Tracing the path through which migrants from Vietnam began to play a role as shopkeepers in Halle reveals the mutuality of interests that emerged between the local city leadership striving to competitively improve the national and global positioning of their city and migrants who generally chose to have a public presence as businesspeople rather than as members of an 'ethnic community'. A core of the migrants who ran small clothing shops, fruit and vegetable shops, and restaurants in Halle had been professionals or students in Halle in the GDR period. After a period of uncertainty immediately after unification they were allowed to stay if they opened small businesses. These migrants' transnational networks and family ties simultaneously played a role in their efforts to succeed as locally based entrepreneurs and in the initial efforts of city leaders to redevelop the city's commercial sector. These connections and the subsequent business sector upon which they were built also helped to recruit migrants into a city generally seen as unwelcoming to foreigners.

Phuong Schmidt's history is illustrative. Trained in Law and Pedagogy in Hanoi, and the child of a university professor, she came to Halle after unification to visit her sister, who had a university degree but had already established a clothing shop. This sister used distribution networks that stretched from nearby Leipzig back to China, the source of many of the inexpensive items sold in the shop. Through a Vietnamese woman who had originally studied in an elite graduate programme in Halle, Phuong then met Bernd, her future husband, who was native to the city and to Germany. Their courtship took place in the meetings and conferences of an Esperanto club that they both had joined.

Bernd was unable to find a job in the depressed local economy, so the couple decided to open a women's clothing shop. Bernd and Phuong drew on her sister and brother-in-law's entrepreneurial experience and networks and a loan from Bernd's father, who had some savings. The shop also provided part-time employment for an experienced German shop assistant. Through her marriage and her business Phuong started to identify with Halle and Germany as well as with Hanoi and Vietnam. She said that she 'felt like a German' because Halle was her 'second home'. She maintained strong family ties in Vietnam.

Phuong's example of an emplacement that extends to an identity not only with her city of settlement but with the nation state through the dual pathways of business ownership and intermarriage cannot be said to be typical of migrants of Vietnamese background or other migrants in Halle. She is also not unique. Among the 22 business owners we interviewed in the course of the research four told us about intermarriages. Nor is Phuong's example of hiring a German worker unusual. We found German workers as employees in businesses owned by people of Nigerian, Vietnamese, and Indian backgrounds. As city leaders noted, some people of migrant background were providing employment for local unemployed people of German background.

These German employees expressed varying kinds of relationships with their employers. One young woman who worked in an Indian *imbiss* situated in the city's central marketplace explained that her relationship to the Indian owner preceded her employment. She said,

> I often went to [the restaurant in Halle that he owns] with a friend of mine. It's like a big family there! We all sat together and talked. The boss—everybody calls him Bobby—is very friendly to me. He often talks to me and hugs me and so on.

Not all relationships to employers were so cordial, but even the most anti-migrant of the employees of German origin, a rather angry middle-aged woman who worked in a tele-café located near the central marketplace, exempted her Indian-born boss and all those of Indian background from her condemnation of 'foreigners'.

20.7 Structural Forces, Changing Times, and Business Failure

Not all migrant businesses were able to survive in Halle. Those that did not provide the necessities of daily life had the most difficulty surviving, particularly when the city faced hard times as a result of the downturn of the global economy after the bursting of the high-tech bubble in 2000. Detailing the struggles of these businesses makes clear that their failure was not a reflection of migrants' cultural difference but of the ongoing restructuring of the city economy within global economic downturns. In this conjuncture city developers in Halle with German and EU funding sought to regenerate the city centre in ways that primarily benefited large-scale international chains and real-estate and construction interests.

An examination of two business failures in our sample of migrant businesses—Elite Foods and Beautiful Dream Gifts, which both were positioned to sell to an upscale cosmopolitan customer base rather than to the urban poor—can clarify these points. The fate of these businesses paralleled that of a city centre non-migrant-owned business that sold upscale gifts from craftspeople located around the world and fashions crafted locally by people of German background.

Elite Food was owned by Helga, a German woman married to Zaher, a Turkish man. It is important to note, in terms of assessing the relationships between migrant-owned businesses and the local structural context of Halle, that although his German was not fluent, Zaher, through his marriage to Helga, was well-incorporated into the local political and social structure. Helga, a native with a fierce love of her city, had extensive local social networks. These became publicly visible when many years after their relationship began the couple decided to legally marry and the wedding guests included city officials.

Helga and Zaher located their shop on a section of a street in the city centre set aside as an urban pedestrian mall and dedicated by urban planners as the 'high street' of the city. However, when our research began in 2001, the most desirable section of the street had four migrant-owned shops: two selling inexpensive clothing and cheap goods, and an ice cream stand. In contrast to these businesses, Elite Foods seemed to meet the upscale aspirations of the city planners. It featured the type of expensive imported fruits, olives, and candies sought by consumers who desired high-end commodities. Some of these were Turkish but of a quality and price not accessible to the poor of the city.

The second elite-oriented migrant business in our sample was Beautiful Dream Gifts, a shop filled with African jewellery and art that the shop owner wished to market to consumers who sought to validate their cosmopolitan tastes through such purchases. The shop's interior and merchandise, and even its wrapping paper, were designed to cater to this market. Beautiful Dream Gifts was owned by Evelyn, a woman from Nigeria, and her husband, Stephan, a retired businessman who was of German ancestry and grew up in a neighbouring village.

Unfortunately, at the turn of the millennium businesses in Halle faced a global economic downturn as well as the price inflation that accompanied the conversion from the German currency to the euro. In this climate it was increasingly difficult for small businesses to compete with well-capitalized corporate-owned businesses for the custom of a diminished number of upscale consumers in Halle. This situation was made more difficult when Halle developers, interested in catering to a high-end market, sought to do so through a second wave of urban regeneration that placed national and international conglomerates in the shopfronts of the city centre.

While Helga and Zaher held onto their valuable corner high-street location for a few years after the downturn, eventually they were unable to compete with a food market set up in an upscale department shop, which was located just down the street and directly on the market square. Concurrently, their profit margin was destroyed by the currency conversion, which almost doubled wholesale prices in the region at a time when their customer base would not support higher retail prices. Meanwhile, many migrant businesses in the city centre that had been selling inexpensive goods found new locations with cheaper rents on the periphery of the city, but Elite Foods and Beautiful Dreams, poised to market to Halle's new cosmopolitans and requiring a central location, went out of business.

In the last days of their gift shop Evelyn and Stephan sought to find new markets by participating in what they thought was an open-air crafts fair. To Evelyn's dismay, when they arrived they found that the event was funded by an organization external to the city which sought migrant integration through multiculturalism and intercultural understanding. The few small migrant organizations in Halle—generally active only at such events—and some migrant families had been contacted to display goods, foods, or crafts such as hair braiding that were seen as ethnic and exotic. Evelyn was discomforted by such marketing because she did not want to position her business or herself within an ethnic niche and vowed no further participation in such an event.

20.8 Conclusion

Several points are crucial in understanding the relationship between the efforts of Halle's leaders to reposition and re-empower the city and the efforts of migrants to secure emplacement in the city through small business. These points all contribute to an analytical perspective that extends beyond the ethnic lens. None of these businesses exclusively served customers of the shop owners' own ethnicity or even a migrant customer base. Most of the clothing shops, fruit and vegetable stands, carryout kiosks, and fast-food restaurants served natives and migrants alike, and given the demographics of the city, most of their customers could be identified as 'German'. None relied solely on the same or single-ethnicity supply chains. Many had workers or co-owners who were natives of Germany.

Unlike many other cities, for a period of at least 15 years small businesses provided a particularly welcoming economic niche for migrants in Halle. Migrants could successfully compete, not because they arrived with an entrepreneurial culture or past experience but because local people also did not have such skills and the city needed small businesses to fill its empty city centre shopfronts. In this context the political, economic, and social leadership of Halle were supportive of migrant businesses and saw them as assisting the city's efforts to reposition itself and rebirth after German unification and deindustrialization. That is to say, migrants' emplacement in Halle through businesses was shaped by the positioning of the city at a particular period of time and within a situation shaped by political and economic forces in Germany, in Europe, and globally.

Those businesses that failed did so not because of the cultural differences of their owners or workers but because of the changing global, national, and local processes of restructuring. As a result of these rapid changes, businesses that could flourish shortly after German reunification might be unsustainable in the economic climate of the following decades. It is important to note that in the same period many of the businesses owned or franchised by international chains also failed, as prey to larger forces and the poverty of a large proportion of the population. Some of the migrant-owned businesses that served this impoverished population persisted, either in their original locations or elsewhere in the city. Hence, to understand the success or failures of migrant businesses it is not enough to speak of the everyday practices of urban people and the presence or absence of ethnic categorization. These practices and these categorizations reflect, are shaped by, and in turn contribute to the constitutions of the local, the national, and the transnational within uneven hierarchies of power. Such a perspective provides new ways to approach the issue of migrant emplacement.

At the same time the ongoing regeneration of the city centre proved a threat to some migrant businesses. Many but not all were pushed out of the city centre when shopfronts were rebuilt and rents raised in an area of the city designated for redevelopment. Meanwhile, the telephone-calling shops were displaced by the growth of the mobile phone industry and the availability of mobile phone networks throughout the world. Depending on the relative political, economic, and cultural positioning of the city and its response to the global neoliberal agenda, migrant businesses can play different roles at different times, not only in terms of the emplacement of migrants in the city but also in terms of the efforts of the city to shape itself for competition within a global market. Migrant retail businesses may revitalize urban areas from which other entrepreneurs have withdrawn. They may provide needed goods and services that are not being supplied by other means, including food and services to the native population whose quality of life would be poorer, or cost of living higher, without migrant businesses.

City developers and policy-makers should recognize people of migrant background not as actors confined to and representing a niche of ethnic diversity but as active agents of neoliberal urban regeneration. As such, they may, in particular contexts of redevelopment, open up ethnically framed business. However, in all cases, and often within networks of emplacement that are not visible through an ethnic lens, they participate in the reshaping of urban fortunes and in the repositioning of the city. As participants in such processes, people of migrant background may advocate and strengthen neoliberal discourses that legitimate growing social and economic inequalities. Or, as they confront these inequalities and the displacements and insecurities that accompany them, people of migrant background may join movements for justice and against various forms of structural adjustment.

As Fox and Jones (2013) note, to understand people of migrant background scholars need to do more than critique the ethnic lens. In response, we have offered an analytical framework that moves beyond a 'view from below' that remains confined by descriptions of the 'everyday' practices. This framework facilitates examination of the dynamics between migrants and situated by networked institutions of power. Such an examination will make clear that migrants do not live in a world apart but are shaped by and contribute to the processes through which globe-spanning institutions, networks, and struggles become emplaced in time and space.

References

Aldridge, H. E., & Waldinger, R. (1990). Ethnicity and entrepreneurship. *Annual Review of Sociology, 16*, 111–135. doi:10.1146/annurev.so.16.080190.000551.

Amelina, A., Nergiz, D. D., Faist, T., & Glick Schiller, N. (Eds.). (2012). *Beyond methodological nationalism: Research methodologies for cross-border studies*. London: Routledge.

Barjak, F. (2001). Regional disparities in transition economies: A typology for East Germany and Poland. *Post-Communist Economies, 13*(3), 289–311. doi:10.1080/14631370120074849.

Bates, T. (1994). Social resources generated by group support networks may not be beneficial to Asian immigrant-owned small businesses. *Social Forces, 72*(3), 671–689. doi:10.2307/2579776.

Beck, U. (2002). The cosmopolitan society and its enemies. *Theory, Culture & Society, 19*(1–2), 17–44. doi:10.1177/026327640201900101.

Binnie, J., Holloway, J., Millington, S., & Young, C. (Eds.). (2006). *Cosmopolitan urbanism*. London/New York: Routledge.

Bonacich, E., & Modell, J. (1980). *The economic basis of ethnic solidarity: Small business in the Japanese American community*. Berkeley: University of California Press.

Borjas, G. J. (1994). The economics of immigration. *Journal of Economic Literature, 32*(4), 1667–1717.

Brenner, N., & Theodore, N. (Eds.). (2002). *Spaces of neoliberalism: Urban restructuring in North America and Western Europe*. Malden/Oxford: Blackwell Publishing.

Business Week. (2000). *Unsung heroes: Europe's immigrant entrepreneurs are creating thriving businesses—And thousands of jobs*. http://www.businessweek.com/2000/00_09/b3670019.htm

CeChemNet. (2008). *CeChemNet—Central European chemical network*. TIME 4 Saxony-Anhalt. http://www.sachsen-anhalt.de

City Population. (2011). *MM. Germany: Halle: City with county rights, Sachsen-Anhalt*. http://www.citypopulation.de/php/germanysachsenanhalt.php?adm2id=15002

CLIP. (2010). *Ethnic entrepreneurship: Case study: Frankfurt am Main, Germany*. Dublin: Cities for Local Integration Policies. http://eurofound.europa.eu/sites/default/files/ef_files/pubdocs/2011/211/en/1/EF11211EN.pdf

Cohen, R. (1997). *Global diasporas: An introduction*. London: UCL Press.

Constant, A., Shachmurove, Y., & Zimmermann, K. (2007). What makes an entrepreneur and does it pay? Native men, turks, and other migrants in Germany. *International Migration, 45*(4), 71–100. doi:10.1111/j.1468-2435.2007.00420.x.

Deakins, D., Smallbone, D., Ishaq, M., Whittam, G., & Wyper, J. (2009). Minority ethnic enterprise in Scotland. *Journal of Ethnic and Migration Studies, 35*(2), 309–330. doi:10.1080/13691830802586468.

Florida, R. (2003). Cities and the creative class. *City & Community, 2*(1), 3–17.

Fox, J. E., & Jones, D. (2013). Migration, everyday life and the ethnicity bias. *Ethnicities, 13*(4), 385–400. doi:10.1177/1468796813483727.

Geohive. (2012). *Germany: Sachsen-Anhalt*. http://www.geohive.com/cntry/de-15.aspx

Giddens, A. (1984). *The constitution of society: Outline of the theory of structuration*. Berkeley: University of California Press.

Glick Schiller, N. (2003). The centrality of ethnography in the study of transnational migration: Seeing the wetlands instead of the swamp. In N. Foner (Ed.), *American arrivals: Anthropology engages the new immigration* (pp. 99–128). Santa Fe: School of American Research Press.

Glick Schiller, N., & Çağlar, A. (2008). Beyond methodological ethnicity and towards city scale: An alternative approach to local and transnational pathways of migrant incorporation. In L. Pries (Ed.), *Rethinking transnationalism: The meso-link of organisations* (pp. 40–61). Abingdon/New York: Routledge.

Glick Schiller, N., & Çağlar, A. (2009). Towards a comparative theory of locality in migration studies: Migrant incorporation and city scale. *Journal of Ethnic and Migration Studies, 35*(2), 177–202. doi:10.1080/13691830802586179.

Glick Schiller, N., & Çağlar, A. (2011a). Downscaled cities and migrant pathways: Locality and agency without an ethnic lens. In N. Glick Schiller & A. Çağlar (Eds.), *Locating migration: Rescaling cities and migrants* (pp. 190–211). Ithaca: Cornell University Press.

Glick Schiller, N., & Çağlar, A. (2011b). Locality and globality: Building a comparative analytical framework in migration and urban studies. In N. Glick Schiller & A. Çağlar (Eds.), *Locating migration: Rescaling cities and migrants* (pp. 60–83). Ithaca: Cornell University Press.

Glick Schiller, N., Çağlar, A., & Guldbrandsen, T. C. (2006). Beyond the ethnic lens: Locality, globality, and born-again incorporation. *American Ethnologist, 33*(4), 612–633. doi:10.1525/ae.2006.33.4.612.

Harvey, D. (2006). *Spaces of global capitalism: A theory of uneven geographical development.* London: Verso.

International Building Exhibition Urban Redevelopment Saxony-Anhalt. (2010). http://www.iba-stadtumbau.de/index.php7iba2010-en

Kitching, D., Smallbone, D., & Athayde, R. (2009). Ethnic diasporas and business competitiveness: Minority-owned enterprises in London. *Journal of Ethnic and Migration Studies, 35*(4), 689–705. doi:10.1080/13691830902765368.

Kloosterman, R., Van Der Leun, J., & Rath, J. (1999). Mixed embeddedness: (In)formal economic activities and immigrant businesses in the Netherlands. *International Journal of Urban and Regional Research, 23*(2), 252–266. doi:10.1111/1468-2427.00194.

Laurence, J. (2011). The effect of ethnic diversity and community disadvantage on social cohesion: A multi-level analysis of social capital and interethnic relations in UK communities. *European Sociological Review, 27*(1), 70–89. doi:10.1093/esr/jcp057.

Light, I. (1972). *Ethnic enterprise in America: Business and welfare among Chinese, Japanese and Blacks*. Berkeley: University of California Press.

Light, I., Barnard, R. B., & Kim, R. (1999). Immigrant incorporation in the garment industry of Los Angeles. *International Migration Review, 33*(1), 5–25. doi:10.2307/2547320.

Masurel, E., Nijkamp, P., & Vindigni, G. (2004). Breeding places for ethnic entrepreneurs: A comparative marketing approach. *Entrepreneurship & Regional Development: An International Journal, 16*(1), 77–86. doi:10.1080/0898562042000205045.

Min, P. G., & Bozorgmehr, M. (2000). Immigrant entrepreneurship and business patterns: A comparison of Koreans and Iranians in Los Angeles. *International Migration Review, 34*(3), 707–738. doi:10.2307/2675942.

National League of Cities. (2011). *Congress of cities and exposition*. Washington, DC: National League of Cities.

Pécoud, A. (2000). Thinking and rethinking ethnic economies. *Diaspora, 9*(3), 439–462. doi:10.1353/dsp.2000.0018.

Pécoud, A. (2004a). Entrepreneurship and identity: Cosmopolitanism and cultural competencies among German-Turkish businesspeople in Berlin. *Journal of Ethnic and Migration Studies, 30*(1), 3–20. doi:10.1080/1369183032000170141.

Pécoud, A. (2004b). Do immigrants have a business culture? The political epistemology of fieldwork in Berlin's Turkish economy. *Journal of the Society for the Anthropology of Europe, 4*(2), 19–25. doi:10.1525/jsae.2004.4.2.19.

Pieterse, J. N. (2003). Social capital and migration: Beyond ethnic economies. *Ethnicities, 3*(1), 29–58. doi:10.1177/1468796803003001785.

Portes, A. (1995). *The economic sociology of immigration: Essays on networks, ethnicity, and entrepreneurship*. New York: Russell Sage.

Rath, J. (2006). *Entrepreneurship among migrants and returnees: Creating new opportunities.* http://www.un.org/esa/population/migration/turin/Symposium_Turin_files/P05_Rath.pdf

Rath, J. (2011). *Promoting ethnic entrepreneurship in European cities*. Luxembourg: Eurofound Publications Office of the European Union.

Rath, J., & Kloosterman, R. (2000). Outsiders' business: A critical review of research on immigrant entrepreneurship. *International Migration Review, 34*(3), 657–681. doi:10.2307/2675940.

Waldinger, R. (1986). Immigrant enterprise: A critique and reformulation. *Theory and Society, 15*(1–2), 249–285. doi:10.1007/BF00156934.

Wimmer, A., & Glick Schiller, N. (2003). Methodological nationalism, the social sciences, and the study of migration: An essay in historical epistemology. *International Migration Review, 37*(3), 576–610. doi:10.1111/j.1747-7379.2003.tb00151.x.

Chapter 21
Mediated Communication and Migration in Europe: A Contribution to the Ongoing Debate

Ricarda Drüeke

21.1 Introduction

Media and communication have always played an important mediating role in the negotiations of migration and citizenship, as Urry (1999: 318) rightly states: 'Citizenship has always necessitated symbolic resources distributed through various means of mass communication'. Consequently, media are fundamental to the processes of belonging, identity, and migration. European nation states have developed specific institutions and norms which regulate who may be treated equally and who is different and should either be deported or assimilated into the majority culture. The defining of such external and internal boundaries goes along with the making of national identities – which are also transmitted via the mass media – and thus with the inclusion of one's 'own' and the exclusion of the 'other' in a community (see Bauman 2004). Sassen (2006) stresses that contemporary identities are always at least partially constituted by the practices of those who are excluded from them. Therefore, public discourses about migration-related issues have become a pivotal arena around which sameness and otherness are constructed. Public and political discourses on migration are very closely connected to the media discourses, as Wodak (2011) has shown in her study of European migration policies.

The research on migration within the field of communication studies is currently dominated by two main premises (for an overview, see Geißler and Pöttker 2009): first, studies on media and migration take a national research perspective, viewing migration as a linear process with the aim of integrating migrants into their respective societies. In these studies migrants are regarded as a homogeneous group, despite all the differences among them. Second, the focus tends to be on the traditional mass media, which are produced and consumed on the national level. As

R. Drüeke (✉)
Department of Communication, University of Salzburg, Salzburg, Austria
e-mail: ricarda.drueeke@sbg.ac.at

A. Amelina et al. (eds.), *An Anthology of Migration and Social Transformation*, IMISCOE Research Series, DOI 10.1007/978-3-319-23666-7_21

a consequence, the traditional mass media usually depict migrants in a stereotypical manner, and in the discussion of media usage migrants are considered to be a problem group that has certain deficiencies compared with members of the majority society. In the face of current developments, however, these assumptions seem poorly founded. Globalization, transnationalism, digitalization, and mediatization evoke a variety of transformation processes in societies as well as in the media system (see Hepp 2009b), and boundaries established by nation states are no longer appropriate to determine the rules of belonging (see Benhabib 2004). A social transformation perspective (see Chap. 2, in this volume) allows analysing the struggle for representation and recognition with respect to changing forms of political institutions, nation-states as well as the media. Furthermore it provides insights into the diversification of migration-related issues and the media. The aim of this contribution is to discuss how to conceptualize research on media and migration that takes into account the ongoing transformation and the challenges of these processes. In doing so, it raises concerns over linear constructions of nation, identity, and migration, as well as over dichotomies such as between 'information' and 'entertainment' and between 'public' and 'private' and their respective roles in media processes. This chapter is organized as follows. First, the gaps in and the shortcomings of the previous research are discussed based on a review of studies on media and migration in the Western Europe an context. Then, concepts from communication studies are presented that address the changing meanings of culture, identity, and politics, as well as the changing conditions in which media operate. In the conclusion I highlight the importance of these concepts for the theoretical understanding of the current transformation processes and of mediated communication.

21.2 Media and Migration: The State of the Research

In the following I will provide an overview of the current state of and indicate the gaps in the recent media–migration research from German-speaking and other European countries. Most of the work on the media coverage of migration has focused on how the medial representation of migrants has been connected with insecurity, crime, rioting, welfare sponging, and other predominantly negative attributions (see e.g. Baker et al. 2008; Geißler and Pöttker 2009), and, more recently, with religious fanaticism and terrorism (Poole and Richardson 2006; Hafez and Richter 2008). Thus, different groups of migrants are associated with implicit or explicit ideas of 'good citizenship', and a distinction is drawn between 'desirable' and 'undesirable' citizens, ideas that also determine what is 'successful' or 'failed' integration (Klaus and Drüeke 2011). Research on media–migration interaction is often concerned with the integrative effects of media and therefore the media role in processes of integration of migrants into the majority society (Geißler and Pöttker 2009). Questions about the role of journalism in the integration of migrants have also arisen in this context, as has the question of how the European Union influences the meanings of multiculturalism in the media (Bonfadelli 2007). Both in print and in audiovisual media images and representations of migrants vary depending primarily on social status, national origin, and gender (Lünenborg and Fürsich 2014). In her study of German television Röben (2013: 119–121) notes that asylum seekers from North Africa and migrant workers from Eastern Europe are often depicted in relation to their 'usefulness' or as a 'burden on the German welfare system'. In German television documentaries women with headscarves are used to symbolize oppression and religious alienation (Paulus 2008). Media–migration research rarely focuses on the ways in which migrants themselves produce and use media. Studies of media production have shown that migrants are still underrepresented in many fields. Particularly among private broadcasters, migrants are scarcely visible as editors or in production; more migrants can be found at public broadcasters, though not in numbers equal to their proportion of the population (Röben 2013: 131). The media usage patterns of migrants are often associated with the question of integration, with the use of native-language media being seen as a factor of disintegration. However, migrants use media in various different ways, and the use of native-language media does not prevent successful integration, as studies have shown, because such media do not distinguish between 'here' and 'there' (Kissau and Hunger 2010). The results of a study by Sauer (2010) confirm this finding: Turkish migrants in Germany use complementary media, even if they have strong ties to Germany.

Thus, on the level of media representation research has focused on national implications, with ethnicity being used as a racializing category (see Dijk 2012). In analyses of the representation of migrants, ethnicity often functions as a strategy to naturalize and culturalize 'the Other'. Here the research and studies on migration and media focus primarily on comparing integrative and/or disintegrative media processes, meaning that it is assumed that the media can either contribute to the integration of various social groups, or they can prevent their integration, such as through what has been called 'media ghettos'. For a long time a broadcast model of distribution predominated in relation to migration issues; television and radio in particular were associated with a national audience. Integration in this context refers less to a movement than to a desired actual condition that migrants should attain. This approach implicitly assumes the homogenization of culture and regards its heterogeneity as dangerous (Pöttker 2009). The shortcoming of these approaches is that they provide a very limited understanding of migration processes and of the reproduction of stereotypical images of migrants that influences the evaluation and classification of the analysis. Migration-related issues are constituted in multiple ways within and through socialcultural networks and mediated everyday practices. Mediatization, and particularly digitalization, in relation to media are decisive factors in the transformation of media processes. The role of the mainstream media itself changes through differentiation, and the consumption and production of media is less national and more networked, as I will demonstrate in the following sections.

21.3 Mediatization, Migration Processes, and Social Transformation

In order to trace and examine the ongoing transformation processes, this section focuses on the concepts and discourses that are relevant to questions of migration and the media because they provide additional, more precise explanations, particularly explanations of social changes. It introduces some studies that serve to illustrate this conceptual tool, and discusses their contribution to migration research in the field of communication studies. Figure 21.1 below visualizes the main arguments of this section.

Migration is considered to be a prominent driver of processes of transformation of media and society, and part of a broader global change. These processes change the conditions of media production and of the organization of national media, as well as the meanings of identity, culture and politics. In Fig. 21.1 this is indicated by arrows. Processes of media and society that are affected are: (1) the transationalization of nation states, as well as of media usage and production; (2) the deterritorialization of media and culture, which means that culture is not merely bound to geographical territories, and communication is related to an increasing global communicative connectivity (Hepp 2008); and (3) the mediatization of society. The term 'mediatization' is used to describe and grasp theoretically the fundamental change of culture and society as a function of the transformation of media, and highlights the meta-character of the processes (see Hepp and Krotz 2014). This has two main aspects: the mediatized forms of social and cultural life, and mediated communication: 'media in the long run increasingly become relevant for the social construction of everyday life, society, and culture as a whole' (Krotz 2009: 24). Technological connectivity, the concepts of home and homemaking, and those of belonging and identity have been among the key issues in studies of transnational migration and the migrant experience.[1]

There are three interwoven dimensions that can serve as a useful starting point for developing an appropriate understanding of mediated communication and migration processes in the face of ongoing transformations.

1. *Questioning the binary-coded assumptions of media research*: Dichotomies such as between 'entertainment' and 'information', 'political' and 'popular' communication, and 'native' and 'foreign' culture reflect the manifoldness of sources of belonging and identity with regard to migration-related issues. Therefore, it is necessary to broaden the theoretical perspective (see e. g. Klaus and Lünenborg 2012).
2. *The social dimension: Plural media publics*: Further research on migration and media should be aware of the fact that the public sphere, as a norm, is realized in the form of plural publics (Fraser 2005). Migration-related issues are debated in

[1] Transnational migration is defined as the social practices of individuals and collectives organized across a multi-sited sociospatial framework (see Amelina 2012).

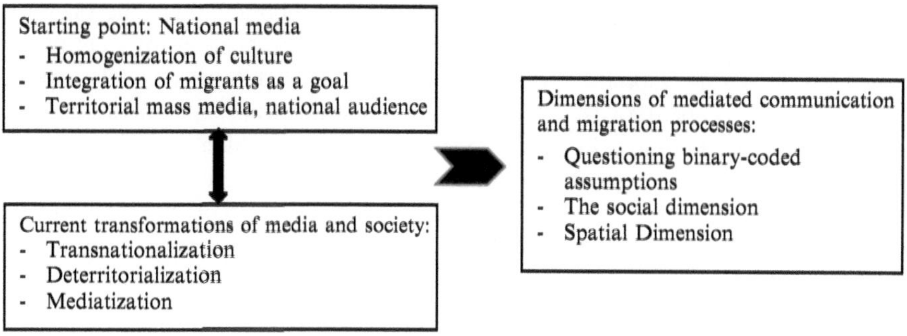

Fig. 21.1 Visualization of the current transformation processes

plural mediated publics, in which heterogeneous meanings emerge and which are not confined by national boundaries.

3. *The spatial dimension: Mediated spaces of identity*: When mediatization is used as an analytical trope, it becomes apparent that identity and belonging are dynamic and open-ended spatial processes rather than static categories. In addition, transnational connectivity in and through media come to the foreground, as do networks of media that extend beyond national boundaries (Steinmaurer 2014).

In the following I will describe each of these dimensions in more detail and situate them within the debate on media and migration, with particular attention to their significance for further research.

21.3.1 Questioning the Binary-Coded Assumptions of Media Research

Establishing European borders, and in particular a European culture with common religious norms, is by no means accomplished by making reference to value-neutral categories. Said (1995), for example, exposes taken-for-granted mental mappings as constructions that are strongly connected to categories of race, class, and gender. Mass media are centrally involved in the production, reproduction, and modification of differentiations that lead to the construction of what are generally called 'Western' norms and values (see e.g. Klaus and Drüeke 2011). They thus play an influential role in the decision of which individuals belong to the nation and which do not. This is indicative of the complex interconnectedness of different markers of belonging in the media's coverage of migration. Media content constructs spaces for identification where identities are formed and defined along dimensions such as gender, class, race, culture, and religion. As a consequence, cultural dimensions of citizenship are used as important indicators to determine entitlement to permanent residence and citizenship, and media debates are used as a means to constantly redefine cultural and normative constructs of 'nation' (Klaus and Lünenborg 2012). The ongoing social transformation processes indicate, moreover, that perceptions of identity are constantly changing. Communities are not imagined and formed solely within national borders; they often exist as cultural communities whose members share the same norms, one example being the European Community, which identifies as democratic and Christian. These change processes, which are based on more than just ethnic or national cultures, call for expanded theoretical concepts that allow us to understand the relationship between media and migration. Markers of cultural citizenship are of prime importance in all debates on a common European identity, as shown in a study of debates in the Austrian press on whether or not migrants should be granted citizenship rights. The ideal citizen in these debates is a white male with a proclivity for high culture (Klaus and Drüeke 2011). These markers are instrumental in shifting the debate from the rights of citizenship and residence to the obligation to be part of the culture.

Cultural studies, and gender studies in particular, show that the very concept of culture is politically dimensioned because these concepts are mutually dependent, so it is impossible to separate the cultural from the political (see e.g. van Zoonen 2005). But it is not only the conditions of culture and identity that are changing; the traditional distinction between political and popular communication is being called into question as well, as the construction of identity in the media through a variety of communication processes makes apparent. This means that even supposedly 'popular' communication—and not just the communication of traditional political actors such as governments or civil societies, which is mirrored in the mass media most of the time—may have an influence on how the migration issue is covered. These forms of communication are also important for negotiating identities, and therefore citizenship and belonging, but they are often viewed as non-political or pre-political, or even, as in the traditional research on the public sphere and the media, as non-informative. In contrast to a narrow definition of the public sphere, a broader definition presupposes no social field to be apolitical, because the coexistence of people, and any connection between them, is potentially political (Pateman 1988). The 'gendering' of political communication could be linked to reflections on democratic participation in order to call into question the conception of political citizenship according to its inclusions and exclusions (Klaus and Lünenborg 2012).

Gender media studies address the fact that systematic distinctions such as between 'public' and 'private', and the related distinction between 'entertainment' and 'information', appear to be fragile (see Mendes and Carter 2008). In a narrow understanding of media and communication, entertainment and popular genres are marginalized and devalued on the grounds that they do not pertain to serious information and deliberation (van Zoonen 2005: 143). For example, popular formats such as soap operas are not credited with producing better citizens, and thus cannot be considered to be political. However, entertainment and popular formats have an explicit political component in that they include diverse groups of citizens. Similarly, Saxer (2007) argues that 'politainment'—i.e. the blending of politics and entertainment—encourages at least a temporary political inclusion of marginalized citizens such as migrants, and that therefore a variety of formats can be described as political.

Thus the reception of these popular formats could be used for the construction of identity and the construction of meaning in the context of the current living situation of the individuals concerned, both of which are politically connoted actions. Not only is high culture relevant to this, but everyday and popular cultures are also central to contemporary societies, and are a part of politics (Dörner 2006: 223). Other partial spaces for migrants are being opened, particularly through talent shows and daily soaps, which grant citizen status through cultural participation (see Dietze 2008). Representations of migrants that resemble everyday life can be found mainly in popular formats, but also in the celebrity pages of magazines and newspapers, both of which present migrants as a natural part of society (see Lünenborg and Fürsich 2014). When research on the representation of migrants in the media and on the use of media is based on more than just traditional information programmes, a wide range of media representations and uses is revealed.

The conceptual broadening of established approaches softens dichotomous assumptions and emphasizes the relational character of binary categories. If the public and the private realms are not seen as opposites, more participatory spaces for migrants become visible. The representations and functions of entertainment formats highlight an extension of traditional communication research and show the fragility of hegemonic interpretation patterns of identity. Changing cultural distinctions raise questions of belonging, which conflict with and call into question the concept of citizenship as a national construct.

21.3.2 The Social Dimension: Plural Media Publics

The constructions of identity and belonging are not the only element that is changing; the forms in which these negotiations take place are subject to constant change as well. Public spheres are a central component of communication processes, and media communication helps to determine which public is or which publics are formed and become visible. These transformation processes, which above all proceed transmedially and transnationally, are currently characterized on a variety of levels: transnationalization can be seen on the discourse level because topics of nationally or culturally coded contexts are negotiated away, and transnational networks are recognizable on the actors' level and can be seen on the operating-range level in terms of addressing and mobilizing new formations (Fraser 2005). Supranational organizations such as the EU foster a new European and/or transnational public sphere, but in an increasing global communicative connectivity transnational public spheres also appear through mediated communication that is not confined by national boundaries. Research in the area of gender studies has drawn attention to the productive dissolution of socially constructed dichotomies, thus critically challenging the concept of a single public sphere. Feminist researchers in particular have highlighted the important role of plural publics in bringing about the change in the public discourse. In this sense alternative publics, subaltern publics, or counter-publics are a resource for modernization, and they play a central role in theories of the public. Examples include religious groups and social movements such as workers', peace, and environmental movements. The historical and the later women's movements emerged simultaneously in different countries and were linked internationally (Wischermann 2004). Functioning public spheres are based on processes of negotiation, understanding, and misunderstanding, as well as on interpretation and reinterpretation (Benhabib 2004). Different types of publics can be distinguished by the complexity of the communicative forums or arenas they involve or by their social segmentation. Their formation is bound to shared interests, spaces, and experiences that are produced discursively and relationally. Migrants and migrant networks, then, create various publics in which identities and narratives can be expressed, explored, and strengthened.

Both historically and in the current debates the concept of 'public sphere' is often viewed in relation to a national public; as a consequence, numerous conceptions of 'the public' have emerged from the nation state context (see Fraser 2005). From a normative perspective, public spheres only have political legitimacy if all of those affected by a decision have an equal opportunity to participate in the informal process of opinion formation. However, processes of opinion formation are often shaped by political elites. The public sphere is therefore based on a hierarchical arrangement of various publics with unequal access to measures of resources and normative power. Marginalized groups, then, form counter-publics because they do not see their interests represented in the hegemonic public sphere. The basis for a growing debate about the transnationalization of public spheres can be seen in the context of globalization, which goes hand in hand with the comprehensive transformation of nation states (Nash 2007). Transnational publics, in this understanding, involve new connections between national public spheres and the emergence of what are considered 'supranational' publics and federations of countries, such as the EU.

Communication processes and their boundaries are changing, particularly as a result of the establishment of transnational and transcultural public spheres. New collective identities and identification possibilities that are being offered by mediated communication come to the foreground, such as hybrid diasporic and cosmopolitan identities. However, to be able to consider these transnational processes, we must recognize the fact that there is a variety of multiple public spheres with political relevance. New, sometimes transnational communities form through exchanges across national boundaries, thus promoting the social participation of migrants (see Hepp 2009a). Transcultural communication not only becomes possible, it is also a central component of everyday life and provides relevant reference points for identity building (Hepp 2010). Various scholars have shown that the Internet functions as a space for diasporic communities and enables new forms of communication (see e.g. Komito 2011). When we talk about transnational public spheres and media consumption across borders, we should also discuss the concept of 'diaspora'., This is not about the question of what contribution the media can make to the integration of minorities into a host society, but much more about the role the media can play in the articulation of different existing transnational diasporas. Plural media publics can transform the way people relate to space and place, specifically for members of a diaspora, by creating a transnational public sphere in which narratives of history, culture, democracy, and identity can be forged (Komito 2011).

In Europe ethnic and diasporic media are seen as part of a lively public sphere, with minorities and their media becoming increasingly visible (see Deuze 2006). They are thus part of the culture of participation, and migrants can be active producers, allowing for attention to be focused on diversity and minorities, as well as on participation. The analysis of the media repertoires of migrants reveals the complexity of transactions with the media. Ethnic and diasporic media are directed at particular ethnic groups who share a sense of belonging across national boundaries. Thus an imagined community and a common culture are built on transnational public spheres. Culture is developed at the intersection of local, national, and transnational spaces (Georgiou 2005). Transnational media call the hegemony of national spaces into question, resulting in the potential for a more critical approach to media and for the emergence of new cultures (Aksoy and Robins 2009). In addition, the national aspect of the media has changed due to the emergence of globalized media industries. Media consumption is varied and involves television, radio, and the Internet; it is characterized not only by prime-time television, with its hegemonic interpretations of the framing of questions of migration and integration, as Macgilchrist and Böhmig (2012) found in their study of the Sarrazin debate in Germany, but also by a variety of public spheres that are formed through blogs and participatory media. Dekker and Engbersen (2012: 15–17) argue that new communication channels opened by social media can transform migrant networks and thus facilitate migration through four key functions: (1) by strengthening ties with family and friends; (2) by creating weak ties to individuals who can assist in the process of migration; (3) by creating a network of latent ties; and (4) by creating a rich source of insider knowledge on migration.

This perspective brings to the foreground the use and production of media by and for migrants, as well as the formation of communities beyond national borders. It shows the opportunities for participation that diverse public spheres strengthen; these are made particularly clear by transnational media mergers and diasporic media communities.

21.3.3 The Spatial Dimension: Mediated Spaces of Identity

In his book *Imagined Communities* Benedict Anderson (1983) regards cultural systems such as nation states as identity spaces in which identity positions are predefined. In this view the nation is an imagined community which distinguishes itself from other communities and whose members assume the existence of certain norms, values, and attributes that bind them together. For example, the imagined community of Europe is based on its self-understanding as a space in which democracy, human rights, and liberty have been realized as paramount goods (Said 1995, see also Chap. 22 on the subject of European identity). The struggle over identity is often linked to gender relations. Media saturate our everyday spaces with images of other places and other imagined or real spatial orders, so that the politics of media images cannot be separated from the politics of space. The dialectics of belonging and alienation, and of self and system, are integral to the experience of media spaces (Couldry and McCarthy 2004: 3). Moreover, thinking of space and the public sphere together allows the analysis of a differentiation of communication processes with regard to identity and migration-related issues according to the different levels of the public involved in the social process of negotiation. Issues of integration and disintegration, inclusion and exclusion, and conflict and consensus are negotiated through communicative practices, which include cultural interpretation disputes, and are decided in social negotiation processes. Like other social spaces, communication spaces are supplied with diverse constructions and representations. In communication processes—and thus also in and through the media—virtual, symbolic, and non-material spaces emerge through the positioning of people and the negotiation and development of identity options and constructions. The new spatial ambiguities, such as globalization and the emergence of new information and communication technologies, reinforce these changes. The media also produce, reproduce, and modify such differentiations in mostly symbolic and imaginary spaces. Communication channels opened by social media transform migrant networks by creating virtual spaces that offer knowledge about migration, provide assistance in processes of migration, and strengthen ties between migrants, even over long distances (Dekker and Engbersen 2012).

Newer approaches used in communication studies emphasize the mutability and the possibilities for change offered by space (Couldry and McCarthy 2004), meaning that spaces and their boundaries are part of an ongoing cultural, social, and societal transformation, and that they do not have fixed meanings but rather generate different interpretations and possibilities for use and awareness (Hepp 2008). Communicative processes are therefore part of processes of the social formation of identity and belonging. Thus, the analyses of communication spaces focus on the wider social context of migration and critically challenge hegemonic cultural norms and values. Essentially, the consideration of sociospatial aspects allows for the examination of mediated forms of communication in transnational spaces without reducing them to national, mass media, or institutional forms. New spaces for migrant collectives emerge primarily in social media, which combine online and offline entities (McGregor and Siegel 2013: 11–13).

The book *Spaces of Identity* by David Morley and Kevin Robins (1995) has been playing a major role in the spatial turn in communication research. Morley and Robins assume that today it is not so much physical constraints as symbolic constraints that function as the framework of cultural communities. They show that in Europe the media offer primarily an ethnic white identity, so that there is no space for other social groups such as migrants and diaspora communities. Yet it is also clear that the existence of multiple transnational interactions across national borders does not diminish the importance of nation states as sites for the production and reproduction of social power. For instance, the headscarf debates in Austria and various other European countries show how manifest physical spaces and spaces for identification are constructed, from which veiled women are excluded (see Drüeke et al. 2012, see also Chap. 19, in this volume). However, new spaces of identity are also opened up for migrants as well; for example, the emerging transnational spaces are shown on posters and in images on websites that are created by transnational activists and that demonstrate the subjectivity of migrants in the European Union (see Doerr 2010).

Identities are offered through the media that break through partially hegemonic discourses. These identities not only provide more ready-made elements of the host culture for migrants to identify with but also show more images and interpretations of identity and belonging that emphasize the incompleteness and diversity of these concepts.

21.4 Conclusion: Reflecting on Media and Migration

The media themselves can no longer be understood solely in the context of a nation state or as insular media systems, nor can migration be reduced to economic, social, or demographic factors. The media also play a role in how migration is framed, in how the meanings of migration are produced, and in how mediated communication is changing processes of identity formation. Mediated processes of migration can be understood as places of conflict in which meanings and positions are fought over. In the context of this contribution I have confined myself to describing the underlying conditions, which I have illustrated using example studies. This contribution can serve as a guide for describing media and migration processes in relation to social transformation processes. The consideration of recent theoretical approaches such as gender studies and cultural studies forms the basis for a research perspective that can be used to examine the impact of processes of social and community transformation on communication and the media. The discussion of the three dimensions has shown that it is necessary to question the diverse assumptions underlying the current media–migration research. The political and media debate is not only influenced by mass media and institutional politics but has also been increasingly shaped by civil societies, social movements, and new and old forms of protest. Transcultural and transnational models of communication suggest that migration movements and the related cultural processes cannot be analysed properly by focusing exclusively on nation states because the places and spaces of communication expand and take on new forms (see Hepp 2009b). Dichotomies in the description of media and communication processes fall short of explaining mediated communication and migration processes; the expansion of these concepts shows the diversity of media representations and the consumption patterns of migrants, and emphasizes the relational character of attributions. The consideration of the social and spatial dimensions of communication extends the concept of the public sphere and, moreover, regards media spaces as identity spaces which appear to be polysemic rather than homogeneous.

References

Aksoy, A., & Robins, K. (2009). Türkisches Satellitenfernsehen: Auf dem Weg zur Entzauberung des Anderswo. In U. Hunger & K. Kissau (Eds.), *Internet und Migration: Theoretische Zugänge und empirische Befunde* (pp. 73–97). Wiesbaden: VS-Verlag für Sozialwissenschaften.

Amelina, A. (2012). Socio-spatial scales as social boundaries? Or: How do migration studies profit from including 'space' in the sociology of social boundaries. *Migration Letters, 9*(3), 273–288.

Anderson, B. (1983). *Imagined communities: Reflections on the origin and spread of nationalism*. London: Verso.

Baker, P., Gabrielatos, C., Khosravinik, M., Krzyżanowski, M., McEnery, T., & Wodak, R. (2008). A useful methodological synergy? Combining critical discourse analysis and corpus linguistics to examine discourses of refugees and asylum seekers in the UK press. *Discourse & Society, 19*(3), 273–306. doi:10.1177/0957926508088962.

Bauman, Z. (2004). *Identity: Conversations with Benedetto Vecchi*. Cambridge/Malden: Polity Press.

Benhabib, S. (2004). *The rights of others: Aliens, residents and citizens*. Cambridge: Cambridge University Press.

Bonfadelli, H. (2007). Die Darstellung ethnischer Minderheiten in den Massenmedien. In H. Bonfadelli & H. Moser (Eds.), *Medien und Migration: Europa als multikultureller Raum?* (pp. 95–116). Wiesbaden: VS Verlag für Sozialwissenschaften.

Couldry, N., & McCarthy, A. (2004). *MediaSpace: Place, scale, and culture in a media age*. London/New York: Routledge.

Dekker, R., & Engbersen, G. (2012). How social media transform migrant networks and facilitate migration. *Global Networks, 14*(4), 401–418. doi:10.1111/glob.12040

Deuze, M. (2006). Ethnic media, community media and participatory culture. *Journalism, 7*(3), 262–280. doi:10.1177/1464884906065512.

Dietze, G. (2008). Casting Shows und Cultural Citizenship: "Deutschland sucht den Superstar" als BONGO für Beheimatung von Migranten. *Medien-Journal, 32*(3), 19–30.

Dijk, T. A. (2012). The role of the press in the reproduction of racism. In M. Messer, R. Schroeder, & R. Wodak (Eds.), *Migrations: Interdisciplinary perspectives* (pp. 15–29). Vienna: Springer.

Doerr, N. (2010). Politicizing precarity, producing visual dialogues on migration: Transnational public spaces in social movements. *Forum: Qualitative Social Research/Sozialforschung, 11*(2), 1–27.

Dörner, A. (2006). Medienkultur und politische Öffentlichkeit: Perspektiven und Probleme der Cultural Studies aus politikwissenschaftlicher Sicht. In A. Hepp & R. Winter (Eds.), *Kultur – Medien – Macht: Cultural Studies und Medienanalyse* (pp. 219–236). Wiesbaden: VS Verlag für Sozialwissenschaften.

Drüeke, R., Kirchhoff, S., & Klaus, E. (2012). Positioning the veiled woman: An analysis of Austrian press photographs in the context of the European headscarf debates. In C.-M. Pascale (Ed.), *Social inequality & the politics of representation: A global landscape* (pp. 190–208). Thousand Oaks/London/New Delhi/Singapore: SAGE.

Fraser, N. (2005). *Transnationalizing the public sphere*. www.republicart.net/disc/publicum/fraser01_en.pdf

Geißler, R., & Pöttker, H. (Eds.). (2009). *Media – Migration – Integration: European and North American perspectives*. Bielefeld: Transcript.

Georgiou, M. (2005). Diasporic media across Europe: Multicultural societies and the Universalism–Particularism Continuum. *Journal of Ethnic and Migration Studies, 31*(3), 481–498. doi:10.1080/1369183050058794.

Hafez, K., & Richter, C. (2008). Das Islambild von ARD und ZDF: Themenstrukturen einer Negativagenda. *Fachjournalist, 3*(2008), 10–16.

Hepp, A. (2008). Translocal media cultures: Networks of media and globalisation. In A. Hepp, F. Krotz, S. Moores, & C. Winter (Eds.), *Connectivity, networks and flows: Conceptualizing contemporary communication* (pp. 33–58). Cresskill: Hampton Press.

Hepp, A. (2009a). Localities of diasporic communicative spaces: Material aspects of translocal mediated networking. *The Communication Review, 12*(4), 327–348. doi:10.1080/10714420903344451.

Hepp, A. (2009b). Differentiation: Mediatization and cultural change. In K. Lundby (Ed.), *Mediatization: Concept, changes, consequences* (pp. 139–158). New York: Peter Lang.

Hepp, A. (2010). Comparing transnationally and transculturally: Leaving container thinking. *Medien & Zeit, 25*(4), 4–9.

Hepp, A., & Krotz, F. (2014). Mediatized worlds – Understanding everyday mediatization. In A. Hepp & F. Krotz (Eds.), *Mediatized worlds: Culture and society in a media age* (pp. 1–18). Basingstoke: Palgrave Macmillan.

Kissau, K., & Hunger, U. (2010). The internet as a means of studying transnationalism and diaspora. In R. Bauböck & T. Faist (Eds.), *Diaspora and transnationalism: Concepts, theories and methods* (pp. 245–266). Amsterdam: Amsterdam University Press.

Klaus, E., & Drüeke, R. (2011). More or less desirable citizens: Mediated spaces of identity and cultural citizenship. *Global Media Journal, 1*(2), www.db-thueringen.de/servlets/DerivateServlet/Derivate-24461/GMJ2_klaus_drueeke_final.pdf

Klaus, E., & Lünenborg, M. (2012). Cultural citizenship: Participation by and through media. In E. Zobl & R. Drüeke (Eds.), *Feminist media: Participatory spaces, networks and cultural citizenship* (pp. 197–212). Bielefeld: Transcript.

Komito, L. (2011). Social media and migration: Virtual community 2.0. *Journal of the American Society for Information Science and Technology, 62*(6), 1075–1086. doi:10.1002/asi.21517.

Krotz, F. (2009). Mediatization: A concept with which to grasp media and societal change. In K. Lundby (Ed.), *Mediatization: Concept, changes, consequences* (pp. 21–40). New York: Peter Lang.

Lünenborg, M., & Fürsich, E. (2014). Media and the intersectional other: The complex negotiation of migration, gender, and class on German television. *Feminist Media Studies, 14*(6), 959–975. doi:10.1080/14680777.2014.882857.

Macgilchrist, F., & Böhmig, I. (2012). Blogs, genes and immigration: Online media and minimal politics. *Media, Culture & Society, 34*(1), 83–100. doi:10.1177/0163443711427201.

McGregor, E., & Siegel, M. (2013). *Social media and migration research* (UNU-MERIT Working Paper Series #2013-068). Maastricht: United Nations University/Maastricht Graduate School of Governance. www.merit.unu.edu/publications/wppdf/2013/wp2013-068.pdf

Mendes, K., & Carter, C. (2008). Feminist and gender media studies: A critical overview. *Sociology Compass, 2*(6), 1701–1718. doi:10.1111/j.1751-9020.2008.00158.x.

Morley, D., & Robins, K. (1995). *Spaces of identity: Global media, electronic landscapes and cultural boundaries*. London/New York: Routledge.

Nash, K. (2007). Transnationalizing the public sphere: Critique and critical possibilities. *Theory, Culture & Society, 24*(4), 53–57. doi:10.1177/0263276407080093.

Pateman, C. (1988). *The sexual contract*. Stanford: Stanford University Press.

Paulus, S. (2008). Ethnisierung von Geschlecht und die diskursive Reproduktion von Differenz in der Fernsehdokumentation "Fremde Nachbarn. Muslime zwischen Integration und Isolation". In U. Wischermann & T. Thomas (Eds.), *Medien – Diversität – Ungleichheit: Zur medialen Konstruktion sozialer Differenz* (pp. 125–139). Wiesbaden: VS Verlag für Sozialwissenschaften.

Poole, E., & Richardson, J. E. (Eds.). (2006). *Muslims and the news media*. London/New York: I.B. Tauris.

Pöttker, H. (2009). Successful integration? Media and polish migration in the German empire at the turn of the 20th century. In R. Geißler & H. Pöttker (Eds.), *Media – Migration – Integration: European and North American perspectives* (pp. 9–26). Bielefeld: Transcript.

Röben, B. (2013). *Medienethik und die "Anderen": Multiperspektivität als neue Schlüsselkompetenz*. Wiesbaden: Springer.

Said, E. W. (1995). *Orientalism: Western conceptions of the orient*. London: Penguin.
Sassen, S. (2006). *Territory, authority, rights: From medieval to global assemblages*. Princeton: Princeton University Press.
Sauer, M. (2010). Mediennutzungsmotive türkeistämmiger Migranten in Deutschland. *Publizistik, 55*(1), 55–76. doi:10.1007/s11616-010-0074-5.
Saxer, U. (2007). *Politik als Unterhaltung: Zum Wandel politischer Öffentlichkeit in der Mediengesellschaft*. Konstanz: UVG Verlagsgesellschaft.
Steinmaurer, T. (2014). Mediatized connectivity: Historical traits of telephony and theoretical considerations about a new dispositive of communication. In A. Hepp & F. Krotz (Eds.), *Mediatized worlds: Culture and society in a media age* (pp. 91–106). Basingstoke: Palgrave Macmillan.
Urry, J. (1999). Globalization and citizenship. *Journal of World-Systems Research, 5*(2), 311–324.
van Zoonen, L. (2005). *Entertaining the citizen: When politics and popular culture converge*. Lanham: Rowman & Littlefield.
Wischermann, U. (2004). Feminist theories on the separation of the private and the public: Looking back, looking forward. *Women in German Yearbook, 20*, 184–197.
Wodak, R. (2011). 'Us' and 'them': Inclusion and exclusion – Discrimination via discourse. In G. Delanty, R. Wodak, & P. Jones (Eds.), *Identity, belonging and migration* (pp. 54–77). Liverpool: Liverpool University Press.

Part V
Outlook for Researching Migration and Social Transformation Beyond Eurocentrism

Chapter 22
The 'European' Question: Migration, Race, and Post-Coloniality in 'Europe'

Nicholas De Genova

22.1 Introducing … the 'European' Question

What is 'Europe'?
Who is a 'European'?

Social transformation in Europe today revolves around these constitutive but ever unasked questions, which I enfold together as the 'European' Question. The pioneering African American intellectual W.E.B. Du Bois famously articulated the 'ever unasked question' routinely posed implicitly to Black Americans: 'How does it feel to be a problem?' (Du Bois [1903] 1982: 43). This dilemma undeniably persists for all those people racialized as not-white, in the United States and Europe alike. However, this question's pertinence for the presumptively 'true' or 'real' Europeans has also become increasingly apparent: each nationalidentity has become problematic in new ways. In this regard, the long-standing German obsession with self-interrogation in the extended aftermath of the Nazi Holocaust – whether sincere, cynical, or evasive – is simply the exception that proves the rule. This is due in no negligible measure to the extent to which these presumptively self-evident and fundamental 'national' identities have been destabilized in unprecedented and unforeseen ways by the mere presence and lived practices of migrants and their progeny. Moreover, 'European'-ness, that rather broader and more encompassing figure, is once again a kind of elusive master signifier, perennially plagued with ambiguities and uncertainties even as its salience seems ever more pronounced.

N. De Genova (✉)
Department of Geography, King's College London, London, UK
e-mail: n.degenova@gmail.com

A. Amelina et al. (eds.), *An Anthology of Migration and Social Transformation*, IMISCOE Research Series, DOI 10.1007/978-3-319-23666-7_22

Today all of Europe has become obsessed with its identity. But … *What is 'Europe'?* And … *Who is a 'European'*?[1]

Social movements during the nineteenth and twentieth centuries were commonly pressed to address various political problems in terms, for example, of 'the Jewish question' (or, in the United States, 'the Negro question'), 'the national question', and 'the woman question'; thus, they approached these questions from the largely unexamined vantage point of relative privilege and power. In these opening years of the twenty-first century we can justifiably say that these famous 'questions' have been succeeded in Europe by the Migration Question. Today, however, in the extended aftermath of the end of the Cold War and especially now, amid the shocks of the global crisis of capitalism, what I will call 'the "European" question' has become a problem of a new significance and magnitude—above all in Europe itself. The European question, therefore, can serve as a crucial index for vital historiographic and ethnographic research into the contemporary post-colonial dynamics of social transformation, in a manner that identifies and underscores the centrality of migration and racialization processes.

If 'Europe' presents itself increasingly as a question (or indeed as a problem) for Europeans, moreover, this is no less true in Europe's increasingly amorphous externalized border zones, and beyond. There is no stable space of 'Europe' towards which the figure of 'migration' can be understood to move, as from an imagined periphery towards a presumably fixed centre. Indeed, the racialized ramifications within the space of 'Europe' of such increasingly blurred ('external') boundaries have prompted Étienne Balibar (2009) to suggest that Europe has indeed become one big borderland. Furthermore, as Sandro Mezzadra argues, invoking the work of Dipesh Chakrabarty, 'movements and struggles of migration in Europe […] are displacing and de-centering Europe on the level of everyday life. They are provincializing it' (Mezzadra 2010; see also Chap. 17, in this volume).

22.2 The Spectre of Disintegration

The figure of 'migration' itself consequently signals a murkier series of preoccupations about the migrants themselves (De Genova 2010). The Migration Question thus gets transposed into the Migrant Question, and it is indeed around this 'problem' that much of the academic research on migration has itself been fundamentally constituted. The very categories of thought that commonly frame discourses of

[1] Nahum Chandler poses practically the same questions: 'Who counts, can be given an account, or can be given, as European? Who, or what, then, (is) Europe?' (Chandler 2013: 51), in the context of asking another question that is nonetheless quite pertinent to the manner in which I am framing the central inquiry pursued in this essay. He asks: 'What if a certain "Europe" might come to imagine that one W.E.B. Du Bois—Negro, African, Afro-Caribbean, African American, Black, American, European American, White, European, etc.—is one of its most distinguished practitioners of thought from the nineteenth and twentieth centuries?' (Chandler 2013: 50).

migration, including scholarly discourses, tend to present migrant mobility as a definite sort of 'problem' that implicitly threatens the presumed normative good of 'social cohesion' and commands various formulae for enhancing the processes for the 'inclusion' of migrant 'outsiders', or perhaps for compelling those 'foreigners' to figure out how to appropriately 'integrate' themselves. In short, the dominant discourses of migration reveal a persistent anxiety about the inexorable forces of post-colonial social transformation. No doubt these same analytical (but deeply normative and politicized) categories have by now begun to be subjected to a fair measure of critical, deconstructivist energy. But... What *is* 'Europe'? *Who* is a 'European'? These are questions that have been left insufficiently deconstructed. They are questions that concern us in profound and indeed intimate ways.

In the wake of decolonization on a global scale, coupled now with many decades of transnational, intercontinental, post-colonial migrations that are the harvest of empire, Europe today, much like Germans confronting the Nazi past, is forced to contemplate the legacies of its historical crimes. Whether in good conscience or bad faith, whether honestly, cynically, or with clumsy dissimulation, furthermore, these acts of post-colonial contemplation are never separable from palpably practical deliberations and decisions over policy questions that intractably take the nativist form: 'What should *we* do with *them*?' (De Genova 2005: 56–94). Thus, as a sort of response to the hegemonic entrenchment of the Migration Question, we must critically formulate the 'European' Question from the vantage point of the cross-border mobility of migrants and the enduring coloniality that contemporary borders imply.

Much as the migration question in Europe is always already an at least implicitly *racial* question, the European question requires us to examine 'European'-ness itself as a racial problem—a problem of post-colonial whiteness (see also Chap. 19, in this volume). As Salman Rushdie once sardonically affirmed, with regard to the British context in the aftermath of the 1981 'race riots', in a rather forthright reply to Du Bois' ever- unasked question:

> You talk about the Race Problem, the Immigration Problem, all sorts of problems. If you are liberal, you say that black people have problems. If you aren't, you say they are the problem. But the members of the new colony have only one real problem, and that problem is white people. [...] racism, of course, is not our problem. It's yours. We simply suffer from the effects of your problem (Rushdie [1982] 1991: 138).

How, then, may we begin to examine anew the problem of European identity and the contradictory and competing productions of a European space as racial formations and racial projects? This question, I contend, is the ever unasked question always posed implicitly whenever the topic or theme of 'migration' is addressed in the contemporary European context.

22.3 'Neo'-Nationalisms?

Whereas 'the national question' was posed historically, particularly in Europe, as one concerning the emancipation and self-determination of subordinated national 'minorities', today the problems of 'national identity', 'national culture', 'national values', and of course also 'national sovereignty' present themselves primarily as *majoritarian* projects, articulated first and foremost in relation to migration, if not plainly against migrants. If the European question tends to manifest itself as a resurgence of nationalisms, how may we begin to analyse these contemporary expressions of ostensibly national identity and prerogative across Europe as distinctly post-colonial racial projects? From the standpoint of migration and what we might call 'the new Europeans' of colour, what is the specificity of, for instance, the Greek problem, or the British problem? The fascistic paramilitary operations of Golden Dawn in Greece and the comparatively feckless thuggishness of the English Defence League are clearly distinct socio-political phenomena, but how substantially different are these manifestations of the new European nativist politics of national identity from the standpoint of those whom they target as the objects of their contempt and animosity? From the standpoint, in other words, of those whom they seek to terrorize, how different are they, really?

Racist far-right parties in Europe tend to articulate their reactionary anti-immigrant populism not only in terms of a pluralistic and differentialist incompatibility between their putative 'national culture' and the 'foreignness' of migrants but also in the idiom of the purportedly legitimate politics of citizenship, which promotes the national priority of 'natives' under the overt rubric not of racial supremacism but rather of the presumptive birthright entitlements of 'the nation' or 'the people'. Nevertheless, the emphatically 'national' gesture is transparently and unapologetically equated with a belligerent politics of hostility to migrants. That is to say, whether explicitly racist or not, these 'neo'-nationalisms are overtly and unabashedly exclusionary. Hence, the generic figures of 'immigration' and the diffuse politics of 'foreignness' suffice to reanimate race in terms that commonly, and perhaps increasingly, are articulated as nation: in terms of the 'national' identity of the 'natives' (De Genova 2005, 2013: 56–94). The national question has thus reasserted itself in Europe today in the form of a variety of profoundly racialized projects from which there is of course no immunity for the native-born European children and grandchildren of the migrants, who commonly remain permanently inscribed as being 'of migrant background' or indefinitely categorized (in some instances, officially, juridically) as (non-citizen) 'foreigners'.

In spite of their ostensibly nationalist militant particularisms, each of these nativist movements from one country to the next is remarkably similar to all the others. Perhaps most revealingly, then, among the various nationally identified offshoots of the English Defence League there has subsequently also arisen the *European* Defence League. Likewise, the rapid emergence in late 2014 of a neo-Nazi/nationalist anti-immigrant movement in Germany, defined specifically by its anti-Muslimracism, has very tellingly designated itself to be a movement of 'Patriotic

Europeans'. Thus, we must be alert to the emergence of new forms of expressly 'European' conviviality, particularly as these may articulate aversion or antagonism to (non-European) migrants.

22.4 Rumours of War, Premonitions of Death

One rather dramatic manifestation of these new formations of 'European' identity is evidenced by the ideological framework that motivated Anders Breivik's bloodbath in Norway, in which a far-right nationalist project of racial whiteness, castigating 'multiculturalism' and principally targeting white Norwegians in a fury of racial 'sanitation', explicitly upheld its specifically anti-Muslim racism by emphatically affirming a renewed devotion to an image of pan-European community, albeit one associated with the pre-modern notion of Christendom. In these ways, and despite its apparent recourse to a kind of neo-medievalism, the historical specificity of the present crisis is clearly distinguished also by its enunciation within the now routinized ideological rubric of the so-called Global War on Terror, protracted warfare and neo-colonial military occupations in predominantly Muslim countries, and the dramatic escalation of securitization generally. It is indisputable that Muslim migrants in particular have borne an inordinate burden of suspicion and hostility in Europe during recent years (see also Chap. 18, in this volume).

Regardless of 'antiterrorist' pretexts and pretences, however, these security state measures figure migration in general as a principal target (De Genova 2007). Indeed, the apparently more generic derision toward 'foreigners' often tends to do the work of one variety of specifically anti-Muslim racism. However, it is also the case that the very category 'Muslim' tends to be conflated with a whole racialized class constellation. Hence, Houria Bouteldja, spokesperson for the Parti des Indigènes de la République in France, unpacks the contemporary 'Muslim question' in Europe:

> I would even say that 'Muslim' also denotes 'resident of a poor neighbourhood'. It is sometimes a euphemism for 'banlieue'. Its meaning is pejorative [...]. In France, Islam is above all a religion of the poor and of immigrants [...]. The white European identity that dominated the world for 500 years is in decline. The voices—often hysterical—raised in the media against Islam fundamentally express a fear of this decline [...]. Whites are losing their historical centrality [...] and they see all these non-whites, wrongly identified with Islam, as a threat to their identity (Bouteldja 2012a).

Thus, it becomes ever more evident that the European question, particularly in the form of a question regarding the crisis of European prestige and prosperity, entails a persistent conflation of migration, race, and 'Muslim' identity as relatively floating signifiers for the intrinsically contradictory mediation of the contemporary, protracted post-colonial agony.

It is noteworthy here that the ideological short circuit that affiliates 'the Muslim' with migration (and hence, 'foreign'-ness) is in no sense coincidental. As Gil Anidjar argues persuasively, 'the Jewish question' and 'the Muslim question' were always co-constituted, but notably were construed to signal figures of alterity that were presumed to be respectively 'internal' and 'external' to Europe, the former as a 'theological' enemy, the latter as a 'political' one (Anidjar 2012: 22–23). In effect, we can add that the 'internal' menace was figured as a *corrosive* one, whereas the 'external' threat was always perceived to be an *invasive* one. Inasmuch as the racialized figure of 'the Muslim' has most recently been hyperbolically affiliated with the anomic aggression and fanatical violence of 'foreigners' (whether internal or external), furthermore, David Theo Goldberg contends that this monstrous menace has come to stand for death itself: 'the fear of violent death, the paranoia of Europe's cultural demise [...] the fear of the death of Europe itself' (Goldberg 2006: 346).

22.5 In Living Colour

It is not sufficient to direct our critical scrutiny only towards the violent outbursts and fascistic movements that have been steadily advancing and normalizing a more broadly anti-immigrant agenda. We must also interrogate the methodological and normative nationalist complacencies of liberal and many left-wing political frameworks, including some varieties of would-be 'critical' migration studies, as well as many anti-racist movements that leave the nationalist presuppositions of an assimilationist politics of 'integration' unexamined (see also Chaps. 17 and 19, in this volume). This is particularly important when so many of the official ideologies of the European nation states themselves avow a kind of putatively anti-racist universalism that, however paradoxically, is systematically mobilized to accuse migrants of parochialism and 'fundamentalism'.

While we may be particularly attentive to new or revised racial formations that are specifically refracted through (Christian) religious identities, as with Breivik, we must also be alert to others that aggressively promote a Eurocentric variety of secularism which equates a specifically European or 'Western' civilization with universalism. In these latter articulations 'European' values are juxtaposed with 'foreign' ones; universalism becomes one more militant particularism; and the demand for compulsory 'integration' becomes a ruse that polices, penalizes, and disciplines migrants' alleged 'foreignness'. This ideological hypocrisy is denounced in the founding statement of the French Movement of the Indigenous of the Republic that culminated in the creation of the Parti des Indigènes de la République (PIR):

> Ideologues recycle the theme of 'clash of civilisations' in the local language of the conflict between the 'Republic' and 'communitarianism' [...]. Under a term of 'fundamentalism' never defined, the populations of African, Maghrebian or Muslim origin are now identified as the fifth column of a new barbarism that threatens the West and its 'values' (MIR 2005).

In short, for those racialized as 'Muslim', secularism gets converted into 'a weapon against us' (Bouteldja 2012b). Ultimately, then, such assertions of pronouncedly European 'universalism' affirm the opposite: a pluralistic and relativistic conception of fundamental 'cultural' incompatibility (and, by implication, the impossibility of migrant 'assimilation'). In the aftermath of decolonization such projects may now be less confident about their global 'civilizing missions', but they have revitalized their supremacist pretensions and their self-satisfied assertiveness about a differentialist politics of national/'European' prerogative and migrant marginalization.

The post-coloniality of Europe today can productively be considered in light of the profound radicality of the PIR. The PIR have not been reticent about the urgency of their own commitment to begin asking and answering the European question. Composed predominantly of 'native'-born citizens of France—'second-generation' and 'third-generation' youth of colour—the PIR proclaim themselves to be *indigènes* (a term of specifically French colonial provenance referring to colonial subjects or colonized 'natives'). Because they have been compelled to 'live the experience of colonial racism' within France, as its ostensible citizens, they provocatively announce themselves to be the *indigènes*—i.e. the colonized natives—of the Republic. Indeed, they thereby repudiate the treacherous egalitarian promise of citizenship itself, repudiate their (post-)colonial racial subjugation, and call for 'the decolonization of the Republic' (MIR 2005). Their principal slogan, '*Le PIR est avenir!*' ('The PIR is the future!'), is a remarkable double entendre which affirmatively announces the political coming of age of French-born youth of colour, and makes a bold claim upon their own post-colonial entitlement to define the future of France. More directly, however, the slogan simultaneously asserts its more customary idiomatic sense: '*Le pir est avenir*' means 'The worst is yet to come!'. Thus, playfully destabilizing all of the encrusted conceits of the dominant ideology of French republicanism, and also forcefully interrogating the racial complacencies of the French (white) left, the PIR unapologetically rejoice in their own insurgent and incorrigible audacity. Here are the new 'Europeans' indeed!

22.6 Remembering European Civilization

Whether the European question manifests itself as a resurgence of nationalist particularism or as one of universalistic secularism, we must begin to analyse these contemporary discourses and practices as distinctly post-colonial racial projects. Indeed, the supranational configuration of a new 'Europe' and its concomitant 'European' identity, which has been underway now for many years (particularly since the end of the Cold War), can only be apprehensible in terms of a historically prior, comparably supranational formation of European 'community', one that was predicated historically on Europe's colonial relation to the globe, and similarly constituted on the material and practical basis of a global regime of white supremacy (Du Bois 1910, 1915, 1917, [1920] 1971). Here, after all, lest we forget, we are speaking precisely of *Europe*.

What is this place called 'Europe'? How did the European nation states come about historically? What was the material basis of European wealth and aggrandizement? This of course was an uneven history in which not all European nation states were equal; the variety of particular national histories is surely not a monolith. Indeed, an essential feature of European history has always been the subjugation of some Europeans by others (see also Chap. 6, in this volume). Nonetheless, the foundation of specifically European prestige and prosperity for hundreds of years was precisely colonial empire. Across Europe's long and sordid colonial history the overwhelming majority of Europe's labouring classes did not live in Europe but rather inhabited the vast expanse of colonized lands in Africa, Asia, and the Americas (Du Bois 1915, 1917, [1920] 1971; Orwell 1939).

The crisis of that earlier (pre-Cold War) supranational European 'community' of colonial powers was set in motion by the era of decolonization, which was itself a fundamental condition of possibility for the particular dynamics of bipolar fracture that prevailed during the Cold War. Here, then, it is instructive to recall that the twentieth century had been inaugurated by W.E.B. Du Bois' famous proclamation of 'the problem of the color line' as the defining and decisive global fault line of the century (DuBois 1900b: para. 2, para. 19; see also Du Bois [1903] 1982: 3; Chandler 2006, 2013). What is considerably less well known, however, is that Du Bois also insisted elsewhere that 'the *civilization* of the twentieth century is European' ([1900a] 2013: para. 7; emphasis added).[2] Hence, one could productively extrapolate that the problem of European 'civilization' was precisely 'the problem of the colour line' or, even further, that a defining dynamic of European 'civilization' as such was that same notorious and nefarious 'colour line'. In the largely unknown early essay in which he makes this latter proposition, titled 'The Spirit of Modern Europe', Du Bois furthermore affirms that the modern achievements of Europe must be apprehensible as having an effectively global configuration, referring provocatively to 'that European civilization of which we all today form a part' ([1900a] 2013: para. 42). Notably, Du Bois returns to this gesture four decades later, on the first page of the first chapter of his autobiographical text *Dusk of Dawn: An Essay Toward an Autobiography of a Race Concept*, in which he refers quite frankly to 'the world-wide domination of white Europe' as 'this European civilization [in the folds of which] I was born and shall die, imprisoned, conditioned, depressed, exalted and inspired. Integrally a part of it and yet, much more significant, one of its rejected parts' ([1940] 1968: 3). In the intervening years, moreover, Du Bois had come to more forcefully underscore how European power and prestige figured centrally in the ordering of a modern, twentieth-century world premised upon what he memorably called 'the divine right of white people to steal' (Du Bois [1920] 1971: 48). Confronted with the 'new imperialism' that had culminated in the ghastly bloodbath of the First World War, Du Bois soberly declared: 'We darker men say: This is not Europe gone mad; this is not aberration nor insanity; this *is* Europe' (Du Bois [1920] 1971: 40; emphasis in original; see also Du Bois 1917).

Perhaps paradoxically, as the twentieth century ended, our current century has been prominently distinguished by the fervent invention and fortification of a new border around a newly reunited Europe, a bordering that may be understood to be nothing less than yet another redrawing of the global 'colour line'. Perhaps still more paradoxically, European border policing has been increasingly externalized, so that supposed would-be migrants are often apprehended and subjected to detention and deportation (and sometimes multiple serial detentions and deportations)

[2] Here, notably, one of the explicit polemical aims of Du Bois' essay is to compel a recognition among his U.S.-based audience 'that after all America is not the centre of modern civilization' ([1900a] 2014: para. 27).

before they have even crossed the territorial border of any European state, designated to be 'illegal migrants' violating the borders of 'Europe'—without ever having set foot in 'Europe'. The European Union has been exceptionally innovative in this regard, enlisting states not only in North Africa but also in sub-Saharan Africa and beyond its eastern and southeastern borders, as 'junior partners' deputized to do the work of policing the effectively virtual European border (see also Chaps. 7 and 9, in this volume).

Today, in the extended aftermath of decolonization for the hundreds of millions of people who formerly were largely confined to the mass prison labour camps that were Europe's colonies, Europe is now confronted with migrants and refugees from those same countries. The escalation and dramatic expansion of migrant mobility in the late twentieth century, therefore, must be apprehensible as the historical successor to the mass global immobilization of labour in Europe's colonies during the preceding era. Consequently, a profound and enduringly poignant expression of the migrant struggle in Europe has long been the declaration: 'We are here because you were there.' Hence, in the face of this inevitable harvest of empire, the mobility of the vast majority of people from formerly colonized countries—indeed the vast majority of humanity—is now pre-emptively illegalized (see also Chap. 10, in this volume).

22.7 Space of Mobilities

The creation of a formalized European space of mobility, whereby EU citizens and residents may cross national borders without passport checks, has been configured, in fact, as largely reserved 'for Europeans only' (see also Chaps. 7 and 9, in this volume).

Here it is instructive to recall the 'guest worker' migration regime that prevailed in much of Western Europe between the calamitous destruction of the Second World War and the more recent era in which migrant 'illegality' has proliferated (see also Chap. 17, in this volume). When the guest worker regime came to an end a new regime premised on asylum effectively foreclosed most other routes for legal migration, and required migrants to now refashion their mobility accordingly. Labour migration thereby assumed the only permissible form: that of refugees fleeing persecution and seeking asylum. Predictably, the inevitable result was an ever increasing and ever more aggressive outcry against the allegedly 'fake' or 'bogus' asylum seekers. By the 1990s, then, the European asylum system had succeeded to produce the material and practical conditions of possibility for a burgeoning influx of illegalized migrants.

To make this point more forcefully: judging it on the basis of its real effects, the European asylum system is precisely not a system for granting asylum to refugees. It routinely and regularly denies the great majority recognition as legitimate asylum seekers, and ordinarily grants 'refugee' status to less than 15 % of applicants.[3] It is premised upon a comprehensive suspicion of people seeking asylum, and is effectively designed to disqualify as many applicants as possible as allegedly 'bogus' asylum seekers. In terms of its real effects and of what it actually produces, therefore, the European asylum system is a regime for the production of migrant 'illegality' (see De Genova 2002, 2005: 213–249).

Subsequently, we have seen only more and more detention for migrants and asylum seekers, with ever greater numbers subjected to plainly punitive recrimination deriving strictly from their non-citizen status.[4] The dramatic expansion and routinization of deportation and migrant detention expose the enormous investment of energy and resources to maintain a European order partitioned by increasingly militarized or securitized borders (see also Chaps. 9 and 10, in this volume). The regulation of borders is never merely a matter of exclusion, however. Detention camps obviously serve as extraterritorial dumping grounds for human beings who are deemed to be 'undesirable' and 'out of place', sanitizing the official borders that are supposed to verify a tidy sociopolitical order of 'European' sovereignty. However, what is less apparent is that in many cases detention centres are not closed prisons but rather provide a kind of solution for housing destitute and homeless migrants. Furthermore, many, and even the majority, of the migrants and asylum seekers detained in such camps are in fact not deported but eventually released. Thus, a key aspect of these detention camps is to decelerate the momentum of migrant mobilities, operating effectively as disciplinary decompression chambers for migrants' trajectories as the migrants commence their more or less protracted apprenticeships as Europe's 'irregular' labor force (De Genova 2002: 429), beginning of course with the severities and deprivations of the extended process of illegalized border crossing itself, including various periods of being stranded in detention or elsewhere en route.

22.8 The Illusion of Wholeness

In order to formulate the European question, fundamentally and ever increasingly fashioned in opposition to the post-colonial spectre of a mob of mobile (non-white) non-Europeans, I have been invoking a notion of Europe in the singular. The European question nonetheless implies the need to defetishize all notions of

[3] In 2012, in the extended aftermath of the events of the Arab Spring, and amid ongoing civil wars in Syria, Afghanistan, and Somalia, and political and economic turmoil in Eritrea, in the enlarged EU-27 first-instance 'refugee' recognition was only 13.9 %, with an additional 10.4 % of applicants denied 'refugee' recognition but granted 'subsidiary protection', and another 2 % granted authorization to stay for humanitarian reasons, in the first instance. In other words, 73 % of all asylum applications were rejected in the first instance (see Eurostat 2013).

[4] An EU-commissioned report on detention revealed in 2006 that there were then at least 130 detention centres in the 25 EU member states (EP 2007). At the time this was probably an underestimate; certainly by now the actual number is much higher, especially once we take into account all of the work of interdiction that transpires beyond the continental territorial limits of Europe itself on behalf of the European border enforcement regime.

'Europe' as a reified monolith. From the Balkans to Chechnya, the unstable and anxious question about Europe's boundaries has been repeatedly re-posed—from within (see also Chaps. 7 and 9, in this volume). Glenda Garelli and Martina Tazzioli have incisively cautioned against transposing the habits of methodological nationalism into an analogous, and comparably uncritical, methodological Europeanism (Garelli and Tazzioli 2013: 300; see also Chap. 5, in this volume). Furthermore, it is important not to collapse the concept of 'Europe' into the EU in an uncritical reflex of methodological EU-ropeanism. The differential layering of relative inclusion within the new (post–Cold War) European project has been pronouncedly salient, for instance, over the course of the gradual accession of various eastern European states to the European Union (see also Chaps. 6 and 7, in this volume). Furthermore, in spite of its campaign for admission to this European constellation, Turkey has remained, at least for now, resolutely 'beyond the pale', and demarcates a decisive frontier. Notably, in precisely this capacity of European frontier Turkey, along with the countries along the southern coast of the Mediterranean, has become a decisive 'holding area', a zone of migrant 'transit' where, in a manner that is analogous to the detention camps but now writ large, human mobility is critically decelerated or temporarily suspended.

The diversity within the larger European constellation refers us to a profoundly uneven history: the ways in which the colonial projects of some European nation states often began 'at home' with the subjugation of their European neighbors, or with the 'internal' colonization of purportedly 'backward' provinces of their presumptive 'national' territories). The legacies of the Cold War, furthermore, have ensured that many regions of 'the East' of Europe have been a crucial reserve of migrant labour both within and across the borders of EU citizenship and mobility (see also Chaps. 6 and 16, in this volume).

Hence, while 'European' may signify racial whiteness, in general, it seems probable that 'European'-ness is also increasingly asserted and affirmed to distinguish the racialized difference between one category of 'foreigners' in European spaces (such as 'Eastern European' migrants in the UK) and the complex field of racialized categories that pertain to those migrant 'foreigners' understood to be decidedly non-European ('Africans', 'Arabs', 'Asians'). These sorts of crude racial distinctions are complicated further when they exist alongside 'native' Europeans who are not racialized as white (such as the European-born children and grandchildren of migrants from formerly colonized countries). Here one could similarly contemplate the racialized indeterminacy or instability of such categories as 'Bulgarian' or 'Romanian' in Western European contexts, where these ostensible 'national' labels often euphemize Roma identities and become inextricably conflated with 'Gypsy' racial alterity, and thereby further exacerbate the anti-Roma hostilities of 'white' (or 'European') Bulgarians, Romanians, and other 'Eastern Europeans'. Thus, the slippages and re-entrenchments of the difference between Eastern European 'whiteness' and Eastern European Roma non-whiteness are a revealing fault line.

In this regard, it is crucial to sustain critical attention to the enduring legacies of anti-Semitism and, especially, anti-Roma racism because these 'internal' figures of European alterity continue to animate the revitalized projects of both 'European' identity and European 'national' identities as post-colonial racial formations. In the era of European integration, Roma communities in particular have been pronouncedly Europeanized[5]: now, increasingly figured as 'Europe's largest ethnic minority' (see e.g. EC 2010), a monolithic 'Roma' construct serves to agglomerate and homogenize diverse communities dispersed across multiple 'national' territories. This minoritizing gesture enfolds the Roma within Europe but re-inscribes them as a singular 'ethnic' alterity that is finally 'European' only inasmuch as it is racialized as effectively non-European—the preeminent perennial (and, by implication, recalcitrant) exception. This is perhaps nowhere more flagrantly evident than in the forcible evictions of Roma settlements and the de facto deportability of the Roma in spite of their putative (EU) citizenship. As Liz Fekete notes, in the face of this newly reanimated 'pan-European racism' against them the Roma can only encounter 'Europe' as something approximating 'a huge open prison' (Fekete 2014: 68).

One could also consider the racialization of Muslim identities, such that 'Bosnian' or 'Chechen' come to demarcate racialized liminal figures, oddly located in the unstable and uneasy borderlands of 'Europe' but simultaneously in the greater orbit of Turkey and 'Turks' as a long-entrenched orientalized Other standing at perhaps the most extreme and enduring border of 'Europe' (see also Chap. 18, in this volume).[6] In this manner 'European' comes to encompass a variegated and contradictory continuum or nexus of racialized formations of whiteness that extend towards a series of 'off-white' or 'not-quite-white' borderland identities. Indeed, it is precisely this inescapable and vexing incoherence that always necessarily attends to all racial meanings, categories, distinctions, and discriminations.

Thus, if 'Europe' may indeed be said to be a racial formation of post-colonial whiteness, this certainly does not mean that all Europeans are equally 'white' or 'white' in the same ways. Like the racial formation of whiteness itself, the homogenizing character of a racial formation of 'European'-ness or European whiteness is precisely devoted to obfuscating and suturing what are otherwise very profound and consequential differences and inequalities. As David Roediger explains, 'It is not merely that 'whiteness' is oppressive and false; it is that 'whiteness' is *nothing but* oppressive and false [...]. Whiteness describes not a culture but precisely [...] the empty and therefore terrifying attempt to build an identity based on what one isn't and on whom one can hold back' (Roediger 1994: 13; emphasis in original). As with whiteness, then, so we may posit of 'European'-ness: it has historically acquired a spurious semblance of integrity or coherence solely on the basis of its presumptive derision for and subjugation of all that is produced as non-European. The constitutive contradictions and intrinsic antagonisms of 'European'-ness are precisely what the homogenizing racial formation of whiteness serves to superintend and recode.

---

[5] I am indebted to Can Yildiz for bringing this particular feature of the contemporary conjuncture of Roma racialization to my attention.

[6] As an expression of its racial populism, Ataka (the 'Attack' Party) in Bulgaria has been known to contend that Bulgaria is still under the control of 'Turks'.

22.9 'European' Futures?

What, finally, is the future of Europe? Today, in the throes of economic crisis, the fragility of the European Union in particular, and the volatility of Europe more generally, are plainly visible. The scapegoating of migrants and an ever more hostile climate of immigration restriction have become standard features of the reactionary politics of misery and expanding precarity. Everywhere migrants are nonetheless central to the ongoing social and political re-definitions of European space (see also Chap. 17, in this volume). How are migrants' sociopolitical and spatial practices actively creating a new Europe and consolidating an alternative European future, in spite of escalating antagonism? Recalling the slogan of the PIR in France, is 'the worst' 'yet to come'? Is it even conceivable that the future will not belong to the 'colonized natives' of Europe, the inheritors of all the colonial subjects who have brought forth the post-colonial migrations that have already permanently and radically altered the social fabric of European life? The European question is as much about this struggle over the future as it is about accounting for the colonial past and the post-colonial present. If we begin to formulate research in terms of these vital questions—from the critical vantage point of those who are conventionally produced as 'outsiders' to Europe, in spite of their very substantive social locations within Europe—we may indeed begin to initiate a critical deconstruction of these sociopolitical processes as they are taking place in the present, in ongoing and unresolved struggles, the stakes of which implicate us all.

References

Anidjar, G. (2012). On the European question. *Forum Bosnae, 55*, 13–27.

Balibar, É. (2009). Europe as borderland. *Environment and Planning D: Society and Space, 27*(2), 190–215. doi:10.1068/d13008.

Bouteldja, H. (2012a). *Islamophobia: When the Whites lose their Triple A rating*. http://www.decolonialtranslation.com/english/islamophobia-when-the-whites-lose-their-triple-a-rating.html

Bouteldja, H. (2012b). *Mohamed Merah and I: Houria Bouteldja's speech in the name of '2012: Printemps des quartiers populaires' (2012: Spring of the poor districts) in Bagnolet, the 31st of March 2012*. http://www.decolonialtranslation.com/english/mohamed-merah-and-I.html

Chandler, N. D. (2006). The figure of W. E. B. Du Bois as a problem for thought. *CR: The New Centennial Review, 6*(3), 29–55. doi:10.1353/ncr.2007.0014.

Chandler, N. D. (2013). *Toward an African future – Of the limit of world*. London: Living Commons Collective.

De Genova, N. (2002). Migrant "Illegality" and deportability in everyday life. *Annual Review of Anthropology, 31*, 419–447. doi:10.1146/annurev.anthro.31.040402.085432.

De Genova, N. (2005). *Working the boundaries: Race, space, and "Illegality" in Mexican Chicago*. Durham: Duke University Press.

De Genova, N. (2007). The production of culprits: From deportability to detainability in the aftermath of "Homeland Security". *Citizenship Studies, 11*(5), 421–448. doi:10.1080/13621020701605735.

De Genova, N. (2010). Migration and race in Europe: The trans-Atlantic metastases of a post-colonial cancer. *European Journal of Social Theory, 13*(3), 405–419. doi:10.1177/1368431010371767.

De Genova, N. (2013). Spectacles of migrant 'illegality': The scene of exclusion, the obscene of inclusion. *Ethnic and Racial Studies, 36*(7), 1180–1198. doi:10.1080/01419870.2013.783710.
Du Bois, W. E. B. (1910, August 18). The souls of White Folk. *The Independent, 69*, 339–342.
Du Bois, W. E. B. (1915). The African roots of war. *Atlantic Monthly, 5*, 707–714.
Du Bois, W. E. B. (1917). Of the culture of White Folk. *Journal of Race Development, 7*, 434–447.
Du Bois, W. E. B. ([1900a] 2013). The spirit of modern Europe. In N. D. Chandler (Ed.), *The problem of the color line at the turn of the twentieth century: The essential early essays* (pp. 139–166). New York: Fordham University Press.
Du Bois, W. E. B. ([1900b] 2013). The present outlook for the dark races of mankind. *A.M.E. Church Review, 17*(2), 95–110. Reprinted in N. D. Chandler (Ed.), *The problem of the color line at the turn of the twentieth century: The essential early essays* (pp. 111–138). New York: Fordham University Press.
Du Bois, W. E. B. ([1903] 1982). *The souls of Black Folk*. New York: Signet.
Du Bois, W. E. B. ([1920] 1971). The souls of White Folk. In W. E. B. Du Bois (Ed.), *Darkwater: Voices from within the veil* (pp. 29–52). New York: AMS Press.
Du Bois, W. E. B. ([1940] 1968). *Dusk of dawn: An essay toward an autobiography of a race concept*. New York: Schocken Books.
EC. (2010). *Communication from the Commission to the Council, the European Parliament, the European Economic and Social Committee and the Committee of the Regions: The social and economic integration of the Roma in Europe*. Brussles: The European Commission. http://eur-lex.europa.eu/LexUriServ/LexUriServ.do?uri=COM:2010:0133:FIN:EN:PDF
EP. (2007). *The conditions in centres for third country national (detention camps, open centres as well as transit centres and transit zones) with a particular focus on provisions and facilities for persons with special needs in the 25 EU member states*. Brussels: European Parliament, Directorate-General Internal Policies, Policy Department C, Citizens Rights and Constitutional Affairs. http://www.detention-in-europe.org/images/stories/2008%20eu-ep-detention-centres-report.pdf
Eurostat. (2013). *Asylum in the EU27: The number of asylum applicants registered in the EU27 rose to more than 330 000 in 2012* (Eurostat news release 48/2013). Luxembourg: Eurostat Press Office. http://epp.eurostat.ec.europa.eu/cache/ITY_PUBLIC/3-22032013-BP/EN/3-22032013-BP-EN.PDF
Fekete, L. (2014). Europe against the Roma. *Race & Class, 55*(3), 60–70. doi:10.1177/0306396813509196.
Garelli, G., & Tazzioli, M. (2013). Migration discipline hijacked: Distances and interruptions of a research militancy. *Postcolonial Studies, 16*(3), 299–308. doi:10.1080/13688790.2013.850048.
Goldberg, D. T. (2006). Racial Europeanization. *Ethnic and Racial Studies, 29*(2), 331–364. doi:10.1080/01419870500465611.
Mezzadra, S. (2010). Anti-racist research and practice in Italy. *Darkmatter*, 6. http://www.darkmatter101.org/site/category/issues/6-challenging-italian-racism
MIR. (2005). The call of the indigenous of the Republic: "We Are the Indigenous of the French Republic!" Mouvement des Indigènes de la Rėpublique. http://www.decolonialtranslation.com/english/AppelEng.php
Orwell, G. (1939). Not counting niggers. *The Adelphi*, 7. http://www.orwell.ru/library/articles/niggers/english/e_ncn
Roediger, D. R. (1994). *Toward the abolition of whiteness: Essays on race, politics, and working class history*. London/New York: Verso.
Rushdie, S. ([1982] 1991). The new empire within Britain. In S. Rushdie (Ed.), *Imaginary homelands: Essays and criticism 1981–1991* (pp. 129–138). London: Granta Books; Penguin.

Index

A. Amelina et al. (eds.), *An Anthology of Migration and Social Transformation*, IMISCOE Research Series, DOI 10.1007/978-3-319-23666-7

I

L

M

N

P